CAMBRIDGE TE>
HISTORY OF POLITI(

GW01018088

——

G. W. F. HEGEL
Political Writings

CAMBRIDGE TEXTS IN THE
HISTORY OF POLITICAL THOUGHT

Series editors

RAYMOND GEUSS

Lecturer in Philosophy, University of Cambridge

QUENTIN SKINNER

Regius Professor of Modern History in the University of Cambridge

Cambridge Texts in the History of Political Thought is now firmly established as the major student textbook series in political theory. It aims to make available to students all the most important texts in the history of western political thought, from ancient Greece to the early twentieth century. All the familiar classic texts will be included but the series seeks at the same time to enlarge the conventional canon by incorporating an extensive range of less well-known works, many of them never before available in a modern English edition. Wherever possible, texts are published in complete and unabridged form, and translations are specially commissioned for the series. Each volume contains a critical introduction together with chronologies, biographical sketches, a guide to further reading and any necessary glossaries and textual apparatus. When completed, the series will aim to offer an outline of the entire evolution of western political thought.

For a list of titles published in the series, please see end of book.

G. W. F. HEGEL

Political Writings

EDITED BY

LAURENCE DICKEY

Professor of History, University of Wisconsin-Madison

and

H. B. NISBET

*Professor of Modern Languages, University of Cambridge,
and Fellow of Sidney Sussex College*

TRANSLATED BY

H. B. NISBET

CAMBRIDGE
UNIVERSITY PRESS

PUBLISHED BY THE PRESS SYNDICATE OF THE UNIVERSITY OF CAMBRIDGE
The Pitt Building, Trumpington Street, Cambridge CB2 1RP, United Kingdom

CAMBRIDGE UNIVERSITY PRESS
The Edinburgh Building, Cambridge, CB2 2RU, UK http://www.cup.cam.ac.uk
40 West 20th Street, New York, NY 10011–4211, USA http://www.cup.org
10 Stamford Road, Oakleigh, Melbourne 3166, Australia

First published 1999

Printed in the United Kingdom at the University Press, Cambridge

Typeset in Ehrhardt 9.5/12 pt [WV]

A catalogue record for this book is available from the British Library

Library of Congress Cataloguing in Publication data

Hegel, Georg Wilhelm Friedrich, 1770–1831.
[Selections. English. 1999]
Hegel: Political Writings/edited by Laurence Dickey and H. B. Nisbet:
translated by H. B. Nisbet.
p.   cm. – (Cambridge Texts in the History of Political
Thought)
Includes bibliographical references and index.
ISBN 0 521 45369 0 – ISBN 0 521 45975 3 (pbk.)
1. Political science. 2. State, The. I. Dickey, Laurence Winnant.
II. Nisbet, Hugh Barr. III. Title. IV. Series.
JC233.H44613   1999
320.1′.01–dc21   98–44357 CIP

ISBN 0 521 45369 0 hardback
ISBN 0 521 45975 3 paperback

Contents

Editors' note

Although this volume has been a joint endeavour from the beginning, each of the editors had special tasks to perform in assembling the volume. The translation was the work of H. B. Nisbet, who has also used the translator's preface and the glossary to explain some of the finer points of rendering Hegel's difficult German into English. The general introduction was written by Laurence Dickey, who was also responsible for the chronology of Hegel's life and career and the editorial notes. Laurence Dickey, however, is greatly indebted to H. B. Nisbet for the many contributions he generously made to each of these parts of the book. Indeed, H. B. Nisbet not only provided suggestions and information that considerably improved the editorial notes but also commented extensively on various drafts of the general introduction. His observations on these drafts – as to style and to the structural balance of the argument – proved immensely helpful.

Laurence Dickey and H. B. Nisbet would respectively like to express their thanks to two colleagues for their friendship and support over many years: they accordingly dedicate this volume to Marc Raeff and Hans Reiss.

General introduction

In 1964, T. M. Knox and Z. A. Pelczynski published their well-known edition of what they called Hegel's 'minor' political writings.[1] They claimed that these writings were 'a most valuable supplement' to Hegel's major political work, the *Philosophy of Right* (henceforth *PR*). In addition, they saw the minor works as in some ways providing 'a clearer insight into Hegel's basic political ideas' than *PR*, a work which, they noted, was filled with metaphysical arguments, esoteric vocabulary, and obscurities associated with Hegel's life-long commitment to the ideals of speculative philosophy. By contrast, the minor writings were 'relatively free' from the jargon of metaphysics and addressed in plain language 'topical political issues' of the day. The down-to-earth quality of these works, in turn, prompted Knox and Pelczynski to present them as journalistic pieces that showcased Hegel's talents as a 'publicist'.[2] If, in that capacity, Hegel could be seen struggling with practical rather than metaphysical problems, then so much the better for appreciating his realistic political outlook.

On a deeper level, though, Knox and Pelczynski wished to use the writings in their edition to introduce students to a more 'liberal' Hegel, one whose ideas were more in line with the mainstream of western political thinking.[3] This Hegel, they argued, while certainly not absent from *PR*, is clearly on display in the minor political writings, for in these, he reveals himself as a supporter of constitutional government and as a critic of absolutism, autocracy, and reaction. To bolster this thesis, Knox and Pelczynski show how, in the minor writings, Hegel was 'the resolute opponent of . . .

vii

étatisme' from the beginning to the end of his career, from the essay
on *The German Constitution* (henceforth *GC*, pp. 6–101 below),
begun in the late 1790s, to the essay entitled *On the English Reform
Bill* (henceforth *ERB*, pp. 234–70 below), published just before his
death in 1831.

The stress here on the long-term continuity of development in
Hegel's political thinking is important, because it calls into question
the conventional view of him as having become the philosopher of
the reactionary Prussian state after 1818, the year in which he
assumed the chair of philosophy at the University of Berlin, Prussia's new but most prestigious university.[4] On the basis of the minor
political writings, Knox and Pelczynski seek not only to correct the
misconception of Hegel as a reactionary but also to draw attention
to what they call the 'rational' core of his political philosophy.[5]
Going further still, they argue that, once we recognise that Hegel
was a 'champion of political rationality', it is incumbent on us to
treat him as a western-style political thinker rather than as a thinker
who upheld the values of 'Prussianism'.[6]

To make this line of argument convincing, Knox and Pelczynski
have to play down two crucial aspects of Hegel's political thinking,
both of which, they contend, are 'metaphysical' and can be found
prominently displayed in *PR* as well as in sections of the *Lectures
on the Philosophy of History* (henceforth *PH*). On the one hand, in
PR, Hegel consistently discusses the modern state in terms of his
'general theory of ethical life' (*Sittlichkeit*). On the other hand, he
insists in *PH* that the emergence of the modern state is inseparable
from a growing realisation among certain groups of Protestants that
Sittlichkeit fulfils religious as well as political needs in the modern
world. As Knox and Pelczynski see it, this mixing of religious and
political values in the concept of *Sittlichkeit* results in a theory of
the modern state that is metaphysical. It is their contention that
Hegel's minor political writings, by way of contrast, show him to
be a practical and pragmatic thinker who 'can be read, understood,
and appreciated without having to come to terms with his
metaphysics'.[7]

Viewed in this way, Knox and Pelczynski's edition of the minor
political writings seems to offer more than just a 'supplement' to
our knowledge of Hegel's political ideas. Rather, its aim seems to
be to make him appear a more liberal, rational, and mainstream

political thinker than he has been taken to be in the past. But they are able to do so only by explaining away the metaphysical dimension of his political thought, especially as it relates to the idea of *Sittlichkeit*. The present edition of his political writings is informed by the converse view that any attempt to rehabilitate Hegel's political thought by ignoring its metaphysical aspects will necessarily be one-sided and unsatisfactory.

After all, as J. Ritter has observed, Hegel knew very well that his conception of *Sittlichkeit* was to a large extent grounded in 'metaphysical' assumptions and was part of a long tradition of philosophical thinking in which the political sphere functioned as a point of mediation between universals and particulars, wholes and parts, divine things and human things, and so on.[8] But in Hegel's judgement, the boundaries of the political sphere were becoming so narrowly drawn in his own age that citizens were on the verge of becoming depoliticised. In this context, he wished from the 1790s on to recall citizens to public life and civic engagement by identifying the political sphere, with the help of his own metaphysical theory of the state, as a point where human beings can aspire to higher things. And he proposed to do so mainly by using the idea of *Sittlichkeit* to stretch the boundaries of the political in directions that would permit him to bring religious and ethical considerations into the political sphere.

It is for this reason, of course, that Hegel has been accused of 'transposing politics to the metaphysical plane'[9] and condemned – especially by liberals – for mixing religious and political values in a way that deified the state in relation to society and to individuals.[10] But whereas liberals tend to believe that *Sittlichkeit* plays an instrumental ideological (i.e. metaphysical) role in the subordination of 'individual rights' to the 'superior rights of the state',[11] Hegel in fact envisaged *Sittlichkeit* as an ideological tool for extending the scope of citizenship from the private to the public sphere. In this respect, one of the great shortcomings of Hegel scholarship is that it has been so convinced that *Sittlichkeit* is an anti-liberal conception that it has forgotten the challenge which the philosophy of *Sittlichkeit* posed to that reactionary alliance of throne and altar that dominated Prussian public policy during the Restoration.[12]

In the light of these considerations, this volume seeks to give students of Hegel's political ideas access to texts which do justice to the *metaphysical* as well as the *practical* aspects of his thinking. To this end, five of the texts included in this volume (discussed in part II of the introduction below) show in detail why Hegel became a philosopher of *Sittlichkeit* and what practical problems he thought could be addressed, perhaps even resolved, by means of this concept. At the same time, our volume includes three texts (discussed in part I of the introduction below) in which he adopts a comparative historical perspective on the evolution of feudalism in Europe in order to examine current political conditions in several of the major European states. The three texts in question are not metaphysical, and they do not feature *Sittlichkeit* as their organising principle. But these texts, especially *GC* and *ERB*, are extremely interesting because they show Hegel drawing conclusions about political life in the modern world from remarkable comparative analyses of recent political developments in England, France, and Germany.

In this general introduction we provide an overview of some of the major themes Hegel develops both in his more metaphysical and his more practical political writings. Both groups of writings are important for developing a historical understanding of his political ideas. We refrain, therefore, from using the labels 'major' and 'minor' to characterise these writings, for no useful historical purpose is served by privileging one group of writings as against the other. As a matter of presentation, however, we discuss the practical essays first because, in his own manner of thought-progression, Hegel liked to proceed from historical-empirical to philosophical-metaphysical concerns.

I The European states in comparative political perspective

Although Hegel devoted much attention throughout his life to developing a metaphysical view of political life, he also engaged in more practical political commentary. Indeed, four of his political works fall into this category – the fragment of a 1798 pamphlet entitled *The Magistrates Should be Elected by the People* (henceforth *M*); *The German Constitution* (*GC*; 1798–1802); the equally long essay on the proceedings of the Estates Assembly in Württemberg in 1815–16 (1817; henceforth *PWE*); and *On the English Reform Bill*

(*ERB*; 1831). Of these, two testify to Hegel's abiding interest in the political affairs of his native Württemberg; one tries to explain the relationship between state and society in England by examining the politics of the English Reform Bill from a unique non-British perspective; and one, while explaining the breakdown of the Holy Roman Empire in the seventeenth and eighteenth centuries, offers a remarkable analysis of the historical processes which, according to Hegel, accounted for the different paths of political development followed by England, France, and the German states in early modern European history.

In some respects, these four pieces, three of which are translated here,[13] all try to identify institutional and cultural obstacles to what Hegel regarded as truly political reform in the modern world. For example, in *M*, he tries to find an institutional mechanism in Württemberg through which initiatives for responsible political reform could flow. But in whichever institutional direction he turns, he discovers good reasons for pursuing his political objectives by other means. Thus, as he surveys the political landscape in Württemberg, he becomes uneasy about leaving the responsibility for reform either in the hands of government officials (even if they are enlightened) or in the control of the various Councils of the Württemberg Estates.[14] At the same time, he expresses reservations about the wisdom of empowering the people to make such decisions.[15]

Given his perception of ever-narrowing institutional options, Hegel proposes to revitalise public life in Württemberg in a relatively new and progressive way: by politicising citizens through 'publicity' (*Publizität*). Since the 1780s, reform-minded Germans had advocated publicity – i.e. the dissemination and public discussion of information relative to the public good – as a means of raising public consciousness concerning political matters. In *M*, Hegel endorses this view. And by suggesting that 'enlightened and upright' (p. 5 below) citizens should actually form themselves into a citizens' association which would operate outside of Württemberg's official political institutions, he also underlines the need for citizens to create associations among themselves through which they could participate in the decision-making political process. He thereby develops a view of political associations which had already been common among German political reformers since the 1760s. *M* is important in this respect because it shows how, in certain circumstances, the inertia of public institutions frustrated political reformers in Germany to the point where they had no option but to identify extra-political groups (Hegel's 'body' of citizens) as agents of the public good. This attitude, as it turns out, is responsible for much of the discussion in the twentieth century about the supposedly 'unpolitical' Germans.[16]

In *GC*, Hegel continues to emphasise the need for citizens to be actively involved in German public life (pp. 23, 96, 98 below). In his view, such action must involve their participation in the exercise of rulership (pp. 22–3 below). It is not enough, he argues, for citizens to pay lip-service to the abstract cultural ideals of cosmopolitanism or to endorse the utopian political ideals of revolutionary democracy. Nor, he adds, should they measure political participation in terms of a 'theory of happiness' (*Glückseligkeitslehre*) or eudaemonism whereby civil liberties are expanded by the government in exchange for the citizens' acquiescence in the government's wishes in all political matters. Indeed, like some 'republicans' of the German Enlightenment, Hegel associates civic engagement with the exercise of political liberty rather than with enhanced civil liberty.[17] In accordance with this view, he holds up to citizens the ideal of the *Staatsbürger* (p. 22 and 277 n 25 below) – that is, the ideal of the citizen who understands that sharing in and promoting the public good constitutes not only the mark of a mature citizen, but of a truly civilised people as well.[18] It is true, as Rudolf Vierhaus has pointed out, that the patriotic discourse of the late German Enlightenment encompassed a wide range of meanings,[19] many of which downplayed (if they mentioned it at all) the importance of active participation by the citizens in the political decision-making process.[20] But as Vierhaus suggests, if the idea of the *Staatsbürger* called citizens to active civic engagement, it did so without supporting the extension of suffrage to everyone. From what Hegel says in *GC*, we can see that, for him at least, patriotic discourse did entail civic engagement for everyone.

In *GC*, Hegel reveals his commitment to participatory government in two important ways. First of all, like the enlightened German patriots of the late eighteenth century, he uses a discussion of the feeble political condition of the German Empire to emphasise the need for more 'public spirit' (*Gemeingeist*) among Germans.[21] He develops this point in a remarkable way, for he relates the decrepit political condition of the Empire to the stages by which feudalism had evolved as a system of social organisation in European history.[22] Proceeding historically, he draws attention to three features of feudalism: (1) it had once been the common form of social organisation in Europe and Britain; (2) it gave impetus to the emergence of representative government in Europe and Britain; and (3) it had Germanic origins, arising 'in the forests of Germania' as he puts it in *GC* (p. 63 below). Secondly, he then explains how the interplay between various historical forces in feudal societies – especially in the domains of law, property, and politics – led to different systems of government in France, England, and the states of the German Empire.

In the end, his point is that, while feudalism degenerated into despotism in France (p. 65 below) and into an institutional system of controlled political anarchy in the German Empire (p. 57 below), it evolved under different circumstances in England into a constitutional form of government – a system of representative government (i.e. limited monarchy) – which, as Montesquieu had noted, showed great flexibility in maximising the liberty of citizens in ever-changing economic circumstances. Following Montesquieu (who appealed to German thinkers for this as well as other reasons),[23] Hegel argues that German liberty found its most mature political expression in England. Accordingly, in *GC*, he sees valuable political lessons for the Germans in English constitutional history.

Hegel's discussion of the evolution of feudalism as a social and political system originates and culminates in celebrations of Germanic liberty. This allows him to take pride in his German heritage, while at the same time associating himself with modern English political institutions and values. This strategy – whereby he depicts England as a fellow 'Germanic' community – helps us to locate his position in the political landscape of the 1790s. For as it turns out, his admiration for England's political institutions is not only close to that of Montesquieu but also mirrors a view of England proclaimed in Germany by the so-called 'Hanover Whigs' during the closing decades of the eighteenth century.[24]

In the 1780s, for example, these Hanoverians had praised English constitutional liberties in order to encourage German princes to moderate their rule and to initiate a range of English-style reforms, many of which demanded that the economic interests of non-landed groups as well as landowners be represented in government.[25] In addition to asking for a more representative government throughout the system of German states, the Hanoverians (e.g. Ernst Brandes) had also complained bitterly about the way in which absolute princes in Prussia and Austria had turned their states into 'machine states', with the result, as Brandes puts it, that these states had lost their character as organic communities.[26] In *GC*, Hegel reiterates many of the points which the Hanoverians had made before him.

If *GC* has many affinities with the pre-revolutionary political outlook of the Hanoverians, it also voices complaints about the French Revolution which echo those articulated by the Hanoverians throughout the 1790s. Hegel's view in *GC* is that the Revolution not only polarised European political discourse but forced a false political choice upon citizens, insisting that they choose between absolute tyranny on the one hand or absolute freedom on the other. He registers his dissatisfaction with this political choice by expanding on the idea of the 'machine state' (pp. 21–5 below).[27]

Hegel had addressed the issue of the machine state several times in the 1790s.[28] Early in *GC* (p. 22 below), he associates this idea with Prussia – just as the Hanoverians had done. However, in the course of the 1790s, he became persuaded – perhaps by Friedrich Schiller[29] – that the revolutionary state in France also exhibited the qualities of a machine state. So, in *GC*, he adds France to the list of machine states, thereby collapsing the political differences between revolutionary French democracy and Prussian absolutism (p. 25 below). Both forms of government, he now proceeds to argue, are inappropriate ways of dealing politically with the increasingly fragmented (i.e. 'atomised') character of modern life; he indeed declares that the machine state is the political correlate of modern atomism.[30] This argument, of course, enables him to present himself as the voice of moderation between political extremes. The Hanoverians had done much the same thing in the 1790s.

In 1831, reacting to the political debate in England over the Reform Bill, Hegel revisits several of the themes which he had earlier discussed in *GC*.[31] In *ERB*, which he published shortly before he died, his main concern is to show how a large part of the agricultural class in Britain failed to become property owners during the 'transition from feudal tenure to property' (p. 248 below). This development, he notes, created socio–economic problems in Britain, for, without the protection of certain provisions of the old feudal law, agricultural workers were dependent for their livelihood on the ability of economic markets to absorb them as free labourers.[32] Given the growing European awareness of the cyclical character of market production patterns,[33] which Hegel had become aware of in the late 1810s,[34] the gloomy prospect of agricultural workers becoming a permanent pauper class was, in his and others' judgement, a disturbing possibility.

In *ERB*, Hegel uses the depressed condition of the propertyless agricultural class, which was a European as well as a British phenomenon, as a point of departure for analysing the Reform Bill. How, he asks (p. 239 below), will the Reform Bill enable Parliament to respond to the pauperisation of Britain's rural population? It is significant that he does not simply allow English supporters and opponents of the Reform Bill to answer this question for him, for neither group, he reports, has taken much interest in the plight of the agricultural workers. Instead, he first frames the question in comparative historical terms and then puts it to the English political class in the light of the way in which the 'civilised states on the Continent' (pp. 239, 264 below) had responded to the social distress of agricultural workers in their own countries. This comparative procedure, which he had used to great effect in *GC* to discuss the evolution of feudalism in Europe and Britain, produces one of the principal themes of *ERB*: namely that, in comparison with the continental countries, England is politically backward in matters relating to the 'material rights' (p. 255) of its citizens.

This evaluation of England, of course, stands in sharp contrast to that which Hegel had developed in *GC*. Perhaps with his own earlier celebration of English constitutional liberty in mind, he says in *ERB* that Europeans had once been 'impressed' (p. 238) by the way the English government had been able to maximise the liberty of the citizens by constantly balancing and adjusting the claims of positive law *vis-à-vis* the private rights of groups and individuals. Throughout *ERB*, however, he contends that, in the course of the eighteenth century, the constitutional balance in England had shifted significantly – to the detriment of the monarchy and to the advantage of the long-standing privileges and private rights of particular propertied groups.[35]

On the basis of their property, Hegel observes, these groups are both represented in Parliament and control it. In this respect, he says, propertied interests in England represent a 'class' in

Parliament – a class, however, which is not without its own internal tensions between its agricultural and commercial components, as well as between financial and manufacturing interests within the commercial group itself. Although he draws attention to these tensions within the English political class, he treats them as less important than the fact that the propertied class as a whole seems to be quite indifferent to the material well-being of the propertyless agricultural workers (pp. 254–6 below). In these circumstances, he thinks, the depressed economic and psychological condition of the bulk of the rural population in England will not be addressed by political means – that is, through the agency of the Reform Bill. In fact, he believes that the 'non-recognition' of the material rights of the propertyless will turn social paupers into political revolutionaries.[36]

According to Hegel, the continental states had reacted in a more responsible way to the pauperisation of their agricultural workers. They had been able to do so, he argues, because of the concerted efforts of a group of dedicated and well-trained civil servants who, while working through the due power of their respective monarchs, developed social legislation that provided state assistance to those whose well-being had been adversely affected by the transition from feudal tenure to property. Indeed, like many German liberals of the 1820s and 1830s,[37] Hegel thinks it is incumbent on the state to accept some responsibility for ensuring the material rights of all citizens.

Throughout the 1820s, he associates this kind of state-sponsored interventionism with what he calls the 'police' (*Polizei*) function of government.[38] He does not, of course, wish to restrict the function of the state to matters which involve only the material needs of citizens – which is why, in a lecture of 1824–5, he limits the focus of 'police' legislation to questions of welfare and physical need as distinct from those which involve *Sittlichkeit*.[39] But just because he separates the welfare and ethical functions of government does not mean that a state which takes heed of the material well-being of its citizens has achieved its end in a teleological sense. On the contrary, Hegel's expectation is that, to enable civilised people to realise themselves fully as human beings, states must help their citizens to form themselves into truly ethical communities. It is, however, the English government's lack of an ameliorative 'police' function that induces Hegel to depict England as politically backward in comparison with the legislative achievements of the civilised states of the Continent.[40] But since neither England nor the continental states had, in his opinion, yet reached the level of *Sittlichkeit*, he refrains from talking about that realm – the ethical life of the state – altogether. As we shall soon see, this was despite the fact that *Sittlichkeit* was very much on his mind at the time when he wrote *ERB*.

Obviously, this criticism of English political institutions stems, in part, from the comparative perspective which Hegel brings to his analysis of the Reform Bill. But throughout *ERB*, he also criticises the English political class more directly, faulting it both for the (false) 'pride' (p. 251) it allegedly took in its own private rights and for the excessively narrow and self-serving way in which it reduced political questions about the common good to economic questions about what was good for the particular interests of particular individuals within Britain's propertied class.[41] In the past, he concedes, the English had been right to take pride in the rationality of their political institutions (p. 238 below), especially in the way in which those institutions defended private rights against encroachments of the absolute state. In the face of changing historical circumstances, though, that pride had impeded the promulgation of legislation which would address the socio-economic distress of Britain's agricultural class.[42] Just as the Germans had once had to overcome the illusions they had formed about themselves as a unified people, so now the political class in England had to see that social justice in modern market societies occasionally requires the state to abridge the private rights of some for the sake of a more comprehensive social justice.[43]

Throughout *ERB*, Hegel suggests that, in the absence both of a strong monarchy and of any inclination on the part of the government to improve the training of civil servants, and in the absence of any commitment by the middle class to extend voting rights to non-propertied groups, England's political class will fail to respond to the social situation of the pauper class. It would be wrong to interpret this concern as evidence of any desire on Hegel's part to have 'persons' rather than 'property' represented in Parliament.[44] This certainly is not his intention. (Nor was it the intention of many liberal reformers in England in the 1820s.)[45] But, as he had already noted in the 1790s in the face of lessons drawn from the French Revolution,[46] if governments fail to minister to the needs (i.e.

'material rights') of impoverished citizens, then those citizens, when driven by 'external necessity' (p. 251 below), will sooner or later not only seek non-political ways to achieve social justice for themselves but will do so in the name of those 'formal principles of abstract equality' (p. 255 below) which had underpinned radical French thinking on the rights of citizens since 1789 (pp. 264–70 below). In this context, Hegel speculates, citizens who are not represented in Parliament will eventually find voices among politically ambitious 'new men' in Parliament to articulate the concerns of the propertyless in the language of 'French abstractions' (p. 265 below). This combination of political ambition and social distress, he fears, will lead to revolution rather than reform in Britain.

Although Hegel invokes the civilised states of the Continent as a means of exposing the myopic political vision of the English ruling class, it would be wrong to assume that he is recommending the 'police state' as a model for Britain to emulate. On the contrary, his argument unfolds within a conceptual framework in which four types of modern political regime are either discussed or alluded to: (1) the *laissez-faire* regime of liberal political economy; (2) the interventionist regime of qualified liberalism; (3) the political regime of French revolutionary democracy; and (4) the ethico-political regime of *Sittlichkeit*. In his view, the first, second, and fourth types constitute an evolutionary pattern which moves modern societies on towards true liberty. The third type, by way of contrast, interrupts that progression; and it is the failure of the first type of regime to transform itself into the second that paves the way for the third type to emerge in history. In this respect, Hegel sees the regime of *Sittlichkeit* as the mature expression of a liberal progression in history and the French Revolution as a threat to liberal values rather than an agent of them. To understand why he holds that view, we need to examine the idea of *Sittlichkeit* more closely.

II Hegel as a philosopher of *Sittlichkeit*

The origins of Sittlichkeit *in Hegel's early writings*

That the concept of *Sittlichkeit* plays a major role in Hegel's political philosophy is beyond dispute. As is well known, it is central to the argument of *PR* (1821), his greatest political work, and it figures prominently in *PH* (1827–31), especially in the section included in this volume (pp. 197–224 below). To understand how *Sittlichkeit* came to command so much of Hegel's attention it is necessary to look at his long-term development as a political thinker.

First of all, it is important to realise that the concept of *Sittlichkeit* is already present in his so-called 'early theological writings'.[47] In these writings, which he composed between 1793 and 1800, he studies the civil history of religion in the ancient world, especially among the Greek, Roman, and Jewish peoples. He himself emerges as a religious optimist who believes that Christianity has the potential to become what he variously calls a 'rational' or 'virtue-' or 'public' or 'folk religion'.[48] By these designations, he means to suggest that Christianity is a religion that asks individuals to assume responsibility for acting ethically in the world. This is especially true, he says, if one's view of Christianity is based on what he identifies as the 'religion of Jesus' (*die Religion Jesu*) as distinct from the 'Christian religion'.[49] The latter, he argues, is a 'private religion';[50] the former is a religion of *Sittlichkeit* that was optimistic about the capacity of human beings both to cope with sin and to realise the 'spark' of divinity which God had originally implanted in them. Given these premises, Hegel says, Jesus expected Christians to carry Christian principles into the world through their ethical actions, forming communities of religious fellowship in the process. In the language of the religious history of Christianity, Hegel could be said to view the latter as an 'ethical religion' whose task was to persuade Christians to strive for perfection in their individual and communal lives. *Sittlichkeit* is the word he often uses in the early theological writings to give ideological focus to this conviction.[51]

Secondly, in the early 1800s (just after he started to teach philosophy at the University of Jena), Hegel begins formally to organise his thinking around the idea of *Sittlichkeit*. He does so most conspicuously in his essay on *Natural Law* (henceforth *NL*; pp. 102–80 below), a work which he published in two instalments in 1802 and 1803. In this essay, he announces his intention of becoming a philosopher of *Sittlichkeit*. In so doing, he makes comments on *Sittlichkeit* that anticipate arguments which he develops later in *PR* (e.g. on the differences between *Moralität* and *Sittlichkeit*). Not for nothing has *NL* been described as the 'first philosophy of right'.[52]

Although Hegel scholars have long been aware of the importance of this essay, the pivotal role which it plays in the development of Hegel's political ideas has not always been fully appreciated. For one thing, if *NL* is read in the light of Hegel's earlier religious arguments concerning *Sittlichkeit*, then it becomes clear that the philosophy of *Sittlichkeit* expresses in new terminology the optimistic view of human nature which he had developed in his earlier theological writings. For example, at a number of places in the latter (as well as at several places in the present volume), he grounds his optimism regarding human nature, and the capacity of human beings to form themselves into communities of fellowship, in the 'fact' that God created human beings in his own image and likeness.[53] From this 'fact', Hegel derives the notion that human beings have a spiritual essence which, with God's help, they can cultivate – but only if they are of a mind to do so. As they are more or less successful in this endeavour, they become more spiritual, more mature, and more capable of Christianising the world through their ethical actions. Or – to use another of Hegel's formulations from the 1790s – by striving for ethical and spiritual perfection in their lives, human beings begin to 'approach' God.[54]

In *NL*, Hegel struggles to find ways to express this optimism about the human spirit (*Geist*) in philosophical terms. To achieve this end, he develops a distinction, insisting throughout the essay that human beings are not initially formed 'by nature' for what they are meant to be 'by nature'.[55] On the still deeper philosophical level of ontology, he sometimes registers this distinction in *NL* by differentiating between 'existence' and 'essence'. In the case of the individual, the latter represents potential being, the former immediately existing being. At other times, he equates the idea of existence with the 'subject' and the idea of essence with a 'substance' that is immanent in the subject but has not yet been either developed in the subject's self-consciousness or translated by the subject into ethical action in the world.

Whatever the terminology, the point of philosophy for Hegel in 1802–3 is twofold: to 'awaken' human beings to what is immanent in them (i.e. to their *Geist*);[56] and to urge them to organise their communities in accordance with this immanent substance which, when externalised, becomes *Sittlichkeit*.[57] In other words, subjective individuals have to realise themselves as ethical substance in the external world – to think of themselves, that is, not as isolated existential beings with immediate natures but as communal beings with spiritual natures.

Two pivotal arguments of *NL* follow from this. Firstly, the philosophy of *Sittlichkeit* implies that human beings can realise their communal natures only when they begin to envisage themselves as spiritual rather than as natural beings. This explains why Hegel talks so much in this essay about the externalisation of inner dispositions (e.g. ethical intuitions, rational spirit, ethical reason, ethical nature) and about the differences between the 'natural' and the 'ethical'.

Secondly, Hegel indicates in *NL* that the impulse towards *Sittlichkeit* involves an elevation and expansion of consciousness which reveals the shortcomings of a life lived in accordance with the Kantian doctrine of *Moralität*. Indeed, as Hegel sees it, *Moralität* is a sophisticated form of philosophical subjectivism which, while undoubtedly high-minded, ultimately contributes to the isolation of human beings from one another.[58] For this reason, he offers *Sittlichkeit* as a corrective to *Moralität* on the grounds that, in the final analysis, *Moralität* is inimical to community (i.e. in the terminology of *NL*, it is *unsittlich*). In this respect, the movement from *Moralität* to *Sittlichkeit* that is so central to the arguments of *NL* and *PR* is governed by the same concerns that induced Hegel to identify *Sittlichkeit* as an agent of religious fulfilment in the early theological writings. Throughout the writings in the present volume, he indicates again and again that *Sittlichkeit* as religious *praxis* is related to the transformation of *Moralität* into *Sittlichkeit*.

Sittlichkeit *and Protestantism in the development of Hegel's political thinking*

If, as we have seen, the discussion of *Sittlichkeit* in *NL* foreshadows much of the argument of *PR*, then *PR* registers Hegel's intention of making *Sittlichkeit* an agent of Protestant religious fulfilment as well. Nothing like this can be found in the writings from the early Jena period.[59] Indeed, during the early Jena years (1801–3), Hegel connects Protestantism with religious and philosophical values that were, for him, alarmingly subjectivist in nature, scope, and purpose.[60] As we have seen, he deliberately develops his conception of *Sittlichkeit* in *NL* as a corrective to moral subjectivism in philosophy; and from some of his other writings of 1801–2 we learn that he also believes that *Sittlichkeit* provides a communal religious alternative to the privatising and atomising tendencies of Prot-estantism.[61] There is even evidence in these other writings that he considered *Moralität* to be the philosophical expression of Prot-estant subjectivism.[62] Thus later, when he declares in the Preface to *PR* that Protestantism is destined to become the agent of *Sittlich-keit* in the modern world,[63] he commits himself to becoming a phil-osopher not only of *Sittlichkeit* but of Protestantism as well. This development means that there is discontinuity as well as continuity between *NL* and *PR*.

In the light of Hegel's embracing of Protestantism and his will-ingness to put the Protestant 'principle' at the centre of his concep-tion of *Sittlichkeit* as essential to modern freedom,[64] the present edition of his political writings includes four texts that testify to the increasing importance he attached to Protestant values in his discussions of *Sittlichkeit*, the modern state, and the philosophy of history. These texts, two of which have never before been translated into English, all date from his so-called Berlin period (1818–31) – the time when his philosophy was in the ascendant in Germany in general and throughout the Prussian educational system in particular.[65]

As these texts confirm, Hegel develops during his years in Berlin a theory of the modern state in which Protestantism becomes a political ideology through the agency of *Sittlichkeit*, and *Sittlichkeit* becomes an agent of Protestant religious fulfilment in the course of Hegel's various reflections on the philosophy of history. For stud-ents of his political ideas, this means that the philosophy of *Sittlich-keit* can no longer be grasped by studying *PR* alone. Indeed, despite its monumental character, *PR* should not be viewed as the culmi-nation of Hegel's development as a thinker. Rather, in keeping with the trajectory of his political thinking in Berlin, it is more accurate to see *PR* as the beginning of a project in which he tries to explain the political interplay between Protestantism and *Sittlichkeit* in terms of a philosophy of history in which the modern state occupies a central place. It is in fact in his reflections on history that he develops an agenda for political change in Europe as well as in Prussia; and *Sittlichkeit* is the point on which his meditations on history, politics, and religion converge.

The first of the texts in question is the *Inaugural Address* that Hegel delivered in 1818 at the University of Berlin (henceforth

BIA; pp. 181–5 below).[66] Although it has never before been translated into English, it has drawn the attention of Hegel scholars for
several reasons. For some, *BIA* offers proof of his servility before
the idol of the Prussian state and of his willingness to act as a
spokesperson for its reactionary religious and political policies.[67]
Others have interpreted *BIA* as an integral part of an ambitious
effort by a group of liberal reformers in the Prussian bureaucracy
to develop a mental culture in the university which would offset
attempts by political forces on the right and the left to shape the
direction of education in Prussia's leading university.[68] Still others
see *BIA* as aimed at philosophical subjectivists (e.g. J. F. Fries)
who, Hegel thought, had debased philosophy by reducing it to matters of mere feeling.[69] Finally, some read *BIA* as a call to the young
people of Germany to become more engaged in public life[70] – first
through their achievements in education (*Bildung*) and then by
applying what they have learned about 'the ethical power of the
spirit' (*die sittliche Macht des Geistes*) to public life.

For our present purposes, what is intriguing about *BIA* is the
way in which Hegel argues for Germany's emerging supremacy in
European philosophy. Although he had held this view since at least
1802,[71] he clearly regards his call to Berlin as part of this broader
European pattern of cultural development.[72] To this end, he uses
BIA to outline a fourfold agenda for the cultivation of philosophy
and the sciences in Germany.

Firstly, as part of his life-long antipathy towards subjectivism, he
pleads for a shift in the focus of philosophy from 'feeling' to 'thinking'.[73] Secondly, he identifies the university as the particular place
where, among other things, people can begin to think seriously and
freely about the universal, essential, and spiritual substance of 'ethical life' (*Sittlichkeit*).[74] Next, he suggests that Germany has become
the custodian of the 'sacred light' of philosophy at this particular
moment in history because the 'world spirit' (*Weltgeist*) demands
emancipation from the 'religious', 'philosophical', and 'ethical' shallowness of French thinking.[75] (Though he does not say so in *BIA*,
he states in 1817, in *PWE*, that the movement of philosophy from
France to Germany has a political dimension which involves defining political rationality in terms of *Sittlichkeit* rather than
'atomism'.[76]) Finally, he is convinced that, as philosophy shifts from
France to Germany, the 'spiritual culture' (*Geistesbildung*) of Europe

will become not only more German but more Protestant as well. For him, this means that education and learning will be less Catholic (i.e. 'hierarchical' and 'closed') and more open to 'laymen' (*Laien*) and to critical ways of thinking that are essential for the cultivation of the sciences.[77]

If *BIA* held up high-minded ideals for Prussia and Protestants to aspire to in 1818, Hegel's Latin oration of 1830 on the tercentenary of the Augsburg Confession – now for the first time translated into English (henceforth *AC*; pp. 186–96 below) – again appears to extol the 'cause' of Prussian and Protestant values. But the political circumstances in which Hegel delivers *AC* are very different from those that existed in 1818. For while there were few signs in 1818 of the coming political and religious reaction, by 1830 an alliance of throne and altar dominated the Prussian state, ensuring that a reactionary religious and political agenda would be at the centre of public life in Restoration Prussia. It is well known that the various groups that had formed this alliance (e.g. orthodox Lutherans, neo-Pietists, and advocates of 'feudal theology' and the 'ideology of patrimonialism') distrusted Hegel as much as he disdained them.[78] Given this mutual suspicion, which surfaced in Prussia as early as 1818,[79] the question to ask is this: is the 'cause' which Hegel promotes in *AC* the alliance's or his own?[80]

To answer this question, we need to bear three things in mind. Firstly, by 1820, shortly after his arrival in Berlin, Hegel wrote the famous Preface to *PR*. In this Preface, he continues his assault on subjectivism by reiterating the need to shift the focus of philosophy from feeling to thinking.[81] In so doing, however, he adds a religious dimension to the discussion, arguing that, in Protestantism, feeling stands to thinking as an immature Lutheran attitude towards religion stands to a mature Hegelian one. As the Preface reveals, Hegel uses the progression from feeling to thinking to exhort Protestants to turn their inner-directed piety outwards – towards *Sittlichkeit* and civic engagement.[82] Throughout *AC*, he underscores this point. It could not have gone down well with either the orthodox Lutherans or the neo-Pietists, both of whom encouraged inner-directed piety and embraced what Hegel called Luther's doctrine of 'faith in feeling'.[83]

Secondly, the 1830 oration's repeated references to Protestantism as a 'lay' religion are designed to operate on two different rhetorical levels. On the one hand, Hegel shows that Luther's doctrine of conscience and his understanding of 'subjective freedom' abolished priestly control of Christianity by Catholics. On the other hand – and here Hegel draws on arguments he had developed in the 1790s[84] – he implies that orthodox Lutheranism had itself fettered the spirit of Protestant religious freedom in order to preserve the letter of orthodoxy. As was the case with Catholicism before it, this 'positive' form of Lutheranism cut Protestants off from free access to God by denying them the capacity to realise in their ethical lives the 'spark' of divinity within them. Such an observation could not have pleased members of the alliance of throne and altar in Prussia.

Finally, *AC* illustrates how Hegel uses history to promote his own Hegelianised version of Protestantism's role in the modern political world. He does this in several ways. To begin with, he suggests that, as Protestants become more mature in a *spiritual* sense, their piety should become more ethically and communally focused in a *religious* sense. Secondly, he indicates that, while Protestantism had its origins in Luther's Reformation, the Lutheran doctrine of inner-directed 'subjective freedom' itself needed to be reformed – that is, it needed to be re-directed outwards before Protestantism could provide constructive 'principles of action' for the organisation of communal life in the modern world. Thirdly, he thereby associates himself with an older tradition of Protestant discourse which had raised questions as to whether the scope of Luther's Reformation extended to matters of 'life' (*Leben*) or was limited to matters of 'doctrine' (*Lehre*) alone.[85] For Hegel – and this is very clear in *PH* (pp. 197–224 below) – Luther's Reformation had succeeded admirably in reforming Christian doctrine by providing a religious sanction for subjective freedom (i.e. freedom of conscience); but it had fallen short of reforming Christian life. Thus, like others before him, Hegel distinguishes between a 'first' and a 'second Reformation'.[86] The first Reformation, he implies in *AC*, gives us the idea of 'freedmen' (*liberi*) in terms of abstract theory; the second Reformation demands that human beings become 'genuinely free' (*liberti*) in terms of the practice of piety in life. As Hegel understands it, *Sittlichkeit* is the agent of the latter, but not of the former.

Thus, at the end of *AC*, when he speaks of the Protestant 'cause', Hegel is referring to Protestant norms that were neither those of

Lutheran orthodoxy nor those of the existing Prussian state.[87] Rather, these norms expressed the values of a liberal Protestant humanist who, for religious and political reasons, wished to turn Lutheranism 'inside out' by insisting that subjective freedom can be realised in the world only through the agency of *Sittlichkeit*.[88] In this respect, *AC* calls on Prussia to complete the work which, in retrospect, Hegel thought the Reformation had begun.

Towards the end of *AC*, Hegel alludes to political developments in France. His comments follow remarks on how different the political histories of Catholic and Protestant nations had been in Europe in the eighteenth and early nineteenth centuries. In various of his Berlin lectures in the 1820s, he had devoted more and more attention to this theme,[89] the results of which can be seen in two other works from his late Berlin period included in the present volume: the famous section on modern history from *PH* (pp. 197–224 below), and the section on *The Relationship of Religion to the State* from the 1831 lectures on the philosophy of religion (henceforth *RRS*).

At the outset, it is worth noting that both of these texts contain material that Hegel added to his lectures after the Revolution of 1830 in France. This allows students of his political ideas to measure continuity and change in his political thinking before and after the Revolution.[90]

Of the two texts, *PH* is the more important. It shows Hegel developing a philosophy of history in which subjective freedom evolves historically into *Sittlichkeit* as the focus of Protestant piety shifts from doctrine to life and from feeling to thinking. His claim is that, in so far as Protestants act to realise *Sittlichkeit* in the world, they become progressively more free – both as citizens and as Christians.[91] Since increasing freedom is, in Hegel's judgement, part of God's plan for human salvation in history, he has no reservation about designating a political association – the state rather than society – as the sphere in which *Sittlichkeit* has to be developed in order for humanity to realise its divine essence in the modern world.

Obviously, Protestant values inform much of this argument. And scholars have been right to note that Hegel's conception of modern freedom unfolds in accordance with a Christian philosophy of history.[92] But with only a few exceptions, Hegel scholars have badly misconstrued how the Protestant aspects of his philosophy of history shape the story he tells about freedom's progress in the world as it advances from the Reformation through the Enlightenment to the French Revolution. The conventional view of his understanding of modern freedom has long been that (1) it starts with Luther's doctrine of religious individualism; (2) it is then shaped by the Enlightenment (i.e. secularised and rationalised) into a philosophy that celebrates the critical thinking of free, morally autonomous, and self-determining individuals; and (3) it culminates in the political individualism of the French Revolution.[93] In keeping with this, it has been said that Hegel regarded the French Revolution as 'a kind of political Reformation' because it gave priority to the exercise of private judgement in political as well as religious life.[94]

Now, this judgement may certainly be applied to Novalis, who in the late 1790s called the French Revolution a 'second Reformation'.[95] But whereas Novalis used the idea of a second Reformation to link the religious anarchy of the Reformation with the political anarchy of 1789, Hegel used the same idea to separate Hegelianised Protestantism from political anarchy. Therefore, to interpret him as if he were saying in a positive sense that the French Revolution was a kind of political Reformation is a serious error, for it makes it impossible to explain all the negative things which he has to say throughout his life about the subjectivism of Luther's Reformation, the abstractionism of the Enlightenment, and the unfreedom of the French Revolution. In addition, it overlooks his interpretation of the Reformation–Enlightenment–Revolution sequence as, respectively, the religious, philosophical, and political moments of a single process of 'atomisation'. Clearly, in his Berlin period, Hegel means to use the idea of a 'second Reformation' to distance himself from the atomising tendencies of each of these major historical events. So, far from seeing 1789 as marking the political fulfilment of Protestant freedom – which, instructively, was the basis of the French theocrats' charge in the 1790s that Protestantism was responsible for the anarchy of the French Revolution – Hegel identifies the 'second Reformation' simultaneously as an agent of *Sittlichkeit* and as an ethical, political, and religious corrective to the atomistic course which European history had been following since the Reformation.

In this respect, the close connection which he draws in *PH* between Protestantism, *Sittlichkeit*, and the second Reformation aims at reasserting human control over the direction of history in the face of anarchy and atomisation. This means, in turn, that his idealised view of religious and political community is predicated on the idea of *Sittlichkeit* becoming a new form of *praxis* for Protestants and burghers alike. It is an ideal, in short, that urges a people to take collective responsibility for its own future through the agency of political association. If a people does so, Hegel says, spirit will triumph over nature in history.

Sittlichkeit *and the critique of civil society*

Given what these four texts from Hegel's Berlin period say, it should be apparent that his Berlin project required the boundaries of the political to expand in a religious direction, one that would be consistent with his understanding of the course of European history since the Reformation. It is worth observing, though, that this is the second time he had sought to expand the scope of the political sphere. He had done so for the first time as a young man in *NL* – when he began to include economic factors in his understanding of the role which *Sittlichkeit* might play in the political sphere in the modern world.

His youthful project of assimilating economics to politics undoubtedly culminates in *PR*.[96] But it is in *NL* that he first begins to write in detail about the triangular interplay between *Sittlichkeit*, economic processes, and the loss of political liberty in the ancient (and presumably modern) world. As we have seen, he wishes in *NL* to use *Sittlichkeit* to ennoble human beings by raising the focus of their ethical and religious lives above the narrow concerns of immediate existence. But from his readings in political economy in the late 1790s he had learned how economic and social developments can together not only militate against ethical uplift, but erode existing communal ties as well.[97] As *NL* shows (pp. 147–9 below), he explains the loss of *Sittlichkeit* from antiquity onwards as a result of the people's growing fixation with their immediate existence – with their private lives, that is. In this context, he explains how privatising processes in economics, property law, and morality produced a class of citizen-proprietors whose primary interest lay more in acquiring economic possessions and securing them legally than in participating in public life through membership of a political association. In *NL*, he connects this development with the depoliticisation of Roman political life. And by calling these citizens *bourgeois* (see p. 151 below), he suggests that privatising processes similar to those which had depoliticised Roman citizens were drawing the burgher, as *bourgeois*, away from public life in the modern world too.[98]

Given the lofty ideal of *Sittlichkeit* that he brought to *NL* from the early theological writings, it cannot be surprising that Hegel depicted the *bourgeoisie*, and their privatised notion of *Moralität*, as an obstacle to the realisation of *Sittlichkeit* among human beings. Thus, one of the principal aims of *NL* is to repoliticise the *bourgeoisie* – that is, to persuade them of the need to develop that political part of their natures which, while 'immanent' within them, still remained to be developed. To do this, Hegel idealises the notions of citizenship and of membership in the political community and holds them up to the *bourgeoisie* of his own day as ideals to which they ought to aspire. In this respect, *NL* must be interpreted as marking the moment when *Sittlichkeit* becomes for Hegel a political as well as an ethico-religious ideal.

But there is more to it than this, for the ideological connection which he draws between *Sittlichkeit* and citizenship is constructed with an eye to how developments in economics and property law 'atomise' society and isolate citizens from one another. Such developments occur, Hegel explains, because economic expansion creates opportunities for individuals to realise themselves outside the political sphere. As *NL* argues, the more citizens come to define liberty in 'civil' rather than 'political' terms, the more subjective and self-regarding they are likely to become.

For all that, Hegel does not blame the *bourgeoisie* for being *bourgeois*. They are as they are because, in his opinion, the organisation of civil society actually encourages individuals to put their private lives before the public good. At best, this arrangement creates depoliticised individuals who hold high personal standards of *Moralität* and are industrious, frugal, and honest.[99] At worst, the organisation of civil society produces a mental outlook that is conducive to what scholars from Carl Schmitt to C. B. Macpherson have called 'possessive individualism'.[100]

In the end, what is important about the economic aspect of *NL* is that it induces Hegel to designate the sphere of *bourgeois* liberty –

the sphere of political economy, private property, property law, *Moralität*, and subjectivism in philosophy and religion – as a depoliticised sphere of atomised individuals who, paradoxically, are *unsittlich* even though – or perhaps precisely because – they are 'moral'. Needless to say, this formulation largely anticipates the view of civil society later expounded in *PR* – that is, in *NL*, Hegel begins to develop *Sittlichkeit* as an alternative – at once political, ethical, and religious – to the way in which life is organised in the civil sphere. In so far as the civil realm is the preserve of liberal values – and Hegel says as much in *PH* (pp. 217–19 below) – his conception of *Sittlichkeit* tends to be critical of those values because they underestimate the role of political association in public life. But in so far as *Sittlichkeit* is the agent of civic Protestantism and of a repoliticised *bourgeoisie*, he intends that it should promote rather than discourage participation in public life.[101] As recent studies of Berlin in the 1820s have shown, it took civic courage to do this in the face of Prussia's illiberal power structure.[102] It would seem fair to say, therefore, that after stretching the boundaries of the political sphere in the direction of economics, Hegel turns round and stretches them in the other direction. By initiating the first move, he becomes open to – and develops an appreciation of – many of the values of economic liberalism. With the second move, however, he registers his growing discontent not only with economic liberalism but also with many of the values of liberalism itself.

The dialectic of Sittlichkeit *and Hegel's myth of the state*[103]

In many interpretations of Hegel's political philosophy, his strategy of stretching the boundaries of the political first one way then another constitutes the 'dialectic of *Sittlichkeit*'.[104] Within the framework of that dialectic, it is often argued, Hegel discusses several other key conceptual movements: from inner- to outer-directed piety; from *Moralität* to *Sittlichkeit*; from parts to wholes; from particulars to universals; from burgher as *bourgeois* to burgher as *citoyen*; from civil society to the state; from *Gesellschaft* to *Gemeinschaft*; from the first to the second Reformation; and, within the framework of Franco-German relations, from 'atomism' to *Sittlichkeit* and from Catholicism to Protestantism. The enormous importance which he attaches to the transformative power of *Sittlichkeit*, however, has been viewed by generations of Hegel scholars as grounded in metaphysics and rooted in an attempt to turn the world, especially the political world, 'upside down' (to borrow a phrase from Schopenhauer's mid-nineteenth-century critique of Hegel's theory of the state).[105]

Among critics of Hegel's political philosophy, the dialectic of *Sittlichkeit* invariably leads to a glorification of political power that is sustained by a myth of the state in which free and autonomous moral persons are reduced to the status of bees in a hive. Ralf Dahrendorf is especially clear on the ideological dynamic here,[106] arguing that the 'dialectic of *Sittlichkeit*' turns 'the world . . . upside down so that the myth of the state becomes reality [i.e. the universal] and the tangible reality of society [a congeries of particulars] a kind of ground fog above which one has to rise'.[107] In this inverted world, Dahrendorf continues, citizens become subjects, liberty is defined in terms of obligations, rights evolve into duties, and questions of justice become questions of mere legality. Just as vehemently, he denounces Hegel's dialectic of *Sittlichkeit* for abolishing the rights of 'free persons' in the name of 'membership' of the state.[108]

In his representation of Hegel's position, Dahrendorf self-servingly associates the free person with *Moralität* and the member of the state with *Sittlichkeit*. Thus, as the dialectical process unfolds, the free person gives way to the member of the state in the same way that *Moralität* gives way to *Sittlichkeit*. The process unfolds in this way, Dahrendorf says, because Hegel's metaphysics values wholes more than parts. Dahrendorf is convinced, moreover, that this way of thinking underpins the widespread belief in the myth of the state in German history.[109]

Sittlichkeit *and Hegel's concept of political association*

Any rehabilitation of Hegel as a political thinker must explain why the dialectic of *Sittlichkeit* does not, as Ernst Barker insinuates, transform free persons into bees who operate in accordance with the 'instinctive automatism of the hive'.[110] This question must be addressed here.

The idea that Hegel reduced free persons to the status of bees is indefensible. After all, as his writings make perfectly clear, he never proposes to eliminate subjective freedom from human life or to

abolish the institutions of civil society, which is the sphere of subjective freedom *par excellence*. With regard to the latter, Cassirer
correctly notes that Hegel's doctrine of *Sittlichkeit* never aimed – as
totalitarian regimes do – at assaulting and obliterating civil
society.[111] In the same connection, Carl Schmitt argues that, for
Hegel, *Sittlichkeit* has less to do with abolishing individual morality
for the sake of strengthening the sovereignty of the state than with
creating within the political sphere an association in which citizens
can think in common about the purpose and direction of public
life.[112] This, Schmitt says, is why the 'state is qualitatively distinct
from society and higher than it' in Hegel's political philosophy.[113]

The fact that Hegel approaches the political sphere with the idea
of promoting membership of a political association rather than with
that of buttressing the sovereignty of the state can be grasped if we
distinguish between his 'idealisation' of membership in the political
sphere and subsequent German 'idolisations' of the state.[114] This
distinction helps us to see how indictments of Hegel's conception
of *Sittlichkeit* often result from interpreting a call for citizens to join
together in political association as an 'invitation to totalitarianism'
(to borrow a phrase from Sheldon Wolin).[115] After all, identifying
the political sphere as an agent of 'universal values' does not necessarily entail granting the state unlimited power in the exercise of its
sovereign 'will'.[116] Aristotle understood this with reference to
Plato;[117] and Hegel understands it with reference to modern
totalitarians.

Is it at all surprising to think that Hegel envisaged the political
sphere in this way? Hardly, for there is a long tradition in western
political thinking, one with which he is often associated when he is
described as the 'modern' Aristotle,[118] in which the meaning of political membership turns far more on questions about the character
of the good life in an ethical sense than on questions about sovereignty. In this tradition, a political association is judged to be
superior to non-political associations (of the sort found in civil
society) because, through membership of a political association,
individuals form themselves into a community of fellowship whose
purposes are truly comprehensive. Membership in a political association, therefore, makes each individual responsible for the whole,
and not just for a part of the whole that may be of particular interest
to the individual citizen or to the group to which that citizen

belongs. It is, therefore, in view of its purpose that Aristotle and Hegel deem membership of a political association to be qualitatively superior to membership of non-political forms of association. There is accordingly a hierarchy of value here, but no involuntary subordination of the individual to the state.[119]

Indeed, in this tradition of political thinking, a middle way does exist between anti-individual collectivism (totalitarianism) and depoliticised individualism (liberalism). Accordingly, it is easy to see why, for Hegel, membership in a political association need not involve engulfment of the individual by the state. Rather, the chief function of *Sittlichkeit* seems to be to reassert the importance of what – following Wolin – we might call the 'politicalness' of citizenship in the modern world.[120] For in Hegel's hands, *Sittlichkeit*'s main aim is to focus the attention of citizens – as *bourgeoisie* and as Protestants – on ethical and spiritual values that they may have, or potentially have, in common with each other. *Sittlichkeit* is the ideological centrepiece of such a community.

Notes to general introduction

1 For much of what follows, see the long introduction to Knox and Pelczynski's edition of *Hegel's Political Writings*, pp. 5–137 (henceforth *KP*).

2 In 1872, a translation of a section of one of Karl Rosenkranz's many books on Hegel appeared in *The Journal of Speculative Philosophy* (vol. 6). It was entitled 'Hegel as Publicist' and made many of the points which Knox and Pelczynski advance here.

3 Some Hegel scholars perceived this as a provocative act. See the essays collected in Kaufmann (1970), especially the one by Sidney Hook.

4 A claim made famous by Haym (1857), pp. 355ff.

5 *KP*, p. 36.

6 For the 'Prussianism' argument, see Knox's sensible and still important essay of 1940 in Kaufmann (1970), pp. 13–29. The essays collected in Stewart (1996), pp. 53–128, also discuss the charge of Prussianism.

7 *KP*, p. 136.

8 Ritter (1982), pp. 36ff, develops this point in his famous essay of 1956 entitled 'Hegel and the French Revolution'.

9 *KP*, p. 136.

10 Schopenhauer (1974), p. 153, took this view in the early 1850s. A

modern essay on this theme can be found in Stewart (1996), pp. 289–300.

11 See, for example, Dahrendorf (1967), p. 193.

12 On the religious aspects of this alliance, see Bigler (1972); for a more politically focused study of the alliance, see Berdahl (1988).

13 Although *PWE* is a remarkable work, we have chosen not to include it in this volume of writings for a variety of reasons. For one thing, it dwells at great length on esoteric and antiquarian matters peculiar to the political history of Württemberg. What is more, many of the broader themes that Hegel does develop in it are dealt with in other essays included in this collection. An English translation of extracts from *PWE* can be found in Hegel (1964), pp. 246–94.

14 In *PWE*, Hegel associates himself with a reform impulse within Württemberg's government. By contrast, he is sharply critical of the obstructionism (i.e. unreflective traditionalism) of the Estates.

15 Harris (1972), p. 430, explains how similar Hegel's position is here to the one articulated by Charles Fox, the liberal English reformer.

16 The themes addressed in this paragraph have been the focus of much recent scholarly interest in the politicisation of German thinking in the late eighteenth century. Helpful essays on 'publicity', the 'association' movement, and the 'unpolitical German' argument can be found in Vierhaus (1987), and in the essays collected in Hellmuth (1990) and Schmidt (1996).

17 Klippel (1990) is particularly helpful in sorting out the differences between civil and political liberty in German thought in the late eighteenth century.

18 In one of his early theological writings, he had already declared his intention of repoliticising the idea of the *Staatsbürger*. See Hegel (1948), p. 284.

19 Vierhaus (1987), p. 96.

20 *Ibid.*, pp. 101–4.

21 In Hegel's mind, promoting such a spirit was a precondition of the exercise of the *Gemeinwillen* of citizens in the public sphere.

22 The interpretation of feudalism as an evolving system of social organisation was a widespread tendency in eighteenth-century European thought. For a view of British developments, especially on how the evolution of property shapes political institutions, see Smith (1987), pp. 71–2, 74, and 103.

23 Montesquieu's importance for German political thinking in the late eighteenth century has been discussed by Vierhaus (1987), pp. 9–32.

24 Hegel began studying Montesquieu in the mid-1790s. The Hanoverians, who were champions of Montesquieu in Germany, were also Anglophiles, very much aware of the dynastic connection between Hanover and England.
25 Useful information on these points can be found in McClelland (1971), esp. pp. 33–7.
26 See Brandes (1808), pp. 38–44 and 50ff. Although they were not published until 1808, Brandes's essays date back to the 1770s. Parry (1963), pp. 180–3, discusses the role of the machine state in eighteenth-century German political thinking.
27 Beiser (1992), pp. 304ff, discusses the Hanoverians' response to the French Revolution in terms of the machine state.
28 See, for example, the fragment of 1796 in Harris (1972), pp. 510–12; and Hegel (1948), p. 156.
29 We refer here to Schiller's *On the Aesthetic Education of Man*. Hegel (1984b), p. 36, called this work a 'masterpiece'. Schiller discusses the machine state in Letter 6: see Schiller (1967), pp. 33–7.
30 In 1801, Hegel identified Fichte as the thinker who had connected the two. See *GW*, vol. IV, p. 58.
31 Similarities between the earlier and later essays confirm that there is a high degree of continuity in Hegel's practical approach to modern political life throughout his career.
32 Waszek (1988), esp. pp. 157ff, provides an excellent analysis of the role of free labour in the evolution of Hegel's thinking about political economy and market societies.
33 This awareness is usually associated with arguments advanced by J. C. L. de Sismondi in the late 1810s.
34 Avineri (1985) shows that Hegel was aware of the theory of economic cycles in 1819–20 – in lectures he gave in Berlin. Similar arguments concerning over-production and the like can be found in *PR*, p 267. (It is important to note that in these instances Hegel is discussing factory work in England, not just the hardships faced by propertyless agricultural workers.)
35 In *SL* (p. 350), Montesquieu attributes the decline of monarchical power in England to the growing participation of the nobility in commerce.
36 As early as 1819–20, Hegel had been concerned about the kind of response the 'non-recognition' of such rights by the political class would provoke among the poor: see *PR*, pp. 453–4. It is the lack of any meaningful response, he implies, that turns a class of paupers into a 'rabble'.

37 On these German liberals, see Sheehan (1973).
38 Hegel discusses the 'police' function of government in *PR*, pp.
   259ff. A good definition of how Hegel uses the term 'police' can
   be found in the editorial note in *PR*, p. 450: '[it] includes all the
   functions of the state which support and regulate the activities of
   civil society with a view to the welfare of individuals. Thus it
   includes public works (e.g. highways, harbours, and waterways),
   all economic regulatory agencies, and also what we would call the
   "welfare" system'. Under no circumstances should this concept be
   uncritically equated with the policy of an authoritarian government
   or police state.
39 For the full quotation, see Waszek (1988), p. 197.
40 There is evidence in the writings of J. S. Mill and of various
   Saint-Simonians in those years that some progressive thinkers outside Germany admired the achievements of Prussia's civil servants.
41 Hegel appears here to be taking his cues from various statements
   in the *Morning Chronicle* (January 1828) concerning the 'ignorance
   and imbecility' of England's ruling class: see Petry (1976), pp.
   56–7.
42 Compare Hegel's line of argument with that developed by Turgot
   (1977) in his famous eulogy of Gournay (1759) in which the per-
   sistence of 'vestiges' of feudalism in England are explained as a
   consequence of a 'republican' reluctance to use state power to
   effect reform, even when the reform is deemed progressive.
43 Waszek (1988), pp. 196ff, discusses this topic in terms of what he
   calls 'Hegel's qualifications of liberalism'.
44 The contrast between 'property' and 'persons' in England goes
   back to the 1770s – specifically to Major Cartwright's criticism of
   Parliament for its failure to expand the basis of political representation. The argument surfaced again in 1818 in the pages of the
   Edinburgh Review, in James Mackintosh's criticism of Bentham for
   having seemingly aligned himself with Cartwright on the issue of
   universal suffrage. Mackintosh's fear was that expansion of the
   suffrage would not only pit 'property' against 'opinion' but would
   lead to political revolution as well. Mackintosh's views are important in the present context because they are those of a liberal
   reformer, and because there is evidence – adduced by M. J. Petry
   in 1976 – that Hegel's views on the Reform Bill mirrored those of
   the group in England around Mackintosh and James Mill.
45 See Petry (1976), esp. pp. 13 and 56–7, for some striking similarities of attitude.
46 *Ibid.*, pp. 56–7, alludes to James Mill's political strategy of using

the threat of revolution on the part of others to win reforms from the government. Hegel, we have seen, (*M*, p. 2), had used the same strategy in 1798 (although he did not learn it from Mill).

47 These writings, not published until 1907, inaugurated a new era of Hegel scholarship. Much of what was published at that time has now been translated into English. The most famous of these writings are translated in Hegel (1948). For some of the other translated pieces, see Hegel (1984a).

48 These terms are used in Hegel (1948), pp. 71–4, 77, 81, and 92 n 25; and in Hegel (1984a), pp. 45, 56, 72, 81, and 94.

49 See Hegel (1948), pp. 71–4, 86. Lessing (1956), p. 106, had already drawn this distinction in 1780.

50 Hegel (1984a), pp. 47, 79–80, and 87.

51 See Hegel (1984a), pp. 45–6, 93, 106, 109, 115–16, 132, 135, and 154.

52 See Hyppolite (1996), pp. 35ff. Hegel delivered his first formal set of lectures on the philosophy of right in 1817. Student notes on these lectures have recently been discovered and published in Hegel (1995). The editors of these lectures refer to them as 'Hegel's first philosophy of right'. Obviously, Hyppolite thinks *NL* deserves that designation.

53 The argument concerning man as an 'image' or 'likeness' of God has long been associated with religious optimism and ethical perfectionism. For its background in the ancient world, see Jaeger (1961), esp. p. 99. O'Regan (1992) offers an excellent discussion of the role which 'the theology of the image' plays in Hegel's thought. Similarly, Steven Ozment (1969: esp. pp. 35–46) discusses the image and likeness argument in the thought of German mystics of the late Middle Ages (e.g. in Tauler). Tauler, of course, is a thinker whom Hegel studied in the 1790s.

54 Hegel (1984b), p. 41. In the history of Christian thought, the idea of 'approaching' or 'drawing near to' or 'assimilating' to God has often been associated with that of man as God's image and likeness (referred to in note 53 above). Towards the end of his life, Hegel discusses this relationship at length in *AC* (p. 187–8 below).

55 Late in his life, in *PH*, he still has recourse to this distinction. See p. 309 n 19 below.

56 Throughout the 1790s, Hegel uses the word 'awaken' to explain what occurs when human beings become receptive to ennobling religious instruction. See, for example, Hegel (1948), p. 71.

57 See Hegel (1984a), pp. 45–6, 95–9, and 154–7. Hegel discusses 'the process of externalisation' in philosophical language in *FK*, p. 57.

58 The argument is developed in *FK*, pp. 55–66 and 147–52. At this time, Schelling also held this view. See Schelling (1966), pp. 95–6.
59 In *FK* and *NL*, Hegel repeatedly links Protestantism with subjectivism. At this time, however, he hesitates to associate his search for a new religion of *Sittlichkeit* with a reform of Protestantism. That change will come later.
60 See, for example, *FK*, p. 57.
61 *Ibid.*, pp. 151–2.
62 Both, he says (*FK*, p. 149), delight in 'deification of the subject'.
63 *PR*, pp. 14–16. Here he argues that *Sittlichkeit* prevents the penetration of 'atheism' into the 'ethical world'. Implicit in this formulation is the idea that atheism and atomism are connected in civil society.
64 Among Hegel scholars, Harris is almost alone in appreciating the circumstances in the early 1800s in which Hegel began to Protestantise *Sittlichkeit*. See Harris (1983), pp. 505 and 515–16, and Harris (1993), p. 49 n28.
65 Toews (1980) is excellent both on the limited extent of Hegel's influence in Prussia and on the way in which his philosophy worked its way into the Prussian educational system.
66 *BIA* is similar to, but more fully developed than, the inaugural address Hegel delivered in Heidelberg in 1816 (henceforth *HIA*).
67 See for example, Haym (1857), pp. 355ff.
68 Rosenberg (1958) and Sheehan (1989), p. 431. The particulars of the political situation at the university around 1818 are discussed by Jaeschke and Meist (1981), pp. 29–39; by Hoover (1988); and by Crouter (1980).
69 Avineri (1972), p. 118; Toews (1980), pp. 59–60.
70 This view is supported by what Hegel says in 1817 in *PWE*. See Hegel (1964), p. 259.
71 *FK*, p. 57.
72 Hegel's growing commitment to this pattern of development has been remarked upon by Clark Butler. See the commentary in his splendid edition of Hegel's correspondence (Hegel 1984b: pp. 122, 300–2, 317, and 324).
73 Hegel continues to contrast feeling and thinking throughout the 1820s. See the discussion in Dickey (1993).
74 In a letter of 1816, he writes '[Among Protestants] our universities and schools are our churches'. See Hegel (1984b), pp. 327–9. On the basis of this remark, it appears that Hegel sees Protestant Prussia as an agent of common or collective culture rather than of an individualising one.

75 In *HIA*, Hegel refers to the 'sacred fire' which has been passed from nation to nation since antiquity. In this earlier address, he also likens Germany's mission to that once undertaken by the Jewish people.

76 See Hegel (1964), p. 263.

77 To appreciate the Protestant dimension of *BIA*, one needs to understand the connection Hegel had been making since 1805 between advances in science and an emerging liberal Protestant outlook. For the background to this connection, see Hegel (1984b), pp. 104–8 and 326–9.

78 Berdahl (1988) discusses each of these groups.

79 For the situation in 1818, see Jaeschke and Meist (1981), pp. 29–39; Hoover (1988); and Crouter (1980).

80 Dickey (1993), pp. 331–4, explains some of the religious conflicts in Prussia in 1830.

81 *PR*, pp. 12–18.

82 See *PR*, p. 16, where Hegel associates *Sittlichkeit* with the 'right kind of piety'.

83 *PR*, p. 22.

84 See Hegel (1948), esp. pp. 105, 121–2, and 127.

85 Hegel contrasts 'doctrine' and 'life' as early as 1793. See Hegel (1984a), p. 55.

86 Although these terms were used by Protestants in the early modern period of European history, our usage of them refers to the important historiographical debate that surrounds them today. On this debate, see the collected essays in Schilling (1986). References to late sixteenth- and early seventeenth-century thinkers who used these terms can be found in the same collection – in the essays of P. Munson (pp. 296–7) and W. Neuser (pp. 379–85) – as well as in Schilling (1992), pp. 273–4.

87 Although the use of Protestant norms to criticise Prussia is often discussed in relation to the Young Hegelians' critique of the Prussian state in the late 1830s, it is already present in Hegel's writings in the 1820s. Jaeschke (1983), p. 37, has understood this very well.

88 Despite his biases against Hegel, Schopenhauer (1995), p. 16, was one of the first to appreciate how and why Hegel proposed to turn Christianity 'inside out'. Schopenhauer was critical of that turn. In the early twentieth century, George Santayana (1968, p. 111) indicted Hegel for the same reason, citing the inside-out movement of his religious thinking as evidence of Hegel's alleged Calvinism.

89 Many of the additions Hegel makes to the 1827 and 1830 editions

of the *Encyclopedia of the Philosophical Sciences* contain comments on Catholicism and Protestantism as political ideologies.

90 Jaeschke (1983) shows how important the matter of continuity and change in Hegel's political thinking is with regard to the Revolution of 1830 in France. The issue is crucial for Hegel scholars since much of the animus against Hegel as a political thinker arises from the perception – articulated by J. G. Droysen (1808–84) in 1831 – that Hegel was a 'philosopher of the Restoration' because he criticised the 1830 Revolution. See Nicolin (1970), p. 431, for Droysen's remark.

91 They do not, however, become more free as self-regarding individuals. Rather, they gain more freedom by becoming members of a political association.

92 See, for example, Ritter (1982), pp. 184–5.

93 We summarise Pelczynski's argument in *KP*, pp. 128–37.

94 *KP*, p. 38.

95 See Novalis (1996), p. 71. The structure and direction of Novalis's argument mirrors the negative view of the French Revolution advanced by one of the main theorists of the Catholic counter-revolution in France in the 1790s, namely Joseph de Maistre: see de Maistre's diatribe of 1798 against Protestantism and the French Revolution in de Maistre (1884), pp. 63–97. It is the link between Protestantism and the French Revolution in Catholic thinking that forced Hegel to separate the second Reformation from the Revolution.

96 Riedel (1984), pp. 107–56, offers an astute analysis of this development in Hegel's thinking.

97 See Hegel (1948), pp. 156–7 and 284.

98 In 1762, in *On the Social Contract*, Rousseau had contrasted *bourgeois* and *citoyen* (Rousseau, 1978, p. 54 n). Among German thinkers in the 1790s, similar contrasts abounded. Hegel's distinction may be understood, in part, as having evolved from that discussion.

99 Hegel elaborates this point in 1802–3 in his long essay *System of Ethical Life*, translated in Hegel (1979), pp. 99–177.

100 In 1932, Schmitt (1996, p. 62) used this phrase in discussing *NL*. Macpherson (1962) develops the idea in his famous study of English political thought in the seventeenth century.

101 Harris (1993, p. 49 n 28) uses the phrase 'civic Protestantism' to characterise the religio-political aspect of *Sittlichkeit* in Hegel's writing after 1802.

102 See Knudsen (1990).

103 The phrase 'dialectic of *Sittlichkeit*' comes from Dahrendorf (1967), pp. 188ff. He uses it in conjunction with an argument about the German fascination with the 'myth of the state'. In the English translation of Dahrendorf's German, *Sittlichkeit* is misleadingly rendered 'morality'; we therefore use the German here.

104 See, for example, Santayana (1968), where this dialectic is discussed in terms of what Santayana calls the 'migratory ego'.

105 Schopenhauer (1974), pp. 144 and 162.

106 Dahrendorf (1967), pp. 188ff, bases his analysis of Hegel's political ideas on the connection between the dialectic of *Sittlichkeit* and the myth of the state. Both, as it turns out, reduce free individuals to the status of bees in a hive (p. 122). Schopenhauer (1974), pp. 147 and 153, twice uses the beehive image to disparage Hegel's theory of the state.

107 Dahrendorf (1967), p. 193.

108 *Ibid.*, pp. 122 and 188–93.

109 For a discussion which distances Hegel from the myth of the state in German history, see Cassirer (1946), pp. 311–47, esp. p. 338.

110 Barker (1957), p. xvii.

111 Cassirer (1946), p. 346.

112 Schmitt (1996), pp. 24–5.

113 *Ibid.*, p. 24.

114 Cassirer (1946), p. 347, makes this all-important distinction.

115 Wolin (1960), p. 434.

116 Schmitt (1996), p. 24, suggests that a state may be 'universal' without being 'total'. The inclusion of 'will' in the latter distinguishes it from the former.

117 Aristotle, *Politics*, 1261a 17–25, 1263b 8–15, and 1263b 30–40.

118 Royce (1919), p. 214.

119 In formulating the above argument, we found Wolin (1960), pp. 429–34, helpful (although Wolin is not discussing Hegel here). In *NL*, p. 114, Hegel speaks of 'non-subjugated oneness' as the key to *Sittlichkeit*.

120 Wolin (1960), p. 431.

Chronology of Hegel's life and career

1770   Born 27 August in Stuttgart, Germany. His father
       was a minor civil servant in the state government
       of Württemberg.

1773–1788 Schoolboy years, during which his mother dies
       (1783).

1788–1793 Attends the University of Tübingen. Holds a ducal
       scholarship to study theology in the famous
       theological seminary (*Stift*). Develops friendships
       with his classmates Hölderlin and Schelling.
       Observes the polarisation between Kantians of the
       'letter' and 'spirit' at the university. Composes in
       1793 the important 'Tübingen Essay' in which
       religious and theological themes are addressed.

1793–1800 Unable to secure a university position, is employed
       as a tutor – first (1793–96) by a wealthy family in
       Berne, Switzerland, and then (1797–1800) by a
       family in Frankfurt. Reads widely during these
       years and writes extensively on the civil history of
       religion in the ancient world (the 'early theological
       writings'). Becomes interested in, and writes on,
       political affairs in Berne, Württemberg, and the
       German Empire. Probably begins to study political
       economy around 1798.

1801–1807 Following his father's death in 1799, receives an
       inheritance which allows him to accept an
       unsalaried teaching position in philosophy at the

University of Jena (helped by Schelling, who is already teaching there). Co-edits *CJ* with Schelling and begins to write philosophical essays, including *The Difference between Fichte's and Schelling's System of Philosophy* (1801). Publishes *FK* and *NL* in *CJ* (1802–3). Offers lectures throughout the Jena period (1801–7) which culminate in the publication of the *Phenomenology of Mind* (1807).

1807–1816   Napoleon's occupation of much of Germany results in the closing of the University of Jena. Unemployed, Hegel accepts a position as a newspaper editor in Bamberg (1807). Becomes principal of a *Gymnasium* (secondary school) in Nürnberg one year later. Marries in 1811; son born in 1812. (In 1806, he had fathered a child out of wedlock.) Volume I of the *Logic* published in 1812, volume II in 1816.

1816–1818   Accepts an appointment to teach philosophy at the University of Heidelberg in 1816. Among other things, he sees his role as combating the pernicious influence of Fries in philosophy. Within the student movement of these years (the *Burschenschaften*), which was dominated by Fries's students, Hegel's own students offer an ideological alternative to the nationalistic and anti-semitic views of the Friesians. Publishes the *Encyclopedia of the Philosophical Sciences* and *PWE* in 1817. Also begins in 1817 to lecture on the philosophy of right.

1818–1831   Called to Berlin to teach philosophy, gaining the appointment in preference to Fries. As political reaction grows in Prussia and central Europe after 1818, Hegel's liberal supporters in the bureaucracy lose much of their influence. Important figures in the university and government distrust Hegel and persecute his students. Publishes *PR* in 1821 and is accused – by Fries among others – of 'servility' to the Prussian state. Beginning in 1821, lectures regularly on religion, art, the history of philosophy, and the philosophy of history. In 1827 and 1830 greatly expanded versions of the *Encyclopedia* appear. Many of the additions to this text incorporate changes he had been making in his lectures during the 1820s. Takes ill in a cholera epidemic and dies 14 November 1831.

Translator's preface

Hegel's writings, particularly his more abstract and systematic works, confront the translator with numerous problems. The principles which I have followed in translating the more abstract texts in this collection – especially *On the Scientific Ways of Treating Natural Law*, but also *The Relationship of Religion to the State* and parts of the extract from the *Lectures on the Philosophy of History* – are identical with those which I followed in my translation of Hegel's *Elements of the Philosophy of Right* (Cambridge, 1991; published in the same series as the present volume) and which I described in detail in my preface to that translation (pp. xxxv–xliv). The most important of these principles is the need to adopt consistent renderings of key expressions in Hegel's system and to avoid confusion between similar or related terms with different nuances of meaning; the English equivalents for all such terms are listed, with explanatory comments where necessary, in the glossary towards the end of this volume.

One of the main difficulties in translating the present collection was due to the fact that the texts included in it vary considerably in form and subject matter and were written at widely separated stages of Hegel's career, from his earliest phase as a writer to the last year of his life. Their style and linguistic register are correspondingly varied, from the impassioned youthful rhetoric of the early pamphlet *The Magistrates should be Elected by the People* (1798) to the discursive historical prose of *The German Constitution* (1798–1802), the dense abstraction of the essay on *Natural Law* (1802–3), the academic formalities of the Berlin *Inaugural Address* (1818), the

Ciceronian Latin of the *Address on the Tercentenary of the Augsburg Confession* (1830), and the political journalism of *On the English Reform Bill* (1831). One of the consequences of this variety is that the kind of terminological consistency which is possible and desirable in translating the systematic works of Hegel's later years could not be sustained throughout the collection: for example, words which, in a given work or period, are invested with semi-technical or programmatic meanings (as with such terms as *aufnehmen/Aufnahme*, *Bestimmtheit*, and *Potenz* in the essay on *Natural Law*) may subsequently revert to their traditional meanings or be abandoned altogether in favour of new expressions whose meaning is itself subject to further variation. Considerations such as these explain why some of the renderings listed in the glossary to this volume differ from those in the corresponding glossary to my translation of Hegel's *Philosophy of Right*, and why a greater number of alternative renderings for certain terms are listed here than were listed in the earlier glossary. In translating the less technical pieces in the present collection such as the essays on *The German Constitution* and *On the English Reform Bill* – I have made greater concessions to readability and naturalness of English expression than were feasible in translating the more abstract and systematic works; in such cases, I followed the same procedure as I did many years ago in translating the (relatively non-technical) Introduction to Hegel's *Lectures on the Philosophy of World History* (Cambridge, 1975).

As on previous occasions, I have consulted – and frequently benefited from – the work of earlier translators. In particular, I am indebted to T. M. Knox's translation of the essay on *Natural Law* (University of Pennsylvania Press, 1975; reprinted 1982) for its illuminating renderings of some of Hegel's most obscure and idiosyncratic formulations. It must, however, be said that the overall accuracy of Knox's translation of this work, and of the works translated in his and Z. A. Pelczynski's edition of *Hegel's Political Writings* (Oxford, 1964), is lower than that of some of his other translations, such as that of the *Philosophy of Right* (Oxford, 1942). For example, I was able to correct over seventy substantial errors and omissions in his translation of the essay on *Natural Law*, almost as many in that of the essay *On the English Reform Bill*, and well over a hundred in his translation of *The German Constitution*; these included such basic mistakes (page references to the Knox–

Pelczynski edition) as 'France' instead of 'Franconia' for *Franken* (pp. 187, 224, 226), 'they became subjects' instead of 'they acquired subjects' for *sie bekamen Untertanen* (p. 203), 'mercenaries' instead of 'paymasters' for *Soldherren* (p. 219), 'early in 1800' instead of 'at the end of 1800' for *zu Ausgang des Jahres 1800* (p. 226), 'possession of abbeys' instead of 'filling of offices' for *Besetzung der Ämter* (p. 232), 'for more than 150 years' instead of 'more than 150 years ago' for *vor mehr als anderthalbhundert Jahren* (p. 306), and many more.

J. Sibree's translation of the *Philosophy of History*, first published in 1858 but still in widespread use (revised edition by Dover Publications, New York, 1956), cannot strictly be described as a translation at all, for much of it consists of loose paraphrase, with Sibree's own elaborations and interpretations, often with serious misunderstandings, masquerading as Hegel's text. In welcome contrast, the translation by P. C. Hodgson, R. F. Brown, and J. M. Stewart of *The Relationship of Religion to the State* (in Hegel's *Lectures on the Philosophy of Religion*, ed. Peter C. Hodgson, 3 vols., Berkeley, Los Angeles, and London, 1984–87, volume I, pp. 451–60) is generally reliable and workmanlike, despite a handful of errors, and I was glad to adopt various of their renderings.

Two items in this volume are translated into English for the first time, namely Hegel's *Inaugural Address* at the University of Berlin and his Latin *Address on the Tercentenary of the Augsburg Confession*. Johannes Hoffmeister's edition of the latter text (in volume XI of his edition of Hegel's *Sämtliche Werke*, Hamburg, 1956, pp. 30–55) includes a parallel German translation by Georg Lasson, with Hoffmeister's revisions; but this contains so many omissions and inaccuracies that I found it preferable to work directly from Hegel's original Latin.

All but two of the texts in this volume are translated from Hegel's *Werke*, edited by Eva Moldenhauer and Karl Markus Michel (20 vols., Suhrkamp Verlag, Frankfurt am Main, 1970). The originals can be found in volume I, pp. 268–73 (*The Magistrates should be Elected by the People*), volume I, pp. 461–581 (*The German Constitution*), volume II, pp. 434–530 (the essay on *Natural Law*), volume X, pp. 399–404 (the Berlin *Inaugural Address*; my translation also takes account of the corrections to this text in Hegel's *Gesammelte Werke. Kritische Ausgabe*, ed. Deutsche Forschungsgemeinschaft, Hamburg, 1968–, volume XVIII, pp. 11–18), volume XI, pp.

83–128 (*On the English Reform Bill*), and volume XII, pp. 491–97, 502–8, and 520–40 (*Lectures on the Philosophy of History*). The *Address on the Tercentenary of the Augsburg Confession* is translated from volume XI of Hoffmeister's edition of the *Sämtliche Werke* (see previous paragraph), and *The Relationship of Religion to the State* is translated from Hegel's *Sämtliche Werke*, ed. Hermann Glockner (20 vols., Stuttgart, 1927–30), volume XV, pp. 256–67.

Square brackets are used throughout the English translations to indicate material interpolated by the translator. Such material includes original German terms where it seemed to me helpful to supply these after their English equivalents (see glossary for further explanation), and English words or phrases which I have added to complete the sense or otherwise facilitate comprehension of Hegel's argument, but for which no equivalent is present in the German text. As in my translation of the *Philosophy of Right*, I have retained both of the devices which Hegel employs to mark paragraph divisions, namely a new line plus indentation for major divisions, and a dash before the beginning of a new sentence for minor divisions.

I am indebted to Laurence Dickey for his scrutiny of the translated texts.

H. B. Nisbet

Abbreviations

The translator's preface provides references to the German editions
of Hegel's works which are translated in this volume.

AC	Hegel,	*Address on the Tercentenary of the Submission of the Augsburg Confession* (25 June 1830)
BIA	Hegel,	*Inaugural Address, Delivered at the University of Berlin* (22 October 1818)
CJ		*Critical Journal of Philosophy*. Some of the items in *CJ* are translated in Harris (1985).
CPR		Immanuel Kant, *Critique of Pure Reason*, 2nd edn (1787), tr. Norman Kemp Smith (London, 1958)
CPrR		Immanuel Kant, *Critique of Practical Reason* (1788), tr. Lewis White Beck (Indianapolis, IN, 1956)
ERB	Hegel,	*On the English Reform Bill* (1831)
FK	Hegel,	*Faith and Knowledge* (1802), tr. W. Cerf and H. S. Harris (Albany, NY, 1977)
GC	Hegel,	*The German Constitution* (1798–1802)
GG		*Geschichtliche Grundbegriffe*, eds. O. Brunner, W. Conze, and R. Koselleck (8 vols., Stuttgart, 1972–97)
GW	Hegel,	*Gesammelte Werke*, ed. Deutsche Forschungsgemeinschaft (20 vols., Hamburg, 1968–)
HIA	Hegel,	*Inaugural Address, Delivered at the University of Heidelberg* (28 October 1816). The German

xlix

		text can be found in *GW*, vol. XVIII (Düsseldorf, 1995)
KP		Refers to Z. A. Pelczynski's 'An Introductory Essay' in *Hegel's Political Writings*, tr. T. M. Knox, ed. Z. A. Pelczynski (Oxford, 1964), pp. 5–137.
M	Hegel,	*The Magistrates should be Elected by the People* (1798)
NL	Hegel,	*On the Scientific Ways of Treating Natural Law, on its Place in Practical Philosophy, and its Relation to the Positive Sciences of Right* (1802–1803)
PH	Hegel,	*Lectures on the Philosophy of History* (1827–1831)
PR	Hegel,	*Elements of the Philosophy of Right*, ed. Allen Wood, tr. H. B. Nisbet (Cambridge, 1991)
PWE	Hegel,	*Proceedings of the Estates Assembly in the Kingdom of Württemberg 1815–1816*. An extensive excerpt can be found in Hegel (1964), pp. 246–94.
RRS	Hegel,	*The Relationship of Religion to the State* (1831)
SL		Montesquieu, *The Spirit of the Laws* (1748), trs. A. Cohler, B. Miller, and H. Stone (Cambridge, 1989)
SR		Johann Gottlieb Fichte, *The Science of Rights* (1796–1797), tr. A. E. Kroeger (London, 1970). The German original, *Grundlage des Naturrechts nach Prinzipien der Wissenschaftslehre*, appears in Fichte's *Werke*, vol. I/3 (Stuttgart, 1966).
Werke	Hegel,	*Werke: Theorie Werkausgabe*, eds. E. Moldenhauer and K. M. Michel (20 vols., Suhrkamp Verlag, Frankfurt, 1970)

The Magistrates should be Elected by the People[1]

[On the recent internal affairs of Württemberg, in particular the inadequacies of the municipal constitution][2]

(1798)

To the people of Württemberg

It is time that the people of Württemberg ceased to vacillate between hope and fear, to alternate between expectancy and frustrated expectations.[3] I will not say that it is also time for everyone who, in the midst of change or in preserving the old, seeks only his own limited advantage or the advantage of his class [*seines Standes*] and consults only his own vanity, to renounce these paltry desires, to cast aside these petty concerns, and to fill his soul with concern for the general [good]. For men of nobler aspirations and purer zeal, it is time above all to focus their undirected [*unbestimmten*] will on those parts of the constitution which are founded on injustice, and to apply their efforts to the necessary change which such parts require.

Peaceful satisfaction with the present [*dem Wirklichen*], hopelessness, and patient acceptance of an all-too-vast and omnipotent fate have given way to hope, expectation, and courage to face the new. A vision of better, juster times has come to life in the souls of men, and a longing and yearning for a purer and freer destiny has moved all hearts and alienated them from the present reality [*der Wirklichkeit*].[4] The urge to break down paltry barriers has fixed its hopes on every event, every glimmering [of change] – even on

I

criminal actions. From what quarter could the people of Württemberg expect more just help than from the Assembly of their Estates? Time and deferment of the satisfaction of their hopes can only refine their longing and separate the pure from the impure; yet it can only intensify the urge to remedy a genuine need, and any delay will make the longing eat more deeply into men's hearts, for it is not just a fortuitous attack of light-headedness which will soon pass away. You may call it a paroxysm of fever, but it can end only with death, or when the diseased matter has been sweated out. It is the effort of a still robust constitution to expel the illness.[5]

The feeling that the political edifice as it still exists today cannot be sustained is universal and profound. The anxiety that it may collapse and injure everyone in its fall is also universal. – With this conviction in our hearts, is this fear to become so powerful that it will be left to chance to decide what shall be overthrown and what shall be preserved, what shall stand and what shall fall? Ought we not ourselves to try to abandon what cannot be sustained, and to examine with a dispassionate eye what makes it unsustainable? Justice is the only yardstick for such a judgement, and the courage to do justice is the only power which can honourably and peacefully remove the unstable edifice and produce secure conditions in its place.

How blind are those who like to believe that institutions, constitutions, and laws which no longer accord with men's customs, needs, and opinions, and from which the spirit has departed, can continue to exist, or that forms in which feeling and understanding no longer have an interest are powerful enough to furnish a lasting bond for a nation [*eines Volkes*]![6]

All the attempts of pompous bungling to restore confidence in constitutional elements and arrangements in which no one any longer has faith, and to conceal the gravediggers behind a screen of fine words, not only cover their ingenious instigators with shame, but also prepare the way for a much more terrible outburst in which vengeance will ally itself to the need for reform and the ever-deceived, ever-oppressed mass will mete out punishment to dishonesty.[7] To do nothing when the ground shakes beneath our feet but wait blindly and cheerfully for the collapse of the old building which is full of cracks and rotten to its foundations, and to let oneself be crushed by the falling timbers, is as contrary to prudence as it is to honour.[8]

2

If a change has to happen, then something has to be changed. So banal a truth needs to be stated, given the difference between fear which must and courage which will; for whereas those who are driven by fear may well feel and admit that change is necessary, they nevertheless display the weakness, as soon as a start has to be made, of trying to hold on to everything they possess. They are like a spendthrift who is obliged to cut his expenditure but cannot dispense with any article he has hitherto required and has now been advised to do without, and who refuses to give up anything – until he is finally deprived of dispensable and indispensable alike. No nation [*Volk*], including the Germans, can afford to display such weakness. In the cold conviction that a change is necessary, they should not be afraid to scrutinise every detail; the victim of injustice must demand the removal of whatever injustice they discover, and the unjust possessor must freely give up what he possesses.

This strength to rise above one's own small interests for the sake of justice is presupposed in the following enquiry, as is the honesty to will this end, and not just to pretend to do so. Only too often, wishes and zeal for the common good conceal the reservation 'in so far as it coincides with our own interest'. Such willingness to consent to every reform takes fright and grows pale as soon as demands are made of those who express it.

Far from this hypocrisy, let each individual and each class [*Stand*] look first to themselves to weigh up their own rights and circumstances before they make demands on others and look outside themselves for the cause of the evil; and if they find themselves in possession of inequitable rights, let them strive to restore the balance in favour of others. Anyone who wishes may regard this demand to begin with oneself as blind and ineffectual, and the hope for this kind of injustice set aside for [. . .]⁹

So long as it is not in one's power to reform or reverse those reforms which have already been attempted and found to be harmful, it is as well not to go beyond those changes whose consequences can be foreseen and assessed throughout their entire extent, and to be content with eliminating the sources of abuse.

Both in earlier and more recent times, the primary cause of all the troubles of the provincial assembly [*Landschaft*] was the presumptuousness of the senior officials.¹⁰ The Council [*Ausschuß*], of course, found it very convenient to employ men to speak and write on its behalf (or even, at a pinch, to think for it). Meanwhile, a large proportion of the Council's members spent their income in comfortable ease, and no doubt looked after their own spiritual welfare on the side, leaving the country's affairs to run their course as providence and its leaders wished. To be sure, the common herd fared badly if one of its herdsmen proposed to lead it east, and another west. The majority naturally followed the one who had the key to the hayloft, who could tempt them with fairer words and more ably conceal his wolfish nature beneath his sheep's clothing. In this way, the Council – and with it the country – was led by the nose by the Council's officials.[11]

The Council itself was never presumptuous. But its consultants and lawyers were. It was merely indolent, and it unthinkingly put its name to all the high-handed actions of these officials. It was they who seduced the Council into a [degree of] generosity towards the Court which was equalled only by the frivolity of the reasons which were adduced in order to justify such expressions of devotion. It was they whom the Court sought to enlist, because it was sure of attaining its end once it had managed to harness the lawyers and consultants to its interests. It was they who determined whether the complaints and wishes of individual classes [*Stände*] were to be heeded. It was they who took charge of the incoming documents and kept their existence secret from the Council until such time as they chose to bring the relevant matter up for discussion. And in fact, no priest has ever exercised greater control over the consciences of his penitents than these political confessors did over the official consciences of the Councillors to whom they were answerable.[12]

The consultants in the narrower sense had, incidentally, nothing to do with financial matters. They were not privy to the operations of the secret account. The self-interest of the members of the Council could therefore expect no favours from them. They were not consulted over the making of appointments, and they played no direct part in any election. This ensured that the lawyers were at a marked advantage, even if they were without talents or knowledge. But even in the elections, the indirect influence of the consultants was unmistakable. A candidate for office had every hope of outdoing the favourite of a lawyer if the most influential consultant was his friend and advocate.

Fortunately, the Council has also at times had right-minded and well-disposed men as consultants;[13] and although they did keep the Council on leading-strings – because it had not learned to walk unaided – they never (or at least not knowingly and deliberately) led it into the mire.

As far as the Diet is concerned, the dangerous influence of this monstrous officialdom has increased rather than diminished. We have grown accustomed to regarding the consultants as essential elements of the provincial assembly's constitution [*der landschaftlichen Verfassung*]. Their official sphere of influence has been enlarged. They have reaped benefits from the rivalry of the deputies. They have contrived to make themselves independent of the Council, their employer and judge in official matters. Until the Diet [was set up], the Council could dismiss an incompetent consultant without argument, and it did so on more than one occasion. Now, perhaps, the consultant might demand that the ruler, to whom he betrays the interests of the provincial assembly [*Landschaft*], should be his judge [. . .]

[. . .] as long as everything else remains as it was, as long as the people do not know their rights, as long as there is no collective spirit [*Gemeingeist*], and as long as the power of the officials remains unchecked, popular elections would serve only to bring about the complete overthrow of the constitution.[14] The chief priority is to place the right of election in the hands of a body of enlightened and upright men who are not dependent on the Court.[15] But I fail to see what kind of election might give us any expectation of an assembly of this kind, however carefully one defined active and passive [kinds of] eligibility [. . .]

The German Constitution (1798–1802)[1]

[Introduction]

Germany is no longer a state.[2] The older teachers of constitutional law had the idea of a science in mind when they dealt with the constitutional law of Germany, and they accordingly set out to specify a concept of the German constitution. But they could not reach agreement on this concept, and their modern counterparts finally gave up looking for it. The latter no longer treat constitutional law as a science, but as a description of what is present empirically without conforming to a rational Idea; and they believe that it is only in name that they can describe the German state as an empire or body politic.

There is no longer any argument about which concept the German constitution falls under. What can no longer be related to a concept [*begriffen*] no longer exists. If Germany were supposed to be a state, we could only describe the present condition of the state's dissolution as anarchy (as a foreign scholar[3] of constitutional law did), were it not that the parts have reconstituted themselves into states which have retained a semblance of unity,[4] derived not so much from a bond which still exists as from the memory of an earlier one. In the same way, fallen fruit can be seen to have belonged to a particular tree because it lies beneath its branches; but neither its position beneath the tree nor the shade which the tree casts over it can save it from decomposition and from the power of the elements to which it now belongs.

6

The health of a state generally reveals itself not so much in the tranquillity of peace as in the turmoil of war.[5] The former is a state [*Zustand*] of enjoyment and activity in isolation, in which government is a wise paternalism which makes only ordinary demands upon its subjects; but in war, the strength of the association between all [individuals] and the whole is displayed, both in the extent of the demands which this association has managed to impose on individuals and in the worth of what the latter are prepared to do for it of their own initiative and inclination [*Trieb und Gemüt*].[6]

Thus, in the war with the French Republic, Germany has found by its own experience that it is no longer a state. Both in the war itself and in the peace which concluded it, it has become aware of its political condition. The following are the tangible results of this peace: some of the finest German territories have been lost, together with several million of the country's inhabitants; a burden of debt, which weighs more heavily on the southern than on the northern half, prolongs the misery of war far into the peace; and apart from those states which have come under the rule of the conquerors, and hence also of foreign laws and customs, many others will lose what is their highest good, namely their existence as independent states.

The present peace affords an opportunity to consider the inner causes, or spirit, of these results, which are merely the external and necessary appearances of this spirit. Besides, this consideration is in itself worthy of anyone who does not simply surrender to current happenings but recognises the event and its necessity. By such recognition, he distinguishes himself from those who see only arbitrariness and chance through the eyes of their own vanity, and thereby convince themselves that they would have exercised wiser and more effective control over all that happened. For most people, such recognition is of importance only because they [can derive enjoyment from][a] it and from the intelligent judgements on individual things which it makes possible, not in order that they may learn by experience how to act better on a future occasion. For there are very few people who can act in these great events in such a way as to direct

---

[a] *Translator's note*: *Werke* (p. 463) fills the bracketed lacuna in Hegel's text with the words *brüsten können* ('can brag about'). I find no evidence in the passage for this pejorative term, and conjecture instead *unterhalten können* ('derive enjoyment from') or some similar expression.

their course, whereas the others must serve the events with understanding and insight into their necessity. But those who learn from the experience of mistakes which are[b] an expression of inner weakness and imprudence are not so much those who have made the mistakes: on the contrary, they are merely confirmed in their habit of making them. It is others who take note of [*kennenlernen*] them and are enabled by this insight to profit accordingly; and if they are at all capable of doing so, and if their external circumstances make this possible, they are in possession of an insight which may well be lacking in the thought of a private individual.

The thoughts which this essay contains can have no other aim or effect, if expressed publicly, than that of promoting an understanding of what is, and hence a calmer attitude and a tolerant moderation both in words and in actual contact [with events]. For it is not what is that makes us impetuous and causes us distress, but the fact that it is not as it ought to be; but if we recognise that it is as it must be, i.e. that it is not the product of arbitrariness and chance, we also recognise that it is as it ought to be.[7] But it is difficult for human beings in general to rise to the habit of trying to recognise and think [in terms of] necessity. For between the events and their free apprehension they interpose a mass of concepts and ends, and they expect what happens to conform to these. And when it doubtless turns out otherwise in most cases, they get round their concepts by arguing that, whereas these were governed by necessity, the events were governed by chance. For their concepts are just as limited as their view of things, which they interpret merely as individual events and not as a system of events ruled by a spirit; and whether they suffer from these events or merely find that they contradict their concepts, they find in asserting their concepts the right to complain bitterly about what has happened.

It is no doubt recent developments above all which have afflicted the Germans with this vice. In the perpetual contradiction between what they demand and what happens contrary to their demand, they appear not only censorious but, when they talk only of their concepts, untruthful and dishonest; for they attribute necessity to their concepts of right [*Recht*] and duties, whereas nothing happens

---

[b] *Translator's note*: I follow T. M. Knox (p. 144) in reading *sind* ('are') for Hegel's *ist* ('is').

in accordance with this necessity, and they are themselves all too accustomed on the one hand to a constant contradiction between their words and the deeds [of others], and on the other to trying to make of the events something quite different from what they really are, and to twisting their explanation of them to fit certain concepts.

But anyone who tried to understand [*kennenlernen*] what normally happens in Germany by looking at the concepts of what ought to happen – namely the laws of the state – would be utterly mistaken. For the dissolution of the state can be recognised primarily from the fact that everything is at variance with the laws. He would likewise be mistaken if he took the form[c] assumed by these laws to be the true ground and cause of this dissolution. For it is precisely with regard to their concepts that the Germans seem dishonest enough not to acknowledge anything as it is, and not to present it as either more or less than the facts actually warrant. They remain true to their concepts, to right and the laws, but the events tend not to correspond with these, so that whichever party [*Seite*] stands to gain an advantage by doing so strives to reconcile the two by means of words with the force of concepts. But the concept which embraces all the others is that Germany is still a state today only because it once was a state, and because those forms whose inner life has [now] departed are still with us.

The organisation of that body known as the German constitution took shape in [the context of] a life quite different from that which later invested it and does so now. The justice and power, the wisdom and valour of times gone by, the honour and blood, the well-being and misfortune of long-deceased generations and of the manners and relationships which perished with them, are [all] expressed in the forms of this body. But the course of time, and of the culture [*Bildung*] which develops within it, has cut the destiny of that age off from the life of the present.[8] The structure in which that destiny resided is no longer supported by the destiny of the present generation;[d] it stands without sympathy for the latter's interests and is unnecessary to them, and its activity is isolated from

---

[c] *Translator's note: Werke* reads *Form*, whereas Rosenkranz, *Hegels Leben* (Berlin, 1844), p. 241 reads *Farbe* ('colour'). The word is indistinct in the original manuscript.

[d] *Translator's note: Geschlechts*; Hegel's manuscript reads *Schicksals* ('destiny' or 'fate'), which is plainly an error.

the spirit of the world. If these laws have lost their former life, the vitality of the present age has not managed to express itself in laws. The vital interest of each has gone its own way and established itself separately, the whole has disintegrated, and the state no longer exists.

This form of German constitutional law is deeply grounded in that quality for which the Germans have become most famous, namely their drive for freedom.[9] It is this drive which did not permit the German people to become subject to a common political authority [*Staatsgewalt*], [even] after all the other peoples of Europe subjected themselves to the rule of a common state. The obduracy of the German character has never yielded sufficiently for the individual parts [of Germany] to sacrifice their particular characteristics to society, to unite in a universal [whole], and to discover freedom in common, free subjection to a supreme political authority.

The quite distinctive principle of German constitutional law has an unbroken connection with the condition of Europe [as it was] when the nations participated directly in the supreme authority, and not indirectly through laws. Among the peoples of Europe, the supreme political power was a universal authority in which each was accorded a kind of free and personal share; and the Germans have not wished to transform this free personal share, which is dependent on the arbitrary will, into a free share independent of the arbitrary will and consisting in the universality and force of laws. Instead, they have based their most recent condition entirely on the foundation of the previous condition of an arbitrary will which, though not opposed to law, is nevertheless lawless.

The later condition arises immediately out of that condition in which the nation constituted a people without being a state. In that age of ancient German freedom, the individual stood on his own in his life and his actions; his honour and destiny were not based on his association with a class [*Stand*], but on himself. Relying on his own sense and powers, he was either destroyed by the world, or shaped it to please himself. He belonged to the whole by virtue of custom, religion, an invisible living spirit, and a few major interests. Otherwise, in his activity and deeds, he did not allow himself to be limited by the whole, but imposed restrictions on himself, without fear or doubt, solely on his own [initiative]. But what lay within his sphere was so very much and so completely himself that it could not even be called his property; on the contrary, he would put life and limb, soul and salvation at risk for what belonged to his sphere, for what we would describe as [only] a part and [for which we] would therefore risk only a part of ourselves. He knew nothing of that division and calculation on which our legal arrangements depend, so that it is not worth the trouble of risking one's neck for a stolen cow or openly setting one's individuality against a power – like that of the state – which is ten times or infinitely superior [to one's own]; instead, he was completely and wholly [involved] in what was his own. (In French, *entier* means both 'entire' and 'obstinate'.)[10]

Out of this self-willed activity, which alone was called freedom, spheres of power over others were shaped by chance and character, with no regard for a universal and with little restriction by what is known as political authority; for the latter, as opposed to individuals, scarcely existed at all.

These spheres of power were fixed by the passage of time. The parts of the universal political power became a multiplicity of exclusive property, independent of the state itself and distributed without rule or precept. This manifold property does not constitute a system of rights, but a collection without principle, whose inconsistencies and confusion required the most acute perception to rescue it as far as possible from its contradictions whenever a collision occurred; or rather, it required constraint and superior strength [for the conflicting elements] to be reconciled with one another, but as far as the whole was concerned, it required above all the most special divine providence for it to survive at all.[e]

Political powers and rights are not offices of state designed in accordance with an organisation of the whole, and the services and duties of individuals are not determined by the needs of the whole. On the contrary, every individual member of the political hierarchy, every princely house, every estate [*Stand*], every city, guild, etc. – everything which has rights or duties in relation to the state – has

---

[e] *Translator's note*: (Deleted passage in Hegel's MS): German constitutional law is therefore a collection of private rights; every individual part of the state, every princely house, every estate [*Stand*], every town, guild, etc., everything which has rights in relation to the state, has acquired these for itself; the state had in the first instance no other function in this regard but to confirm that it had been deprived of its power.

acquired them for itself; and in view of this reduction of its power, the state has no other function but to confirm that it has been deprived of its power. Consequently, if the state loses all authority, and individual ownership [*Besitz*] rests on the power of the state, the ownership of those who have no other support but the power of the state, which is virtually nil, must necessarily be very precarious.

The principles of German public law [*öffentliches Recht*] should therefore not be derived from the concept of the state or the concept of a specific constitution such as monarchy, etc., and German constitutional law is not a science based on principles but a register of the most varied constitutional rights acquired in the manner of civil law [*Privatrecht*].[11] Legislative, judicial, spiritual and military powers are intermingled, divided, and combined in the most irregular manner and in the most disparate proportions, just as diverse as the property of private individuals.

The political property of every member of the German body politic is most carefully defined by decrees of the Imperial Diet,[12] peace treaties, electoral contracts [*Wahlkapitulation*], domestic settlements, decisions of the Imperial Court, etc. The care devoted to this has been extended, with the most religious punctiliousness, to absolutely everything, and years of effort have been devoted to apparently insignificant things such as forms of address, orders of procession and seating, the colour of various furnishings, etc. Given the utmost precision with which it determines every circumstance relating to right, however trivial, the German state must be credited with the best organisation in this regard. The German Empire, like the realm of nature in its productions, is unfathomable on a large scale and inexhaustible on a small scale, and it is this aspect which fills those who are initiated into the infinite details of the [various] rights with such wonder at the venerability of the German body politic and with such admiration for this most scrupulous system of justice.

This [system of] justice, whereby each part is maintained in separation from the state, stands in absolute contradiction to the necessary claims of the state on its individual members. The state requires a universal centre – a monarch and Estates – in which the various powers, foreign relations, defence, and their relevant finances etc. are united, a centre which not only directs [the whole] but also has the necessary power to assert itself and its resolutions and to keep the individual parts in [a state of] dependence on itself. On the other hand, the individual estates are assured by right of almost complete – or rather wholly complete – independence. If there are aspects of independence which are not expressly and solemnly defined in electoral contracts, decrees of the Imperial Diet, etc., they are [nevertheless] sanctioned in practice – a more important and comprehensive legal title [*Rechtsgrund*] than all the others. The German political edifice is nothing other than the sum of the rights which the individual parts have extracted from the whole, and this justice, which watches carefully to ensure that no power remains in the hands of the state, is the essence of the constitution.

Even if the unfortunate provinces which come to grief through the helplessness of the state to which they belong should denounce its political condition; even if the head of the Empire and the patriotic estates which first came under pressure should vainly appeal to the others for collective action; even if Germany should be pillaged and abused – the constitutional lawyer will know how to demonstrate that all this is wholly in accordance with rights and with practice, and that all these misfortunes are trifles in comparison with the operation of this [system of] justice. If the unfortunate manner in which the war has been conducted derives from the behaviour of individual estates, one of which contributed no contingent at all and very many of which sent raw recruits instead of soldiers; if another paid no Roman Months,[13] a third withdrew its contingent at the hour of greatest need, many concluded peace agreements and treaties of neutrality, and the great majority, each in its own way, nullified the defence of Germany – constitutional law can [nevertheless] prove that the estates had a right to behave in this way, a right to plunge the whole into the greatest danger, havoc, and misfortune. And since these are rights, the individuals and the whole must most rigorously guard and protect such rights [even the right] to be destroyed completely. There is perhaps no more fitting motto for this legal edifice of the German state than this:

Fiat iustitia, pereat Germania![14]

It is a feature of the German character – if not a rational one, then at least to some extent a noble one – that it regards right in general, whatever its basis and consequences, as something sacrosanct. If, as seems very likely, Germany should entirely cease to exist as a separate independent state, and [with it] the German nation as a people, it would still be gratifying to observe that, amidst the spirits of destruction, the fear of the law [*Recht*] was still conspicuous.

The political condition and constitutional law of Germany would afford such a spectacle if Germany could be regarded as a state; its political condition would have to be viewed as legal [*rechtliche*] anarchy,[15] and its constitutional law as a legal system opposed to the state. Yet everything supports the conclusion that Germany should no longer be regarded as a unified political whole, but rather as a collection of independent and essentially sovereign states. But it is said that Germany is an empire or body politic under a common imperial head and within an imperial union. There can be absolutely no objection to these expressions as legal titles; but an enquiry dealing with concepts is not concerned with these titles (although the definition of the concepts [in question] may clarify what such titles may mean). Admittedly, such expressions as 'empire' and 'imperial head' are often treated as concepts, and they must act as stop-gaps when the need arises.

The teacher of constitutional law who can no longer call Germany a state because he would then have to concede various consequences which flow from the concept of a state but which he finds inadmissible, adopts the expedient – since Germany is not supposed to be regarded as a non-state either – of treating the title 'empire' as a concept. Or, since Germany is neither a democracy nor an aristocracy, but ought essentially to be a monarchy – although the Emperor is not supposed to be regarded as a monarch either – the Emperor's title of 'Imperial head' is adopted as an expedient, even within a system in which determinate concepts rather than titles are supposed to predominate.

To apply the completely general concept of 'Imperial head' to the Emperor is to consign him to the same category as the former Doge of Venice and the Turkish Sultan. Both of these are likewise heads of state, but the former was the very limited head of an aristocracy, while the latter is the most unlimited head of a despotism. And since the concept of a head [of state] applies to the most diverse range of supreme political authority, it is completely indeterminate and consequently valueless. It purports to express something, but has in fact expressed nothing at all.

Such meaningless expressions should be avoided in scientific and historical [contexts], even if the German character requires them as stop-gaps in actual life. For given the inherent stubbornness of the Germans in sticking firmly to their own will in civil life, and given the separate and irreconcilable interests of the state in [the sphere of] politics, if there are other important reasons why unity should nevertheless be achieved in these two areas, there is no better means [of attaining it] than by finding a general expression which satisfies both [parties], and which nevertheless respects the will of each. In this case, the difference remains as before; or if one party really must give ground, the same general expression at least allows it to avoid admitting that it has done so.

The Germans have for centuries kept up a semblance of unity with the help of such general expressions, although no party has in fact renounced one iota of its claims to independence. Reflection on this matter, particularly if it aims to be scientific, must stick to concepts, and in judging whether a country is a state, it must not waste its time with general expressions, but should consider what degree of power remains to that [body] which is to be called a state; and since it appears on closer examination that what is generally described as constitutional law [*Staatsrecht*] consists [in fact] of rights *against* the state [*Rechte gegen den Staat*],[16] the question arises of whether, in spite of this, the state still [possesses] a power by virtue of which it really is a state. And if one looks more closely at what is required for this purpose, comparing it with the situation of Germany in this respect, it will emerge that Germany can in fact no longer be called a state. We shall [now] review the various principal powers which must be present within a state.

I The Concept of the State

A mass of people can call itself a state only if it is united for the common defence of the totality of its property.[17] Although this is in fact self-evident, it should nevertheless be pointed out that this union should not only have the intention of defending itself, but actually does defend itself by force of arms, whatever power and success it may have. For no one will be able to deny that Germany is united in law and in words for its common defence; but we cannot distinguish here between laws and words on the one hand and deeds and actuality on the other, or say that Germany defends itself collectively at least in law and in words, if not in deeds and actuality. For property and its defence through a political union are things which refer exclusively to reality [*Realität*], and whose ideal equivalent [*Idealität*] is anything but a state.

Plans and theories have a claim to reality in so far as they are *practicable*, but their value is the same whether they exist in actuality or not; a theory of the state, on the other hand, can be called a state and constitution only in so far as it actually exists. If Germany were to claim to be a state and constitution despite the fact that the forms of these were devoid of life and their theory lacked actuality, it would be stating an untruth; but if it actually promised in words [to provide] a common defence, we would have to attribute this either to senile weakness, which still has volition but is no longer able [to put it into practice], or to dishonesty, which does not keep its promises.

For a mass [of people] to form a state, it is necessary that it should form a common military force and political authority. But the manner in which the particular effects and aspects of the union which result from this are present, or the particular constitution [which is chosen], is irrelevant to the formation of an authority by a mass [of people]. The ingredients required for this particular operation may in any case be present in the most diverse ways; and in a specific state, there may even be complete irregularity and disparity in such matters. In considering these, we must distinguish between two things: between what is necessary for a mass [of people] to become a state and common authority, and what is merely a particular modification of this authority and does not belong to the sphere of the necessary but, in conceptual terms, to the sphere of greater or lesser improvement and, in terms of actuality, to the sphere of chance and arbitrary will.

This distinction has a very important aspect for the peace of states, the security of governments, and the liberty of peoples. For if the universal political authority demands of the individual only what is necessary for itself, and places appropriate limits on the measures required for the performance of this necessary service, it may in other respects grant the citizens their living freedom and individual [*eigenen*] will and even leave considerable scope for the latter.[18] In the same way, the political authority, which is concentrated in the government as its necessary centre, is looked on less enviously by the individuals on the periphery if it demands [only] what is necessary and what everyone can recognise as indispensable to the whole. It thereby avoids the danger that, if the central political authority is responsible both for what is necessary and for more arbitrary things, and if both are demanded with equal strictness as [requirements] of the government, the citizens may also confuse the two and, if they grow equally impatient with both, they may place the necessary demands of the state in jeopardy.

The manner in which the whole political authority exists in a supreme point of convergence [*Vereinigungspunkt*] must be relegated to that part of the state's actuality which is governed by chance. Whether the authority is vested in one [person] or many, whether the one or the many are born to such majesty or elected to it, is of no importance in relation to the one essential factor [*das einzig Notwendige*], namely that a mass [of people] should form a state; it is just as irrelevant as the uniformity or lack of uniformity of civil rights among the individuals who are subject to the universal political authority. We are not in any case concerned with that inequality of nature, talents, and mental energy [*Energie der Seele*] which creates a much more considerable difference than does inequality of civil circumstances. The fact that a state counts among its subjects serfs, burghers, free nobility, and princes who in turn have subjects themselves, and that the relationships of these particular classes [*Stände*], even as particular members of the polity, do not exist in a pure form but in endless modifications, does as little to prevent a mass [of people] from forming a political authority as does the fact that the particular geographical members [of the state] constitute provinces with different relations to the inner constitutional law.

As far as actual civil laws and the administration of justice are concerned, neither identical laws and legal processes nor identical weights, measures, and currency would make Europe a state; nor does their diversity nullify [*aufheben*] the unity of a state. If it were not inherent in the very concept of the state that the more precise determinations of legal relationships involving the property of individuals in opposition to other individuals do not impinge on the state as a political authority – for the latter has to determine only its own relationship to property – the example of nearly all European states could teach us as much, because the most powerful of the genuine states have utterly disparate laws. Before the Revolution, France had such a multiplicity of laws that, in addition to the Roman law which obtained in many provinces, Burgundian law, Breton law, etc. prevailed in others, and almost every province, indeed almost every city, had a particular inherited law. A French writer truthfully said that anyone who travelled through France changed laws as often as he changed post-horses.

Another question extraneous to the concept of the state is which particular power is responsible for legislation, and what relative share the various estates or citizens in general have in this process.[19] Likewise irrelevant is the character of the courts of law – whether, in the various instances of the administration of justice, the members inherit their office, are appointed to it by the supreme authority, or are freely entrusted with it by the citizenry or nominated by the courts themselves. It is also immaterial what the scope of a specific court's jurisdiction is, whether this has been determined by chance, whether there is a common supreme court for the entire state, etc.

Equally independent of the state is the form of administration in general; it may likewise lack uniformity, as may the institutions of the magistracy, the rights of cities and estates, etc. All these circumstances are only relatively important for the state, and the form of their organisation is irrelevant to its true essence.

In all European states, unequal taxes are imposed on the various classes according to their material worth; but there is even more inequality on the ideal side, namely in their rights and duties and in the origin of these. The inequality of wealth gives rise to an inequality of contributions to the state's expenditure, but this is so little a hindrance to the state that the more modern states are in fact based on it. It is just as little affected by the inequality of contributions by the different estates of nobility, clergy, and the burghers and peasantry; and apart from everything that is called privilege, the reason why these estates contribute in different proportions lies in the difference between the estates [themselves], for the proportion can be determined only in terms of what they produce, not in terms of the essential aspect of what the contribution is levied on, namely in terms of work – for work cannot be quant-ified and is inherently unequal.

It is also fortuitous whether the different geographical parts of a state are differently weighted [for tax purposes], what transform-ations and subordinate systems the taxes pass through, whether a city receives the land tax, a private individual the ground rent, an abbey the tithes, the nobleman the hunting rights, the [rural] com-mune the grazing rights, etc. from one and the same field, and whether the various estates and bodies of all kinds develop their own arrangements with regard to taxation. All such fortuitous cir-cumstances remain external to the concept of political authority, to which, as the central point, only the determinate quantity [of tax-ation] is necessary, whereas the unequal proportions in which the contributions flow in are irrelevant as far as their origin is con-cerned. Besides, the entire fiscal arrangements may in any case lie outside the state while the latter is nevertheless very powerful, as in the old feudal system, in which [the vassal], in serving the state in emergencies, at the same time supplied all his needs by his per-sonal efforts, while the state derived from its own domains the income it required for other purposes. Alternatively, it is also con-ceivable that all expenditure might be financed in the latter manner, in which case the state [in question], even as a monetary power – which a state has to be in modern times – would not be a centre of taxation; on the contrary, what the state collected as taxes, given the actual arrangements applying to most of these, would be on the same footing of particular right [*Recht*] as [the income of] other people whose relationship to the state was that of private individuals.

In our times, the links between members [of a state] may be equally loose, or even non-existent, as far as customs, education, and language are concerned; and identity in these respects, which was once a pillar of national union, now counts as one of those fortuitous circumstances whose nature does not prevent a mass [of people] from constituting a political authority. Rome or Athens, and even any small modern state, could not have survived if the many languages in use in the Russian empire had been spoken within their frontiers, or if the customs of their citizens had been as varied as they are in Russia (or as customs and culture [*Bildung*] are even in any major city in a large country). Diversity of language and dialect, the latter of which makes divisions more vexatious than does total incomprehensibility, and diversity of customs and culture among the separate estates, which makes it almost impossible for people to recognise one another except by their outward appearance – such heterogeneous and at the same time most powerful elements could be overcome and held together in the enlarged Roman Empire only by the weight of superior power, just as they are in modern states by the spirit and art of political organisation. Consequently, disparity of culture and customs has become a necessary product, as well as a necessary condition, of the continued existence of modern states.[20]

It is in religion that the innermost being of mankind is expressed and in which, as a fixed centre, human beings can still recognise themselves, even if all other external things scattered around them are of no consequence. Only by this means could they manage to trust and be sure of one another, despite the inequality and mutability of their other relationships and situations. But even the need to find identity at least in this sphere has been found superfluous in modern states.

Even in the northern part of Europe, religious unity has always been the prerequisite of a state. No alternative was known, and without this original oneness, no other oneness or trust seemed possible. At times, this bond has itself become so powerful that, on certain occasions, it has suddenly transformed peoples who had previously been alien to one another or national enemies into a *single* state. A state of this kind has been not just a holy community of Christians, nor a coalition uniting their interests and the activity associated with these, but a *single* secular power and state which, as a *single* people and army, has also conquered the homeland of its own eternal and temporal life in a war against the East.[21]

Neither before this time nor after the fragmentation [of Christendom] into nations [*Völker*] has a shared religion prevented wars or united the nations into a single state – no more than religious diversity causes any state to break up in our own times. Political authority, as pure political right [*Staatsrecht*], has managed to separate itself from religious authority and its right, to preserve sufficient stability of its own, and to organise itself in such a way that it has no need of the Church; it has thereby returned the Church to that condition of separation from the state which it occupied in relation to the Roman state at the time of its origin.

Admittedly, in those political theories which, in our own times, have either been propounded by would-be philosophers and teachers of human rights or realised in vast political experiments,[22] everything we have excluded from the necessary concept of political authority – except the most important [aspects] of all, namely language, culture [*Bildung*], customs, and religion – is subordinated to the immediate activity of the supreme political authority. As a result, it is determined by this authority, and all these aspects [referred to above] are drawn into it even in their smallest ramifications.

It is self-evident that the highest political authority must exercise ultimate control of the internal relations of a people and of their organisation as determined by chance and the arbitrary will of former times, and ensure that these factors do not impede the main activity of the state; on the contrary, the latter activity must secure itself above all these, and to this end, it must not spare the subordinate systems of rights and privileges. But it is a great advantage of the older European states that, while their political authority is secure in respect of its needs and functions, it leaves free scope for the citizens' own activity in individual aspects of judicial procedure [*Rechtspflege*], administration, etc. – both in the appointment of the necessary officials and in the conduct of current business and the application of laws and conventions.

Given the size of modern states, it is quite impossible to realise the ideal of giving all free men a share in the discussion and resolution [*Bestimmung*] of universal political issues. Political authority must be concentrated in one centre, both for the implementation [of decisions] by the government, and for the decisions themselves. If popular respect ensures that this centre is secure in itself and immutably sanctified in the person of a monarch chosen by birth and in accordance with natural law, the political authority can freely allow the subordinate systems and bodies, without fear or jealousy, to regulate a large part of the relationships which arise in society, and to maintain them in accordance with the laws; and every estate, city, village, commune, etc. can enjoy the freedom to do and implement for itself what lies within its province.[23]

Just as the laws on such matters have gradually arisen as a hallowed tradition directly out of custom itself, so the legal constitution, the institutions of the lower judiciary, the corresponding rights of the citizens, the rights of city administrations, the collection of taxes (whether national or those required for the needs of the cities themselves) and the lawful application of such taxes – everything is this category has come together of its own accord and developed by itself, and it has likewise maintained itself ever since it first emerged.

The highly complex organisation of the ecclesiastical establishments is not the work of the supreme political authority either, and the whole [ecclesiastical] estate maintains and renews itself more or less internally. – The large sums spent annually on the poor in a large state, and the extensive arrangements made for this purpose throughout all parts of a country, are not financed by state-imposed charges, nor is the whole establishment maintained and run on the state's instructions. The mass of property and income devoted to this end derives from foundations and gifts by individuals, just as the whole establishment and its administration and operation [are] independent of the supreme political authority. In the same way, the majority of internal social arrangements for each specific area of need have been created by the free action of the citizens, and their continuance and life are sustained by this very freedom, undisturbed by any jealousy or anxiety on the part of the supreme political authority – except that the government to some extent protects them, or limits the excessive growth of any part of such arrangements which might suppress other necessary parts.

It is, however, a basic prejudice of those recent theories which have been partially translated into practice that a state is a machine with a single spring which imparts movement to all the rest of its infinite mechanism, and that all the institutions which the essential nature of a society brings with it should emanate from the supreme political authority and be regulated, commanded, supervised, and directed by it.[24]

The pedantic craving to determine every detail, the illiberal jealousy of all direction and administration by an estate, corporation, etc., of its own affairs, this pusillanimous carping at all independent activity on the part of the citizens[25] – even if its significance is purely general and of no relevance to the political authority – has been dressed up in the guise of rational principles. According to these principles, not one farthing of the communal expenditure for the relief of poverty in a country of twenty or thirty million inhabitants [may be spent] unless it has first been not merely approved, but ordained, controlled, and inspected by the supreme govern-

ment. As for educational provisions, the appointment of every village schoolmaster, the expenditure of every penny on a pane of glass
in the village school or the parish council chamber, the appointment
of every toll-clerk, bailiff, or village magistrate should be directly
instigated and effected by the highest governmental authority; and
in the entire state, every morsel of food, from the soil that produces
it to the mouth that consumes it, should follow a course that is
examined, computed, corrected, and ordained by state, law, and
government.

This is not the place to argue in detail that the centre, as the
political authority and government, must leave to the freedom of
the citizens whatever is not essential to its own role [*Bestimmung*]
of organising and maintaining authority, and hence to its external
and internal security, and that nothing should be so sacred to it as
the approval and protection of the citizens' free activity in such
matters, regardless of utility; for this freedom is inherently sacred.

But as far as utility is concerned, if we are to calculate the advantage that is gained if the citizens administer their own affairs
through particular bodies, their own judicial procedure, their own
appointments to the offices required for this purpose, etc., three
calculations are necessary. The first concerns the tangible factor, i.e.
the money which thereby accrues to the supreme political authority;
the second concerns the ingenuity [*Verstand*] and efficiency with
which all the operations of a machine proceed at a regular pace, in
accordance with the shrewdest calculation and the wisest ends; but
the third concerns the vitality, the contented spirit and free and
self-respecting confidence which result if the individual will has a
share in universal affairs (in so far as their ramifications are contingent from the point of view of the supreme political authority).

As to the first calculation (concerning tangible advantage), the
state whose principle is universal mechanism fancies that it has an
undoubted advantage over the state which leaves [matters of] detail
largely to the rights and individual action of its citizens. But it
should be noted in general that the former state cannot possibly
have the advantage unless it imposes altogether heavier taxes. For
when it takes over all branches of administration, judicial procedures, etc., it simultaneously incurs all the associated costs; and
if the whole [state] is organised as a universal hierarchy, these costs
must also be covered by regular taxation. Conversely, the state

which leaves it to interested individual groups [*Einzelheiten*] to make the necessary arrangements for such purely contingent individual matters as the administration of justice, costs of education, contributions to poor relief, etc., and to bear the associated costs, will find that these costs are met in a form other than by taxation. Whoever requires a judge, an advocate, or a teacher, or who cares for the poor on his own initiative, alone bears the cost. No tax is levied, and no one pays for a court, an advocate, a teacher, or a clergyman unless he requires one. Similarly, if [someone] is elected to [one of] the lower positions of authority in a court of law or the administration of civic or corporate affairs, and if he is elected by the members themselves, that person is paid by the honour which is thereby done to him; but if he is employed by the state, he must demand that the latter pay him, because this inherent honour is no longer present. Even if more money might have to be spent by the people in the first of these two cases than in the second (although this is unlikely), the effects in each case are as follows. The first makes the difference that no one spends money on something which he finds unnecessary, on something which is not a universal need of the state; and the second produces an actual saving for everyone. The overall effect is that the people feel themselves treated in the first case in a rational manner and in accordance with necessity, and in the latter case with trust and freedom; and this is what constitutes the main difference between the second and third types of calculation [referred to above].

The mechanistic hierarchy, highly ingenious and dedicated to noble ends, extends no trust whatsoever towards its citizens, and therefore cannot expect any from them in return. It has no confidence in any achievement whose direction and execution it did not itself organise; it therefore prohibits voluntary donations and sacrifices, and displays to its subjects its conviction of their lack of understanding, its contempt for their ability to judge and perform what is conducive to their private welfare, and its belief in universal depravity. It therefore cannot hope for any lively activity or support from the self-confidence of its citizens.

There is a difference here which is too great to be grasped by a statesman who takes account only of what can be quantified in precise figures. This difference can be seen most obviously in the prosperity, well-being, probity, and contentment of the inhabitants of the one state, as compared with the apathy, baseness (which constantly turns into effrontery), and poverty of the other. In matters of major importance where only the contingent aspect of the event is outwardly visible, a state of the latter kind determines this very contingency and renders it necessary.

It makes an infinite difference whether the political authority is organised in such a way that everything on which it can rely is in its own hands (although for this very reason it cannot rely on anything else), or whether, apart from what is in its own hands, it can also rely on the free allegiance, self-confidence, and individual enterprise of the people – on an all-powerful, indomitable spirit which the hierarchical state has expelled and which lives only where the supreme political authority leaves as much as possible in the care of the citizens themselves. Only the future can tell how dreary and spiritless life will be in a modern state like that which the French Republic has become,[26] in which everything is regulated from above, and where nothing of universal significance is entrusted to the management and execution of interested sections of the people – if, that is, the present pedantic style of government can survive. But what [sort of] life and what aridity prevails in another similarly regulated state, namely Prussia, will strike anyone who enters its first village or observes its complete lack of scientific and artistic genius, and who does not measure its strength in terms of the transient energy which a solitary genius was able for a time to extract from it.[27]

Thus, we do not only distinguish between that necessary element within a state which must remain in the hands of the political authority and be directly determined by it, and that element which, though absolutely necessary for the social cohesion of a people, is contingent as far as the public authority as such is concerned. We also regard a people as fortunate if the state allows it considerable freedom in subordinate activities of a universal kind, and we likewise regard a political authority as infinitely strong if it can be supported by a greater spirit of freedom, untainted by pedantry, among its people.

Thus, the illiberal demand that laws, the administration of justice, the imposition and collection of taxes, etc., language, customs, culture [*Bildung*], and religion should be regulated and governed from a single centre is not fulfilled in Germany; on the contrary, the most disparate variety prevails in these matters. But this would not prevent Germany from constituting a state it if were organised in other respects as a political authority [. . .]²⁸

[II History and Critique of the Constitution of the German Empire]

[*1. The Armed Forces*]

The propagation of this warlike talent proves in itself that these hosts of armed men are not idle. For centuries, no major war has been waged among the European powers in which German valour has not invariably won honour, if not laurels, and in which rivers of German blood have not been shed.

Despite its populousness, the warlike talents of its people, and the readiness of its rulers to shed their blood, and despite its wealth of resources – both living and inanimate – required for warfare, no land is more unprotected, more incapable of self-defence – let alone conquest. Neither its attempts to defend itself nor even its aspirations to do so are significant or creditable.

It is common knowledge that the armed forces [of the Empire] consist in the military units of the larger and smaller estates. As far as the latter are concerned, these armies, regiments [*Heere*], contingents, or whatever we choose to call them are usually soldiers who can perform only police functions or parade duties, not warriors who know nothing higher than the fame of the regiment and service to which they belong. The military spirit which lifts the heart of every warrior in a great regiment when he hears the words 'our army', this pride in his estate and service [which is] the soul of a fighting force, cannot prosper in the Town Watch of an Imperial City or the personal bodyguard of an abbot. The kind of respect which the uniform of a great regiment arouses for a hitherto unknown individual who wears it cannot be accorded to the uniform of an Imperial City. When the bravest soldier of a small Imperial estate declares 'I have been in this service for twenty (or thirty) years', his words evoke a quite different feeling and effect from what they would produce if they came from an officer of a great regiment, because the man's own self-esteem and the respect which others have for him grow with the size of the whole to which he belongs; he shares in the fame which the latter has accumulated over the centuries.

The insignificance of these sundry little military units as a result of their small numbers is serious enough without being made even more so by ineptitude and other unfavourable circumstances. Very great disadvantages must ensue if the smaller estates recruit their soldiers, and often appoint their officers, only when war breaks out, and consequently send untrained men into the field; if one estate has to supply the drummers and another the drums, etc.; if the merging of contingents from numerous estates leads to incompatibility of weapons, drill, etc., and to unfamiliarity of the troops with their officers; if each estate is actually entitled to provision its forces itself, so that the greatest disorder prevails in the service and – not to mention the unnecessary expense – operations are hindered by superfluous civilians and camp followers. According to legal theory, a detachment of twenty men from different estates may in fact be served by twenty of their own supply clerks, bakers, etc.. Since the Imperial Register[29] is several centuries old, it no longer reflects the relative size and strength of the estates and consequently gives rise to discontent, complaints, and permanent deficits; it also includes territories whose geographical position can indeed no longer be identified. But these and a hundred other circumstances are so familiar that it is tiresome even to mention them.

Now if the insignificance of the military units of the smaller estates disappears when they come together and coalesce as an Imperial Army, the disadvantages described above, along with innumerable others, render this force less useful in war than any army in the rest of Europe, including even that of Turkey; besides, the very name 'Imperial Army' has had other associations of a particularly unfortunate kind. While the names of other armies, including foreign ones, awaken thoughts of valour and formidable strength, the name of the Imperial Army, if mentioned in German company, used rather to brighten every face, to provoke all kinds of witty reactions according to circumstances and the class [of those present], and everyone would dip into his fund of anecdotes on the subject to entertain the others. Those who consider the German nation serious and incapable of comedy have forgotten the farces of the Imperial wars, which were conducted with every possible appearance of gravity but were at bottom genuinely ridiculous.

While the organisation of the Imperial Army, with all its consequences, has not improved in the slightest, an awareness of the
misfortune it has generated, and of Germany's dishonour, has
diminished the general predilection for jokes at its expense. It is
only because some aspects of its organisation in the last war – for
example, the commissariat – were run illegally and unconsti-
tutionally that its troops were of any use at all.

What is even more of a disadvantage than all these specific features of the Imperial Army is that, in point of fact, no such army
has ever been assembled; and this is the most tangible proof of
Germany's dissolution into independent states.

According to the theory of the basic laws [of the Empire], the
Imperial Army might be a formidable force, but practice, that
powerful principle of German constitutional law, tells a very different story. If only too often one sees a vast number of German
soldiers in the field, one may assume that they are acting not as an
Imperial Army to defend Germany, but rather to inflict internal
injuries on it. What is known as the German constitution is not
only incapable of preventing such wars, but in fact makes them
right and lawful.

The German army is all the more inconsiderable [a force] when
it is mobilised for the protection of Germany. For although the
fivefold contingents of Brandenburg, Saxony, Hanover, Bavaria, and
Hesse are fighting forces in their own right and together make up
a formidable army in which the ineptitude of the smaller associated
contingents disappears from view, they are dependent on something
very different from the laws of Germany, and their contribution to
its defence is just as unreliable and fortuitous as the contribution of
any foreign power.

The Austrian contingent is an exception, for the Emperor, as
monarch of other kingdoms, is obliged to raise its strength far
beyond what his estate requires him to do, given the weakness and
unreliability of the statutory army. He is consequently also obliged
to let Germany enjoy the full range and exercise of his extra-
territorial power. But in the case of the other large contingents, the
Empire cannot count on their statutory strength, or even on their
availability; and even if an estate has supplied its contingent, there
is no guarantee that, in the midst of war and at moments of the
greatest danger, it will not enter into separate treaties of neutrality

or peace with the enemy of the Empire and abandon its beleaguered fellow estates to their own weakness and to the devastating superiority of the enemy.

Despite the fact that the right of the estates, under Imperial law, to form alliances with foreign powers and to choose between foreigners and Germany is limited by the clause 'in so far as such alliances do not conflict with their duties to the Emperor and Empire', this clause is in practice rendered ambiguous as a legal principle, or rather eliminated altogether. Not only the actions of the estates, but also their votes in the Imperial Diet, may ensure that they are prevented by their other commitments from participating in the formation of an Imperial contingent or paying contributions towards the war.

This withdrawal of support for the common defence on the part of the more important estates places others in a helpless position, and this in turn compels them to retreat not just from difficulty and danger, but also from their obligations to the whole. It would be wholly unnatural to demand that they should rely on and contribute to a protection which, as all the world knows, protects nothing at all, and which is legally and constitutionally withheld as a result of the right [of the estates] to form alliances. Under these circumstances, it becomes necessary for the weaker to put themselves under the protection of those powerful fellow estates which are on friendly terms with the enemy, thereby diminishing the overall mass of the collective might. In this way, the powerful estates in question profit not only by a saving of effort, but also by obtaining advantages from the enemy in return for their inactivity. Finally, in weakening the overall mass by the contribution they receive from those whom they compel to accept their protection, they simultaneously derive benefit from the latter in exchange for the protection which they give them.

But even if several large contingents actually amalgamate, their joint effectiveness is prejudiced by the instability of their relationships and the fragility of their alliance. That free disposition of troops which is needed for the successful execution of a military plan is impossible with such bodies, and negotiations rather than orders are required before the plan not just of a campaign, but even of individual operations, can be implemented. Calculations will also inevitably be made as to whether the contingent of one particular estate is being overused while others are spared, and whether the equality of rights is thereby infringed, just as there used to be competition, under other political circumstances, for the most dangerous position, and discontent if a unit was not sent into action.

The jealousy of the different corps, which regard themselves as different nations, and the possibility of their withdrawal at the most critical moments – all such circumstances make it inevitable that an Imperial Army cannot generate an effect commensurate with its considerable numbers and military strength.

If the military weakness of Germany is neither a consequence of cowardice, nor of military inadequacy and unfamiliarity with those skills which, in modern times, are no less necessary[f] than courage if victory is to be won, and if at every opportunity the Imperial contingents offer the strongest proofs of their courage and military sacrifice and show themselves worthy of their ancestors and of the ancient military fame of the Germans, then it is the disposition of the whole and its general dissolution which allow the efforts and sacrifices of individuals and corps to go to waste. This lays a curse on them which nullifies all the effects and consequences of their efforts, however great these may be, and puts them on the same level as a farmer who sows the sea or attempts to plough the rocks.

[2. Finance]

The German political authority is in the same position in *financial matters* as it is in respect of military power; and since the European states have now more or less abandoned the feudal system, finance has become an essential part of that power which must be under the direct control of the supreme political authority.[30]

One extreme of financial organisation is that whereby all expenditure required for a public office, down to [that of] the most humble village magistrate or constable and below (or for some public necessity which is still confined to a single village), as well as all types of revenue, first flows upwards to the supreme political authority in the form of tax, and then back down again to the smallest branches of public activity in the form of state expenditure, through all the

---

[f] *Translator's note:* Reading *nachstehen* for *entstehen*, which, though it appears in both Lasson and *Werke*, is plainly wrong.

intermediate stages of laws, decrees, settlements of accounts, and public officials, no group of whom is in any sense an ultimate authority. The opposite extreme is Germany's complete lack of a financial system.

Germany is not plagued by worries over major political issues and problems concerning what kind of taxes, national debt or public credit is fairest, most economical, or least likely to burden one estate more than another; nor is it troubled by other matters which in other states demand the application of the greatest talents, and in which any mistakes have the most terrible consequences. There is in Germany no superfluous interference by the state in any public spending; on the contrary, each village, town, municipal guild, etc. itself takes care of those financial matters which concern it alone, under the general supervision of the state, but not at its behest. Nor is there any financial institution attached to the political authority itself.

The ordinary finances of Germany are in fact confined solely to the *cameral taxes* [*Kammersteuern*][31] which are paid by the estates for the maintenance of the Supreme Court [*Kammergericht*].[32] They are accordingly very simple, and no Pitt is required to administer them.

The regular costs of the other supreme court of the Empire are in any case borne by the Emperor. A start has been made in recent times to setting up a fund for this purpose by auctioning fiefs on their reversion to the Empire.

Even with regard to that one financial institution just referred to, the [so-called] *Kammerzieler*,[33] there are often complaints that payments are inadequate, and the reason why Brandenburg does not pay the increased amount which was approved several years ago throws an interesting light on the German constitution. Brandenburg withholds payment because it is doubtful whether a majority vote is binding on individual parties in such matters as general contributions to the needs of the state. If there is any doubt about this, the one factor which constitutes a state – namely unity with regard to the political authority – is missing.

Under the principles of the feudal system, the *contingents* are paid and supplied with all their needs by the estates themselves. As already mentioned, pressing needs led several estates to give up exercising this right during the last war, and to negotiate through the Emperor the convenient alternative of a private agreement to establish a joint commissariat. Similarly, smaller estates made no use of their right to send their own soldiers into the field on this occasion, and they came to an arrangement with the larger estates whereby the latter took responsibility for recruiting the contingent which the smaller estates were supposed to provide. This may be the first hint of a change to a new situation in which the estates are no longer responsible for raising their own contingents and supplying their own needs, but instead make financial contributions to a common centre which then takes over these commitments and sees to it that they are met. This might mark the beginning of a transition from separate, and in a sense personal, services to a genuine state organisation of military and financial affairs whereby the latter come under the control of the supreme head, by which means alone the concept of a state is realised. But even if this were so, it is plain that this whole situation has affected only minor estates, and that it was the fortuitous product of temporary circumstances.

As for the expenses which are supposed to be collected under the name of 'Roman Months' to pay for those aspects of a modern war which are not covered by the sending of troops, the same applies to them as to the sending of contingents. Estimates of these cash contributions to the German Empire for military operations have shown that roughly half of the agreed sums were actually received. In the last months of the war before the Congress of Rastatt[34] was convened, published figures of the cash received showed totals of 300 and 400 guilders [per month]; and although in other states the balance of the supreme war chest is not made public at all – especially if it is as small as this – the publication of these figures by the German Empire has had no further effect on the enemy's operations against those of the Empire in war or peacetime.

The principles which prevail here, whereby the decisions of the majority have no binding force on the minority, and the latter, because of its other commitments, cannot assent to the imposition of Roman Months approved by the majority, are the same as those which apply to the duties of the estates in relation to the military power.

Although there was in former times a kind of state authority in financial matters in the shape of *Imperial customs*, taxes paid by Imperial cities, and the like, those times were so far removed from the idea of a state and the concept of a universal [authority] that such receipts were regarded as the exclusive private property of the Emperor and could be sold by him. But what is wholly incomprehensible is that the estates could buy them or mortgage them, in the long run irredeemably, and that even the direct authority of the state could be bought or accepted as security. No clearer sign than this can be found of the barbarity of a people which constitutes a state.

It is nevertheless undeniable that the need to generate finances for Germany has been felt from time to time, and that proposals have been made to establish sources of capital for the Empire as a state. But since the estates could not contemplate setting up this financial authority by laws which required contributions to be made – for this would have produced something akin to a state institution – two things had to be combined: a permanent fund had to be set up for the state, but without imposing a burden on the estates or obligating them in any way. Since this requirement that the estates should neither be [financially] encumbered nor put under any obligation was the overriding consideration, the whole was more of a pious wish than a serious proposition; and with wishes of this kind, a true inner indifference towards the object wished for – or at least a firm determination not to let it cost one anything – tends to hide behind an attitude and demeanour of quite exceptional patriotism. Thus, if the Empire were currently planning to set up a financial institution, and if someone in a company of honest citizens expressed a wish, in the interests of the German Empire, that a mountain of gold might rise up in Germany, and that every ducat minted from it which, on first issue, was not spent on the Empire might at once turn to water, there is no doubt that such a well-wisher would be regarded as the greatest German patriot who ever lived. For the first reaction of those present would be to feel that this would not cost them anything, before it occurred to them that such a wish would not bring one penny into the Imperial treasury; and when this did occur to them, they would find that what had been said was no different from what, despite their own words, they themselves wished for.

Apart from all this, Imperial Diets in the past have not proposed to meet the need for such a fund by drawing on such ideal and purely imaginary sources as these. On the contrary, without any estate having to sacrifice anything of its own, they have suggested that expenditure on Imperial affairs should be paid for out of real and existent territories, just as the hunters [in the story] offered a real bear rather than an imaginary one in payment of their account.[35]

Several hundred years ago, a law was passed specifying that all those territories which had fallen into the hands of other nations should form the basis for an Imperial fund – *when*, that is, the Empire should recover them; and in those wars in which the opportunity to recover them duly presented itself, the Empire has always managed to ensure that it lost even more, thereby increasing the Imperial fund further. Thus, even the loss of the left bank of the Rhine has its consolations: it may be a way of providing a financial endowment for the Empire.

One may be sure that, if a teacher of German constitutional law were reminded of this woeful lack of finances even now, he would defend the perfection of this very aspect of the German constitution in the manner just described. Even if thoughts of this kind, which were cogent enough in their own day, were still able to awaken any hopes which the German character, ever sanguine in such respects, might place in them in the present political situation of Europe and Germany, they are irrelevant when we consider whether Germany possesses that kind of power which is essential to a state in our times, namely a financial power in point of fact and at the time at which we are speaking.

In the past, when one estate incurred costs on behalf of the state in a war fought not against a foreign power but against a rebellious estate on which an Imperial ban had been imposed, there was a special way of meeting this general expenditure and compensating the estate in question. Thus, if the *execution* of bans and other decisions of the Imperial courts was actually put into operation – which is not always the case – the costs were borne by the losing party, i.e. the party defeated not only in law but also in war. The Imperial army of execution in the Seven Years War received no compensation for its trouble. In past ages, this mode of exacting payment for the costs of execution sometimes provided a powerful incentive to execute a ban, since the party which did so retained the territories of the party on whom the ban was executed, with no need for any additional right or other more detailed consideration.

In this way, the Swiss gained possession of most of the old ancestral properties of the Habsburgs, and Bavaria of Donauwörth, etc.

A mass of people which, in view of this dissolution of military power and lack of finances, has not managed to form political authority, is unable to defend its independence against external enemies. It must necessarily see its independence collapse, if not all at once then in gradual stages; it must be exposed in war to all kinds of plundering and devastation, and must inevitably bear the bulk of the cost for friend and foe alike; it must lose its provinces to foreign powers, and since its political authority over its individual members has been destroyed and it has lost its sovereignty over its vassals, it will contain only sovereign states. The mutual relations of these states, as such, will be governed by force and guile, the stronger will expand and the weaker will be devoured, and even the more prominent among them will still be impotent in face of a major power.

[3. Territory of the Empire][36]

The territories which the German Empire has lost over the passage of several centuries make up a long and melancholy list. Since the laws of the constitution in general and of the organisation of political authority have lost their validity and afford little or no scope for discussion, the constitutional lawyers must confine themselves to describing the outward appearances [Zeichen], now empty and meaningless, as symbols of the past, and the claims [embodied in them].[37] On the other hand, these claims evoke that comforting feeling with which an impoverished nobleman cherishes the last reminders of his departed ancestors – a consolation which has the advantage of safety and freedom from disturbance. These [ancestral] portraits cannot raise protests against the present owners of their estates any more than the constitutional claims of the German Empire have ever caused a minister to fear that the latter might contradict him; both the nobleman and the constitutional lawyer can safely abandon themselves to their innocent and harmless amusements.

If the constitutional lawyers still derive pleasure from expounding the Holy Roman (and German) Empire's claims to Hungary,

Poland, Prussia, Naples, etc., it should also be noted that such politically insignificant rights do not pertain to the German Empire as such, but rather to the 'Roman Imperium', the 'Heart of Christendom' and the 'Lord of the World', and that the 'Roman Emperor' and 'King of the Germans', as his title has it, were essentially distinct. The German Empire could have neither the interest, the will, nor latterly the power to assert what might be considered appropriate to the Emperor's role as sovereign, and to uphold so unnatural a union of territories which are separated by their geographical position as well as by the individuality of their peoples – especially since it neither would nor could support even those territories which were integral parts of itself.

Even down to recent times, traces have survived of the [Empire's] connection with the Kingdom of Lombardy; but it cannot be considered an essential part of the German Kingdom proper, especially since it was a kingdom in its own right and also because that recognition as estates of the German Empire which some of its own states had once enjoyed had long since lost its validity. As to those territories which were essential parts of the German Empire and which possessed and exercised the rights of estates within it, almost every Imperial war has ended with the loss of some of them.

This loss in fact assumes two distinct forms. For apart from the actual subjection of German lands to foreign rule and their complete severance from all Imperial rights and duties, it must also be regarded as a loss to the state that so many territories, while retaining all their previous legal and ostensible connections with the Emperor and Empire, at the same time acquired rulers who, though already members – or now becoming members – of the Empire, were also monarchs of independent states. Although this circumstance appears to entail no loss but rather to leave everything as it was, it has nevertheless undermined the basic supports which hold the state together, for it has made the territories in question independent of the state's authority.

Without reverting to earlier times, we shall now confine ourselves to a brief review of the way in which, from the Peace of Westphalia onwards, Germany's impotence and inevitable fate found expression in its relations with foreign powers. We can, of course, deal only with its loss of territories in the peace agreements, for the damage done by war is far greater than any account could encompass.

In the Peace of Westphalia,[38] the German Empire lost all connection not only with the United Netherlands but also with Switzerland, whose independence had long since been attained in practice, but was now formally recognised. This was a loss not of possessions but of claims, and although it was insignificant in itself, it was important for the German Empire, which has often shown that it values chimerical claims and wholly unreal rights more highly than actual possessions. – Thus, in addition, Germany now formally ceded to France the bishoprics of Metz, Toul, and Verdun which it had already lost a century previously. But it was a genuine loss to the Empire when it ceded [to France] the Landgraviate of Alsace – or rather the Austrian part of it – and the Imperial City of Besançon to Spain.

While these territories gave up all their associations with Germany, a greater number retained their legal and theoretical dependence [on the Empire]; but since their rulers were also foreign monarchs, the basis was laid for their real separation in practice. Thus, Sweden acquired Western Pomerania and part of Eastern Pomerania, the archbishopric of Bremen, the bishopric of Verden, and the city of Wismar. The Margrave of Brandenburg (Duke and subsequently King of Prussia) gained the archbishopric of Magdeburg and the bishoprics of Halberstadt, Kammin, and Minden.

Even if the ruler of Brandenburg had not also been a sovereign prince, the effect of this reduction in the number of German estates and their fusion into a single mass would not have been very different, for it would still have created a powerful state which could henceforth resist the German Empire and refuse to submit to its authority, which it could not have done if it had been divided up among several states.

Apart from the reduction just mentioned, several other individual estates such as Schwerin, Ratzeburg, etc. ceased to exist.

Equally destructive for the German state was the fact that under this peace treaty, the German Empire made foreign powers the guarantors of its constitution and internal relations – the same powers which, whether by force or invitation, had interfered in Germany's affairs, laid waste to it from one end to the other, and more or less dictated the [conditions of] peace. It thereby acknowledged its inability to preserve its constitution and its existence as a state, and surrendered its internal affairs to foreign interests.

Other internal weaknesses [were] the granting of privileges to various countries in the matter of appeals, and also to some extent the permitting of a defendant to choose which Imperial court he wished to appear in (for by delaying his choice, the defendant could delay the legal process even further). More serious than all this was the confirmation of the right whereby not only in religious questions – including those relating entirely to the external and purely secular aspects of religion – but also in other matters concerning the Empire as a whole, a majority vote in the Imperial Diet could not be binding. A further weakness was that the German Empire could no longer redeem its rights of sovereignty which had been mortgaged to the Imperial cities – etc.

In the next peace treaty, namely that of Nijmegen,[39] which was conducted without a delegation from the Empire (although the Empire ratified it, including its clause that no objection to it on the part of the Empire should be accepted), the Empire relinquished its sovereignty over the County of Burgundy; a few pieces of territories in the north of Germany changed their rulers; and in the south, the French rights of occupation in German fortresses were modified.

But apart from its losses in peace treaties, the German Empire exhibits some quite unique phenomena which have rarely arisen in other states: in the midst of peace – namely after the Treaty of Nijmegen had been concluded – ten Imperial cities in Alsace, along with other territories, were lost to France.

The Peace of Ryswick[40] was concluded in the presence of an Imperial delegation, but the latter was excluded from the discussions with the foreign ambassadors; it received information only as the Imperial ambassador saw fit, and was duly asked to endorse the agreement. This peace treaty confirmed the French annexation of the territories referred to, while the Empire in turn gained the Imperial fortress of Kehl; but the treaty contained that celebrated clause concerning the religious situation in the conquered territories returned by France, that clause which gave the Protestant estates so much concern and helped to bring so much misfortune to the Palatinate.

In the negotiations over the Peace of Baden,[41] no Imperial delegation took part, nor did the treaty itself bring any immediate change for the German Empire; Austria regained Breisach and Freiburg.

This is in fact the last peace which the German Empire concluded. Since a tabular survey of Imperial history from the Peace
of Baden to the Seven Years War shows neither declarations of war
nor peace treaties, one might well believe that Germany enjoyed the
profoundest peace throughout this long period; but its soil was actually as much the scene of battles and devastation as ever.

The peace treaties which Sweden made with Hanover, Prussia,
Denmark, and Russia after Charles XII's death not only deprived
it of that place among the European powers which its intrepid king
had won for it; it also lost its power in Germany. But the power of
the German state gained nothing in the process, for the territories
which Sweden lost went to German princes, who assumed Sweden's
place as a formidable threat to German unity.

In the Peace of Vienna,[42] Germany lost nothing except its link
with Lorraine, which was in any case tenuous; but this treaty was
never ratified by the Empire.

In the war of the Austrian Succession, Germany was the theatre
of prolonged devastation. Its greatest princes were involved in it,
the armies of foreign monarchs fought each other on German soil,
yet the German Empire was in the depths of peace. Prussia, the
power which had taken Sweden's place, expanded in the course of
this war.

Much more disastrous still – especially for northern Germany –
was the Seven Years War. It is true that the German Empire was
itself at war on this occasion (in order to execute an Imperial ban);
but its friends did not even do it the honour of recognising that it
was at war, or of making peace with it.

Finally, the Peace of Lunéville[43] has not only deprived Germany
of numerous rights of sovereignty in Italy; it has also robbed it of
the entire left bank of the Rhine. This in itself has reduced the
number of princes in Germany, and has laid the basis for reducing
the number of its estates much further still and for making the
individual parts all the more formidable [a threat] to the whole and
to the smaller estates.

If a country is at war, and half of it is either embroiled in civil
conflict, or abandons the collective defence and sacrifices the other
half to the enemy by remaining neutral, it must suffer serious
damage in the war itself and be dismembered when peace returns.
For the strength of a country consists neither in the number of its

inhabitants and troops, nor in its fertility, nor in its size, but solely in the way in which all of this can be used towards the great end of common defence through the rational union of its parts under a single political authority.

[4. Jurisdiction]

Germany does not in itself constitute a political authority in its military and financial affairs. It must therefore be regarded not as a state, but as a mass of independent states, the larger of which act independently even in foreign relations, whereas the smaller must follow some broader movement. The associations which are formed from time to time to pursue some specific end in the name of the German Empire are always partial,[44] and they are set up as the allies themselves see fit, so that they lack all the benefits which the coalitions of other powers may enjoy. For even if such coalitions are short-lived, and even if in certain cases – as in wars – they do not function with the success and energy which they would have if the same power were completely under the control of a single government, they do sensibly adopt the means and measures most appropriate to the end of the coalition, and everything is subsequently directed towards that end. But the coalitions of the German estates are hampered by such formalities, restrictions, and endless considerations – which they have created for this purpose – that the whole functioning of the coalition is paralysed, and it is made impossible in advance to achieve the end which it has set itself.

The acts of the German Empire as such are never acts of the whole, but only of an association of greater or lesser scope. But the means of attaining what the members of this association propose are not chosen with this end in view; on the contrary, the first and sole concern is to adhere to those conditions which preserve the separateness of the members and ensure that they do not become associates.

Such associations are like a heap of round stones which combine to form a pyramid. But since they are completely round and must remain so without interlocking, as soon as the pyramid begins to approach the end for which it was constructed, they roll apart, or at least offer no resistance [to such movement]. Through an arrangement of this kind, these states lack not only the infinite advantage which any political association possesses, but also the advantage of independence, which would enable them to unite with others for specific common ends. For in this instance, they have tied themselves down in such a way that any union is rendered void, or is already worthless from the outset.

Now despite the fact that the German estates have annulled [*aufgehoben*] their union in this way and denied themselves the opportunity of uniting in a sensible manner for temporary or immediate ends as need or emergency requires, the demand is still present that Germany should be a state. The following contradiction is set up: relations between the estates are to be determined in such a way that no state either can or does exist, yet Germany is supposed to count without qualification [*schlechthin*] as a state and likewise wishes to be regarded as a single body. This spirit has for centuries plunged Germany into a series of inconsistencies between its will to render a state impossible and its will to be a state, and placed it unhappily between the estates' resentment [*Eifersucht*] of any kind of subjection to the whole and the impossibility of surviving without this subjection.[45]

The solution to the problem of how it is possible for Germany not to be a state yet [at the same time] to be one is easily found. It lies in the fact that Germany is a state in [the realm of] thought but not in actuality, that formality and reality are separate, so that empty formality belongs to the state, whereas reality belongs to the non-existence of the state.[46]

The system of the state in thought [*des Gedankenstaates*] is the organisation of a constitution which is powerless in all that is essential to a state. The obligations of each estate to the Emperor and the Empire, to the supreme government which consists in the head [of the Empire] in conjunction with the estates, are defined in the most precise manner in an endless number of solemn acts of constitutional law. These duties and rights make up a system of laws which specify precisely the constitutional relationship of each estate and the compulsory nature of its service, and the contribution of each individual estate to the common weal [*das Allgemeine*] is to be made only in accordance with these legal determinations. But the nature of this legal system [*Gesetzlichkeit*] lies in the fact that the constitutional relationship and its associated obligations are not defined by universal laws in the strict sense; on the contrary, the relationship of each estate to the whole is a particular matter – in the same way as in civil rights – which takes the form of a [private] property. This has an essential effect on the nature of the political authority.[47]

An act which emanates from the political authority is a universal act, and by virtue of its true universality, it also bears the rule of its application within itself. What it refers to is universal and identical with itself. The act of the political authority imparts a free and universal determinacy, and its execution is at the same time its application. Since no distinctions can be made in what it applies to, its application must be defined in the act itself, and no refractory or disparate material offers resistance in its application.[48]

If the political authority passes an act to the effect that every hundredth man of a specific age must enlist as a soldier, or that a certain percentage of wealth or a specific tax on every acre of land must be paid, the decree applies to something wholly universal, such as men of a specific age, or wealth, or land, and no distinction is made between some men and others, this or that wealth, and this or that land; the determination [of quantities] applied to a uniform area can be fixed entirely by the political authority. The hundredth man, five per cent, etc. are wholly universal determinations of this kind, and no special measures are needed in order to apply them to the uniform material; for no lines have already been drawn which would first have to be removed or to which those now determined would have to be accommodated, as with the straight line drawn on a tree-trunk to indicate where it is to be cut.

But if the area to which the law is to be applied is [already] determined in multifarious ways from the point of view of the law itself, then the law cannot contain within itself the complete rule of its own application. On the contrary, a distinct application [of the law] is needed for each particular part of the material, and between the law and its execution a distinct act of application intervenes, an act for which the judicial authority is responsible.

An Imperial law cannot therefore furnish a universal rule for [drawing] the requisite lines and divisions as if on a blank sheet, nor execute the actual arrangement [of these] in accordance with one and the same rule of this kind. On the contrary, the material to which an Imperial law applies confronts it with its own determinate characteristics already present, and before the law can be executed, one must first discover to what extent the particular line and shape which each part displays can be reconciled with those prescribed by the law, or how much binding force the universal law has for each part. If contradictions should arise, these questions must be answered by a judicial authority. In the course of such an enquiry, the following conclusions emerge: firstly, while the enquiry is certainly necessary, its organisation is such that it can discover very little; secondly, what it discovers in theory is not subsequently realised, but remains a discovery in thought [alone]; and finally, the whole business of the enquiry is rendered well nigh impossible, because the particular determinacy which the material [already] has stands in the same relation to a universal law as a straight line does to the arc of a circle, so that there is already an incompatibility in advance between a law of the political authority and the determinacy of the universal material upon which this authority acts. In this way, the state in thought [*der Gedankenstaat*] and the system of constitutional law and laws enacted by the state are the straight line, while the area in which the state in thought is to be realised has the shape of a circular line; and everyone knows that the two lines are incommensurable. Nor is it the case that this circular figure renders itself incompatible with the straight line *de facto*; it does not assume the form of violence, illegality, and arbitrariness. On the contrary, the fact that it *is* this incommensurable line is likewise elevated to the form of right [*Rechtsform*]: it acts in accordance with right [*rechtlich*] despite its incompatibility with political right [*Staatsrecht*], and it acts legally despite its incompatibility with the laws of the state.

Thus, if the problem of how Germany can simultaneously be a state and not be a state is to be solved, it must, in so far as it is a state, exist only as a state in thought [*Gedankenstaat*], while its non-existence must possess the reality. Now if the state in thought is to have being for itself, the judicial authority which is to overcome [*aufheben*] the contradiction and apply to actuality what was merely thought, thereby realising it and making actuality correspond to it, must be so constituted that even its application remains merely a thought. Thus, those universal orders [*Ordnungen*] which might transform the country into a state would be paralysed in their transition to reality; and although this transition would itself be posited

43

and decreed – for such arrangements have no meaning unless they are meant to be executed – the act of transition would also be turned into a work of thought [*Gedankending*].[49]

This transition can be paralysed at any one of its stages. A universal ordinance is passed; it is to be put into execution, and in the event of resistance, legal procedures will be instituted. If the resistance offered is not referred to a court of law, the execution in itself remains unimplemented; but if it is referred to a court, a verdict may be delayed; and if a verdict is reached, it may not be complied with. But this judgement in the realm of thought [*Gedankending von Beschluβ*] is supposed to be executed and a penalty imposed, so an order is given to enforce its execution. This order in turn is not executed, so a judgement must follow against those who failed to execute it, in order to compel them to do so. This in turn is not complied with, so a ruling must be given to the effect that punishment shall be carried out on those who fail to carry it out on anyone who fails to carry it out, etc. This is the arid history of how one stage after another in the implementation of a law is turned into a work of thought [*Gedankending*].

Thus, if the judicial authority is to discover how universal obligations towards the Empire are to be rated in comparison with the particular rights of individuals, and if a contradiction between the two is actually referred to a court, it depends on the organisation of that court in its business of pronouncing judgement (irrespective of the subsequent execution of that judgement) whether it does not encounter difficulties in performing even this function and – since the judgement in itself is no more than a thought if it is not executed – whether the arrangement is not such that it does not even get as far as this thought, so that even the latter remains a mere work of thought [*Gedankending*].

Even with regard to the pronouncement of judgement, the very organisation of the judicial authority is such that the essential aspect with which we are here concerned – namely its function of upholding the universal ordinances of the state *qua* state against individuals – is subject to the greatest hindrances. In the judiciary of the Empire, the administration of civil justice and that of constitutional law are intermixed. Constitutional law and civil law are subject to the same courts. The Imperial courts are the supreme courts of appeal for civil actions and for constitutional rights. The scope of their judicial authority in the latter area is already limited, because the most important matters of this kind are the responsibility of the Imperial Diet and are in any case often resolved by courts of arbitration; but it is also subject to endless difficulties even in pronouncing judgement, and is made to depend on a mass of fortuitous circumstances which become necessary conditions of its own ineffectiveness.

This combination of civil and constitutional processes generally has the effect of increasing the volume of business of the existing Imperial courts to such an extent that they are unable to cope with it. It is recognised by the Emperor, the Empire, and the Supreme Court that the Supreme Court is even less equal to the volume of its business than is the Aulic Council.[50]

No evil seems easier to remedy, and nothing simpler to deal with than this. Even without the introduction of several separate courts, the number of judges in the existing courts could be increased. This would simultaneously expedite the conduct of business and allow a single court to be split up into several departments, thereby creating several courts to deal with different areas of business. But it is not possible in Germany to implement so simple a measure as this. It was indeed decided to do so, and the number of assessors in the Supreme Court was increased to fifty; but the German Empire was unable to find the money to pay these [extra] judges. In the course of time their number sank to twelve or even fewer, until it finally rose to twenty-five.

The official statistics show that the annual number of actions pending far exceeds the number of those on which decisions can be given, even if the presentation of a single case sometimes takes only several months (rather than years, as used to happen). It is consequently inevitable, and confirmed by statistical analysis, that many thousands of cases remain undecided, and recourse to petitions remains a necessary evil (even if the worst abuses are a thing of the past, and Jews no longer operate a trade in this item); for since it is impossible for judgements to be delivered on all pending actions, the parties are compelled to make every effort to ensure that their cases are favoured with a court decision.

A thousand other collisions over the nomination of assessors or the *itio in partes*[51] have often immobilised the Supreme Court for several years; and even if the court did not deliberately delay its own proceedings (on the principle of making the great aware of its power), these factors alone impede the course of justice.

Many of these abuses are not encountered in the Aulic Council, whose members are appointed by the Emperor. For example, no case of *itio in partes* has arisen, despite the right to request it; and many forms [of the Council's procedure] are directly conducive to justice [*Recht*] itself, instead of holding it up with pure formalities. It is therefore natural that, in recent times, people have increasingly looked to the Aulic Council for justice.

The need for judicial reform has always been too obvious to be overlooked. But the consequences of the last attempt by Joseph II to organise a visitation of the Supreme Court – a procedure sanctioned by Imperial law but out of use for two centuries – and the reasons why it was terminated before it completed its business, are in general no different from those which characterise the state of Imperial justice at large. In short, while the estates do associate for the administration of justice, they are unwilling, in this union, to give up anything of their mutually opposed existence, based as it is on separation and lack of solidarity; they form an association, but they lack the will for any common purpose.

In this way, jurisdiction in and for itself, quite apart from the execution of its judgements, is impeded. But everyone knows how matters stand with the execution of such decisions of the Imperial courts if they happen to involve constitutional law or important issues connected with it. The more important concerns of this type are not in any case the responsibility of the Imperial courts, but of the Imperial Diet. They are accordingly passed on directly from the legal sphere to the sphere of politics; for when the supreme political authority speaks, it is not applying the laws, but giving them.

Furthermore, matters of major significance (such as the ownership of territories etc.) have even been exempted from the formal procedures of the Imperial Diet. It is laid down by the Compact of Election and other basic laws that decisions on such matters should not be taken by the Imperial courts and the supreme judicial authority, but by amicable agreement between the contending estates; and if this cannot be done by amicable agreement, it must inevitably be settled by war.

The case of the Jülich-Berg succession was so far from being resolved by legal means that it gave rise to the Thirty Years War.[52]

In the case of the Bavarian succession in more recent times, it was once again cannons and politics rather than the Imperial courts which spoke. Even in cases involving less powerful estates, it is not Imperial justice which pronounces the decisive verdict. It is well known that, in the disputes over the succession in the [ruling] houses of Saxony, 206 decisions were issued by the Aulic Council concerning the territories of the extinct lines of Coburg-Eisenberg and Coburg-Römhild, although the most important points were in fact settled by agreement. We have likewise experienced how, in the Liège dispute, the Supreme Court not only pronounced judgement, ordered its execution, and called on several estates to carry it out; in addition, these estates actually fulfilled their obligation. But no sooner had a start been made than the most powerful estate among the executors became dissatisfied with its role as a mere executor of the Supreme Court's judgements, and set to work with good intentions of its own; and when the attempt to resolve the matter by non-legal methods failed, it in turn gave up its role as executor.

In such a delicate situation [as this] where there is a misunderstanding between prince and subject, mediation may be desirable. If, however, after judicial pronouncements have been made, their execution is to be set aside in favour of a further mediation, the whole viewpoint at the stage of development which the case has now reached is shifted, and the essential principle of the constitution is likewise displaced by an influence which seems to offer a momentary benefit; or rather, it becomes apparent on such occasions that this principle has already been displaced long before.

It seems that a distinction must be made here. It is [all] too obvious that the mutual relations between the powerful estates are governed by politics. On the other hand, the lesser estates appear to owe their existence entirely to the constitutional union of the Empire. No Imperial city would consider itself capable of resisting the larger of its neighbouring fellow-estates – no more than a knight of the Empire imagines he can defend his direct dependence on the Emperor against a prince, either on his own or even in association with the rest of the body of knights. The matter speaks for itself, and it is superfluous to quote the fate of the Imperial knights in Franconia. Any attempt, like that of Franz von Sickingen, to conquer an Electoral principality – let alone a successful attempt of this kind – is no longer in the realm of possibility nowadays, just as associations of Imperial cities or abbots can no longer achieve what they could in the past.

Now if it is not the power of the individual estates – nor even their combined power – which preserves them, they appear to owe their existence as relatively independent states and direct subjects of the Empire to nothing other than the Imperial union itself and to the legal constitution established by the prohibition of private warfare [*Landfrieden*].[53] But the question still arises of what it is that preserves this so-called legal relationship, and hence the continued existence of the knights, abbeys, Imperial cities, counts, etc. Obviously, it is not their own power which preserves them, for they lack the power of a state; once again, it is politics which does so.[54] If politics is not immediately recognised as the foundation on which the existence of the less powerful estates rests, this is only because reasoning stops at the Imperial union – which is an intermediate link – as the [supposed] foundation, and forgets what it is that supports this union itself.

States like Lucca, Genoa, etc. managed to survive for centuries without an Imperial union, until they experienced the fate of Pisa, Siena, Arezzo, Verona, Bologna, Vicenza, etc., etc. – in short, one could list the whole gazetteer of cities, principalities, counties, etc. of Italy. That apparently more powerful republic [of Venice] which had previously swallowed up so many independent cities was brought to an end by the arrival of an adjutant who merely conveyed an order from the general of a foreign power.[55] Those states which, in the lottery of fate, scored the few winning numbers in the shape of a slightly longer [period of] independence while several hundred sovereign territories in Italy drew blanks, continued to exist only because of the jealous politics of the greater states around them; and although, in earlier centuries, they had been able to engage in conflict with their powerful neighbours, they had meanwhile – without any external loss – become quite disproportionately weak in comparison with them. But the jealousy of politics is also satisfied by an equal sharing of booty and by parity of expansion and contraction, and in the resultant combinations of interests, states like Venice, Poland, etc. were lost.

The change from the right of private warfare [*Faustrecht*] to politics should not be regarded as a transition from anarchy to constitutionalism. The true principle remains the same, and the change is purely superficial. In the days before the prohibition on private warfare [*Landfrieden*], the injured party or anyone bent on conquest simply struck out at his enemies. In politics, on the other hand, calculations are made before battle is joined, and major interests are not put at risk for the sake of minor gain; but if this gain seems assured, the opportunity is not missed.

Since the mass of German states does not constitute a power, the independence of its parts can be respected only so long as the advantage of other powers requires it and no higher interests or rights of indemnification etc. are involved. As far as interest is concerned, France, for example, when its armies had occupied half of Germany, abolished [*aufgehoben*] the independent states and direct Imperial dependencies in the Netherlands, and among those territories on the left bank of the Rhine which were subsequently ceded to France when peace was restored. It could equally well have abolished the constitutions of the territories on the right bank; and even if this destruction of the independence of so many principalities, counties, bishoprics, abbeys, Imperial cities, and baronies could not have endured, the territories in question would still have been plunged into far greater misfortune [than they were already in]. But politics – namely the need to take account of Prussia and fear of rendering peace more difficult – prevented France from doing so. It was also deterred by the advantage of having a ready-made system for the collection of contributions, which – according to the official French press – were raised 'in meagre amounts' in these territories.

This transition from the state [*Zustand*] of overt power to that of calculated power was not, of course, accomplished all at once; on the contrary, it was made possible by a legal constitution. [Immediately] after the prohibition on private warfare, it was easier to regard Germany as a state than it is today. Under the feudal constitution, the political authority was split up into numerous parts, but because there were so many of them, no individual parts were powerful enough to oppose the whole. But, as if fate had simply not destined Germany for a condition such as this, it soon overcame its aversion to lawlessness and set aside the attempt to establish a firmer framework through the prohibition of private warfare.[56] It did so by means of the deeper interest of religion, which divided the peoples for all time.

49

[*5. Religion*][57]

Amidst all the storms of the lawless state in the age of feuds, the whole still retained a certain cohesion, both in the relation of the estates towards one another and in their relation to the universal [interest]. Even if the fulfilment of obligations seemed to depend not only on the free will of the estates in general, but also on the will of individual estates, and even if the legal bond [*Zusammenhang*] seemed very weak, an inner bond of dispositions [*Gemüter*] nevertheless prevailed. When there was religious unity, and before the rise of the middle class [*Bürgerstand*] brought great variety into the whole, princes, counts, and lords could regard one another more readily and more correctly as a whole, and could accordingly act as a whole. There was no political authority [*Staatsmacht*] opposed to and independent of individuals as there is in modern states; the political authority and the power and free will of individuals were one and the same thing. But these individuals were more disposed to allow themselves and their power to coexist within a [single] state.

But when, with the rise of the Imperial cities, that civic consciousness [*bürgerliche Sinn*] which cares only for individual interests [*ein Einzelnes*] without self-sufficiency or regard for the whole began to gain power, this isolation of [individual] dispositions [*Gemüter*] really required a more universal and positive bond. And when, through the progress of culture [*Bildung*] and industry, Germany was now confronted with the difficult choice of either deciding to obey a universal [authority] or destroying the union altogether, the original German character, which insists on the free will of the individual and resists subservience to a universal, won the day and determined Germany's fate in accordance with its old nature.

In the course of time, great numbers of states had taken shape and trade and commercial wealth became dominant. The intractability of the German character was not directly conducive to the development of independent states, and the old free strength of the nobility could not stand up to the rise of the masses; but above all, that civic spirit [*Bürgergeist*] which was gaining prestige and political significance needed some kind of inner and outer legitimation. The German character seized upon the innermost being [*das Innerste*] of man, upon religion and conscience, and firmly established the isolation [of individuals] on this basis; the separation of the external realm [*des Äußeren*] into states seemed merely a consequence of this.

The original, untamed character of the German nation determined the iron necessity of its fate.[58] Within the sphere which this fate has assigned to them, politics, religion, privation [*Not*], virtue, coercion, reason, cunning, and all the powers that move the human race play out their momentous and seemingly chaotic game on the broad field of conflict that is open to them. Each behaves as an absolutely free and self-sufficient power, unaware of the fact that all of them are instruments in the hands of higher powers – primordial fate and all-conquering time – which laugh at their supposed freedom and self-sufficiency. Even the mighty force of privation has not subdued the German character and its destiny. The universal misery of the wars of religion, especially the Thirty Years War, has rather advanced and reinforced the development of its fate, and its results were a greater and more consolidated separation and isolation.

Religion, far from cutting itself off from the state by its own [internal] division, has in fact introduced this division into the state itself and made the greatest contribution to abolishing [*aufzuheben*] the state.[59] It has become so interwoven with what is known as the constitution that it is a precondition of constitutional rights.

In the particular states of which Germany is composed, even civil rights are tied to religion. The [two] religions have an equal share in this intolerance, and neither is in a position to reproach the other. Despite the intolerance sanctioned by the laws of the Empire, the rulers of Austria and Brandenburg have rated religious freedom of conscience more highly than this legalised barbarity.

The disruption caused by the religious division was particularly acute in Germany because the political bond was looser here than in any other country. The dominant religion was necessarily all the more embittered at those who abandoned it, not only because the religious division destroyed the innermost bond between human beings, but also because this was in a sense almost the only bond [which united them], whereas in other states numerous other links still held firm. Community of religion is a deeper community, whereas the community of physical needs, property, and income is of a lower order,[60] and the demand for separation is inherently more unnatural than the demand that an existing union should be preserved. Consequently, the Catholic Church showed itself more fanatical, because its demand was in general directed towards union and the most sacred aspect of this union. It was prepared at most to admit grace and tolerance, but not right – i.e. it was not prepared to consolidate the [religious] division as Protestantism insisted. The two parties finally agreed to exclude each other from civil rights, and to surround and reinforce this exclusion with all the pedantry of law [*des Rechts*].

The outward appearances are the same: civil rights are denied to Protestants in Catholic territories, and to Catholics in Protestant territories. But the basis seems to be different. The Catholics had been in the position of oppressors, and the Protestants of the oppressed. The Catholics had treated the Protestants as criminals, and denied them the free exercise of their religion in their midst; but where the Protestant Church was dominant, this basis was removed, along with the fear of oppression. The basis of Protestant intolerance could only be either the right of retaliation for the hatred and intolerance of the Catholics[61] – which would have been too unchristian a motive – or distrust in the power and truth of their own faith, and fear that they might easily be seduced by the splendour of Catholic worship and the zeal of its adherents, etc.

In the last century in particular, this perpetual fear that the Protestant faith might be outwitted and surreptitiously overrun, this belief – like that of the watchers on Zion – in their own impotence, this fear of the enemy's cunning prevailed, and became an incentive to fortify the grace of God with untold precautions and legal bulwarks.

This legal position has been asserted with the greatest acrimony whenever it was presented by individuals of the opposite party as a matter of grace. Grace is indeed in one respect inferior to law [*Recht*], for law is determinate, and whatever is legal has lost its arbitrariness for both parties, whereas grace is purely arbitrary in legal terms. But this clinging to pure legality as such also obscured the higher significance of grace, so that for a long time neither party rose above the law or allowed grace to take precedence over law. What Frederick II did for the Catholics and Joseph [II] did for the Protestants was grace in contravention of the rights laid down in the Treaties of Prague and Westphalia. It was indeed in keeping with the higher natural rights of freedom of conscience and the non-dependence of civil rights on faith; yet these higher rights are not only not acknowledged in the religious settlement and the Peace of Westphalia, but are actually excluded by them, and their exclusion was guaranteed with the utmost solemnity by both Protestants and Catholics. From this point of view, these legal guarantees are nothing to boast about; on the contrary, the grace which they reject is infinitely superior.

Religion is an even more important basic determinant of the relationship between the individual parts of Germany and the whole; it has probably contributed most to the destruction of the political union and to legalising this destruction. The era of the religious schism lacked the competence to separate church and state and to preserve the latter despite the separation of the faiths; and the princes could find no better ally in their attempt to withdraw from the supremacy of the Empire than the conscience of their subjects.

The Imperial laws which have gradually developed in consequence have ensured that the religion of every territory and every Imperial city is legally defined, whether as purely Catholic, purely Protestant, or as a parity of the two. But what would happen if a country were to infringe the Treaty of Westphalia to the extent of transferring from one form of purity to the other, or from parity to purity?

Equally fixed is the religion of the votes in the Imperial Diet, the Supreme Court, the Aulic Council, the individual offices and services, etc. The most important of those political matters which are determined by religion is the famous *itio in partes*, the right of one or other religious party not to submit to a majority vote. If this right were confined to religious matters, its justice and necessity would be self-evident. The separation [of the religions] would do no direct harm to the state, because it would affect only those issues which have basically nothing to do with the state. But by virtue of the *itio in partes*, the separation of the minority from the majority is legitimised in all political matters, even if they are unconnected with religion. On [questions of] war and peace, the mobilisation of an Imperial army, or taxation – in short, on all of those few issues which earlier times have left in being as shadows of a [former] whole – the majority vote is not legally binding. Even without resorting to politics, a minority, if it forms a religious party, can obstruct the activity of the state.

It is going too far to draw a parallel, as some people do, between this right and that right of rebellion which is sanctified in some of the various constitutions drawn up over the last decade in France. For Germany must be regarded as a state which has already dissolved; and its parts, which do not submit to a majority [decision] of the whole, should be regarded as independent and self-subsistent states whose divergence, if no joint conclusion can be reached, does not invariably lead to the dissolution of all social bonds or to inevitable civil war.[62]

But while religion has completely torn the state apart, it has also given a remarkable intimation of certain principles on which a state can be based.[63] The religious schism divided people from one another in their innermost being, yet there was still supposed to be a bond between them. This bond must therefore be of an external nature, relating to external things such as warfare, etc. – like the bond which is the principle of modern states. The very fact that the most important parts of constitutional law were interwoven with the religious schism has also woven two religions into the state, thus making all political rights dependent on two (or actually three) religions.[64] This is admittedly contrary to the principle of the state's independence from the church, and to the possibility of there being a state despite the differences of religion; but the principle is in fact recognised, because different religions [really] are present and Germany [really] is supposed to be a state.

Another more important division which is also produced by religion is even more closely linked to the possibility of a state. Originally, votes in general debates and on decisions [of the Imperial bodies] depended entirely on the personal presence of the princes; they had votes only when they appeared in person, and the prince of different and [geographically] separate territories had only *one* vote. His person and his territory, his personality and his quality as representative of the territory, did not appear as distinct. The distinction arose as a result of the religious schism. On which side was a vote to be cast if the prince and his territory were of different religions, and if the Imperial constitution specified that a vote must be allocated to only one religious party?[65]

As a political power, the prince ought not to have been on either of the two sides, but the times were not yet ripe for this. Besides, no one reflected on such matters initially. The ruler of Protestant Neuburg Palatine, who became a Catholic in the seventeenth century, was included among the Catholic voters both in the Imperial Diet and in the Imperial courts, whereas the vote of the Elector of Saxony, who changed his religion at the end of the same century, remained Protestant (as likewise happened when the rulers of Hesse and Württemberg subsequently changed their religion).

Even before all this, only those princes with a territory and subjects of their own were entitled to a seat and a vote in the Imperial Diet, so that a territory seemed inseparable from the concept of membership of the Diet. But this distinction between the personality of the prince and his representation of a territory – even in relation to the German state in general – became more conspicuous and easier to draw when this separation of prince and subjects had already been introduced in the provincial Diet [*Landstände*] of that prince's own territory. The Palatinate, which had no provincial Diet, went over to the Catholic party without resistance, and the struggle of its citizens with their Catholic princes over religious grievances has continued until the most recent times. In Hesse and Württemberg, on the other hand, the separation [of prince and subjects] had already been legalised by the provincial Diet. The religion of these territories was also defended in the context of their relations with the German Empire, and given precedence over the personality of the prince; the latter accordingly appeared in the Imperial Diet not as an individual, but as a representative.

The attention which was devoted to this distinction occasioned by religion has now been extended to other differences, and territories which have come under a single ruler have passed on their individual votes to him. In this case too, the individual as a unit, i.e. the individual personality, is no longer made into a principle, as occurred in the past when even the ruler of various principalities had only *one* vote, or when several princes among whom a single principality was divided each had a vote of his own. The principle now is the ruler in his capacity as a representative.

But just as the food which nourishes the healthy body further undermines a sick one, so too has this true and genuine principle that it is the territory which confers the power and the right to vote contributed all the more to the dissolution of the German Empire since it was applied to the situation in Germany.

[6. The Power of the Estates]

In the course of time, changes in customs, religion, and particularly in the relative wealth of the estates served to disrupt that internal cohesion which relies on character and general interests, so that external legal bonds became necessary to unite Germany into a state once its inhabitants ceased to be one people and became [no more than] a mass.

A theory of such unifying factors is furnished by part of German constitutional law. The old feudal constitution could evolve into that type of modern state on which all those European states which have not undergone a revolution in recent times are more or less modelled – provided that none of the individual vassals was, or could become, excessively powerful.[66] Admittedly, even a mass of weaker vassals can become a power by organising themselves into a solid opposition to the state, as happened in Poland; and the aura which surrounded the [Holy] Roman Emperor could not of itself have given him sufficient power to resist it. But even if the minority in Germany is not bound by the decisions of the majority, this right, based as it is on the *itio in partes*, is nevertheless subject to certain limits. Besides, the activity of the whole cannot be paralysed by an individual veto, but only by a religious party; and even if an individual estate does not for its part consider itself in any way subject to the majority (as when Prussia, in refusing to pay the increased *Kammerzieler*, put forward the principle that it had not yet been established whether decisions of the majority were in any way binding in fiscal matters), and even if each estate makes peace or signs treaties of neutrality on its own account, all such rights and relationships are of later date. It was conceivable that, if the Emperor had possessed sufficient political power on the strength of his hereditary territories, and if the individual vassals had not been able to grow to an overwhelming size, Germany's feudal constitution might have supported the state. It is not the principle of feudalism which has cut off the possibility of Germany becoming a state;[67] on the contrary, the disproportionate expansion of individual estates has destroyed both the principle of feudalism itself and Germany's continued existence as a state.

The power of these individual estates has not allowed the state to develop a power of its own in Germany, and their expansion has made this increasingly impossible. The German character, with its stubborn insistence on independence, has made a complete formality out of everything which might serve to establish a [central] political power and to unite society in a single state, and it has clung to this formality with equal stubbornness. This stubborn attachment to formality can only be interpreted as a resistance to the reality of [political] union, which is averted by the adoption of this formal character [*Wesen*], and this immutability of form is passed off as immutability of substance [*der Sache*].

Just as the Roman Emperors, in putting an end to the anarchy of the Roman Republic and reconstituting the realm as a state, kept all the external forms of the Republic intact, so also in Germany – though with the opposite end in view – all the symbols of the German political union were conscientiously preserved for centuries, even after the thing itself, the state, had disappeared and dissolved (not indeed into open anarchy, but into many separate states). The constitution in fact seems to have undergone no change at all during the thousand years which have elapsed since the time of Charlemagne, for at his coronation, the newly elected Emperor bears the crown, sceptre and orb of Charlemagne, and even wears his shoes, coat, and jewels. An Emperor of modern times is thus identified with Charlemagne as Emperor to such an extent that he even wears the latter's own clothes. Even if the Margrave of Brandenburg now has an army of 200,000 troops, his relationship to the German Empire does not seem to have changed since he had fewer than 2,000 regular soldiers in his pay, for the Brandenburg envoy still presents the Emperor with oats at his coronation, just as he did in the past.

This German superstition regarding purely external forms and ceremony, so ridiculous in the eyes of other nations, does not lack self-awareness. It is a manifestation of the original German character, which clings with unbridled tenacity to its headstrong independence. In the preservation of these forms, the German convinces himself that he can discern the preservation of his constitution. Manifestos and state papers tell exactly the same story.

Mention has already been made of the loss which Germany has suffered at the hands of foreign powers. But for Germany as a state, it must be reckoned as even more of a loss that foreign princes have become the owners of German Imperial territories, and hence also members of the German Empire. Every increase in the power of such a house further detracts from Germany's constitution, which has remained in being only because the house of Austria (which may be described as the Imperial house) has been made strong enough – not by the German Empire, but by the power of its other territories – to offer some resistance to the principle of complete dissolution. Germany's constitution does not even have a guarantee against several German territories combining under a single house, in a perfectly legal manner, through inheritance. On the contrary, since the power of the state itself is consistently treated in the legal form of private property, there can be no question of any resistance to a unification of this kind, which is usually more important in politics than are private and family rights; Naples and Sicily were separated from Spain, and the right of this [Imperial] family to them was recognised in the same way as Tuscany, once it became separate, reverted to the Imperial house.

Just as the old Roman Empire was destroyed by northern barbarians, so also did the principle which destroyed the Roman-German Empire come from the north. Denmark, Sweden, England, and above all Prussia are the foreign powers[68] whose position as estates of the Empire simultaneously gave them a centre outside the German Empire and a constitutionally recognised influence in the Empire's affairs.

In this respect, *Denmark* played only a temporary and short-lived role in the initial years of the Thirty Years War.

The Peace of Westphalia generally consolidated the principle of what was then called German freedom, namely the dissolution of the Empire into independent states. It reduced the number of such states, [and hence] the only possibility which still remained of the whole predominating over the parts;[69] and by fusing independent states into larger ones, it increased the [degree of] separation. It also granted foreign powers the right to interfere in the internal affairs [of Germany], partly by granting them territories within the Empire, and partly by making them guarantors of the constitution.

It has at all times been regarded as [an act of] extreme malevolence if one party in a state which is torn by internal conflict calls on a foreign power for help; and – if there could be any question of punishment when a state is in the process of dissolution – it has even been considered the greatest of crimes. When a state is deeply wounded by civil wars, in the throes of this most terrible of all afflictions and despite the hatred (which surpasses all other hatreds) of such hostile elements, the principle that they ought nevertheless to form a single state still prevails; and even if this union is itself the product of tyranny, the most sacred of human aims – namely the need [*Forderung*] for union – still remains [valid]. But the party which calls on foreign powers to assist it renounces this principle; through its action, it has annulled [*aufgehoben*] the political union, even if its true and conscious intention is simply to find protection, through this foreign help, against an oppression which it is powerless to resist on its own.

In the Thirty Years War, after Denmark's attempt to become Germany's saving genius had failed, and when not just what is known as German constitutional law but all laws in general, without resistance or protest, fell silent before Ferdinand's armies, the noble Gustavus Adolphus made his appearance, almost against the will of the German estates. His heroic death on the battlefield did not allow him to fulfil his role as saviour of Germany's political and religious freedom. Gustavus declared in advance that this was his intention; he entered into the most specific treaties with the German princes on the general affairs of the nation, and placed himself at their head in a spirit of free and noble magnanimity; he defeated the armies of oppression, freeing the lands from this burden and from the even heavier burden of the loss of their religious rights; his camp was a church, and he and his army went into battle singing the most fervent hymns. Through his victories, he restored religion and the rights of which the German princes had been deprived. He did not return the reconquered hereditary lands of the Count Palatine; he kept other territories under his control and had other plans in his head which his death did not permit him to realise, and which the subsequent course of the war allowed his chancellor to fulfil only to the extent that, when peace was restored, the foreign power retained Western Pomerania and part of Eastern Pomerania, the archbishopric of Bremen, the bishopric of Verden and the city of Wismar. In theory, these territories remained dependent on the German Empire, but in practice, they were separated from it and its interest, so that, apart from its political influence as a power – including its legal influence as a guarantor [of the constitution] – Sweden gained a lasting influence, as of right, as a member of the Empire itself.

Human beings are foolish enough to allow their ideal visions of selfless champions of freedom in religion and politics, and the inner warmth of their enthusiasm, to distract them from the truth which resides in power, and so to believe that a work of human justice and dreams of the imagination are secure against the higher justice of nature and truth.[70] But this justice makes use of necessity [*Not*] to compel human beings to accept its authority, in defiance of all their convictions, theories, and inner fervour. This justice, whereby a foreign power which a weak state allows to participate in its internal affairs will also acquire possessions within it, duly expressed itself in the Peace of Westphalia in the case of the Duchy (subsequently the Kingdom) of Prussia: the Prussian Duke received the archbishopric of Magdeburg, and the bishoprics of Halberstadt, Kammin, and Minden. Even if the house of Brandenburg, like the [Swedish] house which now succeeded to the ducal title of Pomerania etc., had not simultaneously been an external foreign power, the reduction in the number of German estates and their amalgamation into a single (albeit domestic) power would still have had the effect of reducing the power of the [Empire in] general, because the previously smaller parts now constituted a power capable of resisting the power of the whole.

Through the peace treaties which it was compelled to make, after the death of Charles XII, with Hanover, Prussia, Denmark, and Russia, Sweden lost that place among the European powers which its valiant king had won for it in so meteoric a fashion, and it likewise lost its power in Germany. But the power of the German state gained nothing in the process, for another centre of resistance to it was already developing ever greater strength. The territories which Sweden lost to Germany neither came directly into the possession of the German Empire to serve as a fund for the Imperial exchequer, nor into that of their own princes, but of princes who were already fellow-members of the Empire and who now in turn became a formidable threat to the unity of the state.

During that profound peace which the German Empire claimed to enjoy while engaged in general warfare, *Hanover*, which now shared a single ruler with England, played a part which nevertheless remained without further consequence; it had no principle to assert which was directly linked with Germany's interest. Neither political nor religious freedom had to be defended, and even in later years, Hanover never rose to that degree of influence in Germany which Sweden, and later Prussia, commanded. England's constitution and all-too-remote interests did not allow it to amalgamate Hanover – and hence its relations with Germany – with England's political relations in the way that had been possible, because of his natural allegiance to his German connection, in the case of the first ruler of Brunswick who ascended the English throne.[71] The divergence of interests between England and the Electorate of Brunswick became most obvious during the Seven Years War, when France was so gratified with its project of conquering America and India through Hanover but realised in the event how little damage the devastation of Hanover did to the English nation. Despite this divergence (and consequently despite the reduced influence of England in Germany), the English monarch remains a member of the German Empire.

In the same war, Germany did not lose Silesia; but that power whose size constitutes the greatest threat to the unity of the German state became larger still by annexing it, and it retained its hold over it in the Seven Years War to which the conquest of Silesia subsequently gave rise. It is true that, in this war, the German Empire declared war on one of its members;[72] but the latter did not do it the honour of recognising it. It may indeed happen that a state against which war is actually waged is not recognised [by its adversary]; but the very fact that war is waged against it amounts to recognition, and the state in question is recognised in full when peace is concluded with it. But the enemy of the German Empire scarcely did it the honour of waging war on it, and its war was not recognised in a peace [treaty]; for no peace was concluded with the German Empire.

This war shared with earlier wars the character of being an internal war between German estates. One group of estates sent its troops to join the Imperial army of execution, in keeping with the decisions of the Imperial Diet; another group of estates abstracted completely from this relationship to the German Empire and allied themselves, as sovereign territories, with *Prussia*. No universal interest was any longer recognised. An old Protestant jealousy of Austria meant that religion became to some extent involved, and this was fostered by the Empress's known Catholic zeal, which had exposed her otherwise maternal heart to intrigues in which Protestants were oppressed within her states, and by certain other circumstances such as the Pope's consecration of the Austrian supreme commander's sword, etc. But the element of animosity which came from this quarter was present on both sides only as a public attitude [*Geist*]; the war itself was not concerned with more general interests of this kind, but only with the private interests of the warring powers.

Since that time, Prussian power has expanded in Poland. The number of German estates has again been reduced by three, namely Bavaria, Anspach, and Bayreuth. In this respect, the results of the war with France have not yet reached their full development.

Thus, it was partly religion and the progress of culture [*Bildung*], partly the fact that the Germans were united not so much by the power of an external political bond as by that of their inner character, and partly the absence of any political principle to limit the supremacy of the individual estates, which dissolved the German state by leaving it bereft of political power. The old forms have remained, but the times have changed, and with them manners, religion, wealth, the position of all political and civil estates, and the whole condition of the world and of Germany. The old forms do not express this actual condition; the two are separate, mutually contradictory, and reciprocally devoid of truth.

Germany arose out of the same condition as nearly all other European states and at the same time as they did.[73] France, Spain, England, Denmark and Sweden, Holland, and Hungary each grew into a single state and have continued as such, whereas Poland has ceased to exist. Italy has broken up, and Germany is disintegrating into a mass of independent states.

Most of the above states were founded by Germanic peoples, and their constitutions have developed out of the spirit of these peoples. Among the Germanic peoples, reliance was originally placed on the arm of every free man, and his will was involved in the nation's deeds. The election of princes, war and peace, and all collective enterprises were decided by the people. Anyone who wished to do so took part in debates in person; whoever did not so wish abstained of his own free will and relied on his common interest with the others.

As manners and way of life changed, each individual became more preoccupied with his own needs and private affairs; the overwhelming majority of free men – the middle class [*Bürgerstand*] proper – had to look exclusively to its own needs and livelihood; the states became larger, the external circumstances became more complex, and those who had to concern themselves exclusively with the latter became a class [*Stand*] of their own; the mass of things required by free men and by the nobility, by those who had to maintain themselves in their position [*Stand*] either by industry or by service to the state, grew larger. Thus, national affairs became increasingly remote from each individual, and responsibility for them therefore became more and more concentrated in a single centre consisting of the monarch and the Estates – i.e. one part of the nation made up of the nobility and clergy on the one hand, who spoke for themselves and in person, and of the third estate on the other, which represented the rest of the people. The monarch looks after national affairs, especially in so far as they concern external relations with other states; he is the centre of political power, and everything which requires legal enforcement emanates from him. The legal power is accordingly in his hands; the Estates have a share in legislation, and they furnish the means which sustain[g] his power.

This *system of representation* is the system of all modern European states. It did not exist in the forests of Germania, but it did emerge from them; it marks an epoch in world history. The continuum [*Zusammenhang*] of world culture [*Bildung*] has led the human race from oriental despotism to a republic which ruled the world and then, through the decay of this republic, to the present mean between the two extremes; and the Germans are the people from whom this universal shape [*Gestalt*] of the world spirit was born.

This system did not exist in the forests of Germania, for each nation must first have gone through its own phases of culture [*Kultur*] independently before it intervenes in the universal world continuum; and the principle which elevates it to universal

---

[g] *Translator's note*: Reading the plural *erhalten* for Hegel's singular *erhält*.

dominion does not arise until its own distinct principle is applied to the rest of the unstable world system [*Weltwesen*]. Thus, the freedom of the Germanic peoples necessarily became a *feudal system* when they overran the rest of the world with their conquests.

Among themselves, in their relations with one another and with the whole, the fief-holders remained what they were before, namely free people; but they acquired subjects, and in doing so, they also entered into a relationship of duty towards the individual whom, without any such relationship, they had freely followed or placed at their head. These contradictory attributes of the free man and the vassal can be reconciled inasmuch as the fiefs were not fiefs of the prince in person, but of the Empire. The individual's connection with the whole people now takes on the form of duty, and his possession of a fief and authority is not dependent on the arbitrary will of the prince, but is legal and proper to himself and hence hereditary. If, in despotisms, the title of a hospodar can have a kind of inherited status, even this has an arbitrary character; or if a hereditary authority of this kind is associated with a distinct and relatively independent state like Tunis, etc., this state is liable to pay tribute – and, unlike fief-holders, it has no share in collective deliberations. In such deliberations, the vassal's personal and representative capacities are combined; as a representative, he acts on behalf of his territory; he is its man, and he stands at the head of its interest with which he is personally identified. Besides, the vassal's own followers, apart from being subjects, have in many states also become citizens; or the individual free men who have not become barons have united into citizens' assemblies [*Bürgerschaften*], and this middle class [*Bürgerstand*] has acquired a further representation of its own.

In Germany, that portion of the middle class which has representation in its own right within the universal state does not also have the status of a subject, and those who are subjects are not separately represented within it; but they are represented through their princes, and they again have representation in relation to their princes within the frontiers of the particular state which they constitute.

Along with its territorial sovereignty, the upper and lower nobility in England lost some of its function of representing a section of the people; but this does not mean that its significance within the state has become entirely personal. The peer with a seat and a vote in the national parliament is, by virtue of primogeniture, the representative of his great family; but the Chancellor of the Exchequer, the younger son of the Earl of Chatham, is simply *Mr* Pitt. Unless he is the eldest son, a nobleman must surmount the same hurdles as all commoners face at the start of their careers, and the path to the highest honours through talent, character, and education is no less open to the commoner than to the son of a duke. Similarly, in the Austrian monarchy, it is part of social convention to address every well-dressed man as *Herr von*; the way to the highest military and political offices is open to everyone, and whoever attains them is elevated to the nobility and treated as its equal (except in those circumstances which, as in England, entail a [right of parliamentary] representation).

[The causes of] France's misfortune must be sought entirely in the complete degeneration of the feudal system and the consequent loss of its true character. When the Estates General ceased to meet, the higher and lower nobility no longer appeared in that character in which its main strength within the political organisation consists, namely its representative function.[74] Conversely, its personal character was developed to an extreme and provocative extent.

From youth upwards, the nobility is exempted by wealth from the sordidness of business and the rigours of deprivation. This, and its inherited carefree attitude, untroubled by affairs, have enabled it to maintain a free state of mind, so that it is more capable of that warlike courage which sacrifices all possessions, all cherished property and habits, in favour of limitation and adaptation to the whole existing order. It is likewise better equipped to deal with state business in a more liberal manner, and is more capable, in such contexts, of a certain freedom which is less dependent on rules and which – according to circumstances, situation and need – can show a greater self-confidence and impart greater freedom and vitality to the mechanical aspects of administration. Thus, if the nobility is at a personal advantage in all states, it must also be freer, and therefore open to possible competition, because its qualities are personal. For the organisation of our states, which is artificial, labour-intensive, and exceptionally demanding in terms of effort, in any case requires the assiduous application and laboriously acquired skills and knowledge of the middle class. Given the previous rise of this class [*dieses*

Standes] and its increased importance in recent times, the way must remain open to the knowledge and skills through which it transcends its [original] character.

This process whereby the difference [between nobility and commoners] is diminished by nature and by most modern states – in Prussia, for example, to some extent in civil affairs, but in England, Austria, and other states in military aspects too – has been taken to an extreme in France. There, judicial positions and a military career are open to[h] them [i.e. members of the middle class], and the purely personal has been made into a principle.

Representation is so intimately bound up with the essence of the feudal constitution in its further development, in conjunction with the rise of a middle class, that it may be classed as the silliest of illusions to regard it as an invention of very recent times.[i] All modern states exist through representation, and only its degeneration, i.e. the loss of its true nature, has destroyed France's constitution (though not France as a state). It came [originally] from Germany, but it is a higher law that any people from which the world receives a new and universal impulse must itself finally perish before all the others, while its principle – though not the people itself – survives.

[7. The Independence of the Estates]

Germany has not developed for itself the principle which it gave to the world, nor managed to sustain itself by it. It has not organised itself by this principle; on the contrary, it has disorganised itself, in that it did not develop the feudal constitution into a political power, but sought at all costs to remain true to its original character whereby the individual is independent of the universal, i.e. the state.[75] It has disintegrated into a mass of states whose mode of

[h] *Translator's note*: Reading *erschlossen* for Hegel's *verschlossen*, as in *Werke*, vol. I, p. 536.
[i] *Translator's note*: (Hegel continues as follows in a marginal addition): By transforming free men into rulers, a feudal constitution – i.e. in modern countries, a state – has been established in which each individual no longer has an immediate will of his own in all national affairs; instead, all obey a whole which they themselves have founded, along with its branches and individuations (i.e. the state and its laws), as a fixed and permanent centre to which each [individual] has a mediate relationship made possible by representation.

subsistence is fixed by solemn mutual treaties and guaranteed by major powers. But this mode of subsistence is not based on their own power and strength; it is dependent on the politics of the major powers.

What true guarantee remains for the existence of these individual states?

Since they lack a true political power, this guarantee can be based only on the venerability of those rights in and for themselves – rights which, over a period of centuries, have been elevated by a multitude of solemn peace treaties to the point where they cannot possibly be infringed. Indeed, it is common practice to treat the mode of political subsistence of the individual states as a moral power, and to impress its sanctity on people's minds [*Gemüter*] so that it becomes something as fixed and inviolable as the universal manners or religion of a people.

But we have often seen the most violent attacks on religion and manners themselves, backed by orders and authority, even in the most recent times in France; and even if such highly dangerous experiments usually lead to the downfall of their instigators – or at least produce only a very ambiguous effect – even religion and manners are exposed to the influences of changing times and to imperceptible change.

But apart from this, manners and religion are of a quite different order from constitutional rights. When we say that nothing can be more sacred than right, then as far as private right is concerned, even grace is superior, because it can relinquish its rights. The right of the state is also superior, for if the state is to survive, it cannot allow private right to prevail in its full force;[76] for even the taxes which it must impose are a suspension [*Aufheben*] of the right of property. And if political rights were to have the force of private rights, they would involve a kind of internal contradiction; for they would imply that those who had firm and reciprocal political rights of this kind stood in a legal relationship under a higher instance which exercised power and authority. But if this were the case, the reciprocal rights in question would no longer be political rights, but private rights or rights of property.

The German Empire is supposed to furnish the basis for a relationship of this kind. But on the one hand, it is already a contradiction in and for itself if not only property, but relationships which directly involve the state, are to have the form of private rights; and on the other hand, since no political power exists any longer in Germany, political rights can no longer be treated as private rights and no longer have the same security and stability as the latter, but fall into the category of political rights in general.

We already know what venerability these political rights have in and for themselves. Every peace treaty – and peace treaties are the true contracts on which the reciprocal political rights of the powers are based – contains the central article that friendship shall prevail between the contracting powers. Apart from this article, it contains a definition of their other relations, especially those which previously gave rise to conflict. Although the central article expresses in general terms the need to preserve a good understanding, it is clear in itself that this is not to be taken in an absolute [*unbedingt*] sense.

The Turkish Empire seems to conduct its relations with foreign powers almost in the spirit [*Sinn*] of being generally at peace with them until it is itself attacked, and the politics of the rest of Europe have only rarely succeeded in embroiling it in a political war. Otherwise, the relations between states are so many-sided, and each individual strand of these relations as defined in a peace treaty has in turn so many aspects, that however precisely they are defined, infinite other aspects remain over which conflict is still possible. No power attacks a stipulated right directly and openly. Rather, differences arise over some undefined aspect and then destroy the peace altogether; through the effects of war, they subsequently undermine the foundations of the other defined rights as well.

This suspension [*Aufhebung*] of mutual political rights occurs only as a result of war. The treaties and the relations defined in them might well remain in being; they are not directly infringed or attacked outright with open force, for treaties are not to be trifled with. But if a conflict arises over other points and circumstances which have not been clearly resolved, everything else which had previously been settled by treaty collapses.

Wars, whether they are described as wars of aggression or as wars of defence (and the parties can never agree over such designations) could be called unjust only if the terms of the [previous] peace treaty stipulated an *unconditional* peace between the parties; and even if we do use such expressions as 'perpetual peace' and 'eternal friendship between the powers', they should be understood as subject to the essential qualification 'until one party attacks or acts in a hostile way [towards the other]'. For no state can be obliged to let itself be attacked or treated in a hostile manner without defending itself, and at the same time to keep the peace.

But the potential modes of hostility are so infinite that the human understanding cannot possibly define them [all], and the more definitions there are, i.e. the more rights are established, the more easily a contradiction can arise between such rights. If one party pursues a right conceded to him as far as the concession allows, he will come into conflict with some other right enjoyed by the other party. One need only look at the reciprocal manifestos and political documents which, in the event of a disagreement between two states, contain accusations concerning the other power's behaviour and justifications of the accuser's own!

Each party bases its own behaviour on rights and accuses the other of infringing a right. The right of state A has been infringed by state B in respect of right a which state A enjoys, but state B maintains that it asserted its own right b and that this cannot be interpreted as an infringement of the right of A. The public takes sides, each party claims it has right on its side, and both parties are right; for it is precisely the rights themselves which come into contradiction with each other.

It is the philanthropists and moralists who decry politics as an attempt and artifice to pursue one's own advantage at the expense of right, as a system and work of injustice.[77] And the carping, indifferent public – i.e. that uninterested, unpatriotic mass whose ideal of virtue is the peace of the alehouse – accuses politics of questionable faith and lack of justice and stability; and if they do at least take an interest in it, they are for that very reason distrustful of the legal form [*Rechtsform*] which the interests of their state assume. If these interests coincide with their own, they will duly defend the legal form; but their own interests rather than the legal form are their true inner motive.

If the philanthropic friends of right and morality did have an interest, they might realise that interests, and hence also rights themselves, can come into collision, and that it is foolish to set up a dichotomy between right and the interest of the state (or, to use a morally more repugnant expression, the advantage [*Nutzen*] of the state).

Right is the advantage of a particular state, specified and acknowledged by treaties; and since, in treaties in general, the different interests of states are specified, despite the fact that these interests, as rights, are infinitely complex, these interests – and hence also the rights themselves – must come into contradiction with each other. It depends entirely on circumstances, on the combinations of power – i.e. on the *judgement* of politics – whether an endangered interest or right will be defended with all the force a power can muster, in which case the other party can also, of course, adduce a right of its own, since it has itself exactly the opposite interest which collides with the first, and hence also a right. Thus, war or some other means must now decide – not which of the rights asserted by the two parties is the genuine right (for both parties have a genuine right), but which right should give way to the other. War or some other means must decide the issue, precisely because both contradictory rights are equally true; hence a third factor – i.e. war – must make them unequal so that they can be reconciled, and this occurs when one gives way to the other.

The venerability and moral power of rights may last and hold firm, but how could these qualities possibly preserve the rights themselves? Because of the indeterminacy of rights, conflict *may* arise, and because of their determinacy, contradictions between them *must* arise, and in the resultant dispute, right must assert itself through its power.

It makes no sense that what are called 'the rights of the German estates' should subsist as a moral power by virtue of their inherent venerability, although – given the contradiction mentioned above – no power is or can be available to uphold them throughout their whole multifarious range. The result would be a situation in which true anarchy – not just passive but active anarchy – prevailed, like the genuine ancient right of private warfare [*Faustrecht*] which, in the constant disputes over such confused ownership, gave temporary possession to the stronger arm and sustained it therein until the arm of its adversary grew stronger.

This situation was remedied, however, by the prohibition on private warfare [*Landfriede*]. This prohibition inaugurated a state of peace among the smaller estates, which is sustained by their impotence in relation to the larger ones. As for the more powerful estates, it has already been noted that the ownership of the Jülich-Cleve[78] inheritance gave rise to the Thirty Years War, and the issue was no more resolved by courts of law than were others such as the Bavarian succession. But apart from this, the number of contentious issues which have led to wars would appear very small in comparison with the infinity of contentious issues which must have arisen from the infinite complexity of rights, and which have been settled peacefully – or rather, left in abeyance. It is well known that the German nobility is embroiled in countless and interminable lawsuits, and that proceedings instituted one or more centuries ago are still pending; in addition, an infinite number of claims – that is, rights which have not been fulfilled – lie buried in the archives of every prince, count, Imperial city, and nobleman. If all these rights were suddenly given a voice, what a confused and endless clamour would result!

Claims are undecided rights. Remission is imposed on them not by judicial decision – for they have not been decided – but by fear of the law [*des Rechts*] (for a claim is always preferable to a right denied, a possible lawsuit preferable to a lost one), and by fear of those with greater power who, if an open feud takes place in their neighbourhood, must, on the basis of the more general legality [*Rechtsgrund*] of modern times, take sides in order to secure their territory and its frontiers; and in this case, those with less power, whether this intervention [of their more powerful neighbours] was directed against them or designed to benefit them, would gain no advantage. Consequently, feuds have come to an end, the prohibition on private warfare [*Landfriede*] has restored peace – i.e. it has silenced the contradiction of rights, but not resolved it – and the party which happens to be in current possession continues to enjoy the legally disputed object (*beati possidentes!*)[79] even if no legal title to it has been established. Thus, what preserves a certain measure of peace in Germany is not a condition – like that of a state – in which possession is determined by right. On the contrary, given the astonishing differences in the power of the estates, their guarantee is fear and politics, not the venerability of the actual rights on which they depend, nor any inner power which these might possess.

Given this lack of political power [*Staatsmacht*] in Germany –

and it is a necessary lack, as has been shown, because the object of such a power, namely the permanent preservation of rights, would be impossible to attain – it is conceivable that the mass of isolated estates, since they are still in the old situation of collaborating towards a universal end when and in so far as the individual estates wish to do so, might revert to their old behaviour. That is, even if they are not already members of a lasting and established union, they might freely come together in times of danger or emergency and thereby constitute a state and a political power [*Staatsmacht*] out of their separate powers in order to meet the current need, both in their internal affairs (if their rights were attacked) and in their external relations (if they were attacked collectively or through one of their particular members).

One specific instance of this kind was [prompted by] the attacks on the Protestant religion in former times, in which the [common] objective did not arise out of the ambition [of the princes] – which was quite indifferent to their subjects – but from the innermost interests of the common people. No other objective could have united the princes and their peoples so unanimously, so freely and with such enthusiasm, to the extent that their other rivalries were forgotten. All other objectives have less impact on the peoples themselves, for other disputed interests may spring to mind again and assert themselves alongside them.

We know, however, what an ignominious end befell the *Smalkaldic League*.[80] The whole League was full of vain and petty aspirations, and was so immersed in smug complacency with regard to itself and its noble work – even before it had done anything – that it disintegrated at the first assaults. Yet even here, some members of the League behaved courageously and actually ventured into battle, whereas the *Protestant Union* of the following century advertised its own complete inanity in advance by the inanities in which it indulged when it first arose, and this quality was fully revealed as soon as it had work to do.

The so-called *League of Princes*[81] opposed to Joseph II, whose behaviour appeared dangerous to many estates, may be regarded as the only other example of an internal association of this kind. The idea of this League made a splendid impression, as much because of the prince who led it as of the prince against whom it was directed, and also because popular opinion was much engaged by numerous writers on both sides, some of whom were talented. The public voice seemed to have some kind of significance here; if Frederick II was surrounded by the glory of his deeds, these deeds belonged to the past, and their result – Silesia in Prussian hands, state control and religious and civil laws in the Prussian territories – was already present; and if nothing more could be expected for the rest of Germany from this direction (and indeed nothing further emerged from it), all the more interest was aroused by the hope that an all-embracing new German century was about to dawn. But there is nothing further to remark concerning the League of German Princes except that it caught the attention of public opinion and aroused many hopes and anxieties. Since it neither acted nor expressed itself, nothing further can be said of its essential character. Brandenburg's independence of the German Empire was established long before, and the possibility that this would have increased or diminished if the League of Princes had been put into operation is something on which there is nothing to be said.

As for free alliances against external powers, these took the place of Imperial wars in the proper sense whenever Germany was not torn by internal conflict but defended itself against an external enemy (Müller,[82] p. 70; alliance with William of Orange against Louis XIV; League of Augsburg, 1686). What the princes and estates did was rather the free will of individual circles of associates than the legal and universally binding resolution of a body politic. Brandenburg still appears in association with the Empire, but not on account of its obligations towards the latter; it acts independently, and its chief end is the Prussian crown.

The wars of this century were internal wars.

In the course of the last war against France, at the moment when danger threatened for Germany, rather more of a common will for the defence of Germany did seem to be developing. Nearly all the German states took part in it, but one cannot identify any single moment at which all of them collaborated simultaneously. On the contrary, the most powerful of them distanced themselves from it for most of the time.

In the Peace of Westphalia, the old independence of the parts of Germany was consolidated – albeit in completely changed circumstances – and Germany was thereby prevented from becoming a modern state with a political power [*Staatsmacht*].[83] Subsequent experience has taught us that the spirit of the age which followed has changed completely, for each individual part has acted for the whole only of its own free will and by agreement; even in the direst emergencies in which interests of the most pressing concern to all parts are involved, no common and united action is to be expected.

In the Peace of Westphalia, Germany's statelessness became organised. Writers like Hippolytus a Lapide[84] have expressed the inner character and tendency of the nation in precise [*bestimmt*] terms. In the Peace of Westphalia, Germany gave up the task of establishing itself as a secure political power [*Staatsmacht*] and abandoned itself to the good will of its members.

One may, if one wishes, regard this confidence with which the common weal of Germany was entrusted to the free will of its parts as an effect of that spirit of integrity of which the German nation is so proud. It sounds admirable if, on the one hand, the power of the state [*Staatsmacht*] is dissolved and placed in the hands of the individual estates [*der Einzelnen*], while on the other hand, there is a demand – and with it an expectation – that these individuals will co-operate freely. The German estates which concluded the Peace of Westphalia would have considered themselves offended by lack of trust if anyone had mentioned to them the possibility that, after this division [of powers], they might disregard the best interests of the whole, and that each [estate] could and would act for its own interest, even if this interest did not coincide with the general interest but ran counter to it. The general context, the obligations of the individuals towards the whole, and the best interests of the latter were most solemnly acknowledged and secured, and at every disagreement on such matters – even if it erupted into the most terrible wars – each of the two parties justified itself legally by detailed manifestos and [legal] deductions.

By these means, the matter is transferred from the sphere of will and particular [*eigenen*] interest to the sphere of insight, and, given a general will to act in the best interests of the whole, it would be up to the understanding to discover the mode of action most conducive to the general good; and if this were determined by the majority, the minority would necessarily have to follow suit. But this is not the case, nor can it be so, not only because no political power [*Staatsmacht*] is present, but also because the individual [estate] has the right to form alliances, make peace, etc. according to its own insight with regard to the general good. If, in the event of disunity and war, someone – of necessity a private individual, for a minister cannot adopt this course – were honestly to believe that the reason for the war was simply a lack of general insight into whether something was in keeping with the good of Germany, and cherished the hope of creating unanimity by acting upon this conviction, the only effect he would produce would be to make himself ridiculous through his good nature. He should try instead to promote the insight that a mode of action which ought to be general is also in keeping with the particular interest of every individual.

It is a widely acknowledged and familiar principle that this particular interest is the main consideration. It cannot be held to contradict rights, duties, or morality; on the contrary, each individual estate, as a particular state, *must* not sacrifice itself to a universal from which it can expect no help, whereas the prince of a specific territory or the magistrate of an Imperial city is invested with the sacred duty of caring for his land and his subjects.

[8. The Formation of National States]

It was the Peace of Westphalia which secured this independent status for the parts [of Germany]. On their own, they would not have been capable of attaining it; on the contrary, their alliance had disintegrated, and both in politics and religion, they themselves and their territories were in the despotic hands of Ferdinand,[85] with no possibility of resistance.

Gustavus Adolphus's campaign might itself be placed in exactly the same class as the campaigns of his successor Charles XII – not with regard to his own person, for he died at the height of his fortune, but with regard to his nation. In both cases, the Swedish power would have failed completely in Germany if Richelieu's politics, continued in the same direction by Mazarin, had not adopted and sustained its cause.

Richelieu was accorded the rare good fortune of being considered its greatest benefactor both by the state of whose greatness he laid the true foundation and by that at whose expense this was done.

Both France as a state and Germany as a state had within them the same two principles of dissolution. In the one, Richelieu destroyed these principles completely and thereby raised it to be one of the most powerful states; but in the other, he gave these principles free rein and thereby annulled [*aufhob*] its continued existence as a state. In both countries he brought the principle on which they were inherently grounded to complete maturity; the principle of monarchy in France, and in Germany the principle of forming a mass of distinct states.[86] Both principles still had to struggle against their opposites; but Richelieu succeeded in guiding both countries to their fixed and mutually opposed systems.

The two principles which prevented France from becoming a single state in the form of a monarchy were the great nobles and the Huguenots;[87] both engaged in wars with the kings.

The great nobles, who included members of the royal family, intrigued with armies against the minister [of the crown]. It is true that the sovereignty of the monarch had long been treated as sacrosanct and elevated above all claims, and the great nobles did not lead armies into the field to claim sovereignty for themselves, but to become the foremost subjects of the monarchs – as ministers, provincial governors, etc. Richelieu's achievement in subjecting them to the political authority in its immediate forms of expression, i.e. to the ministry, has at first glance the appearance of ambition. Those who had been his enemies seem to have fallen victim to his ambition; in their rebellions and conspiracies, they protested their innocence and their dutiful dedication to their sovereign – no doubt with complete veracity – and regarded their armed opposition to the minister in person as neither a civil nor a political crime. But they were defeated not by Richelieu as a person, but by his genius, which linked his person to the necessary principle of the unity of the state and made political offices dependent on the state. And this is what constitutes political genius, i.e. the identification of the individual with a principle; given this association, the individual must necessarily triumph. In terms of ministerial achievement, Richelieu's success in conferring unity on the executive power of the state is infinitely superior to the achievement of adding a further province to a country, or of rescuing it in some other way from adversity.

The other principle which threatened the dissolution of the state was the Huguenots, whom Richelieu suppressed as a political party; his measures against them should by no means be regarded as a suppression of freedom of conscience. They had their own armies,

fortified cities, alliances with foreign powers, etc. and accordingly
constituted a kind of sovereign state. In contrast to them, the great
nobles had formed the League, which had brought the French state
to the edge of the abyss. Both opposing parties were an armed
fanaticism beyond the reach of the political authority. In destroying
the Huguenot state, Richelieu simultaneously destroyed the rights
of the League, and he then disposed of its lawless [*rechtlosen*] and
unprincipled legacy, the insubordination of the great nobles. But
while he eradicated the Huguenot state, he left the Huguenots their
freedom of conscience, their churches, worship, and civil and political rights, on an equal footing with the Catholics. Through his consistent statesmanship, he discovered and practised that toleration
which was implemented more than a century later as the product
of a more cultivated humanity and as the most splendid achievement of philosophy and more refined manners; and it was not ignorance or fanaticism on the part of the French when, in the [Thirty
Years] War and in the Peace of Westphalia, they gave no thought
to the separation of church and state in Germany, made religion
the basis of a distinction between political and civil rights, and
applied in Germany a principle which they abolished [*aufhoben*] in
their own country.

Thus France, as well as England, Spain, and the other European
countries, succeeded in pacifying and uniting those elements which
fermented within them and threatened to destroy the state; and
through the freedom of the feudal system which Germany [*Germania*] taught them, they managed to create a centre which is freely
determined by laws and in which all powers are concentrated
(irrespective of whether it assumes a truly monarchic form or that
of a modern republic, which nevertheless also comes under the
principle of limited monarchy, i.e. a monarchy based on laws).
From this epoch in which the [European] countries developed into
states, we can date the period of the power and wealth of the state
and of the free and lawful welfare of individuals.

Conversely, the fate of *Italy* has run the same course as that of
Germany, except that Italy, since it had already attained a greater
degree of culture, brought its fate sooner to that level of development which Germany is now approaching in full.

The Roman–German Emperors long claimed over Italy a
supremacy which, as in Germany, usually had only so much force –

or indeed any force at all – if it was backed up by the personal power of the Emperor. The Emperors' urge to keep both countries under their rule destroyed their power in both.

In Italy, every point of the country acquired sovereignty. It ceased to be one state and became a host of independent states – monarchies, aristocracies, democracies, just as chance dictated; and the degeneration of these constitutions into tyranny, oligarchy, and ochlocracy even made its appearance for a time. The condition of Italy cannot be called anarchy, for the mass of opposing parties were organised states. Despite the lack of a proper association of states, a large proportion of them always united in joint resistance to the head of the Empire, while the rest united to make common cause with him. The parties of Guelphs and Ghibellines, which at one time extended to Germany as well as Italy, reappeared in the eighteenth century in Germany as the Austrian and Prussian parties (with modifications derived from the changed circumstances).

It was not long after the individual parts of Italy had dissolved the former state and risen to independence that they aroused a desire for conquest on the part of larger powers and became the theatre of wars between foreign powers. The small states, which measured themselves against a power over a thousand times greater than their own, met the inevitable fate of their own downfall, and our regret at this fate is accompanied by an awareness of the necessity and guilt which pygmies bring upon themselves when they square up to giants and are trampled underfoot. Even the larger Italian states, which had grown by devouring a mass of smaller states, continued to vegetate, without strength or true independence, as counters in the schemes of foreign powers. They survived a little longer by their skill and astuteness in abasing themselves at the right moment, and in avoiding total subjection by constantly accepting semi-subjection, although they did not escape the former in the long run.

What became of the mass of independent states – Pisa, Siena, Arezzo, Ferrara, Milan, and those hundreds of states which included every city among them? Or of the families of the many sovereign dukes, margraves, etc., the princely houses of Bentivoglia, Sforza, Gonzaga, Pico, Urbino, etc., and the innumerable minor noblemen? The independent states were swallowed up by larger ones, and these in turn by larger ones still, and so on. One of the greatest, namely Venice, was finished off in our own times by a letter from a French general, delivered by an adjutant. The most illustrious princely houses no longer have sovereignty, nor even political or representative significance. The noblest families have become courtiers.

In that unfortunate period when Italy hastened towards its ruin and was the battlefield in those wars which foreign princes fought over its territories, it both furnished the resources for the wars and was itself the prize of victory. It entrusted its own defence to assassination, poison, and treason, or to hordes of foreign rabble whom their paymasters always found costly and destructive, and often formidable and dangerous; and some of whose leaders rose to the rank of princes. Germans, Spaniards, French, and Swiss plundered the country, and foreign cabinets decided the fate of the nation. Deeply conscious of this state of universal misery, hatred, upheaval, and blindness, an Italian statesman,[88] with cool deliberation, grasped the necessary idea of saving Italy by uniting it into a single state. With rigorous logic, he mapped out the way forward which both the country's salvation and the corruption and blind folly of the age made necessary, and appealed in the following words to his prince to assume the exalted role of saviour of Italy and to earn the fame of bringing its misfortune to an end:[89]

> I have maintained that the Israelites had to be enslaved in Egypt before the ability of Moses could be displayed, the Persians had to be oppressed by the Medes before Cyrus's greatness of spirit could be revealed, and the Athenians in disarray before the magnificent qualities of Theseus could be demonstrated.[90] Likewise, in order for the valour and worth of an Italian spirit to be recognised, Italy had to be reduced to the desperate straits in which it now finds itself: more enslaved than the Hebrews, more oppressed than the Persians, more scattered than the Athenians, without an acknowledged leader, and without order or stability, beaten, despoiled, lacerated, overrun, in short, utterly devastated. And although recently a spark was revealed in one man that might have led one to think that he was ordained by God to achieve her redemption, yet it was seen that he was struck down by misfortune at the highest point of his career. Thus, remaining almost lifeless, Italy is waiting for someone to heal her wounds, and put an end to the ravaging of Lombardy, to the extortions in the Kingdom of Naples and

Tuscany, and to cure the sores that have been festering for so long [. . .] This is a very righteous cause: 'iustum enim est bellum quibus necessarium, et pia arma ubi nulla nisi in armis spes est'[91] [. . .] Everything points to your future greatness. But you must play your part, for God does not want to do everything, in order not to deprive us of our freedom and the glory that belongs to us [. . .] I have no doubt at all that he would be received with great affection in all those regions that have been inundated by the foreign invasions, as well as with a great thirst for revenge, with resolute fidelity, with devotion and with tears of gratitude. What gate would be closed to him? What people would fail to obey him? What envious hostility would work against him? What Italian would deny him homage?

It is evident that a man who speaks with such true gravity was neither base-hearted nor frivolous-minded. As for the first of these qualities, the very name of Machiavelli carries with it the guarantee of disapproval in public opinion, in which Machiavellian principles and obnoxious principles are synonymous. The idea that a state should be constituted by a people has for so long been obscured by the senseless clamour for so-called 'liberty' that the entire misery which Germany suffered in the Seven Years War and in the recent war with France, along with all the advances of reason and the experience of the French obsession with liberty, has perhaps not been enough to establish as an article of faith among peoples or as a principle of political science the truth that freedom is possible only when a people is legally united within a state.

Even Machiavelli's basic aim of raising Italy to statehood is misconstrued by those who are short-sighted enough to regard his work as no more than a foundation for tyranny or a golden mirror for an ambitious oppressor. But even if his aim is acknowledged, it is alleged that his means are abhorrent, and this gives morality ample scope to trot out its platitudes that the end does not justify the means, etc. But there can be no question here of any choice of means: gangrenous limbs cannot be cured by lavender-water, and a situation in which poison and assassination have become common weapons permits no half-measures. Life which is close to decay can be reorganised only by the most drastic means.

It is quite senseless to treat the exposition of an idea directly derived from observation of the Italian predicament as a compendium of moral and political principles applicable indiscriminately to all situations – i.e. to none at all. One must study the history of the centuries before Machiavelli and of Italy during his times, and then read *The Prince* in the light of these impressions, and it will appear not only as justified, but as a distinguished and truthful conception produced by a genuinely political mind of the highest and noblest sentiments.

It may not be superfluous to say something on a matter which is commonly overlooked, namely the other genuinely idealistic demands which Machiavelli makes of an excellent prince, and which have probably never been fulfilled by any prince since his times (not even by the one who refuted him).[92] But what are described as the abhorrent means advocated by Machiavelli must be viewed from a different angle. Italy was supposed to become a state, and this was recognised as a principle even at a time when the Emperor was still regarded as the supreme feudal lord. Machiavelli starts from this general premise; this is his demand and the principle which he opposes to the misery of his country. From this point of view, his procedure in *The Prince* appears in a very different light. What would indeed be abhorrent if done by one private individual to another, or by one state to another (or to a private individual), is now [seen to be] a just punishment. The promotion of anarchy is the ultimate – or perhaps the only – crime against the state; for all crimes which the state has to deal with tend in this direction. Those who attack the state itself directly, not indirectly like other criminals, are the worst offenders, and the state has no higher duty than to preserve itself and to destroy the power of such offenders in the surest way it can. The state's performance of this supreme duty is no longer a means, but a punishment; and if punishment is itself a means, then every punishment of every criminal would have to be classed as abhorrent, and every state would be in the position of using abhorrent means, such as death and lengthy imprisonment, for its own preservation.

Cato the Younger of Rome enjoys the privilege of being invoked by every libertarian agitator.[93] He was the greatest supporter of the plan to make Pompey the sole ruler, not out of friendship for Pompey but because he considered anarchy to be the greater evil; and he killed himself not because what the Romans then still called freedom (i.e. anarchy) had disappeared – for the party of Pompey, of which Cato was a member, was merely a different party from that of Caesar – but because of his stubborn character which would not submit to his despised and hated enemy.[94] His death was a party matter.

The man whom Machiavelli had hoped to see as the saviour of Italy was by all accounts the Duke of Valentinois,[95] a prince who, with the help of his uncle and through his bravery and all kinds of deception, had constructed a state out of the principalities of the Dukes of Ursino, Colonna, Urbino, etc. and the domains of the Roman barons. Even if we discount all the deeds which mere rumours and the hatred of their enemies have imputed to him and his uncle, their memory as human beings is blemished in the eyes of posterity (if posterity should presume to pass such moral judgements); and the Duke and his uncle have perished, though their work remains. It was they who obtained a state for the papal throne, a state whose existence Julius II[96] knew very well how to exploit and to render formidable, and which is still extant today.

Machiavelli ascribes the fall of Cesare Borgia not just to political mistakes, but also to the accident which consigned him to his sick-bed at that most critical moment when Alexander died. But we should rather see in his fall a higher necessity which did not allow him to enjoy the fruits of his deeds or to make them the foundation of an increased power; for nature, as his vices indicate, seems to have destined him rather for ephemeral glory and a purely instrumental role in the founding of a state, and a large part of the power to which he rose was based not on any internal or even external natural right, but was grafted on to the alien branch of his uncle's spiritual dignity.

Machiavelli's work remains a major testimony to his age, and to his own belief that the fate of a people which rapidly approaches political destruction can be averted by a genius. In view of the misunderstanding and hatred which *The Prince* has encountered, it is a noteworthy feature of this work's peculiar fate that, as if by instinct, a future monarch[97] whose entire life and deeds were the clearest expression of the German state's dissolution into independent states made this same Machiavelli the subject of an academic exercise.[98] He opposed him with moral lessons whose hollowness he himself demonstrated both through his own behaviour and quite explicitly in his literary works; for example, in the preface to his history of the first Silesian War, he declares that treaties between states cease to be binding when they no longer serve a state's best interests.

But apart from this, the more astute public, which could not fail to notice the genius of Machiavelli's works yet was too morally inclined to approve of his principles, nevertheless wished, in a well-meaning way, to rescue him [from his detractors]. It accordingly resolved the contradiction honourably and subtly enough by maintaining that Machiavelli was not serious in what he said, and that his entire work was a subtle and ironic persiflage. One can only compliment this irony-seeking public on its ingenuity.

Machiavelli's voice has died away without effect.

[9. The Politics of the Two Great German Powers]

Germany shares the fate which Italy once experienced: it has been the theatre of civil wars for many centuries. But it has also been a theatre for the wars of foreign powers; it has been plundered, robbed, vilified, and despised by friends, and it has usually lost territory when peace was restored. It suffered this fate much later than Italy. Sweden was actually the first foreign power to gnaw significantly at its entrails and to help to demolish the previous unstable system of [political] association. From that time onwards, foreign powers decided Germany's lot. Even before then, it had ceased to inspire any fear abroad. Thenceforth, it ceased to settle its own internal affairs independently and to decide its own course; it has handed over its destiny to others.

But Germany's fate differs essentially from that of Italy in that the states into which Italy had split up were long able, in view of the world situation in general, to assert themselves even against much greater powers, and their disproportion in size had not yet rendered their power equally disproportionate. On the contrary, just as Greece was capable not only of resisting the Persians but also of conquering them, so was a city like Milan able in former times to defy the power of Frederick[99] and to hold out against it; and later still, Venice stood firm against the League of Cambrai.[100] But the possibility of small states resisting large ones has now completely vanished; and the sovereignty of the German states developed mainly at a time when this possibility no longer existed.

Consequently, the German states have not exchanged association for complete separation, but have entered at once into associations of a different kind. The mass [of Germany] has not split up into numerous pieces and then remained fragmented for a time; instead, new centres have formed within the mass, and the parts which broke away from the whole gathered round them to form new masses.

Religion and independent statehood were at one time the interests and focal points round which the German estates rallied, and which together shaped their political system. But those focal points have now vanished. Religion has not only been preserved; the spirit of the times has placed it beyond all danger. Similarly, the estates have now acquired their independence. But alongside the Austrian power, whose claims as a universal monarchy used to give rise to anxiety, the Prussian monarchy has developed. Strong enough in itself, it held its own in the Seven Years War against the power not only of the Austrian monarchy, but of several others too, and since then it has expanded even further in Poland and Franconia.

By virtue of this power, Prussia has ceased to share in the common interest in preserving independence, and it cannot consequently be regarded any longer as the natural centre for those estates which wish to preserve theirs. It may wish to ally itself with other estates; in this respect, it does not depend on the support of the German princes, but can look after itself on its own. Its partnership with the German estates is therefore an unequal one, for it has less need of this partnership than they do, and the benefits [which flow from it] must also be unequal. Prussia itself may [now] give cause for anxiety.

In the last war, four political systems could be discerned in Germany: firstly the Austrian one, secondly, the Imperial one, [thirdly,] the neutral one, and fourthly, the Prussian one.

Austria has had no immediate support, except perhaps from a few lesser princes such as the Bishop of Brixen,[101] who lives in the midst of the Austrian states. As the Imperial house, Austria demands the support and collective co-operation of the German estates, and all the less powerful estates which can preserve some degree of independence only if a German Empire continues to exist – especially those in the south of Germany – have maintained their allegiance to the Imperial system; these include above all the ecclesiastical estates and the Imperial cities.

The third system is chiefly that of Bavaria, Baden, and Saxony, which – without any political association with Austria, Prussia, or the Empire – have acted in accordance with their own particular interest as regards war or peace or neutrality.

The fourth system includes those estates of northern Germany which, through the mediation of Prussia, concluded a treaty of neutrality with France and placed themselves under the protection of Prussia, which undertook to guarantee the peace of northern Germany.

After Prussia had concluded peace with France, several northern states associated themselves with this peace treaty, and, terrified by France's military success in the campaign of 1794, more than half of Germany joined in this neutrality. When the French advanced as far as Bavaria in 1796, the city of Nuremberg wished not only to associate itself with this neutrality, but to turn itself into a town wholly under Prussian jurisdiction. Nuremberg was occupied by Prussian troops after Prussia, on the strength of old claims, had declared itself owner of part of its territory a few years earlier and duly taken it over; it likewise abolished [*aufhob*] the direct dependence on the Empire[102] of many Imperial knights in Franconia. For these reasons, neither Nuremberg nor the knights could obtain any help from the German Empire.

The estates of northern Germany did not undertake to guarantee their neutrality themselves by means of the regional associations usually employed [for this purpose], and Prussia is not one of the [ordinary] members of this confederation, but its head and guarantor; the estates contribute to the costs of the Demarcation Commission.[103] But there is no standing federal council in permanent session; instead, it has assembled only at certain times to discuss and determine the regulation and continued use of these measures and the contributions towards their cost.

But the true political position of the estates came fully to light at the end of 1800[104] when the estates in question, which were not assembled, formed the intention of holding a new assembly. Prussia refused to permit this assembly and debate on the ground that, as the guarantor of peace in the north, it was its responsibility to judge which measures were necessary for this purpose.

When the northern coalition against England's claims concerning neutral shipping seemed to be moving towards war with England, one of the principal members of the league whose neutrality was guaranteed, namely Hanover, was occupied, along with other Imperial cities, by Prussia. It had to disband its own troops and assume responsibility for the maintenance of the Prussian corps. The peace was ratified by the estates of the German Empire, but Prussia promptly had its own independent ratification of the peace announced officially in Paris.

The whole history of the war, the split between the north and south of Germany, the separate conventions of neutrality and peace which the north concluded while the south languished in the most relentless misery and hence found itself totally abandoned by the north, make it clear not only that Germany is split up into independent states, but also that their interests are completely separate; and while the political bond is as loose as it was in the Middle Ages, no free unification can now be expected. When Germany was deprived of the territories on the left bank of the Rhine, and when half of it was overrun and plundered by the enemy, the most powerful of all interests[105] offered no help, either voluntarily or within the terms of its association with the Empire. The other estates had broken off all collaboration, and by having its neutrality guaranteed by a foreign prince, one group of them thereby also surrendered its right to collaborate or to join in future collaboration with the estates at large, and even its ability to discuss such matters with the other estates.

When war broke out once again, Sweden did in fact publicly offer to send its contingent. But it was reported that Prussia had refused to allow it transit through the line of neutrality. Not only in this war, Brandenburg accordingly divorced its interest entirely from that of the German Empire and led other estates to do likewise. It then put them in a position in which it could compel them, legally and by its power as their guarantor, to remain divorced from the Empire. It also deprived the Franconian knights of their direct dependence on the Empire and the Imperial city of Nuremberg of part of its territory, and accepted the complete surrender of the magistrates' powers to the occupying forces in that city's hour of need. It subsequently occupied and disarmed Hanover, with which it was allied for the peace and security of northern Germany, and imposed on it a requisition to maintain the occupying troops. All these circumstances have made clear what had long been the case, namely that Prussia should not be regarded as a German Imperial principality on the same footing as the other estates, nor as an estate capable of accepting the same conditions as other estates within an association, but as a powerful sovereign state in its own right.

Generally speaking, the last [war] has brought more truth into international relations. In so far as the relationship between states is one of power, illusions on this score have vanished, and this relationship has been brought to light and endorsed everywhere; the weaker states have been made to recognise that they cannot claim equal status with the stronger ones. Even if a republic such as Geneva behaved like a sovereign state and prided itself on being the first, εὔχετο,[106] to send an ambassador to the French Republic and to recognise it formally, its relationship with France quickly assumed a different character as soon as it was taken seriously; on the other hand, Bonaparte presented a few cannons to the Republic of San Marino, because in this case, there was no connection which could become a serious issue, but simply an occasion for high-sounding words concerning respect for republics.

The Republic of Geneva has vanished, whereas the independence, peace, and – so to speak – the neutrality of the Batavian, Helvetian, Cisalpine, and Ligurian Republics are guaranteed by strong garrisons.

Such are the relations which link more powerful states with weaker ones according to their true differences in strength.

The relations between Austria and Germany date back to ancient times, and they would necessarily take a very different course if Austria gave up the Imperial crown and, purely as a major sovereign power, subsequently entered into treaties involving mutual protection and guarantees (especially if there were a risk that hard times lay ahead). In this respect, Austria is at a serious disadvantage in comparison with Prussia, for although Austria has old relationships, Brandenburg does not need to enter into any specific relationships in peacetime, while in wartime, it can impose conditions on the hard-pressed and weak who turn to it for help. Since everything is subject to calculation nowadays, these conditions can be made ten per cent less [stringent] than those which are feared from the enemy; or, since the enemy is altogether such an indefinite quantity that everything is to be feared from him, any definite condition whatsoever will seem less [stringent] than the indefinite conditions to be feared from that quarter. In this case, at least the extent of one's loss is known, and this is in itself a major consolation.

It used to be popularly supposed in the Rhineland that, if one part of a state lay within the line of demarcation and the other lay outside it and was liable to pay public and private contributions to the French, and if the provincial assemblies of both parts were supposed to act together for the joint settlement of their liabilities, the part which was under French rule refused to accept parity and equal shares because it expected to lose in the process. This popular opinion may be without foundation; but it does at least give us a general indication of the people's judgement.

[Thus, Brandenburg enjoys the advantage of] either having the more powerful states as its friends or, since it has no other alliances or protective relationships, of treating them as enemies. It can even suspend [*aufheben*] a treaty of guarantee immediately, because this is merely a specific and individual matter, like any other political treaty, and it is in the nature of political treaties that its suspension does not constitute perfidy – as this war in particular has taught us, when so many treaties have been suspended, renewed, and suspended once again. Austria's links with the estates, on the other hand, do [not] seem to be in the same class as ordinary political treaties; on the contrary, whenever it has entered into an ordinary relationship with an Imperial estate, as Prussia can, all the estates feel thereby attacked. With Prussia this seems natural, just as it does with France, etc.

Through its power and its display of the latter in the cases referred to above, Prussia has ceased to be on the same level as the other estates. The latter can find a pure interest in their political independence only among themselves, and in this respect a joint association, a true federation of estates, is conceivable. But it is also no more than conceivable, for some of the estates are themselves so disparate in terms of power that they are not capable of any true and equal association.

An abbey, Imperial city, or such nobility as is directly dependent on the Empire may have less fear of falling victim to the Austrian monarchy's expansionist ambitions than to those of a lesser power. Although the Prussian power is a major monarchy, it is closer to the level of less powerful estates with regard to this capacity for arousing anxiety among small estates and for exploiting minor advantages. For its political art, like that of France, is entirely calculating, and since its military power was [always] disproportionate to its size, it was compelled to seek the sum of small advantages – just as the French Republic consistently acted in accordance with general principles, used all its power to follow these down to the smallest details, and subordinated all particular rights and relationships to the principles in question. One might also say that Prussia's recent policy has not been based on the royal principle of majesty, but on that of the middle class [*Bürgerlichkeit*];[107] its relation to the power of Austria, for example, is like that of a [middle-class] citizen who has laboriously accumulated his assets penny by penny to a free nobleman with inherited wealth whose property is based on his land and remains the same, even if he allows his servants or neighbours latitude in minor matters. His wealth is not a sum – which would be diminished by individual withdrawals – but a permanent and invariable asset.

The lesser estates, whose anxieties over their independence must be greatest, can only rely on associating themselves with a power whose politics and magnanimity give it the will and capacity to guarantee their survival. We have accordingly seen how the ecclesiastical princes, abbots, and Imperial cities have always associated themselves with the Emperor and observed their obligations towards him and the German Empire with the greatest loyalty.

Even if the more powerful Imperial estates wished to form an alliance amongst themselves and devised a method for preventing such a coalition from sharing the fate of all coalitions, and even if the combined strength of their troops formed a power capable of resisting a single great power, they would never be in the position of having to worry about one power only, for this one power would necessarily fear the intervention of other powers against it; but against a consortium of several powers, a coalition would be ineffectual, both because of its inferior military power and because of the scattered geographical position of its members. This position has been shaped along similar lines to that of the territory of great empires. In military respects, it is inherently extremely weak, and since the coalition would be a new development, the states taking part in it would also not be rich enough to surround themselves with rings of fortresses.

The politics of this coalition would have to tie it to this or that greater power according to circumstances, and its fate would be the common fate of a weaker ally or a weak enemy.

The fate of the German estates lies directly between the politics of two great powers. These two powers are now equal inasmuch as their relationship with Germany is primarily a political one – more so in the case of Prussia than in that of Austria, because the latter carries with it the Imperial crown and has consequently been hampered since ancient times by the pressure of an infinite number of rights.

The remaining interests in which the powers formerly differed have now balanced out. It was through this difference of interests that Prussia became great, by allying itself with – or placing itself at the head of – those interests which were opposed to the house of Austria. But time itself has both overcome [*aufgehoben*] the division of interest between Austria and a large part of Germany, and separated Prussia's interest from that of the German estates.

One major interest in whose defence Prussia took a leading part was *religion*.

The German estates themselves (especially Saxony and Hesse in earlier times) and foreign powers (Sweden and France) had formerly defended this interest against the Emperor, and Prussia at that time played no part at all – or, as Brandenburg, only a subordinate part. In the Seven Years War, this interest was still apparent, not so much on the part of the opposing powers as in popular opinion, and it did not fail to have an effect. A kind of distrust still remained, and even if the Protestants did not find themselves attacked as such, they still feared this possibility. They still attributed to the house of Austria the will [to mount such an attack] if it were in a position to do so; as well as the utmost bigotry and the influence of a new and indulgent Pope, of the Jesuits, and of priests in general; and they saw in Prussia the guarantor and – if the worst came to the worst – the saviour of their freedom of faith and conscience.

The politics of the Jesuits, petty and fanatical in its aims, has long ceased to be the politics of the courts. Especially since Joseph II's time, the Protestants have had no need for anxiety on this score. Joseph II's policy was not just the sudden inspiration of a single monarch, which can die away again on his demise; on the contrary, these principles have not only been preserved by his successors, but have also been absorbed as a whole into the fixed body of culture [*Bildung*] and political principles in general.

The predicament of the Protestants in the Palatinate, as the one remaining relic which ran counter to the principles of our age, was subsequently an object of special interest to the Protestant party among the princes of the Empire; but even this has now been rectified. The spirit of the times, the mode of operation of governments, now fixed and based on principles, has dramatically reduced the importance of the *corpus evangelicorum*, and hence also of its supreme head.[108]

The obsession of the Catholic estates with ensuring the supremacy of the Catholic religion has now disappeared, and with it the nefarious means which were formerly employed to induce princes of the German Empire to convert to Catholicism, thereby arousing such an astonishing degree of fear and anxiety among Protestants. The Catholic side no longer places any value on such means, for even on its own account, the state has managed to separate itself from the church, and experience has also shown that such means have produced more ill effects in the shape of mistrust and increased obstinacy than any actual benefit. It was not long before the person of the prince was separated from his country in the context of religion. Even if the prince became a Catholic, the relationship of his country to the Imperial Diet remained Protestant. Indeed, if the prince converted to Catholicism, he lost power within his Protestant country, not only through the mistrust which his conversion generated, but also because he was deprived, by his undertakings [*Reversalien*][109] to respect his subjects' rights, etc., of the influence which a Protestant prince has over the ecclesiastical affairs of his country. He is thereby placed in the position of a Catholic prince of a Catholic country, in which the church is completely independent of the secular power with regard to its property, appointments to offices, and other arrangements, whereas the Protestant prince of a Protestant country is both head of the church and bishop. Furthermore, princely houses which were formerly Catholic have reverted [to Protestantism] in recent times.

Such means [as described above] are no longer employed on the Catholic side: the Jesuit order has been abolished, tolerance has been introduced even in the Catholic countries, and the Protestants have been granted civil rights, despite the ungenerous provisions of the Peace of Westphalia. Consequently, the long lists which constitutional lawyers used to draw up of Protestant princes who went over to Catholicism, the detailed accounts of Jesuit villainy, and the descriptions of the oppression and tribulations of Protestants in Catholic countries have become objects of history devoted to things of the past, rather than nightmares for the present.

With powerful foreign support, the Protestants have long been free from the fear of seeing their faith suppressed by force, while they have never in any case thirsted greatly for the martyr's crown. And the fact that systematic proselytising is no longer practised by any court has also freed them to some extent from their previous mortal fear that they might be cunningly deprived of their faith and surreptitiously robbed of their conscience. The passage of time has in itself given them greater confidence and certainty that they are in possession of the truth. It is a long time since we last heard reports of the Imperial Diet regarding a Catholic confessor as a power to be reckoned with, and presenting demands to the Emperor on this score.

Although freelance writers in Berlin have sought to reawaken this mortal terror among Protestants by making a fearful clamour about suspected Jesuits,[110] this kind of thing is no longer a matter for cabinets or debates in the Imperial Diet. On the contrary, it looks like plain stupidity, or else the outburst of an extremely blinkered attitude or a disagreement between different branches of Freemasonry.

Another concern was to rescue what used to be called 'German freedom' from what was described as '*universal monarchy*' or subsequently even 'the oriental system'.

Since the attention of the whole of Europe has been focused for the last ten years on a people's tremendous struggle for freedom, and all Europe has been in general agitation as a result, it is inevitable that concepts of freedom have undergone a change and been refined beyond their earlier emptiness and indeterminacy. German freedom used to mean simply the independence of the estates from the Emperor. The alternatives were either slavery and despotism, or the abolition of the political union; no third possibility was known in earlier times.[111]

The Spanish and Austrian monarchies have not been combined since the time of Charles V, and the two have been in the hands of quite different families for the last century. Austria has lost large provinces, France and England have risen to the same level of power, and Prussia and Russia have developed; Austria has long ceased to be a monarchy without equal in Europe. A *system of the balance of power in Europe* has taken shape, i.e. a system whereby, in the event of war, all European powers will usually have an interest at stake and each of them (either on its own or simply in proportion to the advantages it has gained) will be prevented from reaping the fruits of even the most fortunate war. Even in their own right, wars have changed so greatly in character that the conquest of a few islands or of a province costs many years of effort and enormous sums of money, etc.

The idea of a universal monarchy has always been an empty word. The fact that it was never implemented when the plan for it was first laid shows that it is impossible to do so, and that it is therefore an empty thought; but in any case, there can no longer be any question of it in more recent times.

Nevertheless, Austria remains predominant in Germany, i.e. more powerful than any single German estate and more powerful than many of them combined. But Prussia has now likewise attained this status. As a danger to the German estates, Austria and Prussia are on the same level. What used to be called German freedom should be on its guard against them both.

[10. Freedom of Citizens and Estates]

As for those two principles whose adoption made it possible for a state to attain great influence in Germany – the threat to Protestantism and the fear of a universal monarchy – the former no longer exists; and as for the second – the quest for expansion at the cost of the German estates – Austria and Prussia are at least on a par, if Austria does not in fact still have certain advantages.

It is evident, however, that ten years of struggle and the misery of a large portion of Europe have taught us enough – at least in terms of concepts – to make us more impervious to the blind clamour for freedom. In this bloody game, that cloud of freedom which nations sought to embrace, only to plunge into an abyss of misery, has evaporated, and certain figures [*bestimmte Gestalten*] and concepts have found their way into public opinion. The clamour for freedom will have no effect; anarchy has been distinguished from freedom, and the realisation that a firm government is necessary for freedom has made a deep impression; but an equally deep impression has been made by the realisation that the people must take part in the making of laws and in the most important affairs of the state. In the organisation of a body which represents it, the people has a guarantee that the government will act in accordance with the laws, and [it can observe in this body] the participation of the general will in the most important matters of general concern.[112] This body has to give the monarch its approval for a proportion of national taxation, especially for extraordinary taxes; and just as in former times the most essential issue, namely personal service, depended on free agreement, the same is true now of money, which comprehends all other factors.

Without such a representative body, freedom is no longer conceivable. All other indeterminate notions and all the empty clamour for freedom disappear when freedom is so defined. This is not something which individuals come to know as a scientific concept through learning or as the result of arbitrary study. This definition is rather a principle which underlies public opinion, and which has become part of sound common sense. Most German states have representation of this kind, and the provincial assemblies of Austria, Bohemia, and Hungary have freely made extraordinary payments to their monarchs for the war with France.

It is more natural for the interest of this German freedom to seek protection from a state which is itself based on this system of freedom. The interests which used to be dominant in Germany have to some extent disappeared. Prussia can consequently no longer associate itself with them, and public opinion can no longer regard any war involving Prussia as a war for German freedom. The true, lasting interest [of the German estates], which has become particularly acute in our time, can find no protection from Prussia. The Prussian provincial assemblies have lost their significance under the pressure of royal power. A new and artificial system of taxation has been introduced in the Prussian territories, and it has also been enforced in the recently acquired territories which used to have privileges and taxes governed by ancient rights and traditions.

The German subjects of Prussia cannot expect help either from the Emperor or from the Imperial courts of justice against this burden of taxes in the Prussian states and against the suppression of their privileges.

Apart from the less powerful estates like the Imperial cities etc., the provincial assemblies of the German territories have a natural interest in looking to the Emperor's court and expecting to find support there for what the world now understands as German freedom – not least because the Emperor's hereditary domains are themselves a state which is based on representation and in which the people has rights, and especially because of the legal help which the Aulic Council can offer.

This kind of freedom has, of course, had to suffer increasingly the more the other kind of German freedom has grown, and the more the power of the state over its individual members has diminished.

In the Peace of Westphalia, the sovereignty – or at least the supremacy – of the Emperor over Imperial cities, a sovereignty which belonged to the Emperors but was mortgaged in the course of time to the cities (i.e. to their magistrates) was declared to be irredeemable. The mayor (or whatever his title was in other cities) appointed by the Emperor must always have commanded a certain respect among the magistrates. They were under a kind of supervision, under the eye of a person who was independent of them and who necessarily carried weight by virtue of his connection with the head of the Empire. After the Imperial cities became completely assured of one kind of freedom when the Peace of Westphalia declared that the political power which had been mortgaged to them was irredeemable, the other kind of freedom suffered all the more. It is well known under how great a burden of taxes, judicial neglect, and debt so many Imperial cities sank, and in general, what inner corruption they experienced. The citizenry had no control over the administration and use of public offices, nor any say in the imposition of taxes; taxation and its expenditure and appointments to public offices have come entirely under the arbitrary control of the magistrates. Some [Imperial cities] have succeeded, with the Emperor's help, in liberating themselves completely from this

'German freedom' of the magistrates; as a result of this system, others were plunged, before the last war, into the greatest embarrassment and financial confusion which the war in no small measure exacerbated.

As for the states ruled by princes, the cameral taxes [*Kammerzieler*] and costs of military contingents, embassies to the Imperial Diet, etc. have been transferred, since the Peace of Westphalia, to the provincial assemblies.

In the year 1670 – twenty-two years after German freedom was achieved through the Peace of Westphalia – the Council of Princes conveyed to the Emperor a memorandum of the Imperial Diet in which the previous mode of contributing to state expenditure by contractual agreement was abolished and the princes were to be left to judge what they considered necessary for the requirements of their country. This extension of their power, whereby the princes of that time would have abolished the entire principle on which modern states are based (with who knows what consequences for their successors) – this extension of (if one may so call it) German freedom was prevented by the Emperor Leopold. He did not ratify the memorandum of the Diet, although it would have entitled him to abolish the territorial rights of his own German lands, Bohemia and Austria. Or if the link, which was still to some extent present, between the Empire and the Burgundian sphere had been reaffirmed, he would also have been entitled by the [recommendation of the] Diet to abolish the rights of the Burgundian estates, which had degenerated into an aristocratic despotism, and to implement those measures over which Joseph II came to grief more than a century later.

As far as the interest of this [kind of] German freedom is concerned, the Emperor's relationship with Germany appears in a different light, very different from that of Prussia. Through the power of time, the great interest of the people returned to its source – but as a need which has not as yet found satisfaction in an appropriate political organisation.

The principle of the original German state, which spread from Germany throughout the whole of Europe, was the principle of monarchy, a political power under a supreme head for the conduct of business of universal concern, in which the people were involved through their representatives.[113] The form of this [monarchic principle] has even survived in what is known as the Imperial Diet; but the substance [*die Sache*] has vanished.

In Europe's protracted oscillation between barbarism and civilisation [*Kultur*], the German state has not fully accomplished its transition to the latter, but has succumbed to the convulsions which accompany it; its members have broken away to complete independence, and the state has dissolved. The Germans have not managed to find the mean between oppression and despotism [on the one hand] – i.e. what they described as universal monarchy – and complete dissolution [on the other].[114]

In its negative sense, the 'struggle for German freedom' signified the endeavour to oppose universal monarchy; in positive terms, it became the attainment of complete independence by each member. In this enterprise, the countries stood by their princes and were at one with them, but they inevitably found that German freedom was not attained when their princes gained their sovereignty – quite the reverse.

But at the same time, the tendency of the provincial assemblies is primarily to favour their own country; they have lost all connection with the whole. In former times, the princes often convened a Provincial Diet before they attended the Imperial Diet, and held joint consultations with their country. That contradiction whereby the provincial assemblies are most strongly opposed to Imperial wars and to contributions towards their cost, yet at the same time owe their existence to the Empire – this division within Germany has taken root universally within the popular mind [*Volksgeist*]. Bavaria, Hesse, etc. regard each other as foreigners; the provincial assemblies, which are in immediate contact with the people, express this division most clearly and regard everything which the prince does through his own connections as alien and as no concern of theirs; they simply wish to remain separate, just as the Swiss wish to remain neutral. But the whole constellation of circumstances goes against such separation. There is no longer any neutrality for a weak state close to – let alone in between – powerful states if the latter are at war; or it can remain neutral in the sense of allowing itself to be plundered and abused by both.

However much our insight may tell us that the interest of the provinces and their assemblies is bound up with the continued existence of a political power in Germany, in the provinces themselves this interest has in practice [*fürs Handeln*] become alien to Germany. Alien to Germany – but who has any concern for that country now, and where might any German patriotism come from?[115] The individual provinces and their assemblies enjoy and recognise whatever passive benefit they may gain from Germany, but they do nothing in return; for it is fundamental to human nature to be interested only in something which we can actively support, with which we can co-operate and share decisions, with which our will can identify itself.[116] The provinces need to find some mode of joint action towards a universal end.

[III Proposals for Constitutional Reform]

It has been the fate of Italy to come for the most part under the authority of foreign powers. Even if a few of its estates – two, three, or thereabouts – have continued to exist for longer as states the size of one or more districts, the majority of them, politically speaking, have gradually become entirely dependent on these great powers and gradually been completely devoured by them (the smaller and ecclesiastical estates being the first to go). If Germany is not to suffer the same fate as this after a few wars, it should re-organise itself as a state. The essential constituent of a state, namely a political power governed by a supreme head with the co-operation of the parts, would have to be established. All inessential elements – the dependence of the administration of justice, the management of revenues, religion – all of these must be excluded from the necessary attributes of a state.

The only way in which the German Empire might continue to exist would be by organising a political power and restoring the German people's connection with Emperor and Empire.

The former could be accomplished by amalgamating the whole military strength of Germany into a single army. In this army, every major prince would be a general by birth, and each would be in charge of his own regiment and appoint its officers, or have detachments from it as his lifeguard and to garrison his capital. Companies or smaller units would be assigned to the smaller estates. The Emperor would, of course, have supreme command of this army. Its costs, which are now paid chiefly by the provincial assembly –

and not, as in earlier times, by the prince from his hereditary domains – would also be borne by the provinces. These costs would be approved annually by the provincial assemblies, all of which would combine to perform this task. This could not be done by delegating some members of the existing assemblies for this purpose, partly because many provinces have no assembly, and partly because the costs would be too great for the very small estates. But given that it would in any case be necessary to divide Germany into military regions in order to raise the army, and to subdivide each district into smaller districts quite independently of other jurisdictions and sovereignties unconnected with the military regions, delegates could be selected from these subdivisions, according to their relative populations, in order to approve the levies required for the maintenance of the state's power.

These delegates would for this purpose form a single body with the Cities Bench of the Imperial Diet; for this Bench has in any case again been depleted by the loss of several cities, and it is uncertain whether it may not suffer further reductions, with consequent benefit in the matter of compensation[117] to some of the smaller cities. Hamburg would also have to be required to send its deputy. – The smallest Imperial cities with one thousand or a few thousand citizens have votes in the Imperial Diet, whereas a whole province like Bohemia or Saxony has none. Such small Imperial cities as still remained would have to allow the territories around them to share in their entitlement to send a deputy.

In any case, no one knows what the [precise] significance of the Cities Bench is. There are three Colleges within the Imperial Diet, but a majority vote is not decisive. If the College of Electors and the College of Princes do not agree, the matter rests, and the College of Cities cannot decide the issue.

The complete change would be that the provinces would now pay directly to the Emperor and Empire that money which they at present grant directly to the princes, and only indirectly to the Emperor and Empire.

The Emperor would again be placed at the head of the German Empire.

The question would arise as to whether the knights' cantons would send deputies to the Council of Princes or to the College of

Cities. They would approve their charitable subsidies along with the others, and as rulers of their domains, they would have to be associated with the College of Princes.

The question would also arise of whether the princes would decide to make a joint contribution from their [personal] domains and other territorial incomes, or whether each would meet part of the cost of his regiment or guard from these sources. At all events, each would be at liberty to contribute as much of his own income as he wished for the embellishment of his regiment, over and above the subsidy it would receive from the Empire as a whole. In the former case, i.e. if the princes authorised and contributed payments from their own domains to a central fund, the knights would have to be associated with them; for in any case, the true nobility – i.e. rulers and owners of knightly estates directly dependent on the Empire – originally belonged entirely to the class of princes and were no different from them in their origin.

The question would also be asked whether the princes should be represented in the College of Electors or the College of Princes by relatives of princely rank, or at least by their most eminent vassals, if they did not wish to appear in person. Besides, in an assembly such as this, the [present] kind of procedure whereby statements are dictated for minuting would not be applicable; there would be oral discussions and votes, and if the representatives were drawn exclusively from princely houses and the most noble families, their talents and brilliance would give an exalted status and appearance to such a princely assembly.

Although all parties might gain if Germany were to become a state, an event such as this has never been the fruit of deliberation, but only of force – even if it were in keeping with the general [level of] culture [*Bildung*], and even if its need were deeply and distinctly felt. The common mass of people in Germany, together with their provincial assemblies, who know only the segregation of communities in Germany and to whom a unification of such communities is something utterly alien,[118] would have to be brought together into a single mass by the power of a conqueror.[119] They would have to be compelled to regard themselves as belonging to Germany.

This Theseus would have to possess enough magnanimity to grant the people he had created out of scattered groups a share in matters of common concern.[120] Since a democratic constitution such as Theseus gave his people is, in our times and within large states, a contradiction in itself, this share would have to be an organisation [of some kind]. And even if he could be assured, by having the direction of the state's power within his hands, that he would not be repaid with ingratitude as Theseus was, he would also have to possess sufficient character to be ready to endure the hatred which Richelieu and other great men who destroyed the particular and distinctive characteristics of their fellows brought upon themselves.

Once the social character of human beings has been disturbed and forced to throw itself into idiosyncrasies [*Eigentümlichkeiten*], it becomes so profoundly distorted that it expends its strength on this separation from others and proceeds to assert its isolation to the point of madness; for madness is simply the complete isolation of the individual from his kind.[121] The German nation may not be capable of intensifying its stubborn insistence on particularity to the degree of madness encountered in the Jewish nation, which is incapable of uniting with others in common social intercourse.[122] Nor may it be able to attain so pernicious a degree of isolation as to murder and be murdered until the state is obliterated.[123] Nevertheless, particularity, prerogative, and precedence are so intensely personal in character that the concept of necessity and insight into its nature are much too weak to have an effect on action itself. Concepts and insight are fraught with such self-distrust that they must be justified by force before people will submit to them.

On the Scientific Ways of Treating Natural Law, on its Place in Practical Philosophy, and its Relation to the Positive Sciences of Right (1802–1803)[1]

It is true that the science of natural law, like other sciences such as mechanics and physics, has long been recognised as an essentially philosophical science and – since philosophy must have parts – as an essential part of philosophy.[2] But it has shared the fate of the other sciences in that the philosophical element in philosophy has been assigned exclusively to metaphysics, and the sciences have been allowed little share in it; instead, they have been kept completely independent of the Idea, within their own special principle. The sciences cited as examples have finally been compelled more or less to confess their remoteness from philosophy. They consequently acknowledge as their scientific principle what is commonly called experience, thereby renouncing their claim to be genuine sciences; they are content to consist of a collection of empirical knowledge [*Kenntnisse*] and to make use of the concepts of the understanding as postulates [*bittweise*], without claiming to make any objective assertion.[3] If whatever has called itself a philosophical science has been excluded from philosophy and from the category of science in general, at first against its will but in eventual acceptance of this situation, the reason for this exclusion is not that these so-called sciences did not originate in philosophy itself and did not maintain a conscious connection with it. For every part of philosophy is individually capable of being an independent science and attaining complete inner necessity, because it is the absolute which makes it a genuine science. In this shape, the absolute is the distinctive principle which stands above the sphere of that science's cognition and freedom, and in relation to which the science partakes of an external necessity. But the Idea itself remains free from this determinacy and can reflect itself in this determinate science just as purely as absolute life expresses itself in every living thing – although the scientific element in such a science, or its inner rationality, does not come to light [within this science] in the pure form of the Idea, which is the essence of every science and exists [*ist*] as this pure Idea in philosophy, as the absolute science. Geometry furnishes a brilliant example, envied by the other sciences, of this distinctive [*eigenen*] yet free scientific development of a science. Nor is it [i.e. the reason why the sciences were excluded from philosophy] because sciences of the kind mentioned above must be denied all reality on the grounds that they are in fact empirical. For just as each part or aspect of philosophy is capable of being a self-sufficient science, so in consequence is each [of these sciences] also in an immediate sense [*unmittelbar*] a self-sufficient and complete image; and in the shape of an image, it can be registered and represented by a pure and felicitous intuition which avoids contamination by fixed concepts.

But the completion of a science demands not only that intuition and image be combined with the logical [dimension] and taken up into the purely ideal [realm]; the separate (though genuine) science must also be divested of its singularity [*Einzelheit*], and its principle must be recognised in its higher context and necessity and thereby itself be completely freed. Only by this means is it possible to recognise the limits of the science, and without this principle, the science must remain ignorant of its limits, because it would otherwise have to stand above itself and recognise in the absolute form the nature of its principle in its determinacy; for from this knowledge [*Erkenntnis*], it would directly obtain the knowledge and certainty of the extent to which its various determinacies were equal. But as matters stand, it can take only an empirical attitude towards its limits, and must at one moment make misplaced attempts to overcome them, and at another suppose them to be narrower than they are, and consequently experience quite unexpected enlargements [of its horizons], just as geometry (which is able to demonstrate, for example, the incommensurability of the diameter [i.e. diagonal] and side of a square, but not that of the diameter and circumference of a circle),*⁴ or even more so arithmetic, and most of all the combination of the two, afford the greatest examples of science groping in the dark at its [outer] limits.

The critical philosophy has had the important negative effect on the theoretical sciences [firstly] of demonstrating that the scientific element within them is not something objective, but belongs to the intermediate realm between nothingness and reality, to a mixture of being and not-being, and [secondly] of inducing them to confess that they are [engaged] only in empirical conjecture [*Meinen*].⁵ The positive effect of the critical philosophy has proved all the poorer from this point of view, and it has not succeeded in restoring these sciences to philosophy.⁶ Conversely, it has placed the absolute wholly within practical philosophy, and in the latter [realm], it [i.e. the critical philosophy] is positive or dogmatic knowledge. We must regard the critical philosophy (which also describes itself as 'transcendental idealism') as the culminating point, both in a general sense and especially in natural law, of that opposition which – like rings on the surface of water which spread concentrically outwards from the point of disturbance until, in tiny movements, they lose their connection with the centre and become infinite – grew ever greater, from weaker beginnings in earlier scientific endeavours through the constraints of barbarism, until it came to understand itself in the critical philosophy by means of the absolute concept of infinity and, as infinity, is in turn superseded. Thus, the earlier ways of treating natural law, and what must be regarded as its vari-

---

* *Hegel's note*: In the introduction to his *Natural Law*, Fichte prides himself somewhat on the simplicity of his insight into the reason for this latter incommensurability, declaring in all seriousness that curved is not [the same thing as] straight. The superficiality of this reason is self-evident, and it is also directly refuted by the former incommensurability of the diameter [i.e. diagonal] and side of a square, both of which are straight lines, and by the quadrature of the parabola. As for the help which he seeks in the same context from 'sound common sense' in the face of the mathematical infinite, [arguing] that a polygon of infinitely many sides cannot be measured, precisely because it is a polygon of infinitely many sides, the same help should be available in dealing with the infinite progression in which the absolute Idea is supposed to be realised. Besides, this gives us no means of determining the main point at issue, namely whether positive infinity, which is not an infinite quantity but rather an identity, should be posited – which amounts to saying that nothing has been determined with regard to either commensurability or incommensurability.

ous principles, must be denied all significance for the essential nature [*das Wesen*] of science. For although they are in [the realm of] opposition and negativity, they are not in [that of] absolute negativity or infinity, which alone is appropriate to science. On the contrary, they no more contain the purely positive than they do the purely negative, for they are mixtures of both. Only an interest based on curiosity concerning the history of science could dwell on them, *firstly* in order to compare them with the absolute Idea and to perceive in their very deformation the necessity with which, distorted by a determinate principle, the moments of absolute form present themselves and, even under the aegis of a limited principle, nevertheless dominate these attempts [at self-representation] – and *secondly*, in order to see the empirical condition of the world reflected in the ideal mirror of science.

For as far as *the second* is concerned, it is indeed the case that both empirical existence [*Dasein*] and the condition of all the sciences will also express the condition of the world, given that all things are connected. But the condition of natural law will do so most directly [*am nächsten*], because natural law has immediate reference to the ethical [*das Sittliche*], the [prime] mover of all human things; and in so far as the science of the ethical has an existence [*Dasein*], natural law belongs to [the realm of] necessity. It must be at one with the ethical in its empirical shape, which is equally [grounded] in necessity, and, as a science, it must express this shape in the form of universality.[7]

As far as *the first* is concerned, the only true distinction that can be recognised as [constituting] the principle of a science is whether that science lies within the absolute, or outside absolute unity and [hence] in opposition. But in the latter case, it could not be a science at all unless its principle were some incomplete and relative unity, or the concept of a relation, even if this were only the empty abstraction of relation itself under the name of attractive force or the force of identity [*des Einsseins*]. Sciences whose principle is not a concept of relation, or is merely the empty force of identity, retain nothing ideal except the first ideal relation which differentiates the child from the world, namely the form of representational thought, in which such sciences present empirical qualities and can enumerate their variety; these would be described primarily as empirical sciences. But since practical sciences are by nature focused on something both real and universal, or on a unity which is a unity of differences, the feelings [*Empfindungen*] likewise, in practical empiricism, must embrace not pure qualities but relations, whether negative ones like the drive for self-preservation or positive ones like love and hate, sociability, and the like.[8] And the more scientific [kind of] empiricism is in general distinguished from this pure empiricism not by having relations rather than qualities as its object, but by fixing these relations in conceptual form and sticking to this negative absoluteness (though without separating this form of unity from its content). We shall call these the *empirical sciences*; and conversely, we shall describe as purely *formal* science that form of science in which the opposition [of form and content] is absolute, and pure unity (or infinity, the negative absolute) is completely divorced from the content and posited for itself.

Although we have thus identified a specific difference between the two inauthentic [*unechten*] ways of treating natural law scientifically – inasmuch as the principle of the first consists of relations and mixtures of empirical intuition with the universal, while that of the second is absolute opposition and absolute universality – it is nevertheless self-evident that the ingredients of both, namely empirical intuition and concept, are the same, and that formalism, as it moves from its pure negation to a [specific] content, can likewise arrive at nothing other than relations or relative identities; for the purely ideal, or the opposition, is posited as absolute, so that the absolute Idea and unity cannot be present. With the principle of absolute opposition or the absoluteness of the purely ideal, the absolute principle of empiricism is posited; thus, with reference to intuition, the syntheses – in so far as they are meant to have not just the negative meaning of cancelling [*der Aufhebung*] one side of the opposition, but also the positive meaning of intuition – represent only empirical intuitions.

In the first place, these two ways of treating natural law scientifically must be characterised more precisely, the first with reference to the manner in which the absolute Idea appears within it in accordance with the moments of absolute form, the second with regard to the way in which the infinite (or the negative absolute) vainly attempts to arrive at a positive organisation. Our exposition of the latter attempt will lead directly to a *consideration of the nature and relationship of the ethical sciences as philosophical sciences, and of their relation-*

ship to what is known as *the positive science of right.*⁹ Although the latter holds itself apart from philosophy and, by voluntarily renouncing it, believes it can escape its criticism, it also claims to have an absolute subsistence and true reality; but this pretension is inadmissible.

[I]¹⁰

With regard to that *way of treating* natural law which we have called *empirical*, it must first be said that we cannot materially concern ourselves with those determinacies and concepts of relation which it fastens upon and affirms under the name of principles; on the contrary, it is precisely this separating out and fixing of determinacies which must be negated.¹¹ The nature of this separation presupposes that the scientific aspect consists solely in the form of unity; and if, in an organic relationship between the manifold qualities into which such a relationship can be divided, a unity is to be found within this multiplicity (and the qualities are not just to be enumerated), some determinacy must be singled out and regarded as [constituting] the essence of the relation. But the totality of the organic is precisely what this procedure fails to grasp, and its remaining aspects, which were excluded from the determinacy already selected, are subordinated to the latter, which is elevated to the essence and end [*Zweck*] of the relation. Thus, in order to define [*erkennen*] the relation of marriage, for example, reproduction, the sharing of goods in common, etc. are adduced, and the whole organic relation is defined and contaminated by [exclusive insistence on] this determinacy, which is elevated into a law as the [supposed] essence [of the relation]. Or in the case of punishment, one determinacy is seized upon – be it the moral improvement of the criminal, the damage caused, the awareness of the punishment among others, the criminal's own awareness of the punishment before the crime was committed, or the need to give this awareness reality by carrying out the threat, etc. – and the detail in question is made the end and essence of the whole. It naturally follows that, since this determinacy has no necessary connection with the other determinacies which can also be brought to light and distinguished, endless agonising takes place to discover their necessary relationship or the dominance of one over the others; and since inner necessity, which is not present in individual detail [*in der Einzelheit*], is lacking, each [determinacy] can very well justify its independence of the others. – Such qualities, picked out from the multiplicity of relations into which the organic is broken up by empirical or imperfectly reflected intuition and then given the form of conceptual unity, are what knowledge of the kind described calls the essence and ends [of the organic whole in question]. And since their conceptual form is expressed as the absolute being of the determinacy which constitutes the content of the concept, they are set up as principles, laws, duties, etc. Of this transformation of the absoluteness of pure form – which, however, is negative absoluteness or pure identity, the pure concept, or infinity – into an absoluteness of the content and of the determinacy which is elevated to [*aufgenommen in*] the form, more will be said in connection with the principle of the critical philosophy; for that transformation which takes place unconsciously in the empirical knowledge presently under discussion is accomplished by the critical philosophy with reflection and as absolute reason and duty.[12]

This formal unity into which thought converts determinacy is also what provides the semblance of that necessity which science seeks; for the unity of opposites, regarded as a real unity in the context of science, is a necessity for the latter. But since the material of the formal unity in question is not the [two] opposites as a whole but only one of them (i.e. one determinacy), the necessity is likewise merely a formal, analytic necessity which pertains only to the form of an identical or analytical proposition in which the determinacy may be presented. On the strength of the absoluteness of this proposition, however, an absoluteness of content is likewise falsely claimed, so that laws and principles are [thereby] constituted.

But since this empirical science finds itself [immersed] in a multiplicity of such principles, laws, ends, duties, and rights, none of which is absolute, it must also have before it the image of, and need for, [both] the absolute unity of all these unconnected determinacies and an original simple necessity; and we shall consider how it will satisfy this demand, which is derived from reason, or how the absolute Idea of reason will be presented in its [different] moments [while] under the domination of the one and the many which this empirical knowledge cannot overcome.[13] On the one hand, it is inherently interesting to perceive how, even in this scientific endeavour and its turbid medium, the reflection and domination of the absolute are still present (though at the same time distorted). And on the other, the forms which the moments of the absolute have here assumed have turned into a kind of prejudice and of unquestioning, universally valid thoughts whose nullity criticism must point out in order to justify science in ignoring them. This proof of their nullity is accomplished most effectively by showing the unreality of the whole ground from which they have sprung, and whose flavour and nature are implemented in them.

In the first place, empirical science conceives of scientific totality as a totality of the manifold or as completeness, whereas true formalism conceives of it as consistency. The former can raise its experiences to universality as it pleases, and pursue consistency in its thought determinacies [*gedachten Bestimmungen*] until it reaches the point where further empirical material which contradicts the previous material, but has an equal right to be thought and expressed as a principle, no longer sustains the consistency of the previous determinacy but forces it to be abandoned. Formalism can extend its consistency as far as the vacuity of its principle – or a content to which it has falsely laid claim – will at all permit; but it is at the same time justified in proudly excluding whatever lacks completeness from its apriorism and its science and in denigrating it as 'the empirical'.[14] For it asserts its formal principles as the a priori and the absolute, thereby implying that whatever it cannot master by means of these principles is non-absolute and contingent – unless it can get out of the difficulty by finding, in the empirical realm at large and between one determinacy and the next, the formal transition of a progression from the conditioned to the condition [itself] and, since the latter is in turn conditioned, so on in an infinite sequence. But in so doing, formalism not only renounces all the advantages it has over what it calls empiricism; in addition, since the conditioned and the condition, as interconnected opposites, are posited as subsisting absolutely, formalism itself sinks totally into empirical necessity and lends the latter a semblance of genuine absoluteness by means of the formal identity, or negative absolute, with which it holds the opposites together.

But this combination of consistency with completeness of picture – whether the consistency in question is the latter (more complete) formal and empty consistency or the former consistency which, with determinate concepts as principles, passes from one of these to the others and is consistent only in its inconsistency – immediately alters the position of multiplicity in relation to pure empiricism. For pure empiricism, everything has equal rights with everything else, and it gives no precedence to any [one] determinacy, since each is as real as the other. We shall return to this topic later in comparing pure empiricism with the scientific empiricism with which we are at present concerned.

After this formal totality, we must consider how absolute unity makes its appearance both as simple unity – which we may call the original unity – and as totality reflected in empirical knowledge [*Wissen*]. Both unities, which are one [and the same] in the absolute and whose identity is the absolute, must appear separate and distinct within this knowledge.

As for the former [absolute] unity, it must first be said that empiricism can have nothing to do with it as that essence of necessity which, for appearance, is an external bond of this unity. For in the essential [kind of] unity, the manifold is immediately annihilated and nullified; and because manifold being is the principle of empiricism, the latter is denied [the possibility of] pressing on to the absolute nullity of its qualities, which for it are absolute and (by virtue of the concept according to which they are purely and simply many) infinitely many. Consequently, this original unity can only signify – as far as is possible – a simple and small number of qualities, which it believes are sufficient for it to attain knowledge [*Erkenntnis*] of the rest. For empiricism, this ideal, in which what counts roughly speaking as arbitrary and contingent is effaced and the smallest necessary quantity of the manifold is posited, is *chaos*, both in the physical and in the ethical realm.[15] In the latter, chaos is sometimes represented by the imagination rather in the image of being – as the *state of nature*; and at other times, it is represented by empirical psychology rather in the form of possibility and abstraction, as an enumeration of the capacities encountered in man – i.e. as the *nature and destiny of man*. In this way, what is declared on the one hand to be utterly necessary, in itself, and absolute, is simultaneously acknowledged on the other to be something unreal, purely imaginary, and a product of thought; in the first case, it is treated as a fiction, in the second, as a mere possibility – which is a blatant contradiction.

For the common understanding, which sticks to the obscure mixture of what is in itself [*was an sich ist*] and what is transient, nothing is more plausible than that it should be able to discover the former by removing all arbitrary and contingent elements from the composite image of the state of law [*des Rechtszustandes*], and that by means of this abstraction, it should at once be left with the absolutely necessary. If [, it imagines,] one mentally subtracts everything that it dimly suspects may belong to the particular and transient, as pertaining to particular customs, to history, culture [*Bildung*], or even the state, we are left with the human being in the image of the bare state of nature, or the abstraction of the human being with his essential capacities, and we have only to glance at it to discover what is necessary. What is recognised as having a connection with the state must therefore also be separated out, because the chaotic image of the necessary cannot contain absolute unity, but only simple multiplicity [*Mannigfaltigkeit*], or atoms with the fewest possible properties.[16] Thus, whatever may come under the concept of a linking and ordering of these [atoms] as the weakest unity of which the principle of multiplicity [*Vielheit*] is capable, is excluded from this multiplicity as an adventitious and later accretion.[17] Now in making this distinction [between unity and multiplicity], empiricism in the first place lacks any criterion whatsoever for drawing the boundary between the contingent and the necessary, between what must be retained and what must be left out in the chaos of the state of nature or the abstraction of the human being. The determining factor here can only be that it [i.e. the required definition] must contain as much as is needed to represent what is encountered in actuality; the guiding principle for this a priori is the a posteriori. If a point is to be made regarding the representation [*Vorstellung*] of the state of law [*des Rechtszustandes*], all that is required in order to demonstrate its connection with the original and necessary – and hence also its own necessity – is to project a distinct [*eigene*] quality or capacity into the chaos, and, in the manner of the empirically based sciences in general, to construct hypotheses for the so-called explanation of actuality, hypotheses in which this actuality is posited in the same determinate character [*Bestimmtheit*], but in a purely formal and ideal shape – as force, matter, or capacity – so that one thing can very readily be grasped and explained in terms of the other.[18]

On the one hand, this dim inkling of an original and absolute unity, a unity which is expressed in the chaos of the state of nature and in the abstraction of capacities and inclinations, does not get as far as absolute negative unity, but seeks only to eliminate a large mass of particularities and oppositions. But there still remains an indefinable mass of qualitative determinacies which likewise have only an empirical necessity for themselves and have no inner necessity for one another.[19] Their only relationship consists in being many, and since this many is for one another and yet is devoid of unity, they are destined to be mutually opposed and in absolute conflict with one another. In the state of nature or the abstraction of man, the isolated energies of the ethical realm must be thought of as embroiled in a war of mutual annihilation.[20] For precisely this reason, however, it is easy to show that, since these qualities are purely and simply opposed to each other and consequently purely ideal, they cannot survive in this ideality and separation as they are supposed to do, but cancel each other out [*sich aufheben*] and reduce each other to nothing. But empiricism cannot attain to this absolute reflection, or to an insight into the nullity of [all] determinacies in the absolutely simple; instead, the many nullities remain for it a mass of realities. But the positive unity, expressing itself as absolute totality, must, for empiricism, be added on to this multiplicity as a further and alien factor; and it is inherent even in this form of linkage between the two aspects of absolute identity that their totality will present itself just as dimly and impurely as that of the original unity. It is easy for empiricism to supply a reason why one of these separated unities exists for the other, or a reason for the transition from the first to the second, for [the activity of] giving reasons in general comes easily to it. According to the fiction of the state of nature, this state is abandoned because of the evils it entails – which simply means that the desired end is assumed in advance, namely that a reconciliation of the elements which, as chaos, are in mutual conflict is the good or the end which must be reached; or a similar reason for change, such as the social instinct, is introduced directly into the notion [*Vorstellung*] of original qualities as potentialities; or the conceptual form of the [human] capacity is dispensed with altogether, so that one can proceed at once to the purely particular qualities of the second unity's appearance, i.e. to the historical as the subjugation of the weak by the strong, etc.

The unity itself, however, can only follow the principle of absolute qualitative multiplicity, as in empirical physics, representing a multiplicity of divisions or relations; that is, it merely replaces the many atomic qualities with further manifold complications of the simple isolated [elements of a] multiplicity which was assumed to be original, i.e. with superficial contacts between these qualities which, for themselves, are indestructible in their particularity and capable of entering into only simple [*leichte*] and partial combinations and mixtures. And in so far as the unity is posited as a whole, it is given the empty name of a formless external harmony called 'society' and 'the state'. Even if this unity – whether it is considered in itself [*für sich*] or, in a more empirical sense, in relation to its emergence – is represented as absolute, i.e. as originating directly from God, and even if the centre and inner essence of its subsistence are represented as divine, this representation [*Vorstellung*] nevertheless again remains something formal, which merely hovers above the multiplicity without penetrating it. God may certainly be recognised not only as the founder of the association, but also as its preserver, and in the latter connection, the majesty of the supreme authority may well be recognised as his reflection and as in itself divine; nevertheless, the divine aspect of the association is an external quality for the associated many, whose relationship with it can only be that between ruler and ruled, because the principle of this empiricism excludes the absolute unity of the one and the many. At this point of the relation, empiricism coincides directly with its opposite principle, for which abstract unity is primary, except that empiricism is not embarrassed by its inconsistencies, which arise out of mixing together things posited as so specifically different as abstract unity and absolute multiplicity; and for precisely this reason, it also has the advantage of not closing the door on views which, apart from their purely material aspect, are manifestations [*Erscheinungen*] of a purer and more divine inwardness [*Innern*] than can arise under the principle of opposition, within which only domination and obedience are possible.

The state of nature, and that majesty and divinity of the whole state of law [*Rechtszustand*] which is alien to individuals and is consequently itself individual and particular, as well as the relation whereby the subjects [*Subjekte*] are absolutely subordinated to this supreme authority,[21] are the forms in which the fragmented moments of organic ethical life are fixed as particular essences and, like the Idea, thereby distorted [*verkehrt*];[22] these moments are that of absolute unity (and of unity in so far as it encompasses the opposition of unity and multiplicity and is absolute totality), and the moment of infinity (or of the nullity of the realities of the opposition in question). The absolute Idea of ethical life, on the other hand, contains both majesty and the state of nature as altogether identical, for majesty itself is nothing other than absolute ethical nature;[23] and there can be no thought, in the real existence [*Reellsein*] of majesty, of any loss of absolute freedom (which is what we should understand by 'natural freedom') or of any abandonment of ethical nature. But the natural, which in an ethical context must be thought of as something to be abandoned, would not itself be ethical and therefore could not remotely represent the latter in its original form. Nor is infinity, or the nullity of the individuals and subjects, in any way fixed in the absolute Idea, or relatively identical with majesty as a relation of subjugation in which individuality [*Einzelheit*] would also be something purely and simply posited. On the contrary, infinity in the Idea is genuine, and individuality as such is nothing and completely at one with absolute ethical majesty; and this genuine, living, non-subjugated oneness is the only genuine ethical life of the individual.[24]

We have accused scientific empiricism – in so far as it is scientific – of positive nullity and untruth in respect of its principles, laws, etc., because it endows determinacies with the negative absoluteness of the concept by means of the formal unity in which it places them, and expresses them as positively absolute, having being in themselves [*an sich seiend*], as end and destiny, principle, law, duty, and right – [all of] which forms signify something absolute. But in order to preserve the unity of an organic relationship which presents this qualitative determination with a mass of such concepts, *one* of the determinacies – expressed as end, destiny, or law – must be given supremacy over the other determinacies within the manifold, and these others must be posited as unreal and as nothing in comparison with it. It is by this application [of reasoning] and its consistency that intuition is nullified as an inner totality; it is therefore by inconsistency that this incorporation [*Aufnahme*] of determinacies into the concept can be corrected and the violence done to intuition overcome, for inconsistency immediately nullifies the absoluteness previously attributed to a single determinacy.[25] From this point of view, the old and utterly inconsistent [kind of] empiricism must be vindicated, not in relation to absolute science as such, but in relation to the consistency of that empirical scientific procedure which we have hitherto been discussing. A great and pure intuition can in this way express the genuinely ethical in the purely architectonic qualities of its exposition, in which the context of necessity and the dominance of form do not become visible – just as in a building which mutely reveals the spirit of its originator throughout its diversified mass, without setting up his actual image concentrated into a single shape within it. In an exposition of this kind, presented with the help of concepts, it is only through ineptitude that reason fails to elevate what it encompasses and penetrates to the ideal form, and so to become conscious of it as Idea. If only intuition remains true to itself and does not allow the understanding to confuse it,[26] it will [admittedly] be inept in its use of concepts (inasmuch as it cannot dispense with these in order to express itself); it will assume distorted shapes in its passage through the consciousness; and it will be both incoherent and contradictory with regard to the concept; but the disposition of the parts and of the determinacies in their modifications does give an indication of the invisible but rational spirit within,[27] and in so far as this manifestation [*Erscheinung*] of the spirit is regarded as a product and result, it will, as a product, correspond perfectly with the Idea.

In these circumstances, nothing is easier for the understanding than to mount an attack on this empiricism, to oppose its inept reasons with alternative ones, to expose the confusion and contradiction of its concepts, to draw consequences of the most extreme and irrational kind from its individual propositions, and in numerous ways to demonstrate its unscientific character.[28] Empiricism justly deserves this treatment, especially if it has scientific pretensions or adopts a polemical stance in relation to science as such. Conversely, if determinacies are fixed and their law is consistently applied to all the aspects which empiricism has brought to light, if intuition is subordinated to them, and if in general what is commonly called a theory is constructed, empiricism can rightly accuse this of one-sidedness; and by virtue of the complete range of determinacies which it brings into play, it is within its power, by [citing individual] instances, to force this theory to adopt a [level

of] generality which becomes totally empty. This conceptual limitation, the fixing of determinacies and the elevation of one selected
aspect of appearance to universality so as to give it precedence over
others, is what in recent times has described itself not just as theory,
but as philosophy and – since it has ascended to more vacuous
abstractions and got hold of purer negations such as freedom, pure
will, humanity, etc. – as metaphysics. It believed it had accomplished philosophical revolutions in natural law, and especially
in constitutional and criminal law, when it dragged these sciences
in one direction or another with such insubstantial abstractions and
positively expressed negations as freedom, equality, the pure state,
etc., or with equally insubstantial determinacies picked up from
ordinary empiricism such as coercion (especially psychological
coercion, with its whole paraphernalia of opposition between practical reason and sensuous motives, and whatever else is at home in
this psychology); and with greater or lesser consistency, it likewise
compelled the science in question to incorporate insignificant [*nich-
tige*] concepts of this kind as absolute ends of reason, rational principles, or laws. Empiricism rightly demands that such philosophising should take its directions from experience. It rightly insists on
stubbornly opposing such a contrived framework of principles. It
rightly prefers its own empirical inconsistency – based as it is on
an (albeit dim) intuition of the whole – to the consistency of such
philosophising; and it prefers its own confusion – for example, of
ethical life, morality, and legality, or, in the more specific case of
punishment, its confusion of revenge, national security, reform [of
the criminal], the carrying out of a threat, deterrence, prevention,
etc. (whether in a scientific context or in practical life) – to the
absolute separation of these various aspects of one and the same
intuition, and to the definition of the latter as a whole in terms of
a single one of these qualities. It rightly maintains that the theory,
and what calls itself philosophy and metaphysics, has no application
and contradicts practical necessity (although this non-applicability
would be better expressed if one were to say that there is nothing
absolute, no reality, and no truth in the theory and philosophy in
question). Finally, empiricism rightly reproaches such philosophising with ingratitude, because it is empiricism which furnishes it
with the content of its concepts and must then see this content
corrupted and distorted by this philosophising; for the determinacy

of the content, as supplied by empiricism, forms, with other determinacies, a complex combination which is essentially an organic
and living whole, and this is killed by such fragmentation and such
elevation of insubstantial abstractions and details to absolute
status.[29]

If empiricism were itself pure and remained so, it would be
fully justified in asserting itself against such theory and philosophy, and in regarding the mass of principles, ends, laws, duties,
and rights not as something absolute, but as distinctions of
importance for that [process of] education [*Bildung*] through
which its own intuition becomes clearer to it. But when empiricism appears to seek a conflict with theory, it usually emerges
that both of them embody an intuition which is already contaminated and superseded by reflection and a distorted reason; and
what professes to be empiricism is merely weaker in abstraction
and shows less initiative, in that it has not itself selected, distinguished, and fixed its own limited concepts [*Beschränktheiten*],
but is tied to concepts which have become firmly entrenched in
general culture [*Bildung*] as 'sound common sense' and hence
appear to have been derived directly from experience. The conflict between such entrenched distortions of intuition and the
newly fixed abstractions offers a spectacle which is necessarily as
motley as the combatants themselves. Each side deploys against
the other at one moment an abstraction, at another some so-called
experience; and on both sides, empiricism is destroyed by empiricism, and [conceptual] limitation by [conceptual] limitation. At
one moment principles and laws are vaunted against philosophy,
which is ruled out as an incompetent judge of those [supposedly]
absolute truths with which the understanding has become
obsessed, at another philosophy is misused for ratiocination in
the name of philosophy.

This relative right which was conceded to empiricism – [at least]
when intuition is the dominant factor within it – against the combining of empirical and reflective elements, refers, it will be recalled,
to its unconscious inner nature. But the intermediate term between
this inner nature and its external expression – i.e. consciousness –
is the area where its deficiency (and hence its one-sidedness) lies;
and its tendency to go against the scientific, its incomplete link with
the concept (with which it only just makes contact and is merely

contaminated in the process), derives from the necessity that multiplicity and finitude should be absolutely submerged in infinity or universality.

[II]

But it is the aspect of *infinity* which constitutes the principle of that apriorism which sets itself against the empirical, and we must now consider this in turn.

In the absolute concept of infinity, the drift of empirical opinion (with its mixing of the manifold with the simple) in relation to the concept is released from its vacillation, and the incomplete separation [of the two elements] is resolved. It is true that, at a lower level of abstraction, infinity is also emphasised (as the absoluteness of the subject) in the theory of happiness in general and especially in natural law, by those systems which are described as anti-socialistic and which posit the being of the individual as the primary and supreme value;[30] but it is not raised to the pure abstraction which it has attained in the idealism of Kant or Fichte.

It is not appropriate in the present context to give an account of the nature of infinity and its manifold transformations. For since it is the principle of movement and change, its essence is itself none other than to be the unmediated opposite of itself; or [to put it differently,] it is the negatively absolute, the abstraction of form. Inasmuch as this is pure identity, it is immediately pure non-identity or absolute opposition; inasmuch as it is pure ideality, it is equally immediately pure reality; inasmuch as it is the infinite, it is the absolutely finite; inasmuch as it is the indeterminate, it is absolute determinacy. That absolute transition to its own opposite which is its essence, and the disappearance of every reality in its opposite, cannot be halted except in an empirical manner, by fixing one of its aspects (namely reality, or the subsistence of the opposites) and abstracting from the opposite of this (namely the nullity of this subsistence). This real opposition consists, on the one hand, of manifold being or finitude, and on the other, of infinity as the negation of multiplicity (or, in a positive sense, as pure unity); and the absolute concept which is thereby constituted supplies, within this unity, what has been called 'pure reason'. But the relation of this pure unity to the manifold being [*dem mannigfaltigen Seienden*] which is opposed to it is also itself a double relationship [*Beziehung*] – either the positive relationship of the subsistence of both, or the nullification of both. Both this subsistence and this nullification should, however, be understood as only partial; for if the subsistence of both were absolute, the two could have no relationship whatsoever, and if the complete nullification of both were posited, there could be no subsistence of either. This partial subsistence and partial negation of both – the opposition of a divisible 'I' to a divisible not-'I' within the 'I' (i.e. in a relationship which, for this very reason, is likewise partial) – is the absolute principle of this philosophy. In the former, positive relationship, the pure unity is called theoretical reason, and in the negative relationship, practical reason; and since, in the latter, the negation of the opposition is primary (so that unity is more subsistent), whereas in the former, the subsistence of the opposition is primary (so that multiplicity [*Vielheit*] is primary and more subsistent), practical reason appears here as real, whereas theoretical reason appears as ideal. – One can see, however, that this definition is wholly concerned with opposition and appearance. For that pure unity which is posited as reason is, of course, negative and ideal if what is opposed to it, namely the many (which is accordingly the irrational), is purely and simply subsistent – just as it will appear more subsistent and real if the many is posited as negated (or rather as what should be negated). But if nature is posited in opposition to reason as pure unity, this irrational many is irrational only because it is posited as the non-essential [*wesenlose*] abstraction of the many, whereas reason is posited as the non-essential abstraction of the one. Regarded in itself, however, this many is just as much absolute unity of the one and the many as unity is; and nature, or theoretical reason (which is the many), must, as the absolute unity of the one and the many, conversely be defined rather as real reason. But ethical reason (which is unity) must, as the absolute unity of the one and the many, be defined as ideal reason, because in the opposition, reality belongs with multiplicity, while identity belongs with unity.

Consequently, in what is known as practical reason, one can recognise only the *formal* Idea of the identity of the ideal and the real, and this Idea should be the absolute point of indifference in these [philosophical] systems.[31] But this Idea does not escape from difference [*Differenz*], and the ideal does not attain reality; for despite the fact that the ideal and the real are identical in this practical reason, the real remains purely and simply opposed [to the ideal]. This real is essentially posited [as] outside reason, and practical reason is [to be found] only in its difference [*Differenz*] from it. The essence of this practical reason is to be understood as a causal relation to the many – as an identity which is absolutely encumbered [*affiziert*] with a difference and does not emerge from [the realm of] appearance. This science of the ethical, which talks of the absolute identity of the ideal and the real, accordingly does not do what it claims to do: its ethical reason is, in truth and in its essence, a non-identity of the ideal and the real.

Ethical reason has already been defined as the absolute in the form of unity; consequently, since it is itself posited as a determinacy, it immediately seems, in this determination, to be posited just as essentially with an opposite. There is, however, a difference [*Unterschied*] here, in that true reality and its absolute are completely free from this opposition to nature, and are the absolute identity of the ideal and the real. The absolute, in accordance with its Idea, is recognised as this identity of different things, whose determinate character [*Bestimmtheit*] is to be unity and multiplicity respectively; and this determinate character is ideal, i.e. it resides only in infinity in accordance with the concept of infinity as indicated above: it is both superseded and posited. Each of the two, the unity and the multiplicity, whose identity is the absolute, is itself a unity of the one and the many. But that unity whose ideal determinacy is multiplicity is the subsistence of the opposites (i.e. positive reality), and it therefore itself necessitates an opposite and double relation. Since the real subsists within it, its identity is a relative one, and this relative identity of opposites is a necessity. Since it [i.e. this unity] thus resides [*ist*] in difference [*Differenz*], its relation itself or the identity of the relation must also be a difference [*ein Differentes*]; that is, both unity and multiplicity must be primary within it. This twofold relation determines the dual aspect of the necessity, or the appearance, of the absolute. Since this twofold relation refers to multiplicity, if we then describe as 'indifference' that unity of different things which stands on the opposite side and in which the reality [of these things], or the many, is superseded, then the absolute is the unity of indifference and relation. And since this relation is a double one, the appearance of the absolute is determined [firstly,] as the unity of indifference and of that relation – or that relative identity – in which the many is primary and positive, and [secondly,] as the unity of indifference and of that relation in which the unity is primary and positive. The former is physical nature, and the latter is ethical nature.[32] And since indifference or unity is freedom, whereas relation or relative identity is necessity, each of these two appearances is the oneness and indifference of freedom and necessity. Substance is absolute and infinite; in this predicate of infinity, the necessity of the divine nature, or its appearance, is entailed, and this necessity is expressed as reality in none other than a double relation. Each of the two attributes itself expresses the substance, and is absolute and infinite, or the unity of indifference and relation. And in the relation, the distinction between them is posited in such a way that, in the relation of the ones, the many is the primary element which stands out from the others, and in the relation of the others, the one is the primary element which stands out from these. But since unity is primary in the relation of ethical nature itself, this nature is free even in this relative identity, i.e. in its necessity. Or, since the fact that unity is primary does not mean that this relative identity is superseded, this second freedom is so determined that, although the necessary is indeed [present] for ethical nature, it is posited negatively. Now if we were to isolate this aspect of the relative identity of ethical nature, and to acknowledge as the essence of ethical nature not the absolute unity of indifference and of this relative identity, but the aspect of relation or necessity, we would be at the same point at which the essence of practical reason is defined as possessing absolute causality, or as being free while necessity is only negative, but for that very reason nevertheless posited. Consequently, this very freedom does not escape from difference; relation or relative identity is made the essence, and the absolute is understood only as negatively absolute or infinite.

The empirical and popular expression through which this notion, which envisages ethical nature solely in terms of its relative identity, has recommended itself so widely is [the claim] that the real, under such names as sensuousness, inclinations, the lower appetitive faculty, etc. (the moment of the multiplicity of the relation), and reason (the moment of the pure unity of the relation) do not coincide (the moment of the opposition of unity and multiplicity); and that reason consists in willing out of its own spontaneity and autonomy, and in limiting and dominating that sensuousness (the moment whereby the relation is determined in such a way that unity, or the negation of multiplicity, has primacy within it). The reality of this notion is based on the empirical consciousness, and on the universal experience of everyone in finding within the self both that division and that pure unity of practical reason (or the abstraction of the 'I') [referred to above]. Nor can there be any question of denying this point of view; on the contrary, it has already been defined as the aspect of relative identity, of the being of the infinite within the finite. But it must at least be stated that it is not the absolute point of view, in which it has been shown that the relation proves to be only a single aspect, whose isolation consequently proves to be a one-sided thing; and [it must also be stated] that, since morality [*Sittlichkeit*] is something absolute, the point of view referred to is not that of morality – on the contrary, there is no morality within it.[33] And as for the appeal to ordinary consciousness, morality [*Sittlichkeit*] itself must be present within this consciousness just as necessarily as that point of view which, since the relation, isolated for itself, is posited not as a moment, but as having being in itself, is the principle of immorality [*Unsittlichkeit*]. The empirical consciousness is empirical because within it, the moments of the absolute appear scattered, co-existent, consecutive, and fragmented; but it would not in itself be an ordinary consciousness if morality [*Sittlichkeit*] were not likewise present within it. That formal philosophy [referred to above] was able to choose among these manifold appearances of the moral and the immoral [*des Sittlichen und des Unsittlichen*] which are present in the empirical consciousness, and it is not the fault of ordinary consciousness, but of philosophy, that it chose the appearance of the immoral and imagined that it had [found] the genuine absolute in negative absoluteness or infinity.

The exposition of this practical philosophy is based on a presentation of what this negative absoluteness can accomplish, and we must review the chief moments in this mistaken attempt to discover a genuinely absolute [quality] in the negatively absolute.

It at once becomes clear that, since pure unity constitutes the essence of practical reason, a system of morality [*Sittlichkeit*] is so much out of the question that not even a plurality of laws is possible; for whatever goes beyond the pure concept, or – since this concept, in so far as it is posited as negating the many (i.e. as practical) is duty – whatever goes beyond the pure concept of duty and beyond the abstraction of a law, no longer pertains to this pure reason. Thus Kant, as the one who presented this abstraction of the concept in its absolute purity, fully recognises that practical reason is completely lacking in any content of the [moral] law and that it can do no more than make the *formal appropriateness* [*Form der Tauglichkeit*] of the will's maxim into a supreme law. The will's maxim has a content and includes a determinacy; the pure will, on the other hand, is free from such determinacies. The absolute law of practical reason is to raise this determinacy to the form of pure unity, and the expression of this determinacy elevated to this form is the law. If the determinacy can be elevated to the form of the pure concept, and if it does not thereby cancel itself [*sich aufheben*], then it is justified and has itself become absolute, through its negative absoluteness, as law and right or duty. But the material [aspect] of the maxim remains what it is, a determinacy or individual quality [*Einzelheit*]; and the universality which its formal elevation confers on it is consequently a purely analytic unity, so that, when the unity conferred on it is expressed in a proposition purely for what it is, that proposition is an analytical one and a tautology. In truth, the sublime capacity of pure practical reason to legislate autonomously consists in the production of tautologies; and the pure identity of the understanding, expressed in theoretical terms as the principle of contradiction, remains exactly the same when applied to the practical form. If the question 'What is truth?', when put to logic and answered by it, provides Kant with 'the ridiculous spectacle of one man milking a billy-goat while another holds a sieve beneath it', then the question 'What is right and duty?', put to and answered by pure practical reason, is of exactly the same kind. Kant recognises that 'a universal criterion of truth would be one which would apply to all knowledge [*Erkenntnisse*], irrespective of the objects of this knowledge, but it is clear that, since this involves abstracting from the whole content of knowledge (although truth is concerned with precisely this content), it is quite impossible and absurd to ask for a test of the truth of this content'[34] (because this test is supposed to have nothing to do with the content of knowledge). With these words, Kant in fact passes judgement on the principle of duty and right which is set up by practical reason. For the latter abstracts

completely from all material [aspects] of the will; any content presupposes a heteronomy of the arbitrary will [*Willkür*]. But our interest here is precisely to establish what right and duty are; we enquire
what the content of the moral law is, and our sole concern is with
this content. But the essence of pure will and of pure practical
reason is to abstract from all content, so that it is self-contradictory
to look to this absolute practical reason for a moral legislation –
which would have to have a content – because the essence of this
reason consists in having no content at all.[35]

Thus, before this formalism can pronounce a law, it is necessary
that some material [aspect], some determinacy, should be posited
to supply its content; and the form which is conferred upon this
determinacy is that of unity or universality. 'That a maxim of your
will must simultaneously count as a principle of universal legislation'[36] – this basic law of pure practical reason implies that some
determinacy which constitutes the content of the maxim of the particular will should be posited as a concept, as a universal. But every
determinacy is capable of being elevated to conceptual form and
posited as a quality [*Qualität*], and there is nothing which could not
be made into a moral law in this way.[37] But every determinacy is
particular in itself, and is not a universal; it is confronted by an
opposite determinacy, and it is determinate only in so far as it has
such an opposite. Each of the two determinacies is equally capable
of being thought; which of the two is to be elevated to unity (or
to be thought), and which is to be abstracted from, is completely
indeterminate and free. If one of them is fixed as subsisting in and
for itself, the other cannot, of course, be posited; but this other can
equally well be thought and (since the form of thought is [of] the
essence) expressed as an absolute moral law. That 'the commonest
understanding, without any guidance', can perform this simple
operation and distinguish what form of maxim is appropriate for
universal legislation or not, Kant shows by the following example.[38]
I ask whether the maxim that I should increase my wealth by all
reliable means can count as a universal practical law if such a means
should present itself to me in the shape of a deposit [with which I
am entrusted].[39] The content of this maxim should thus be 'that
anyone may deny having received a deposit if no one can prove that
he did so'. This question supplies its own answer [according to
Kant], because 'such a principle, as a law, would destroy itself,

since its effect would be that no deposits would be made'. But what contradiction is there in no deposits being made? The absence of deposits will contradict other necessary determinacies, just as the possibility of a deposit will be compatible with other necessary determinacies and consequently itself be necessary. But it is not other ends and material reasons which have to be invoked; on the contrary, the immediate form of the concept is to decide the correctness of the first or the second assumption. But the two opposing determinacies are equally indifferent as far as the form is concerned; each can be conceived as a quality, and this conception can be expressed as a law. If the determinacy of property in general is posited, the following tautological proposition can be constructed: 'Property is property and nothing else besides'; and this tautological production is the legislation of the practical reason already referred to: property, if there is property, must be property. But if the opposite determinacy, i.e. the negation of property, is posited, the legislation of the same practical reason results in the tautology: non-property is non-property. If there is no property, anything which claims to be property must be annulled [*aufgehoben*]. But the interest [at stake] is precisely to prove that there must be property; we are solely concerned with what lies outside the competence of this practical legislation of pure reason, namely with deciding which of the opposing determinacies must be posited. But pure reason requires that this should have been done in advance, and that one of the opposing determinacies should already have been posited; only then can it enact its now superfluous legislation.

The analytic unity and tautology of practical reason is not only superfluous, however, but – in its present application – false, and it must be recognised as the principle of immorality [*Unsittlichkeit*]. The mere elevation of a determinacy to the form of unity is supposed to change the nature of its being; and the determinacy, which by its nature is opposed by another determinacy so that each is the negation of the other and neither is absolute (and as far as the functioning of practical reason is concerned, it is a matter of indifference which of the two it has to deal with, for it supplies only the empty form), is itself supposed to become absolute, as law and duty, by means of this union with the form of pure unity. But whenever a determinacy or individual quality is raised to [the status of] something in itself [*zu einem Ansich*], irrationality and (in a moral

context) immorality [*Unsittlichkeit*] are posited. – The illegitimacy
of this transformation of the conditioned and unreal into something
unconditioned and absolute is easily recognised, and its subterfuges
are easily detected. When the determinacy is elevated to the form
of pure unity or formal identity and the determinate concept is
expressed as a proposition, the result is the tautology of the formal
proposition 'determinacy A is determinacy A'. But the form, as
expressed in the proposition 'the identity of the subject and predicate is an absolute', yields only a negative or formal [statement]
which has nothing to do with determinacy A itself; this content is
entirely hypothetical as far as the form is concerned. But the absoluteness which is present in the proposition by virtue of its form
takes on a wholly different significance within practical reason; for
it is also transferred to the content, which is by nature a conditioned
thing [*ein Bedingtes*], and contrary to its essence, this non-absolute,
conditioned thing is raised to [the status of] an absolute as a result
of this confusion. It is not in the interest of practice to produce a
tautology, and practical reason would not make so much fuss just
for the sake of this empty form (although this is the only power
which it has); but through this confusion of the absolute form with
the conditioned material, the absoluteness of the form is imposed
by stealth on the unreal and conditioned character of the content,
and this inversion and sleight of hand lies at the heart of the practical legislation of pure reason. The true meaning of the proposition
'property is property' is 'the identity which this proposition
expresses through its form is absolute'; but instead, the meaning
'the material [content] of this proposition, namely property, is
absolute' is falsely attributed to it, and any determinacy can at once
be made into a duty. The arbitrary will can choose between opposing determinacies, and it would be sheer ineptitude if, for any [par-
ticular] action, some ground could not be found which not only
possessed the form of probability – as with the Jesuits – but also
acquired the form of right and duty; and this moral formalism is
no better than the moral artifice of the Jesuits or the principles of
eudaemonism,[40] which are one and the same thing.

It should be clearly noted in this connection that the elevation of
a determinacy to the concept must be understood as a [purely]
formal operation, or as implying that the determinacy remains [as
it was], so that matter and form contradict one another (inasmuch

as the former is determinate and the latter infinite). But if the content were genuinely equated with the form, and determinacy with unity, no practical legislation would be possible: the determinacy would simply be annulled. Thus, property itself is directly opposed to universality;[41] but if it is equated with it, it is superseded. – This annulment of determinacy by elevating it to infinity or universality also causes problems for practical legislation. For if the determinacy is such that it itself expresses the superseding of a determinacy, then the elevation of this supersession [*Aufheben*] to universality or supersededness [*Aufgehobensein*] annuls both the determinacy which is to be superseded and the supersession itself; consequently, a maxim which refers to a determinacy of this kind, which is annulled when thought of in terms of universality, would be incapable of becoming the principle of a universal legislation, and would consequently be immoral. In other words, the maxim's content, which is the supersession of a determinacy, contradicts itself if it is raised to the concept. For if the determinacy is thought of as superseded, its supersession no longer obtains; but if this determinacy is supposed to remain [in being], then the supersession which was posited in the maxim is in turn no longer posited – and whether the determinacy remains [in being] or not, it cannot in either case be superseded. But a maxim which is immoral [*unmoralisch*] in principle (because it is self-contradictory) is absolutely rational, and hence absolutely moral, inasmuch as it expresses the supersession of a determinacy; for the rational in its negative aspect is the indifference of determinacies, the supersededness of the conditioned. Thus, the determinate injunction [*die Bestimmtheit*] to help the poor expresses the supersession of the determinacy which is poverty; but if the maxim whose content is this determinacy is tested by raising it to a principle of universal legislation, it will prove to be false, because it annuls itself. If it is thought that the poor should be helped universally, then there are either no longer any poor, or there are only the poor (in which case no one remains to help them), so that in both cases, the help becomes irrelevant; thus, if the maxim is thought of as universal, it cancels itself [*hebt sich selbst auf*]. But if the determinacy which is the condition of the supersession – namely poverty – should remain [in being], the possibility of help also remains, but only as a possibility and not as the actuality implied by the maxim. If poverty is to remain in order that the duty of helping the poor can be fulfilled, this very retention of poverty runs directly against the fulfilment of the duty. Thus, the maxim that one should honourably defend one's fatherland against its enemies, and an infinite number of other maxims, cancel themselves out [*heben sich auf*] whenever they are thought of as principles of universal legislation; for when, for example, the above maxim is extended in this way, the determinacy of a fatherland, like those of enemies and defence, cancels itself out.

Unity neither has the purely negative meaning of the mere supersession of determinacies, nor is it genuine unity of intuition or the positive indifference of such determinacies. Comparison with the latter [kind of] unity will clarify the distorted nature [*Wesen*] of the former from another angle. For the former unity of practical reason is essentially encumbered [*affiziert*] with a difference [*Differenz*], because it is posited either as the fixing of a determinacy, so that others are thereby immediately excluded (or negatively posited), or as an analytic proposition, in which case the identity of this proposition (i.e. its form) immediately contradicts its content. This can also be formulated as follows: given its content, this proposition contradicts the requirement that it should be a judgement. The proposition was supposed to say something, but an identical proposition says nothing, for it is not a judgement, because the relation of the subject to the predicate is merely formal, and no difference between them is posited. Or if the unity is understood as universality, then it refers entirely to an empirical multiplicity, and the present determinacy is opposed to an infinite mass of empirically different determinacies. The unity of intuition, on the other hand, is the indifference of the determinacies which constitute a whole; in this unity, they are not fixed as separate and opposed, but integrated and objectivised. And since this indifference and the different determinacies are completely united, this unity does not involve a division either between indifference as possibility and the determinacies as actualities, or between some of the determinacies as possible and others as actual; on the contrary, it is absolute presence. And in this power of intuition and presence lies the power of morality [*Sittlichkeit*] in general[42] – and, of course, of morality [*Sittlichkeit*] in particular, with which that legislative reason referred to above is primarily concerned, and from which that form of the concept, of formal unity and universality, must rather be kept completely separate. For the essence of morality is immediately annulled [*aufgehoben*] by this very form, in that it renders contingent what is morally necessary by making it appear in opposition to other things; but in morality [*Sittlichkeit*], the contingent – which is identical [*eins*] with the empirically necessary – is immoral [*unsittlich*]. A pain which is [present] is raised by the power of intuition out of [the realm of] sensation, in which it is accidental and contingent, to unity, and [given] the shape of something objective and necessary which has being for itself; and through this immediate unity, which gives no thought to what possibilities formal unity offers on one side or the other, it is preserved in its absolute presentness. But as a result of the objectivity of intuition and the raising [of the sensation of pain] to this unity of being-for-itself, it is genuinely detached from the subject and rendered ideal in the fixed intuition of this unity.[43] If, on the other hand, the pain is compared with other determinacies by the unity of reflection, or thought of as universal and found not to be so, it is in both cases rendered contingent, and the subject thereby recognises itself in its mere contingency and particularity; this cognition is the sensibility [*Empfindsamkeit*] and immorality [*Unsittlichkeit*] of impotence. Or if morality [*das Sittliche*] is concerned with relations between individuals, it is pure intuition and ideality (as in the entrusting of a deposit) which must be held on to and kept free from any interference on the part of formal unity and of the thought of other possible determinacies. The expression of this unity of intuition ('someone else's property entrusted to me is someone else's property entrusted to me and nothing else besides') has a completely different meaning from the universally expressed tautology of practical legislation ('an alien property entrusted to me is an alien property entrusted to me'). For the latter proposition can equally well be confronted by another to the effect that 'something entrusted to me which is not the property of another is not the property of the other'; that is, a determinacy raised to the concept thereby becomes ideal, and the opposite determinacy can equally well be posited. On the other hand, the expression of intuition contains a 'this', a living relation and absolute presence whose possibility is inseparably connected [*schlechthin verknüpft*] with it, whereas any possibility distinct from it, or any [possibility of] otherness [*Anderssein*], is simply annulled, for in this possible otherness lies immorality [*Unsittlichkeit*].[44]

Now if the unity of practical reason were not this positive unity of intuition but had only the negative meaning of annulling the determinate, it would simply express the essence of negative reason or of infinity, of the absolute concept. But because infinity becomes fixed and divorced from the absolute, it shows itself in its essence as being its own opposite. It makes a mockery of reflection, which seeks to pin it down and grasp in it an absolute unity, and it does so by also giving rise to the complete opposite of such unity, namely a difference [*Differenz*] and multiplicity; thus, within this opposition (which reproduces itself infinitely), it permits only a relative identity, and even as infinity, it is consequently its own opposite, namely absolute finitude. And as it thus becomes isolated, it is itself only the powerless form, abandoned by the genuinely nullifying power of reason; it takes up and accommodates determinacies without annulling them, but rather perpetuating them.

It is on the opposition described above, on its fixation as a reality and its incomplete connection [*Verknüpfung*] as a relative identity, that the recent definition of the concept of natural law and of its position within the whole science of ethics [*des Sittlichen*] depends.[45] We must now consider from this more specific angle what has hitherto been examined in general terms, [and so discover] how that separation, insuperable as soon as it was posited, appears in its own distinctive way in the science of natural law.

The absolute concept, which is both the principle of opposition and opposition itself, presents itself – since it is fixed – within this separation in such a way that, as pure unity, it is opposed to itself as multiplicity. As a result, it can remain the absolute concept both in the form of pure unity and in that of pure multiplicity; and in the form of multiplicity, it is not a varied range [*Mannigfaltigkeit*] of differently determined concepts, but is subsumed under unity as well as under multiplicity. The concept *itself* is subsumed in many determinate concepts, and is [nevertheless] not many but one. The absolute concept, being itself a multiplicity, is a mass of subjects, and in the form of pure unity – as absolute quantity – it is opposed to these as its own qualitative and posited being [*Gesetztsein*]. Thus, both [aspects] are posited – an inner oneness of the opposites, which is the essence of both (i.e. the absolute concept), and a division of the concept under the form of unity (in which it is right and duty) and under the form of multiplicity (in which it is the thinking and willing subject). The first of these aspects, whereby the essence of right and duty and the essence of the thinking and willing subject are totally one, is the main aspect of the philosophy of Kant and Fichte (as is, generally speaking, the higher abstraction of infinity). But this philosophy has not remained true to this oneness; instead, although it does acknowledge this oneness as the essence and absolute, it posits the separation into the one and the many just as absolutely, according equal dignity to both. Consequently, it is not the positive absolute which constitutes the essence of both and in which the two are one, but the negative absolute or the absolute concept; furthermore, this necessary oneness becomes formal, and the two opposite determinacies, posited as absolute, accordingly belong in their subsistence to ideality, which is in this respect the mere possibility of both. It is possible for right and duty to have reality independently, as a particular [realm] separate from the subjects and from which the subjects are separate; but it is also possible for the two to be linked.[46] And it is absolutely necessary for these two possibilities to be kept apart and distinguished from one another, so that each may form the basis of a separate science – one concerned with the oneness of the pure concept and the subjects (or the morality [*Moralität*] of actions), the other with their non-oneness [*Nichteinssein*] (or legality), but in such a way that if, in this division of the ethical realm [*des Sittlichen*] into morality [*Moralität*] and legality, these two become mere possibilities, they are both for that very reason equally positive. Admittedly, the one is negative for the other – but both are equally so. It is not that one is the absolutely positive, and the other the absolutely negative; on the contrary, each is both [positive and negative] within their mutual relation, and since both are only relatively positive in the first instance, neither legality nor morality is absolutely positive or truly ethical. But then, since each of the two is as positive as the other, both are absolutely necessary, and the possibility that the pure concept and the subject of duty and right are *not* one must be posited unalterably and without qualification.

The basic concepts of the system of legality flow directly from the above, in the following manner. The pure self-consciousness, the 'I', is the true essence and the absolute, but it is nevertheless conditioned. The condition to which it is subject is that it should progress to real consciousness. In this relation of mutual conditionedness, the two forms [of consciousness] remain totally opposed to one another. The former pure self-consciousness, pure unity, or the empty law of ethics [*Sittengesetz*] – the universal freedom of all – is opposed to the real consciousness, i.e. to the subject, the rational being, and individual freedom – which Fichte, in a more popular manner, expresses as the presupposition that 'loyalty and faith are lost'.[47] On this presupposition, a system is established which aims to unite both the concept and the subject of ethical life, despite their separation (although because of the latter, their union is only formal and external); the resultant relation is called *coercion*.[48] Since this externality of oneness is thereby totally fixed and posited as something absolute which has being in itself, the inner dimension [*Innerlichkeit*], the reconstruction of the lost loyalty and faith, the oneness of universal and individual freedom, and ethical life [in general] are rendered impossible.

We shall refer here to Fichte's exposition as the most consistent and least formal account, which actually attempts to create a consistent system with no need of an ethics [*Sittlichkeit*] and religion that are alien to it. In a system of such externality (as in any system which proceeds from the conditioned to the unconditioned), it is either impossible to discover anything unconditioned, or if something of this kind is posited, it is [merely] a formal indifference which has the conditioned and the different outside it; it is essence without form, power without wisdom, quantity without inner quality or infinity, rest without movement.

The supreme task in an arrangement which works with mechanical necessity so that the activity of each individual is coerced by the general will is one which presupposes an opposition between the individual will and the general will (given that this general will must necessarily be real in those subjects [*Subjekte*] who are its organs and administrators). Oneness with the general will consequently cannot be understood and posited as inner absolute majesty, but as something to be produced by an external relation, or by coercion. But in reality, in the process of coercion and supervision which must in this case be posited, one cannot continue in infinite series and make a leap from the real to the ideal; there must be a

supreme positive point from which coercion in accordance with the
concept of universal freedom originates. But this point, like all other
points, must itself be coerced into coercing [others] in accordance
with the concept of universal freedom; for any point within this
universal system of coercion which were not itself coerced would
depart from the principle [of the whole] and become transcendent.
The question is therefore how this supreme will, by coercion and
supervision, can likewise be made to conform to the concept of
the general will so that the system remains wholly immanent and
transcendental. The only way in which this could happen would be
for the power of the whole to be divided between the two opposing
sides so that the governed are coerced by the government and the
government by the governed. If we assume that the power – and
hence the possible coercion – exercised by the two sides is of
unequal strength, then only one part, rather than its opposite, is
subject to coercion, inasmuch as the one has more power than the
other or the power of both is excessive; and this ought not to
happen. But in point of fact, only the possessor of excess power
is genuinely powerful, for before something can impose limits on
something else, it must be equal to it.[49] The weaker [of the two]
cannot therefore limit the other; both must consequently coerce and
be coerced by one another with equal power. But if in this way
action and reaction, stance and resistance, are equally strong, the
power on both sides is reduced to equilibrium; thus all functions,
actions, and expressions of will are annulled [*aufgehoben*]. This
reduction may be thought of in positive or negative terms; that is,
action and reaction may be posited as existing [*seiend*] and working,
or posited negatively, so that the equilibrium arises because neither
action nor reaction is present. Nor is it a true solution to try to
remedy this stagnation[a] by opening out the direct confrontation [of
the two sides] into a circle of effects, so that the central point of
contact at which the reduction of the opposites takes place may be
annulled [*aufgehoben*] by deceptively leaving the centre empty. In
opposition to the hierarchy of coercion which descends from the
supreme authority [*Gewalt*] through all its ramifications down to
every individual unit [*allen Einzelheiten*], a corresponding pyramid
is in turn supposed to ascend from the latter to an uppermost point

---

[a] *Translator's note*: Literally, 'this death'.

of counter-pressure acting against the downward pressure.[50] The whole is thus supposed to turn round in a circle in which the immediacy of contact would vanish; the forces – in so far as they constitute a mass – would be kept apart, and intermediate elements would create an artificial difference [*Differenz*] so that no single element [*Glied*] would react directly upon the one which moved it (so reducing the two to equilibrium), but always on another element, so that the first would move the last and the last would in turn move the first. But instead of moving, such a *perpetuum mobile* whose parts are all supposed to move one another round in a circle will at once achieve perfect equilibrium and become a perfect *perpetuum quietum*; for pressure and counter-pressure, coercion and exposure to coercion are precisely equivalent, and they are just as directly opposed to one another, and produce the same reduction of forces, as in the original model [*Vorstellung*]. Pure quantity cannot be subverted by such mediation, which brings no difference, true infinity, or form whatsoever into it; on the contrary, it remains, as before, a completely undivided, pure, and shapeless power. It is impossible to compel such a power to conform in this way to the concept of universal freedom, for no authority can be found outside it, and no division can be established within it.

For this reason, the expedient of a purely formal distinction is in turn adopted. *Actual* power is admittedly posited as *one*, and as united in the government; but it is contrasted with *possible* power, and this possibility is supposed as such to be capable of coercing the actuality in question. This second, powerless existence of the general will is supposed to be in a position to judge whether the power has deserted the first [existence of the general will] with which it is associated, and whether or not this power still accords with the concept of universal freedom.[51] Indeed, the general will is supposed to supervise the supreme power in general, and, if a private will takes the place of the general will within it, to wrest the power from this private will; the manner in which this is supposedly accomplished is by a public declaration, possessing absolute force, of the complete nullity of all actions of the supreme political authority from that moment onwards. What should and may not happen is for the power to detach itself on its own independent judgement, as this would amount to insurrection; for this pure power consists solely of private wills, which are consequently unable to constitute themselves as a collective [*gemeinsame*] will. But it is the second collective will [referred to above] which declares that this mass [of private wills] is united as a community, or that the pure power is also united with the general will, since the general will is no longer present in the former powerholders. Whatever determinate element [*Bestimmtheit*] is posited as a means of enforcing anything against the supreme power must be invested not just with the possibility of power, but with real power. But since this power is in the hands of other representatives of the collective will, it is able to thwart [the efforts of] any such determinate element [*Bestimmtheit*], and to nullify whatever operations are entrusted to the ephorate – such as supervision, the public declaration of the interdict, and whatever formalities it may devise.[52] And it does so with the same right as those who were made responsible for the business of the [proposed] determinate element [*Bestimmtheit*]; for such ephors are likewise just as much private wills as the others, and whether the private will of the ephors has detached itself from the general will can just as readily be judged by the government as the latter can be judged by the ephorate – and the government can enforce its judgement absolutely [*schlechthin*]. It is well known that, when a government in recent times set about dissolving a rival legislative power which was paralysing its activity, a man who was himself involved rightly judged – when it was suggested that the establishment of a supervisory commission like Fichte's ephorate would have prevented such an outrage – that such a supervisory council would have been treated just as violently if it had attempted to oppose the government.[53] – But finally, even if those in supreme authority voluntarily agreed to permit these secondary representatives of the general will to summon the community to choose between the government and the supervisors, what could one do with such a mob, which also interferes in all private affairs, which is itself remote from public life, and whose education has not equipped it to be conscious of the collective will or to act in the spirit of the whole, but to do precisely the opposite?[54]

What this has shown is that, if ethical life [*das Sittliche*] is posited solely in terms of relations, or if externality and coercion are thought of as a totality, they cancel themselves out [*sich selbst aufhebt*]. This certainly proves that coercion is not something real and that it is nothing in itself; but this will become even clearer if we demonstrate it in terms of coercion itself, in accordance with its concept and with the determinate character [*Bestimmtheit*] which the relation of this association [*Beziehung*] assumes; for the fact that relation is absolutely nothing in itself is something which must in part be proved by dialectics, and which has in part already been briefly outlined above.

As to those concepts in general which have to do with coercion and which express this same relation, it has in part already been shown that they are insubstantial abstractions, products of thought or figments of the imagination without reality. In the first place, there is the hollow abstraction of the concept of the universal freedom of all, supposedly distinct from the freedom of individuals; then on the other hand, there is the latter freedom of the individual, equally isolated. Each, posited on its own [*für sich*], is an abstraction without reality; but both, as absolutely identical and then posited merely *in terms of* this first basic identity, are a very different thing from those concepts whose significance lies solely in their non-identity.[55] Then natural or original freedom is supposed to be limited by the concept of universal freedom; but the former freedom, which can be posited as subject to limitation, is for that very reason not something absolute. And then it is self-contradictory to construct an idea to the effect that the freedom of the individual, because of the externality of coercion, conforms with absolute necessity to the concept of universal freedom – which simply amounts to imagining that the individual, by virtue of something which is not absolute, is nevertheless absolutely equal to the universal. In the concept of coercion itself, something external to freedom is directly posited. But a freedom for which something is genuinely external and alien is not freedom at all; its essence and formal definition is precisely that nothing is absolutely external [to it].

That view of freedom which regards it as a choice between opposite determinacies (so that if +A and −A are given, freedom consists in determining oneself *either* as +A *or* as −A, and is completely tied to this *either-or*) must be utterly rejected. Anything resembling this possibility of choice is purely and simply an empirical freedom, which is the same thing as ordinary empirical necessity and is completely inseparable from it. Freedom is rather the negation or ideality of the opposites, of +A as well as −A, the abstraction of the possibility that neither of the two exists; something external would exist for it only if freedom were determined solely as +A or solely as −A. But freedom is the direct opposite of this: nothing is external to it, so that no coercion is possible for it.

Every determinacy is in essence either +A or −A, and the −A is indissolubly joined to the +A, just as the +A is to the −A. Thus, whenever an individual has adopted determinacy +A, he is also tied to −A, and −A is for him an external [element] over which he has no control. In fact, because of the absolute link between +A and −A, he would be brought, by the determinacy +A, directly under the alien power of −A, and the freedom which supposedly resides in determining itself either as +A or −A would never escape from necessity. If it determines itself as +A, it has not nullified −A; on the contrary, −A subsists absolutely necessarily for it as an external [element], and the converse applies if it determines itself as −A. Freedom is freedom only in so far as, either positively or negatively, it unites −A with +A and thereby ceases to occupy the determinacy +A. In the union of the two determinacies, both are nullified: $+A − A = 0$. If this nought is thought of only in relation to +A and −A, and the indifferent A itself is thought of as a determinacy and as a plus or minus in opposition to another minus or plus, absolute freedom stands above this opposition, and above any opposition or externality; it is utterly incapable of any coercion, and coercion has no reality whatsoever.

But this idea of freedom seems itself to be an abstraction; and if it were a question of concrete freedom and the freedom of the individual, for example, the existence [*Sein*] of a determinacy − and with it a purely empirical freedom as the possibility of choice − would be posited, and hence also empirical necessity and the possibility of coercion, and in general the opposition of universality and singularity [*Einzelheit*]. For the individual is a single entity [*Einzelheit*], and freedom is the nullification of singularity. By virtue of singularity, the individual is [placed] directly among determinacies, so that something external is present for him, and coercion is accordingly possible. But it is one thing to impose determinacies on the individual under the form of infinity, and another to impose them absolutely. Determinacy under the form of infinity is thereby superseded, and the individual exists [*ist*] only as a free being; that is, inasmuch as determinacies are posited within him, he is the absolute indifference of these determinacies, and it is in this that his ethical nature formally consists. And in so far as individuals in general are different [*different*] – whether in relation to themselves or to something else – and have a relationship [*Beziehung*] to something external, this externality is itself indifferent and a living relationship; and it is in this that organisation and (since totality is [to be found] only in an organisation) the positive [aspect] of ethical life consists. – But the indifference of the individual as a single entity is a negative one in relation to the being of the determinacies; when his being is actually posited as individuality, however (i.e. as a negation which he cannot positively overcome and a determinacy by which the external as such is maintained), all that he is left with is completely *negative* absoluteness or infinity – the absolute negation of both −A and +A, or the absolute elevation of this individual being to the concept. Since −A is an external element in relation to the subject's determinacy +A, the subject is under alien control as a result of this relation; but since the subject can equally well posit its +A negatively as a determinacy and supersede and dispose of it, it remains completely free in face of the possibility and actuality of alien power. If it negates +A as well as −A, it is constrained [*bezwungen*] but not coerced [*gezwungen*]; it would have to suffer coercion only if +A were absolutely fixed within it, because this would allow an infinite chain of further determinacies to be attached to this same subject as a determinacy itself. This possibility of abstracting from determinacies is unlimited; or [to put it differently,] there is no determinacy which is absolute, for this would be a direct self-contradiction. But though freedom itself – or infinity – is the negative, it is also the absolute, and the individual being of the subject is absolute singularity elevated to the concept, negatively absolute infinity, or pure freedom. This negatively absolute [element], this pure freedom, makes its appearance as death, and through his ability to die, the subject proves that he is free and utterly above all coercion. Death is the absolute constraint [*Bezwingung*]; and because this constraint is absolute, or because individuality becomes completely pure individuality within this constraint, and not a positing of +A to the exclusion of −A (an exclusion which would not be a true negation, but merely the positing of −A as something external and at the same time of +A as a determinacy), but the cancellation [*Aufhebung*] of both the plus and the minus, this individuality is its own concept, and consequently infinite. It is the opposite of itself, or absolute liberation, and the pure individuality which is in death is its own opposite, namely universality. Within this constraint, there is accordingly freedom, because it is directed purely towards the cancellation [*Aufhebung*] of a determinacy. It cancels not just one side of this determinacy, but cancels it both in so far as it is posited positively and in so far as it is posited negatively, subjectively as well as objectively; consequently this freedom, considered in itself, remains purely negative in character. Or, since the cancellation [*Aufheben*] itself can also be understood and expressed in positive terms by reflection, the cancellation of both sides of the determinacy will then appear as the wholly equal positing of both sides of whatever is determined.

If this is applied to punishment, for example, it follows that its only rational aspect is retribution; for it is by retribution that the crime is subjected to constraint [*bezwungen*]. A determinacy +A, which was posited by the crime, is complemented by the positing of −A, so that both are nullified; or viewed in positive terms, the determinacy +A is coupled for the criminal with determinacy −A and both are posited equally, whereas the crime posited only one of them. Thus, the punishment is the restoration of freedom; and not only has the criminal remained (or rather been made) free, but the administrator of the punishment has acted rationally or freely. In this, its [proper] determination, the punishment is accordingly something in itself, genuinely infinite and absolute, which therefore carries its own respect and fear within it; it derives from freedom, and even as a constraint [*als bezwingend*], it remains in freedom. But conversely, if punishment is understood [*vorgestellt*] as coercion, it is posited merely as a determinacy and as something wholly finite which embodies no rationality. It falls entirely under the common concept of one specific thing as against another, or of a piece of merchandise with which another commodity, namely the crime, can be bought. The state, as a judicial authority, runs a market in determinacies known as crimes, which it can buy in exchange for other determinacies [known as punishments], and the legal code is the list of current prices.

[III]

But however vacuous these abstractions and the relation of externality to which they give rise may be, the moment of the negatively absolute or infinity (which was noted in this example as determining the relation between crime and punishment) is a moment of the absolute itself which must be identified in *absolute ethical life*. We shall point out the versatility of absolute form (or infinity) in its necessary moments, and show how they determine the shape of absolute ethical life; from this, the true concept and relation of the practical sciences will in turn emerge. Since our primary concern here is to define the relations which all this involves, and hence to emphasise the aspect of infinity, we shall make the positive presupposition that the absolute ethical totality is nothing other than a *people*;[56] this will also become evident from the following moments of the negative aspect which we are considering here.

In absolute ethical life, infinity – or form as the absolutely negative – is nothing other than constraint itself, as interpreted above, elevated to its absolute concept. As such, it does not relate to individual determinacies, but to their entire actuality and possibility, namely life itself. Hence matter is equal to infinite form, but in such a way that its positive aspect is the absolutely ethical, namely [the quality of] belonging to a people; the individual proves his oneness with the people in a negative sense – and in an unambiguous manner – only by [incurring] the danger of death. Through the absolute identity of the infinite, or the aspect of relation with the positive, ethical totalities such as peoples take shape and constitute themselves as individuals, thereby adopting an individual stance in relation to [other] individual peoples. This stance and this individuality are the aspect of reality, and if we think of these as absent, they [i.e. the ethical totalities in question] are [mere] creations of thought; this would be the abstraction of essence without absolute form, and the essence in question would consequently be devoid of essence. This connection [*Beziehung*] of individuality with individuality is a relation, and is accordingly twofold: firstly, it is the positive connection of tranquil and equable co-existence of the two [ethical totalities or peoples] in peace, and secondly, it is the negative connection of the exclusion of one by the other – and both connections are absolutely necessary. With regard to the second, we have already interpreted the rational relation as a constraint elevated to its concept, or as the absolute formal virtue which is courage. It is this second aspect of the connection which posits the necessity of war for the shape and individuality of the ethical totality. In war, there is the free possibility that not only individual determinacies, but the sum total of these, will be destroyed as life, whether for the absolute itself or for the people. Thus, war preserves the ethical health of peoples in their indifference to determinate things [*Bestimmtheiten*]; it prevents the latter from hardening, and the people from becoming habituated to them, just as the movement of the winds preserves the seas from that stagnation which a permanent calm would produce, and which a permanent (or indeed 'perpetual') peace would produce among peoples.[57]

Since the shape of the ethical totality and its individuality are defined as outward-directed individuality and its movement is defined as courage, the negative aspect of infinity which we have just been considering is directly linked with its other aspect, namely the [continued] existence [*Bestehen*] of opposition. The one aspect is infinity, and like the others, it is negative; the first is the negation of the negation, opposition to opposition, and the second is negation and opposition itself in its [continued] existence [*Bestehen*] as determinacies or manifold reality. In the practical realm, these realities in their pure inner formlessness and simplicity – i.e. the feelings – are feelings which reconstruct themselves out of difference [*Differenz*], and which proceed from the supersession [*Aufgehobensein*] of undifferentiated self-awareness to restore themselves through a nullification of the intuitions. They are physical needs and pleasures which, in turn posited for themselves in their totality, obey one single necessity in their infinite complications, and form the system of universal mutual dependence with regard to physical needs and the labour and accumulation [of resources] which these require; as a science, this system is what is known as political economy.[58] Since this system of reality is [rooted] entirely in negativity and infinity, it follows that, in its relation to the positive totality, it must be treated wholly negatively by the latter and must remain subject to the dominance of this relation;[59] whatever is by nature negative must remain negative and may not become a fixture. In order to prevent it from constituting itself on its own account [*für sich*] and becoming an independent power, it is not enough to put forward the propositions that everyone has the right to live, and that the universal [interest] within a people must ensure that every citizen has a livelihood and that complete security and ease of acquisition prevails. The latter proposition, if taken as an absolute principle, would indeed rule out a negative treatment of the system of possession, and would give it complete latitude to become absolutely firmly established. Instead, the ethical whole must ensure that this system remains aware of its inner nullity, and prevent it from growing excessively in terms of quantity and from developing ever greater difference and inequality in keeping with its natural tendency.[60] This does indeed take place in every state, largely unconsciously and in the shape of an external natural necessity which it might well wish to be spared, as a result of ever-increasing expenditure on the part of the state itself; this increases with the growth of the system of possession, and leads to corresponding rises in taxation, thereby reducing possession and making acquisition more difficult. War does most to accelerate this tendency by bringing multiple confusion into the process of acquisition, but also by [encouraging] jealousy on the part of other classes [*Stände*] and placing restrictions on trade, some of them voluntary, others involuntary and the result of incomprehension, etc. This can go to such lengths that the positive ethical life of the state itself allows [people] independence from the purely real [economic] system, and allows the negative and restrictive attitude to be asserted.

In that context [*Beziehung*] in which it has just been considered – and of which physical need, enjoyment, possession, and the objects of possession and enjoyment are various aspects – reality is pure reality; it merely expresses the extremes of that relation. But the relation also contains an ideality, a relative identity of the opposing determinacies; this identity cannot therefore be positively absolute, but only formal. Through that identity which the real element in the nexus [*Beziehung*] of relations attains, possession becomes property, and particularity in general – including living particularity – is simultaneously determined as a universal; by this means, the sphere of right is constituted.[61]

As for the reflection of the absolute in this relation, it has already been defined above in its negative aspect, as a constraint on the subsistence of the real and the determinate. In its positive aspect with regard to the subsistence of the real, indifference can express itself in this determinate material only as an external and formal equality; and the science which deals with this matter can aim only to define the gradations of inequality on the one hand, and – in order to make this possible – to define on the other hand the way in which something living and internal can be posited sufficiently

objectively and externally to be capable of such definition and calculation. The absolute reality of ethical life at this level [*in dieser
Potenz*] is confined to this superficial appearance by the subsistence
of the reality which is present within the opposition.[62] Not only does
the equating and calculating of inequality have its limits (because of
the fixed determinacy which contains an absolute opposition) and,
like geometry, come up against incommensurability; it also necessarily [*schlechthin*] encounters endless contradictions, because it
remains wholly within [the sphere of] determinacy and yet cannot
abstract as geometry does, but – since it is dealing with living
relationships – is necessarily [*schlechthin*] always faced with whole
bundles of such determinacies. In the case of intuition, however,
this [mutual] contradiction of determinacies can of course be remedied and removed by specifying [*Festsetzen*] and adhering to individual determinacies, which allows a decision to be made – and this
is always better than reaching no decision at all. For since there is
nothing absolute in the material [*Sache*] itself, the essential factor is
actually the formal requirement that some decision and definition
or other should be arrived at. But it is quite a different matter for
a decision reached in this way to be in accordance with genuine and
complete justice and morality [*Sittlichkeit*]. For this very specifica-
tion of, and absolute adherence to, determinacies makes such justice
impossible; it is possible only when these determinacies are confused, and it becomes actual only through immediate ethical
intuition, which subjugates the determinacies which were posited
as absolute and adheres only to the whole. – When Plato, in his
simple language, discusses the two aspects of [firstly,] the endless
definition of the infinite incorporation [*Aufnahme*] of qualities into
the concept and [secondly,] the contradiction of their individuality
in relation to intuition, he says:[63]

> It is clear that lawmaking belongs to the science of kingship;
> but the best thing is not that the laws be in power, but that the
> man who is wise and of kingly nature be ruler [. . .] Because
> law could never, by determining exactly what is noblest and
> most just for one and all, enjoin upon them that which is best;
> for the differences of men and of actions and the fact that
> nothing, I may say, in human life is ever at rest, forbid any
> science whatsoever to promulgate any simple rule for every-
> thing and for all time [. . .] But we see that law aims at pretty

nearly this very thing, like a stubborn and ignorant man who allows no one to do anything contrary to his command, or even to ask a question, not even if something new occurs to some one, which is better than the rule he has himself ordained [. . .] So that which is persistently simple is inapplicable to things which are never simple.

The fact that there is still support for the belief [*Gedanke*] that absolute and determinate right and duty with being in themselves [*an sich seiend*] are possible in this sphere of human affairs is a consequence of that formal indifference or negative absolute which has its place only in the fixed reality of this sphere, and which does indeed have being in itself; but in so far as it has such being, it is empty – or [to put it differently,] there is nothing absolute about it except pure abstraction itself, the completely vacuous thought of unity. It is not, for example, a conclusion derived from prior experience, nor should it be regarded as a fortuitous incompleteness in the concrete [sphere] or in the implementation of an idea that is true a priori. On the contrary, it should be recognised [firstly,] that what is here described as an 'idea', and the hope for a better future derived from it, are inherently null and void, and [secondly,] that a perfect legislation, together with true justice in accordance with the determinacy of the laws, is inherently impossible in the concrete realm of judicial authority. As for the first of these impossibilities, since the absolute is supposed to be present in the determinacies as such, it is merely the infinite; and the same empirical infinity and inherently endless determinability is posited here as would be posited if we thought of comparing a determinate measure with an absolutely indeterminate line, or a determinate line with an absolutely indeterminate measure, or of measuring an infinite line or dividing a determinate line absolutely. As for the second impossibility, each of the views [*Anschauungen*] which are the object of jurisdiction – and which are likewise infinite in number and in their variety of forms – is defined in ever more various ways as the mass of definitions increases. This development [*Bildung*] of distinctions through legislation makes each individual view [*Anschauung*] more distinguishable and further developed, and the expansion of legislation is not an advance towards the goal of positive perfection (which, as already shown, has no truth in this context), but only the formal process of increasing development.[64] And in order that the unity [*das Eins*] of the judicial view [*Anschauung*] of right and judgement may become organised as a genuine unity [*Eins*] and whole within this multiplicity, it is absolutely necessary that each individual determinacy should be modified – i.e. partly superseded as an absolute determinacy with being for itself, which is precisely what it professes to be as a law – so that its absoluteness is not respected; and there can be no question of a pure application, for a pure application would involve positing some individual determinacies to the exclusion of others. But by their existence [*Sein*], these others also demand to be taken into account, so that the interaction [of them all], determined not by parts but by the whole, may itself be a whole. The empty hope and formal conception [*Gedanke*] both of an absolute legislation and of a jurisdiction unconnected with the inner disposition [*dem Innern*] of the judge must give way to this clear and definite knowledge.

This examination of the system of reality has shown that absolute ethical life must adopt a negative attitude towards this system.[65] The absolute, as it appears in the fixed determinacy of this system, is posited as a negative absolute, as infinity, which presents itself as a formal, relative, and abstract unity in relation to the opposition. In the former, negative attitude, the absolute is hostile to the system; in the latter, it is itself under its dominion; in neither case is it indifferent to it. But the unity which is the indifference of opposites, and which nullifies and comprehends them within itself, and that unity which is only formal indifference or the identity of the relation between existing [*bestehender*] realities, must themselves be wholly at one as a result of the complete incorporation [*Aufnahme*] of the relation into indifference itself; that is, the absolute ethical realm must take on a perfectly organised shape [*Gestalt*], for relation is the abstraction of the aspect of shape. Although relation becomes wholly undifferentiated as shape, it does not cease to possess the nature of relation: it remains a relation of organic to inorganic nature.[66] But as has already been shown, relation as an aspect of infinity is itself twofold in character: in one case, unity or the ideal comes first and predominates, and in the other, it is the many or the real which does so. In the first case, the relation is properly [to be found] in shape and indifference, and the eternal restlessness of the concept, or infinity, lies in part in the organisation itself as it consumes itself and relinquishes the appearance of life, the purely quantitative, in order to rise up eternally out of its ashes, as its own seed-corn, to renewed youth. And it lies in part in its eternal nullification of its outward difference as it feeds on and produces the inorganic, calling forth from indifference a difference [*Differenz*] or a relation to inorganic nature, then in turn cancelling [*aufhebend*] this relation and consuming both this nature and itself. We shall shortly see what this inorganic nature of the ethical is.[67] But secondly, the [continued] existence [*Bestehen*] of what was nullified is also posited in this aspect of relation or infinity, for precisely because the absolute concept is its own opposite, the being [*Sein*] of difference is also posited along with its pure unity and negativity. Or [to put it differently,] nullification posits something which it nullifies, i.e. the real, so that there must be an actuality and difference which cannot be overcome by ethical life. Since infinity has established itself here in the whole strength of its opposition (not just potentially but in fact), individuality is actually in opposition, and it would not be possible for it to purge itself of difference and be taken up into absolute indifference. If both [aspects], the supersession [*Aufgehobensein*] of the opposition and its subsistence, are to be not just ideal but also real, we must at all events posit a separation and selection whereby reality, in which ethical life is objective, is divided into one part which is taken up absolutely into indifference, and another part in which the real as such is subsistent (and hence relatively identical), and embodies only the reflection of absolute ethical life. What is posited here is a relation between absolute ethical life, as the essence of individuals and wholly immanent within them, and relative ethical life, which is no less real within them.[68] Ethical organisation cannot preserve its purity in reality unless the universal spread of negativity within it is curbed and set aside.[69] We have shown above how indifference appears in existing [*bestehenden*] reality as formal ethical life. The concept of this sphere is the real and the *practical*, in subjective terms with reference to feeling or physical needs and enjoyment, and in objective terms with reference to work and possession; and if this practical realm is taken up into indifference – as can happen in accordance with its concept – it is formal unity, or that *right* which is possible within this realm. Above these two [realms] is a third, the absolute or the *ethical*. But the reality of the sphere of relative unity (or of the practical and legal [*des Rechtlichen*]) is constituted, in the system of this sphere in its totality, as a distinct class [*eigener Stand*].

Thus, two classes [*Stände*] are formed in accordance with the absolute necessity of the ethical. One of these is the class of the free, the individual of absolute ethical life; its organs are the single individuals. From the point of view of its indifference, it is the absolute living spirit, and from the point of view of its objectivity, it is the living movement and divine self-enjoyment of this whole in the totality of the individuals who constitute its organs and members. But its formal or negative side must also be absolute – namely work, which is directed not towards the nullification of individual determinacies, but towards death, and whose product is again not something individual, but the being and preservation of the whole of the ethical organisation. Aristotle defines the proper business of this class as what the Greeks called πολιτεύειν, which means living in and with and for one's people, leading a universal life wholly dedicated to the public interest, or philosophising, while Plato, with his superior vitality, does not wish to regard[b] these two activities as separate but as indissolubly linked.[70] – Then there is the class [*Stand*] of those who are not free, and which has its being [*ist*] in the differentiation [*Differenz*] of need and work and in the right and justice of possession and property; its work deals with matters of detail and consequently does not entail the danger of death. To these must be added the third class which, in the crudity of its non-educative work, is solely concerned with the earth as an element; its work confronts it with the whole [sphere] of need as its direct object, with no intermediate links, and it is consequently itself an unalloyed totality and indifference, like an element. Lacking the differentiated understanding of the second class, it accordingly maintains its capacity, in body and spirit, for formal and absolute ethical life and for courage and a violent death, and is consequently able to reinforce the first class with its numbers and elemental being. – These two classes relieve the first class of a situation [*Verhältnis*] in which reality, partly in its passive and partly in its active aspect [*Beziehung*], is fixed either as possession and property or as

---

[b] *Translator's note*: Reading *sehen* (with *Werke*, vol. II, p. 489) for the *sein* of the first edition.

work, in the same way as, among modern nations, the earning class [*Klasse*] has confined itself to this function [of earning its living] and has gradually ceased to do military service, while valour has become more purified and developed into a particular class [*Stand*] released by the former from the need to earn its living, and for which possession and property, at least, are a contingent matter. The constitution of this second class, in its material aspect, is defined by Plato as follows.[71] The art of kingship removes

> those men who have no capacity for courage and self-restraint and the other qualities which tend towards virtue, but by the force of an evil nature are carried away into godlessness, violence, and injustice [. . .] by inflicting upon them the punishments of death and exile and deprivation of the most important civic rights [. . .] And those in turn who wallow in ignorance and craven humility it places under the yoke of slavery.

And Aristotle places in the same category anyone who is by nature not his own but someone else's, and who is like a body in relation to spirit.[72]

But the relation of one who is by nature someone else's, and who does not have his spirit within himself, to absolutely independent individuality may, in formal terms, be of two kinds – either a relation of the individuals of this class [*Stand*] as particulars to the individuals of the first class as particulars, or a relation of universal to universal. The former relation (of slavery) vanished of its own accord in the empirical phenomenon [*Erscheinung*] of the universality of the Roman Empire: with the loss of absolute ethical life and the debasement of the nobility, the two previously distinct classes became equal, and with the demise of freedom, slavery necessarily came to an end. When the principle of formal unity and equality was enforced, it completely cancelled [*hat . . . aufgehoben*] the true inner difference between the classes, and did not at first bring about that separation between them which was posited above. Still less did it bring about that form of separation whereby their relation to one another, under the form of universality, is one of domination and dependence, and purely that of one whole class to another, so that, even within this relation, the two associated classes remain universal. (In the relation of slavery, on the other hand, the form of particularity is the determining factor; it is not a case of one class against the other – on the contrary, the unity of each group [*Teil*] is dissolved in their real association [*Beziehung*], and individuals are dependent on individuals.) The principle of universality and equality first had to take possession of the whole in such a way as to mix the two classes together instead of separating them. In this mixture, under the law of formal unity, the first class is in fact completely annulled [*aufgehoben*],[73] and the second alone becomes the people.[74] Gibbon portrays this change in the following terms:[75]

> This long peace, and the uniform government of the Romans, introduced a slow and secret poison into the vitals of the empire. The minds of men were gradually reduced to the same level, the fire of genius was extinguished, and even the military spirit evaporated [. . .] Their personal valour remained, but they no longer possessed that *public* courage which is nourished by the love of independence, the sense of national honour, the presence of danger, and the habit of command. They received laws and governors from the will of their sovereign [. . .] The posterity of their boldest leaders was contented with the rank of citizens and subjects. The most aspiring spirits resorted to [. . .] the standard of the emperors; and the deserted provinces, deprived of political strength or union, insensibly sunk into the languid indifference of *private life*.[c]

– This universal private life, and a state of affairs in which the people consists solely of a second class, immediately introduces the formal legal relationship [*Rechtsverhältnis*] which fixes individual being and posits it absolutely; and it was indeed out of such corruption and universal debasement that the most comprehensive development of legislation relevant to this relationship grew and evolved.[76] This system of property and right which, because of the fixation of individuality already referred to, does not consist in anything absolute and eternal but wholly in the finite and formal, must constitute itself as a distinct [*eigenen*] class, really detached and set apart from the nobility, and then be able to expand throughout its entire length and breadth. To this system belong the inherently [*für sich*] subordinate and purely formal questions concerning the rightful basis of property, contract, etc., but also the whole endless expansion of legislation at large on matters which Plato categorises as follows:[77]

[c] *Translator's note*: The italics in this quotation are Hegel's.

These legal issues in contracts made by individuals with other individuals concerning goods or services, as well as [actions] for injury and assault, rulings on the competence and appointment of judges, or on the need to collect or impose tariffs in markets or ports, are matters on which it is unworthy to lay down rules for good and admirable men. For they will easily find out for themselves the many points which have to be settled in this regard, provided that God grants them the blessing of a truly ethical constitution. But if this is not the case, it follows that they will spend their lives regulating and amending many such things, in the belief that they will finally reach the best result; they will live like invalids who, out of intemperance, will not abandon their unhealthy diet, and achieve nothing by their remedies other than producing more varied and more serious illnesses, while constantly hoping to be cured by whatever means they are prescribed. Equally amusing are those who make laws on the matters in question, and constantly amend them in the belief that they will reach a conclusive result – unaware of the fact that they are, so to speak, cutting off a Hydra's head.

It is true that, as licentiousness and disease increase among a people, many lawcourts are opened, and no clearer sign of bad and shameful comportment can be found than that excellent physicians and judges are required not only by bad men and artisans, but also by those who pride themselves on having enjoyed a liberal education, and who are compelled to accept a justice imposed on them by others as their masters and judges and spend much time in courts of law with actions and defences.

This system must simultaneously develop as a universal condition, and must destroy free ethical life whenever it is combined with such circumstances and not separated from them and their consequences from the outset.[78] Thus it is necessary that this system should be consciously adopted, recognised in its [own] right, kept apart from the nobility, and given a class [*Stand*] of its own as its realm in which it can establish itself and develop its full activity by way of its own confusion and the superseding of one confusion by another. The status [*Potenz*] of this class is accordingly determined by the fact that its province is possession in general and the justice which is possible in this context, that it at the same time constitutes a coherent system, and that, as a direct consequence of the elevation of the relation of possession to formal unity, each individual who is inherently [*an sich*] capable of possession is related to all the others as a universal entity, or as a citizen in the sense of a *bourgeois*. For the political nullity which results from the fact that the members of this class are private individuals, these citizens find compensation in the fruits of peace and of gainful employment [*des Erwerbes*], and in the perfect security, both as individuals and as a whole, in which they enjoy them.[79] But the security of each individual is related to the whole, inasmuch as he is released from [the need for] courage and from the necessity (to which the first class is subject) of exposing himself to the danger of violent death, a danger which entails for the individual absolute insecurity in every enjoyment, possession, and right. Through the superseding of this mixture of principles and their constitutional and conscious separation, each of these principles receives its due [*sein Recht*], and only what ought to be is put into effect, namely the reality of ethical life as absolute indifference, and at the same time as the real relation within the opposition which is still present [*im bestehenden Gegensatze*], so that the latter is overcome [*bezwungen*] by the former and this constraint [*Bezwingen*] is itself rendered indifferent and reconciled. This reconciliation consists precisely in the recognition of necessity, and in the right which ethical life accords to its own inorganic nature – and to the chthonic powers – by giving up and sacrificing part of itself to them. For the potency of the sacrifice consists in facing up to [*in dem Anschauen*] and objectifying this involvement with the inorganic, and it is by facing up to it that it is dissolved. By this means, the inorganic is separated out and recognised as such, and thereby itself taken up into indifference, while the living, by relegating what it knows as part of itself to the inorganic [realm] and consigning it to death, simultaneously acknowledges the right of the inorganic and purges itself of it.[80]

This is nothing other than the enactment, in the ethical realm, of the tragedy which the absolute eternally plays out within itself – by eternally giving birth to itself into objectivity, thereby surrendering itself in this shape to suffering and death, and rising up to glory from its ashes.[81] The divine in its [visible] shape and objectivity immediately possesses a dual nature, and its life is the absolute oneness of its two natures. But the movement of the absolute antagonism between these two natures presents itself in the divine nature, which has thereby comprehended itself, as the courage with which this nature liberates itself from the death of the other, conflicting nature. Through this liberation, however, it gives up its own life, because this life exists [*ist*] only in its association with the other life, but is just as absolutely resurrected from it; for in this death, as the sacrifice of the second nature, death is overcome [*bezwungen*]. But appearing in its second nature, the divine movement presents itself in such a way that the pure abstraction of this nature (which would be a merely chthonic and purely negative power) is superseded by its living union with the divine nature. This union is such that the divine illuminates this second nature and, by this ideal spiritual oneness, makes it into its reconciled living body which, as body, simultaneously remains in difference [*Differenz*] and transience and, through the spirit, perceives the divine as something alien to itself. – The image of this tragedy, in its more specifically ethical determination, is the outcome of that legal process between the Eumenides (as the powers of the right which resides in difference) and Apollo (the god of undifferentiated light) over Orestes, played out before the organised ethical entity of the Athenian people.[82] In a [very] human way, the latter, as the Areopagus of Athens, puts equal votes in the urn for each of the two powers, and so acknowledges their co-existence. This does not, however, resolve the conflict or define the connection and relationship between them. But in a divine way, the Athenian people, as the goddess Athena, wholly restores to the god the man [i.e. Orestes] whom the god himself had involved in difference; and by separating those powers, both of which had had an interest in the criminal, it also effects a reconciliation in such a way that the Eumenides would [thereafter] be honoured by this people as divine powers and have their abode in the city, so that their savage nature might enjoy and be pacified by the sight of Athena enthroned high above on the Acropolis, opposite the altar erected to them in the city below.

Tragedy arises when ethical nature cuts its inorganic nature off from itself as a fate – in order not to become embroiled in it – and treats it as an opposite; and by acknowledging this fate in the [ensuing] struggle, it is reconciled with the divine being as the unity of both. *Comedy*, on the other hand (to develop this image further), will generally come down on the side of fatelessness.[83] Either it falls under [the heading of] absolute vitality, and consequently presents only shadows of antagonisms or mock battles with an invented fate and fictitious enemy; or it falls under [the heading of] non-vitality, and consequently presents only shadows of independence and absoluteness. The former is the old (or Divine) comedy, the latter is modern comedy. The *Divine Comedy* [of Dante] is without fate or genuine struggle, because absolute confidence and certainty concerning the reality of the absolute are present in it without opposition, and whatever opposition does bring movement into this perfect security and peace is only an opposition without seriousness or inner truth.[84] This opposition may present itself – in contrast to the divinity which appears as alien and external, though rooted in absolute certainty – as the remnant or dream of a consciousness of isolated self-sufficiency, or as a consciousness of individuality [*Eigenheit*] which, though fixed and firmly held on to, is completely impotent and powerless. Alternatively, the opposition may present itself in a divinity, sensible of itself and inherently conscious, which consciously generates antagonisms and forms of play [*Spiele*] in which, with absolute frivolity, it sets some of its members to compete for a specific prize and gestates its manifold aspects and moments until they are born into perfect individuality and develop organisations of their own. And even as a whole, it cannot treat its own movements as movements in response to fate, but as contingent happenings, and it regards itself as invincible, counts loss as nothing, is certain of its absolute control over every idiosyncrasy and eccentricity, and is aware of what Plato said in another context, namely that a city[d] is remarkably strong by nature.[85] Thus, an ethical organisation such as this will, for example, without risk or fear or envy, drive individual members to extremes of accomplishment in every art and science and skill, and make them special in their field, confident within itself that such divine monstrosities of beauty do not disfigure its shape, but are comic traits which enhance a [particular] moment within it. To cite one specific people, we may regard Homer, Pindar, Aeschylus, Sophocles, Plato, Aristophanes, etc. as such serene enhancements of individual traits. But both in the serious reaction to the increasingly serious nonconformity [*Besonderung*] of Socrates (not to mention the [subsequent] remorse this aroused), and in the teeming profusion and high energy of the

---

[d] *Translator's note*: Hegel uses the Greek term *polis*.

individualisations which were simultaneously emerging, we must not fail to recognise that the inner vitality [of the city] had thereby reached its extreme limits, and that it proclaimed, in the ripening of these seeds, not only its own strength but also the imminent death of the body which bore them.[86] It [i.e. the city] thus had to accept the antagonisms which it had itself provoked (and which it could formerly stir up and pursue as fortuitous events and with corresponding frivolity, even in their more serious and far-reaching manifestations such as wars) no longer as shadows, but as an increasingly overwhelming fate.[87]

But that *other comedy* whose complications are devoid of fate and genuine struggle (because ethical nature is itself caught up in that fate) is of a different class. Its plots are woven in conflicts which are not playful, but of serious significance for this ethical drive (though nevertheless comical for the spectator); and deliverance from these conflicts is sought in an affectation of character and absoluteness which constantly finds itself disappointed and deflated. The ethical drive (for it is not conscious and absolute ethical nature which features in this comedy) must, in short, transform the status quo [*das Bestehende*] into the formal and negative absoluteness of right, and thereby relieve its anxiety over the security of its possessions. It must raise its belongings to a position of security and certainty by means of agreements and contracts with all imaginable clauses and safeguards, deducing the requisite systems from experience and reason as [equivalent to] certainty and necessity itself, and backing them up with the most profound ratiocinations. But just as, according to the poet,[88] the spirits of the underworld saw the plantations they had established in the wilderness of hell swept away by the next tempest, so must the ethical drive observe how the next change, of course (or indeed resurgence) of the earth-spirit washes away half, or even the whole, of sciences which were proved by experience and reason, how one legal system is supplanted by another, how on the one hand humanity takes the place of severity, while on the other the will to power takes the place of contractual security, and how in the world of science and in actuality alike, the most well-earned and assured possessions of rights and principles are utterly destroyed. It [i.e. the ethical drive] must then either conclude that it is its own endeavours, hovering above fate with reason and will, which wear themselves out in such matters and have produced the changes in question, or grow incensed at their unexpected and gratuitous intervention, and first invoke all the gods in face of this necessity, and then resign itself to it. In both cases, the ethical drive, which looks for absolute infinity in these finite things, merely enacts the farce of its own faith and undying illusion which – at its darkest when it burns brightest – is already forlorn and mistaken [*im Unrecht*] when it believes that it rests in the arms of justice, stability, and enjoyment.

Comedy separates the two zones of the ethical in such a way as to allow each full play in its own right, so that in the one, oppositions and the finite are insubstantial shadows, whereas in the other, the absolute is an illusion. But the true and absolute relation is that the one does in all seriousness illuminate the other, each is tangibly [*leibhaft*] connected with the other, and each is the other's serious fate. The absolute relation is accordingly presented in tragedy.

For although, in the living shape or organic totality of ethical life, what constitutes the real aspect of that life is [to be found] in the finite, and therefore cannot in and for itself fully incorporate [*aufnehmen*] its own bodily essence into the divinity of that life, it nevertheless already expresses the absolute Idea of ethical life, albeit in a distorted form. Admittedly, ethical life does not inwardly unite into absolute infinity within itself those moments of the Idea which are of necessity kept apart; on the contrary, it has this unity only as a simulated negative independence, namely as freedom of the individual. But this real essence is nevertheless completely bound up with the absolute indifferent nature and shape of ethical life; and if it must perceive this nature only as something alien, it does nevertheless perceive it and is at one with it in spirit. Even for this real essence, it is of primary importance that the completely pure and indifferent shape and the absolute ethical consciousness should *be*, and it is a secondary and immaterial consideration that this essence, as the real, should relate to it [i.e. the absolute consciousness] only as its empirical consciousness – just as it is of primary importance that an absolute work of art should *be*, and only of secondary importance whether this specific individual is its author, or merely someone who contemplates and enjoys it. However necessary this existence of the absolute may be, it is equally necessary that there should be a division whereby there is on the one hand the living spirit, the absolute consciousness, and the absolute indifference of the ideal and real aspects of ethical life itself, and on the other, that spirit's corporeal and mortal soul and its empirical consciousness, which cannot completely unite its absolute form and its inner essence (although it enjoys its perception of the absolute as something alien, as it were, to itself). In its real consciousness, this spirit is at one with the absolute through fear and trust, as well as obedience; but in its ideal consciousness, it is wholly united with it in religion and the worship of a universal [*gemeinschaftlichen*] God.[89]

But what we [earlier] put on one side in connection with the external form of the first class [*Stand*] is the real absolute consciousness of ethical life. It is consciousness and, as such, in its negative aspect pure infinity and the highest abstraction of freedom – i.e. the relation of constraint [*Bezwingen*] pushed to the point of its own cancellation [*Aufhebung*], or freely chosen violent death; but in its positive aspect, this consciousness is the singularity and particularity of the individual. But this inherent negativity – namely consciousness in general – of which the distinctions just indicated are merely the two aspects, is absolutely incorporated [*aufgenommen*] into the positive, while its particularity and infinity or ideality are absolutely incorporated, in a perfect manner, into the universal and real; this oneness [of universal and particular] is the Idea of the absolute life of the ethical. In this oneness of infinity and reality in the ethical organisation, the divine nature (of which Plato says that it is an immortal animal, but one whose soul and body are eternally born together) seems at the same time to display its rich multiplicity in the highest energy of infinity and in that unity which becomes the wholly simple nature of the ideal element.[90] For although the most perfect mineral displays the nature of the whole in every part which is broken off from its mass, its ideal form is that of mutual externality, whether as the inner form of fragmentation or as the outer form of crystallisation, in contrast to the elements of water, fire, and air, in which each separate part is the perfect nature and representative of the whole, both in its essence and in its form (or infinity). Nor is the real form of such a mineral permeated by the true identity of infinity, for its senses are devoid of consciousness. Its light is a single colour, and it does not see; or it is indifferent to colour, and offers no point of resistance to the passage of colour through it. Its sound is heard when it is struck by an external body, but it does not sound of itself; its taste does not taste, its smell does not smell, and its weight and hardness have no feeling. If it does not share in the individual determinations of sense, but unites them in indifference, it is undeveloped and closed undifferentiatedness rather than that internally self-dividing unity which subordinates its own divisions. In the same way, those elements whose parts are all identical have within them only the possibility, but not the actuality, of difference [*Differenzen*], and have indifference only in the form of quantity, not qualitatively posited indifference. But the earth, as the organic and individual element, extends throughout the system of that element's shapes, from its primal inflexibility and individuality to qualitative characteristics and differentiation. Only in the absolute indifference of ethical nature does it reach its summation, attaining perfect equality of all its parts, and the absolute and real oneness of the individual with the absolute – in that primal aether[91] which, from its self-identical, fluid, and flexible form, disseminates its pure quality through individual formations into singularity [*Einzelheit*] and number, and completely dominates [*bezwingt*] this absolutely unyielding and rebellious system by refining number to pure unity and infinity, so that it becomes intelligence. Thus, the negative can become completely one with the positive by becoming absolutely negative; for the absolute concept is its own absolute and immediate opposite and, as one of the ancients puts it, 'the nothing is not less than the something'.[92] And in intelligence, the form or the ideal is absolute form and, as such, real; and in absolute ethical life, absolute form is combined with absolute substance in the most authentic manner [*auf das wahrhafteste*]. Of those individualised formations which lie between simple substance in reality as pure aether, and substance in its marriage with absolute infinity, none can bring form and qualitative unity to absolute indifference with the essence and substance that are found in ethical life (whether through the quantitative and elemental equality of the whole and the parts, or, in higher formations, through the individualisation which extends to more detailed aspects of the parts themselves), and at the same time bring about the formal unification of the parts into the whole (through the social bond among leaves in plants, in sexual union, or in the gregarious life and collective labour of animals). This is because it is in intelligence alone that individualisation is taken to its absolute extreme – namely to the absolute concept – and that the negative is taken to the absolute negativity of becoming its own unmediated opposite. Thus, intelligence is alone capable of being absolute universality (inasmuch as it is absolute individuality), absolute position [*Position*] and objectivity (inasmuch as it is absolute negation and subjectivity), and the highest identity of reality and ideality (inasmuch as it is absolute difference and infinity, absolute indifference, and totality – actually, in the development [*Entfaltung*] of all oppositions, and potentially, in their absolute nullification and unity).

The aether has disseminated its absolute indifference among the indifferences of light to [create] a multiplicity, and in the flowering of solar systems, it has given birth to its inner reason and totality in expansive form. But whereas these individualisations of light [i.e. the stars] are scattered in multiplicity, those which form their orbiting petals [i.e. the planets] must adopt a posture of rigid individuality towards them, so that the unity of the former lacks the form of universality, while the unity of the latter lacks pure unity, and neither of them embodies the absolute concept as such. In the system of ethical life, on the other hand, the unfurled flower of the heavenly system has closed up again, and the absolute individuals are completely united into universality. Reality – or the body – is in the highest degree at one with the soul, because the real multiplicity of the body is itself nothing other than abstract ideality, and the absolute concepts are pure individuals, so that the latter can themselves be the absolute system. Consequently, if the absolute is that which intuits [*anschaut*] itself as itself, and that absolute intuition and this self-cognition, that infinite expansion and this infinite withdrawal into itself, are completely one – and if both [processes], as attributes, are real – then spirit is higher than nature.[93] For if nature is absolute self-intuition and the actuality of the infinitely differentiated mediation and development [*Entfaltung*], then spirit, which is the intuition of itself as itself – or absolute cognition – is, in the withdrawal of the universe into itself, both the scattered totality of this multiplicity which it [i.e. the spirit] encompasses, and the absolute ideality of this same multiplicity, in which it nullifies this separateness and reflects it into itself as the unmediated point of unity of the infinite concept.[94]

Now from this idea of the nature of absolute ethical life, a relation arises which has still to be discussed, namely *the relation of the individual's ethical life to the real absolute ethical life*, as well as the relationship between the corresponding sciences, namely morality [*Moral*] and natural law.⁹⁵ For since real absolute ethical life comprehends and unites within itself infinity (or the absolute concept) and pure individuality in general and in its highest abstraction, it is immediately the ethical life of the individual; and conversely, the essence of the ethical life of the individual is quite simply the real (and hence universal) absolute ethical life – the ethical life of the individual is one pulse-beat of the whole system, and is itself the whole system. We also note in this connection a linguistic indicator which, though dismissed in the past, is completely vindicated by the foregoing – namely that it is in the nature of absolute ethical life [*Sittlichkeit*] to be a universal or an *ethos* [*Sitten*]. Thus, both the Greek word for ethical life and the German word express its nature admirably,⁹⁶ whereas the newer systems of ethics, which make a principle out of individuality and being-for-itself, cannot fail to reveal their allegiance [*Beziehung*] in [their use of] these words.⁹⁷ Indeed, this internal indicator proves so powerful that, in order to define *their own* enterprise [*Sache*], these systems were unable to misuse the words in question and adopted the word 'morality' [*Moralität*] instead; and although the latter's derivation points in the same direction, it is more of an artificial coinage and consequently does not so immediately resist its debased meaning.

It follows from what has been said, however, that absolute ethical life is so essentially the ethical life of everyone that one cannot describe it as reflected, as such, in the individual; for it is as much the essence of the individual as the aether which permeates nature is the inseparable essence of natural forms [*Gestalten*], and as space, the ideality of nature's appearances, is in no way particular to any of them. On the contrary, just as those lines and angles of the crystal in which it expresses the external form of its nature are negations, so likewise is ethical life, in so far as it expresses itself in the individual as such, negative in character [*ein Negatives*]. For first of all, it cannot express itself in the individual unless it is his soul, and it is his soul only in so far as it is a universal, and the pure spirit of a people.⁹⁸ The positive is by nature prior to the negative; or, as Aristotle puts it:⁹⁹

> The state [*Volk*] is more in accord with nature than is the individual; for if the individual, in isolation, is not self-sufficient, he must – like all [other] parts – constitute a *single* unit with

the whole. But anyone who cannot belong to a community [*wer
... nicht gemeinschaftlich sein kann*], or who requires nothing
since he is self-sufficient, is not part of the state [*Volk*] and is
therefore either an animal or a god.

And secondly, in so far as ethical life expresses itself in the individual as such, it is posited in the form of negation: that is, it is the
possibility of the universal spirit, and the ethical qualities which
pertain to the individual, such as courage or moderation or thrift or
generosity, etc., are negative ethical life (for in the particular sphere
of the individual, no individual characteristic is truly fixed, and no
real abstraction is truly made), and possibilities or capabilities of
partaking in universal ethical life. These virtues, which in themselves are potentialities and have a negative significance, are the
object of morality [*Moral*]; and it can be seen that the relation
between natural law and morality has in this way been inverted,
because only the sphere of the inherently negative properly belongs
to morality, whereas the truly positive belongs to natural law (as its
name suggests).[100] [The task of] natural law is to construct the way
in which ethical nature arrives at its true right. Conversely, if the
negative – both in itself and as the abstraction of externality, of the
formal moral law [*Sittengesetz*], of the pure will and the will of the
individual – along with the syntheses of these abstractions (such as
coercion, the limitation of individual freedom by the concept of
universal freedom, etc.), were defining properties of natural law,[e] it
would then be natural wrong [*Naturunrecht*], for if such negations
are treated as basic realities, ethical nature is plunged into the
utmost corruption and misfortune.

But given that these qualities are the reflection of absolute ethical
life in the individual as the negative (but the individual who is in
absolute indifference towards the universal and the whole), and are
consequently the reflection of that life in its pure consciousness,
they must also be reflected in its empirical consciousness, thereby
constituting the ethical nature of that second class [*Stand*] which is
rooted in firmly established reality – in possession and property as
distinct from courage. Now it is this reflection of ethical life which
corresponds, more or less, to morality [*Moralität*] in the usual

---

[e] *Translator's note*: Literally, 'natural right', which makes possible the subsequent
contrast with 'natural wrong'.

sense – the *formal* positing of the determinacies of the relation as indifferent, as in the ethical life of the *bourgeois* or private person, in which the difference [*Differenz*] of relations is fixed, and which depends on them and is in them.[101] A science of this morality is consequently in the first place a knowledge [*Kenntnis*] of these relations themselves, so that, in so far as they are considered with reference to the ethical realm (a reference which, given the absolute fixity [of these relations], can only be formal), that tautological formulation which was referred to above now comes into its own: this relation is only this relation; and if you are in this relation, then be in it with reference to the same; for if, in actions which have reference to this relation, you do not act with reference to it, you will nullify and cancel [*aufheben*] this relation. The true sense of this tautology likewise directly presupposes that this relation itself is not absolute, and consequently that the morality [*Moralität*] which is based on it is also relative [*etwas Abhängiges*] and not truly ethical. In the light of what was said above, this true sense emerges from the fact that only the form of the concept – i.e. its analytic unity – is the absolute, and hence the negatively absolute, because its content, which is determinate, contradicts the form.

But if those qualities which are truly ethical (inasmuch as the particular or negative appears within them) are wholly taken up into indifference, they can indeed be called ethical qualities; but they can be called virtues only if they are individualised once again with enhanced energy, and if they become – albeit within absolute ethical life – so to speak distinctive living shapes, like the virtues of Epaminondas, Hannibal, Caesar, and a few others. As energies of this kind, they are [particular] shapes, and are therefore not absolute in themselves, no more than are the shapes of other organic products [*Bildungen*]. They are rather a more powerful manifestation of one aspect of the Idea of the whole, and the morality [*Moral*] of virtues, or ethics [*Ethik*] (if we wish to define the morals of morality [*die Moral der Moralität*] in general and use the term 'ethics' [*Ethik*] as a description of virtue), must therefore consist only of a natural description of the virtues.

Now given that ethics is associated with the subjective or the negative, a distinction must be made, within the negative at large, between the negative as the subsistence of difference [*Differenz*] and the negative as the absence of difference.[102] We have already discussed the first of these negatives; but the second, i.e. the absence of difference, presents the totality as something enclosed and undeveloped [*unentfaltet*], in which movement and infinity are not present in their reality. In this negative form, the living principle [*das Lebendige*] is the *development* [*das Werden*] of ethical life, and *education* [*Erziehung*] is by definition the emergent and progressive cancellation [*Aufheben*] of the negative or subjective. For the child, as the potential form of an ethical individual, is a subjective or negative being whose growth to maturity marks the end of this form, and whose education [*Erziehung*] is the correction or suppression [*Bezwingen*] of it. But the positive and essential aspect of the child is that it is nourished at the breast of universal ethical life, lives at first in the absolute intuition of that life as an alien being, increasingly comprehends it, and so becomes part of the universal spirit. It follows automatically that neither the above-mentioned virtues nor absolute ethical life – nor the development of these through education [*Erziehung*] – is an attempt to attain a distinct and separate ethical life, and that it is futile and inherently impossible to strive for an ethical life of a distinct and positive kind. As far as ethical life is concerned, the words of the wisest men of antiquity are alone true: the ethical consists in living in accordance with the ethics [*Sitten*] of one's country; or (with reference to education), as a Pythagorean replied when someone asked him how best to educate his son: 'make him the citizen of a well-managed nation [*Volk*]'.[103]

Thus, the absolutely ethical has its proper organic body in individuals; and its movement and life [*Lebendigkeit*] in the common being and activity of everyone is absolutely identical in its universal and particular forms.[104] We have just considered it in its particularity – though in such a way that its essence is the absolutely identical; but at all events, we have considered it in that identity. Thus, in the *form of universality* and cognition, it must also present itself as a *system of legislation* – so that this system perfectly expresses reality, or the living customs [*Sitten*] of the present. This will ensure that a situation does not arise – as often happens – in which it is impossible to recognise what is right and what has actuality within a people by looking at its laws. Such ineptitude in expressing [a nation's] genuine customs in the form of laws, and the fear of *think-ing*[f] these customs, of regarding and acknowledging them as one's

---

[f] *Translator's note*: Translator's italics.

own, is the mark of barbarism.[105] But this ideality of customs and their form of universality in the laws must also – in so far as it subsists as ideality – in turn be perfectly united with the form of particularity, so that the ideality as such may take on a pure and absolute shape, and thus be perceived and worshipped as the god of the people; and this perception itself must in turn have its active expression [*Regsamkeit*] and joyful movement in a cult.[106]

[IV]

We have so far presented absolute ethical life in the moments of its totality, and constructed its Idea. We have also demolished the distinction which is commonly made in this connection between legality and morality [*Moralität*], along with the related abstractions concerning the universal freedom of formal practical reason, and shown them to be groundless intellectual constructions [*Gedankendinge*]. And we have defined the differences between the sciences of natural law and morality [*Moral*] in accordance with the absolute Idea – not, as it happens, by combining the principles of both, but by cancelling [*Aufhebung*] them and constituting the absolute ethical identity.[107] We have thereby demonstrated that the essence of these sciences is not an abstraction, but the living principle [*Lebendigkeit*] of the ethical, and that the difference between them concerns only their external and negative aspects. We have also shown that this difference is the complete opposite of the other distinction [referred to above], according to which the essence of natural law resides in its formal and negative quality, and that of morality in its absolute and positive quality, but in such a way that even this absolute quality is in truth no less formal and negative [than its opposite]; and what is here described as formal and negative is in fact nothing at all.

Now in order to specify *the relation of natural law to the positive sciences of right*, we need only pick up its threads at the point where we ceased to follow them, and indicate where this relation ends.

From the outset, we should note in general that philosophy arbitrarily defines its own limits in relation to a specific science by means of the universality of the concept of a determinacy or potentiality [*Potenz*]. The specific science is nothing other than the progressive presentation and analysis (in the higher sense of that word) of how that which philosophy leaves undeveloped – as a simple determinacy – in turn branches out and is itself a totality. But the possibility of such a development lies *formally* in the fact that the law of absolute form and totality whereby a determinacy can be further recognised and developed is immediately present in the Idea. But the real possibility is present because such a determinacy or potentiality [*Potenz*] which philosophy has not developed is not an abstraction or genuinely simple atom, but – like everything in philosophy – a reality, and a reality is a reality because it is a totality, and itself a system of potentialities [*Potenzen*]; to present the potentiality as such is the development appropriate to the science in question.[108]

It follows from this that we can declare in advance that a considerable part, if not all, of what are known as the positive sciences of right will fall within a fully developed and comprehensively formulated philosophy, and that they are neither excluded from, nor set at odds with, philosophy by the fact that they constitute sciences in their own right; no true distinction between this body of sciences and philosophy is posited by their having being for themselves [*Fürsichsein*] and being empirically distinct. The fact that they call themselves empirical sciences, some of which have their application in the actual world and attempt to make their laws and procedures acceptable even to ordinary ways of thinking, while others refer to the individual systems of existing constitutions and legislations and belong to a specific people and a specific age, does not create any distinction which necessarily excludes them from philosophy. For nothing needs to be more applicable to actuality than the products of philosophy, or to be more fully justified in relation to the universal way of thinking (that is, the truly universal way, for there are common ways of thinking which are also highly particular); nor does anything have to be so highly individual, alive, and enduring as they do. But before we can discuss the relationship of these sciences to philosophy, we must first establish and define a distinction by virtue of which they are positive sciences.

First of all, the positive sciences include in that actuality to which they claim to refer not only historical material, but also concepts, principles, relations, and in general much that in itself pertains to reason and is supposed to express an inner truth and necessity. Now to appeal to actuality and experience in this context and to defend them against philosophy as positive factors must be recognised as wholly [*an und für sich*] inadmissible. It is impossible that anything which is proved by philosophy not to be real should genuinely occur in experience; and if positive science appeals to reality and experience, philosophy can enunciate its proof of the non-reality – even in an empirical context [*Beziehung*] – of the concept asserted by positive science, and deny that what the latter professes to find in experience and actuality can in fact be found there. Philosophy will of course acknowledge the belief that something of the sort is experienced – [though only as] a random and subjective view. But when positive science professes to discover and identify its ideas [*Vorstellungen*] and basic concepts in experience, it claims to assert something real, necessary, and objective, and not just a subjective view. Philosophy alone can establish whether something is a subjective view or an objective idea [*Vorstellung*], an opinion or a truth. It can allow positive science its own procedure *ad hominem*, and in addition to denying the fact that an idea of that science occurs in experience, it can assert the contrary view that only a philosophical idea can be found there. The reason why philosophy can point to its ideas in experience is directly attributable to the ambiguous nature of what is known as experience. For it is not immediate intuition itself, but intuition raised to an intellectual level, conceived by thought [*gedacht*] and explained, divested of its singularity [*Einzelheit*], and expressed as a necessity, which counts as experience.[109] Thus, the most important aspect of what is singled out in and as experience is not what we may call actuality (with reference to that division which thought introduces into intuition). But once intuition is drawn into the field of thought, opinion must yield to the truth of philosophy. That distinction between what positive science believes it has derived directly from intuition (but by means of which it has itself determined the latter, applying a relation and concept to it), and what does not belong to thinking, is in any case very easy to demonstrate – as is philosophy's complete competence to regulate such matters. Furthermore, this kind of thinking, with its appeals to actuality, tends to be truly positive in its opinions because it is [at home] in opposition and clings to determinacies, and consequently treats products of thought or of the imagination as absolute and derives its principles from them. Thus it always runs the risk that every determinacy [to which it clings] may be proved to it to be the opposite determinacy, and that the opposite conclusions may be drawn from what it itself assumes. Similarly, if the increased density or specific weight of a body is explained by an increase in the force of attraction, it can equally well be explained by an increase in the force of repulsion, for there can only be as much attraction as there is repulsion. The one has significance only with reference to the other, and the extent to which the one exceeded the other would be the extent to which it did not exist at all; consequently, what is supposed to be seen as an increase in the one can be seen precisely as an increase in the other.

For example, in natural law in general or the theory of punishment in particular, a relation may be defined as coercion, while philosophy proves the nullity of this concept and positive science invokes experience and actuality to show that the coercion actually is real and actually does take place. The non-reality of this concept, as proved by philosophy, can, however, be expressed with equal justice and with reference to experience and actuality, so as to argue that there is no such thing as coercion, and that no human being ever is or ever has been coerced. For everything here depends exclusively on the way in which the phenomenon is explained, and on whether, for the purposes of the idea [*Vorstellung*] of coercion, something is regarded as merely external or as internal. Thus, if it is intended to demonstrate the existence of coercion in a given instance, the very opposite can be shown to be true of one and the same phenomenon – namely that it is not a [case of] coercion, but rather an expression of freedom; for the very fact that the phenomenon is elevated to the form of an idea [*Vorstellung*] and thereby determined by internal or ideal factors means that the subject is free in relation to it. And if, in order to eliminate the opposition of internal factors or of freedom, what was supposed to be seen as external coercion is itself internalised and a psychological coercion is accordingly postulated, this internalisation of the external is of equally little help. For thought remains completely free, and psychological or intellectual coercion [*Gedankenzwang*] cannot tie it down. The possibility of cancelling [*aufzuheben*] the determinacy which is contemplated [*vorgestellt*], and which is supposed to serve as coercion, is absolute; if punishment threatens the loss of a [specific] determinacy, it is entirely possible to accept this loss and to give up [freely] what the law proposes to take away by way of punishment. Thus if it is argued, in explanation of a given phenomenon, that the idea [*Vorstellung*] of a [specific] determinacy functions, or has functioned, as coercion, the opposite explanation – i.e. that the phenomenon is an expression of freedom – is likewise entirely possible. The fact that the sensuous incentive – either that which supposedly prompts the action or the legal means which is supposed to deter it – is psychological (i.e. internal) in character, immediately places it in [the realm of] freedom, which can either abstract from it or not; and in either case, freedom of the will is involved. But if it is objected that people *believe* there is coercion (including psychological coercion), and that this is a universal attitude, this is firstly untrue, for it is equally well (and doubtless more universally) believed that an action, or non-action, is the product of free will. Besides, there is no more need to worry about opinion in setting up principles and defining laws than there is for astronomers to be held up in their understanding of the laws of the universe by the opinion that the sun, the planets, and all the stars revolve round the earth, or are no bigger than they seem, etc. – as little as the owner of a ship worries about the opinion that the ship is stationary and the shore is moving past. If each of these were to be guided by opinion, the former would find it impossible to comprehend the solar system, and the latter would tell the oarsmen to stop work or lower the sails. Both would instantly find it impossible to achieve their ends, and immediately become aware of the non-reality of the opinion in question as soon as they tried to concede its reality – just as it was shown above that, if coercion is taken to be a reality (i.e. conceived of [*vorgestellt*] as part of a system within a totality), it immediately cancels [*aufhebt*] itself and the whole.

Given that a determinacy of this kind, upheld by positive scientific opinion, is its own direct opposite, it is equally possible for each of two parties who attach themselves to opposite determinacies to refute the other. This possibility of refutation consists in showing that any [specific] determinacy is completely unthinkable, and that it is nothing at all without reference to its opposite. But because it has being and significance only with reference to this opposite, the latter likewise can and must immediately be present and demonstrated. From the fact that +A is meaningless without reference to −A, it can be proved that −A is immediately present with +A, which one's opponent will take to mean that −A rather than +A is present; but the same can be said in reply to his −A. Often, however, we do not even trouble to do so; and with regard to that freedom, for example, which is opposed to sensuous motives and which, because of this opposition, is no more truly free than they are, we omit to point out that everything which purports to be an expression of this freedom must in fact be explained as an effect of the sensuous motives. This can be done very easily; but it is just as easy to show conversely that what is supposed to be experienced as the effect of a sensuous motive should in fact be experienced as an effect of freedom. Instead, we simply abstract from freedom and assert that it has no place here, because it is internal – or rather moral or even metaphysical – in character. But what is overlooked in this case is that the other determinacy with which we are left (namely coercion, and the sensuous motive whereby this coercion is posited as external) has no significance without the opposite, internal factor (i.e. freedom), and that freedom simply cannot be separated from coercion. If we consider a criminal act from the point of view that it has a *determinate* aim which runs counter to the threatened punishment, and to the sensuous motive which the law introduces by means of this threat, then this determinate aim is described as sensuous, and it will be said that the source of the crime is a sensuous stimulus. But if we adopt the point of view that the act is a [product of] volition, with the possibility of abstracting from the sensuous motive specified by the law, it will appear to be free. Neither view – neither the former determinacy nor the latter possibility – can be ruled out, for the one is absolutely tied to the other, so that each can be directly deduced from its opposite. But the logic of opinion maintains that if a determinacy, or an opposite, is posited, one can then actually abstract from the other, opposite determinacy and eliminate it. Because of the nature of its principle of contradiction, this logic is likewise quite unable to grasp that, in the case of such determinacies, the opposite of each is completely irrelevant in defining one's perception [*Anschauung*], and that in this abstraction and negative being [*Wesen*], one opposite is exactly the same as the other. Nor is it able to grasp that the two together, e.g. freedom contrasted with sensuousness, like sensuousness and coercion, are simply not real, but merely products of thought and figments of the imagination.

Thus, in so far as a science of right is positive (in that it clings to opinions and insubstantial abstractions), its invocation of experience, or of its applicability, by definition, to actuality, or of sound common sense and universal attitudes, or even of philosophy, makes no sense whatsoever.

Now if we look more closely at the basis on which science becomes positive in the manner indicated above, and if we consider in general the basis of appearance [*Schein*] and opinion, we discover that it lies in *form* – in so far as what is ideally opposite and one-sided, and has reality only in absolute identity with its own opposite, is isolated, posited as existing independently [*für sich seiend*], and declared to be real. It is by this form that intuition is immediately cancelled [*aufgehoben*], and the whole is dissolved and ceases to be a whole and a real entity; consequently, this distinction between the positive and the non-positive has nothing to do with content. Through this form, it is possible not only for a purely formal abstraction to be fixed and falsely described as a truth and reality (as indicated above), but also for a true idea and genuine principle to be misunderstood with regard to its limit, and posited outside that area [*Potenz*] in which it has its truth, thereby forfeiting its truth altogether. That a principle belongs to a [specific] area is an aspect of its determinacy; but within that area itself, this determinacy is both present [in] undifferentiated [form] and really permeated by the Idea, which makes it a true principle. It is then recognised as the Idea, appearing in these determinacies as their shape [*Gestalt*], but only as the principle of this [specific] area, so that its limits and conditionality are also thereby recognised. But it is completely divorced from its truth if it is absolutised in its conditionality, or even applied more widely to the nature of other areas [*Potenzen*]. The absolutely clear unity of ethical life is absolute and living, to the extent that neither an individual area nor the subsistence of such areas in general can be fixed. On the contrary, just as ethical life eternally expands them, it just as absolutely breaks them down and annuls [*aufhebt*] them and enjoys itself in undeveloped unity and clarity; and as far as the [specific] areas [*Potenzen*] are concerned, secure in its own inner life and indivisible, it now diminishes one by means of the other, now passes over entirely into one and destroys the others, and in turn withdraws altogether from this movement into absolute rest, in which all are annulled [*aufgehoben*]. Conversely, sickness and the seeds of death are present if one part organises itself and escapes from the authority of the whole; for by isolating itself in this way, it affects the whole negatively, or even forces it to organise itself solely for [the benefit of] this area; it is as if the vitality of the intestines, which serves the whole [organism], were to form itself into separate animals, or the liver were to make itself the dominant organ and compel the entire organism to perform its function. Thus it can happen in the universal system of ethical life that the principle and system of civil right, for example, which concerns property and possession, becomes totally immersed in itself and, losing itself in discursiveness, regards itself as a totality which has being in itself and is unconditional and absolute. The inner negativity of this area [*Potenz*], even in respect of its content (which is the finite in its subsistence), has already been defined above, and it is even more difficult to regard the reflection of the indifference which is possible within this content as absolute. It is equally impossible for the system of acquisition and possession itself, the wealth of a people – or again an individual area [*Potenz*] within this system (whether agriculture, manufactures and factory production, or commerce) – to be transformed into something unconditional.

But an individual area [*Potenz*] becomes even more positive if it and its principle forget their conditionality to such an extent that they encroach upon others and subordinate them to themselves.[110] Just as the principle of mechanics has intruded into chemistry and natural science, and that of chemistry has in turn forced its way into the latter in particular, the same has happened to the philosophy of ethics at various times and with various principles. But in recent times, in the internal economy of natural law, that external justice – or infinity reflected in the subsistence of the finite, and hence formal infinity – which constitutes the principle of civil law [*bürgerliches Recht*] has gained a special predominance over constitutional and international law. The form of a relationship as subordinate as that of contract has intruded upon the absolute majesty of the ethical totality. In the case of monarchy, for example, the absolute universality of the central point and the unitary being of its particular occupant are at one moment interpreted (in the manner of a contract of authorisation) as a relation between a top civil servant and the abstraction of the state, and at the next (in the manner of ordinary contractual relationships in general) as a transaction [*Sache*] between two specific parties, each of whom has need of the other, and hence as an exchange of services; and by relations such as these, which are wholly within the finite realm, the Idea and the absolute majesty [of the ethical totality] are immediately nullified. It is likewise inherently contradictory if, in international law, the relations between absolutely independent and free nations [*Völker*], which are ethical totalities, are defined in the manner of a civil contract, which directly involves the individuality and dependence of the subjects [*Subjekte*] concerned. Thus constitutional law as such could also seek to apply itself entirely to individual matters and, as a perfect police-force, to permeate the being of each individual completely, thereby destroying civic freedom – and this would be the harshest despotism; in this way, Fichte wishes to see the entire activity and being of the individual as such supervised, known, and determined by the universal and the abstraction to which he stands opposed.[111] The moral principle could also seek to intrude into the system of absolute ethical life and to take over public and civil law, and international law as well. This would be the greatest weakness and equally the basest despotism, as well as the complete loss of the Idea of an ethical organisation; for the moral principle – like the principle of civil law – exists only in the finite and individual realm.

In science, such consolidation and isolation of individual principles and their systems, and their encroachment on others, is prevented only by philosophy.[112] For the part does not recognise its limits, but must rather tend to constitute itself as a whole and as an absolute, while philosophy stands above the parts in the Idea of the whole, and thereby keeps each part within its limits; and by the loftiness of the Idea itself, it prevents the parts, in their further subdivision, from proliferating into endless minutiae. In the same way, this limitation and idealisation of the [specific] areas [*Potenzen*] presents itself in reality as the history of the ethical totality, in which the latter fluctuates between the opposites with the passage of time, steadfast in its absolute equilibrium. It sometimes reminds constitutional law of its own determinacy by giving somewhat greater weight to civil law, and at other times creates cracks and fissures in the latter by giving greater weight to the former, thus in general revitalising each system for a time by strengthening its presence within it, and reminding all, in their separate existence, of their temporality and dependence. It also destroys their prolific expansion and self-organisation by suddenly confounding them all on particular occasions, presenting them in their self-absorption and then releasing them, reborn from unity, with a memory of this dependence and an awareness of their own weakness whenever they try to exist on their own [*für sich*].

This character of the positivity of the legal sciences relates to the form in which one area [*Potenz*] isolates itself and posits itself as absolute; and in this respect, not only religion and whatever else [one cares to name], but also every philosophical science can be distorted and contaminated. But we must also consider positivity in its material aspect. For although both what we earlier described as positive and what we are now considering as material belong to the particular realm, what we considered earlier was the external connection of the form of universality with particularity and determinacy, whereas we are now considering the particular as such.

And in this regard, we must above all defend against formalism everything which, in material terms, can be posited as positive. For formalism breaks up intuition and its identity of the universal and the particular, and treats the abstractions of the universal and the particular as opposites; and whatever it can exclude from this emptiness and yet subsume under the abstraction of particularity, it regards as positive. It overlooks the fact that, through this opposition, the universal becomes no less positive than the particular; for as was shown above, it becomes positive through the form of opposition in which it is present in that abstraction. But the real is purely and simply an identity of the universal and the particular, and consequently that abstraction, and the positing of one of the opposites which arise from that abstraction – i.e. of the universal as something which has being in itself – cannot take place. If formal thinking is at all consistent, it must have no content whatsoever if it regards the particular as positive. In the pure reason of formal thinking, all multiplicity and all possibility of discrimination must disappear, and it is impossible to imagine how such thinking could ever arrive at even a minimal number of rubrics and chapter-headings; just as those who view the organism essentially in terms of the abstraction of a vital force ought in fact to regard the limbs and brain and heart and all the abdominal organs as particular, contingent, and positive, and to ignore them altogether.

Ethical life, like all living things, is simply an identity of universal and particular, and it is therefore an individuality and a shape. It embodies particularity, necessity, and relation (i.e. relative identity), but since these are undifferentiated and assimilated to it, it is free in this identity. And although reflection may regard it as particular, it is not something positive or opposed to the living individual, which is consequently associated with contingency and necessity, but is [itself] alive. This aspect is its inorganic nature, but it has organised it as part of itself in its shape and individuality.[113] Thus – to name the most general factors – the specific climate of a nation [*Volk*], and its chronological position in the development of the race in general, belong to necessity, and only *one* link in the far-reaching chain of necessity relates to its present condition. This link should be understood, with reference to the former aspect, in terms of geography, and with reference to the latter, in terms of history. But ethical individuality [*Individualität*] has made itself an organic part of this link, and the determinate character [*Bestimmtheit*] of this link has nothing to do with this individuality, but with necessity; for the ethical vitality of the people consists precisely in the fact that the people has a shape in which its determinate character [*Bestimmtheit*] is present, though not as something positive (in the sense in which we have hitherto used this word), but absolutely united with universality and animated by it. And this aspect is also very important both as a means of recognising how philosophy teaches us to honour necessity, and because this aspect is a whole, and only a limited view confines itself to individual characteristics [*die Einzelheit*] and despises them as contingent; but it is also important because this aspect supersedes the view of individuality [*Einzelheit*] and contingency by showing how these do not hinder life in itself, but that life, by allowing individuality and contingency to [continue to] exist [*bestehen*] as they are of necessity, simultaneously rescues them from necessity, and permeates and animates them.[114] Just because the elements of water and air, to which different parts of the animal kingdom are organically adapted, are individual elements, they are not something positive or dead for the fish and the birds respectively. Equally, *this* [particular] form in which ethical life is organised in this [particular] climate and this [particular] period of a particular culture (or of culture in general) is not [merely] positive in this context. Just as the totality of life is no less present in the nature of the polyp than in the nature of the nightingale or the lion, so has the world spirit enjoyed its weaker or more developed – but none the less absolute – [modes of] self-awareness in each of its shapes; and it has enjoyed itself and its own being in every people and in every ethical and legal whole.[115]

Each stage [in the process] is also externally justified; and this external aspect belongs to necessity as such, for even in this abstraction of necessity, individuality [*die Einzelheit*] is in turn completely cancelled [*aufgehoben*] by the Idea. This individuality of the stage of the polyp and the nightingale and the lion is a potentiality [*Potenz*] within a whole, and it is honoured within this context. Above the individual stages, there hovers the Idea of the totality, but it is reflected back from its whole scattered image in which it perceives and recognises itself; and this totality of the extended image is the justification of the individual [*des Einzelnen*] as subsistent. It is therefore the formal viewpoint which confers the form of particularity on an individuality [*Individualität*] and cancels [*aufhebt*] that vitality in which particularity is real; but where the reality of a particular stage is posited, it is the empirical viewpoint which demands a higher stage. That higher stage is equally present, both empirically and even in its developed reality: the higher development of plant life is present in the polyp, the higher development of the polyp in the insect, etc. Only empirical unreason claims to discern in the polyp the empirical expression of the higher stage of the insect. A polyp which is not a polyp remains only a specific piece of dead matter to which I have an empirical relation [*Beziehung*]; it is dead matter because I posit it as an empty possibility of being something else, and this emptiness is death. But if our concern is with the expression of something higher [*die höhere Darstellung*] without an empirical relation, this can indeed be found, for it must be present in keeping with absolute necessity. – Thus the feudal system, for example, may well appear as something wholly positive. But in the first place, as far as necessity is concerned, it is not an absolute individual [entity], but exists entirely within the totality of necessity. Internally, however, in relation to life itself, the question of whether it is positive depends on whether the nation [*Volk*] concerned has genuinely organised itself as an individuality within it, whether it completely fills the shape of that system and permeates it with its life, and whether the law of these relations is [based on] custom [*Sitte*]. Thus, if it happens that the genius of a nation is weaker and altogether of a lower order (and the weakness of ethical life is at its most acute in barbarism or in a formal culture); if the nation has let itself be conquered by another nation and has had to forfeit its independence (and has consequently preferred misfortune and the shame of lost independence to conflict and death);[116] if it has sunk so crudely into the reality of animal life that it cannot even rise to formal ideality and the abstraction of a universal (so that, in determining relations for its physical needs, it cannot support the relation of right, but only that of personality); or similarly, if the reality of the universal and of right has lost all credence and truth and the nation cannot feel or enjoy the image of divinity within itself, but must place it outside itself and make do with a vague feeling towards it, or with the highly painful feeling of great distance and sublimity – under circumstances such as these, the feudal system and servitude have absolute truth, and this relationship is the only possible form of ethical life, and hence the necessary, just, and ethical form.

It is this individuality of the whole, and the specific character of a nation [*Volk*], which also enable us to recognise the whole system into which the absolute totality is organised. We can thereby recognise how all the parts of the constitution and legislation and all determinations of ethical relations are completely determined by the whole, and form a structure in which no link or ornament was present a priori in its own right [*für sich*], but all came about through the whole to which they are subject. In this sense, Montesquieu based his immortal work on his perception of the individuality and character of nations [*Völker*], and even if he did not ascend to [the height of] the most vital Idea, he certainly did not deduce the individual institutions and laws from so-called reason, nor did he abstract them from experience and then elevate them to universal status. Instead, he understood both the higher relations in the sphere of constitutional law, and the lower determinations of civil relations down to wills, laws concerning marriage, etc., solely in the light of the character of the whole and its individuality. As for those empirical theorists who imagine that their knowledge of the contingent elements in their political and legal systems is based on reason, or derived from common sense itself or even from universal experience, he showed them, in a way which they could understand, that the reason, common sense, and experience from which specific laws are derived are not reason and common sense a priori, let alone experience a priori (which would be absolutely universal), but quite simply the living individuality of a nation [*Volk*][117] – an individuality whose most prominent characteristics [*höchste Bestimmtheiten*] should in turn be understood in terms of a more general necessity.

It was shown above, with reference to science, that each individual area [*Potenz*] can become fixed, with the result that the science [in question] becomes positive; exactly the same must be said of the ethical individual or nation [*Volk*]. For the totality must of necessity present itself within the latter as the subsistence of its scattered determinacies, and that individual link in the chain which the individual or nation occupies in the present must pass on and be replaced by another. As the individual grows in this way, and one area [*Potenz*] becomes more prominent while a second recedes, it can happen that the parts which were organised in the second area find themselves discarded and defunct. This division, in which some parts mature towards a new life while others, which have become firmly established at the stage of one [particular] determinacy, remain behind and see their life flee away, is possible only because the determinacy of one [particular] stage has become fixed and been made formally absolute. The form of the law which was conferred on a specific custom [*Sitte*], and which is the universality or the negative absolute of identity, gives that custom the appearance of having being in itself; and if the mass of a nation [*Volk*] is large, so also is that part of it which has organised itself in that determinacy [referred to above], and the law's consciousness of the latter will predominate over its unconsciousness of the newly emergent life. When custom and law were one, the determinacy was not something positive; but if the whole does not keep pace with the growth of the individual, law and custom become separate, the living unity which binds the members together grows weak, and there is no longer any absolute coherence or necessity in the present state of the whole. In these circumstances, therefore, the individual cannot be understood on its own terms, for its determinacy lacks the life which explains it and makes it comprehensible; and as the new custom likewise begins to express itself in laws, an internal contradiction between the various laws must inevitably arise. Whereas in our earlier discussion, history was only one aspect of the picture and what was necessary was at the same time free, necessity no longer coincides with freedom in the present case, and to that extent, it belongs entirely to history proper. Whatever has no true living ground in the present has its ground in the past – that is, we must look for a time when that determinacy which is fixed in the law but is now defunct was a living custom which harmonised with the rest of the legislation. But the effect of a purely historical explanation of laws and institutions does not extend beyond this specific end of [attaining] knowledge [*Erkenntnis*]; it will go beyond its function [*Bestimmung*] and truth if it is supposed to justify in the present a law which had truth only in a life that is past. On the contrary, this historical knowledge of the law, which can discover the basis of the law only in bygone customs and in a now departed life, proves precisely that, in the living present, the law lacks any sense or significance (even if it still has power and authority because of its legal form, and because some parts of the whole are still in its interest and their existence is tied to it).[118]

But in order to distinguish correctly between what is dead and devoid of truth and what is still alive, we should recall a distinction which a formal approach may overlook, and which will prevent us from mistaking what is inherently negative for the living law, and hence from mistaking the rule of inherently negative laws for the living existence of the organisation. For laws which exempt individual parts and determinacies from the dominion of the whole, which withdraw its authority from them, and which constitute individual exceptions to the universal [rule], are inherently negative, and they are signs of approaching death. This threat to life becomes ever more serious as such negative factors and exceptions multiply, and as those laws which promote this dissolution gain the ascendancy over the true laws which constitute the unity of the whole. Thus, we must count as positive and defunct not only what belongs entirely to a past age and no longer has any living presence but only an uncomprehending and (since it lacks all inner significance) shameless power; on the contrary, whatever consolidates the negative – namely dissolution and separation from the ethical totality – is also devoid of genuinely positive truth. The former is the history of a life in the past, but the latter is the determinate representation [*Vorstellung*] of death in the present. Thus, in a nation [*Volk*] which has experienced dissolution (and Germany is certainly an example), the laws may appear to have truth if we fail to distinguish whether they are laws of negativity and division, or laws of the genuinely

positive and of unity.[119] If laws which organise a whole have significance only for a past age, and refer to a shape and individuality
which were cast off long ago as a withered husk; if their interest
extends only to [individual] parts and they consequently have no
living relation [*Beziehung*] to the whole, but constitute an authority
and rule which are alien to it; if all that embodies a living bond and
an inner unity is no longer in the least appropriate as a means to
their ends, so that this means is neither true nor comprehensible
(for the truth of a means consists in its adequacy to the end), and
this fundamental untruth of the whole ensures that there can be
little truth left in the science of philosophy in general, in ethical
life, and likewise in religion – if all of this is the case, the dissolution
[of the whole] is immediately determined and consolidated, and it
sets itself up in a negative system and thereby gives itself a formal
semblance of knowledge [*Erkenntnis*], and of laws whose inner
essence is nothingness. If the knowledge and science of such a
nation [*Volk*] expresses the view that reason knows and understands
nothing, and that it is [to be found] only in empty freedom as an
escape, and in nothingness and its semblance, then the content and
essence of the negative legislation is that there is no law, no unity,
and no whole.[120] The former untruth is therefore one which is
unconsciously and unintentionally untrue, whereas this second
untruth is one which has formal pretensions and so becomes firmly
established.

Thus, philosophy does not take the particular as positive just
because it is particular; on the contrary, it does so only in so far as
the particular has attained independence as a separate part outside
the absolute context of the whole. The absolute totality, as a necessity, confines itself within each of its potentialities [*Potenzen*], and
produces itself as a totality on this basis. It there recapitulates the
[development of the] preceding potentialities, as well as anticipating
[that of] those still to follow; but one of these is the most powerful
among them, and in its complexion and determinacy, the totality
appears – though without imposing any more restrictions on life
than water does on the fish, or air on the bird. It is at the same
time necessary that individuality should advance through metamor-
phoses, and that everything that belongs to the dominant potentiality should grow weaker and die, in order that all stages of necessity may appear as such within it. But it is in the misfortune of

the transitional period (inasmuch as this strengthening of the new development [*Bildung*] has not purged itself absolutely of the past) that the positive lies. And although nature, within a specific shape, proceeds with a constant movement (not mechanically uniform, but uniformly accelerated), it nevertheless also enjoys whatever new shape it has attained. Though it springs into this shape, it also lingers in it, just as a [mortar-] bomb rushes towards the culmination [of its trajectory] and pauses there for a moment, or as heated metal does not soften like wax, but suddenly goes into flux and remains in this state – for this phenomenon [*Erscheinung*] is a transition to the absolute opposite and is consequently infinite, and this emergence of the opposite from infinity, or from its [own] nullity, involves a leap. The existence [*Dasein*] of a shape in its new-born vigour is initially an existence for itself, before it becomes conscious of its relationship to anything alien to it. So likewise does a growing individuality have both the delight of that leap into a new form and lasting enjoyment within it, until it gradually becomes open to the negative, and its downfall also constitutes a sudden break.

Now the philosophy of ethical life teaches us to understand this necessity, and to recognise the structure [*Zusammenhang*] and determinacy of its content as absolutely conjoined with the spirit, and as its living body; and it is opposed to that formalism which regards as contingent and dead whatever it can subsume under the concept of particularity. But this philosophy at the same time recognises that this vitality of individuality in general, whatever its shape, is a formal vitality; for the limited nature [*Beschränktheit*] of all that belongs to necessity, even if it is absolutely taken up into indifference, is only a part of necessity, not absolute and total necessity itself, so that there is still a disparity between the absolute spirit and its shape. But it [i.e. this philosophy] cannot discover this absolute shape by resorting to the shapelessness of cosmopolitanism, or to the vacuity of the rights of man or the equal vacuity of an international state or a world republic;[121] for these abstractions and formal constructions [*Formalitäten*] contain the precise opposite of ethical vitality, and are essentially protestant and revolutionary in relation to individuality.[122] On the contrary, it must discover [*erkennen*] the most beautiful shape to match the high Idea of absolute ethical life. Since the absolute Idea is in itself absolute intuition, its construction [*Konstruktion*] also directly determines the purest and freest individuality in which the spirit intuits itself with complete objectivity in its shape; and without returning into itself out of intuition, the spirit recognises [*erkennt*] this same intuition, wholly and immediately, as itself, and by this very means, it is absolute spirit and perfect ethical life. At the same time, this ethical life resists any involvement with the negative in the manner outlined above (for it has become self-evident that what we have hitherto described as positive, if considered in itself, is in fact the negative). It confronts the negative as an objective fate, and by consciously granting it an authority and realm of its own through sacrificing part of itself, it purges its own life of the negative and [thereby] preserves it.

Inaugural Address, Delivered at the University of Berlin (22 October 1818)[1]

Gentlemen,

Since today marks my *first*[a] appearance at this university in *that official capacity as a teacher of philosophy* to which I was graciously appointed by His Majesty the King,[2] permit me to say by way of introduction that I considered it particularly desirable and gratifying to take up a position of wider *academic influence* both at this *particular moment* and in this *particular place.*[3]

As far as the *particular moment* is concerned, those circumstances appear to have arisen in which *philosophy* may once again expect to receive *attention* and *love*, and in which this science, which had almost fallen silent,[4] may once more lift up its voice. For not long ago, the *urgency of the times* on the one hand conferred such great importance on the *petty* interests of everyday life, and on the other hand, the *high interests* of actuality, the interest and *conflicts* involved simply in restoring and salvaging the *political totality of national life and of the state*, placed such great demands on all [our] mental faculties and on the powers of all [social] classes [*Stände*] – as well as on

---

[a] *Translator's note*: The frequent use of italics in this text is based on Hegel's manuscript, and was no doubt designed to highlight those words and phrases which he wished to emphasise in delivering his address. In translating the address, I have, as usual, followed *Werke* (vol. XII, pp. 399–404) in the first instance; but in marking Hegel's emphasis, I have been guided rather by the definitive *GW*, and have indicated in the following notes those instances where the wording of the text in the latter edition differs significantly from that of the former.

external resources – *that the inner life of the spirit* could not attain *peace* and leisure; and *the world spirit* was so bound up with actuality and *forced to turn outwards* that it was prevented from turning *inwards* upon itself and enjoying and indulging itself in its proper home.[5] Now once this *stream* of actuality had been checked, and the *German nation* at large had salvaged its *nationality, the basis of all vitality and life*, the time came when, *in addition* to the empire of the *actual* world, the *free realm of thought* might also flourish independently within the *state*. And at all events, the *power of the spirit* has asserted itself to such an extent in the [present] age that only *Ideas*, and what is in keeping with *Ideas*, can now survive, and nothing can be recognised unless it *justifies* itself before *insight* and *thought*.[6] And it is this *state* in particular,[7] the state which has taken me into its midst, which, by virtue of *its spiritual* supremacy [*Übergewicht*], has raised itself to its [present] *importance* [*Gewicht*] in *actuality* and in the *political* realm, and has made itself the equal, in *power* and *independence*, of those *states* which may surpass it in *external resources*. Here, the cultivation and flowering of the *sciences* is one of the most essential *moments* – even of *political life*. In this university – as the central university – the *centre* of all spiritual culture [*Geistesbildung*] and of all science and truth, namely *philosophy*, must also find its place and be treated with special care.

But it is not just spiritual life in general which constitutes a *basic moment* in the existence of *this state*; more particularly, that great struggle of the people, together with its ruler, for independence, for the destruction of soulless foreign tyranny, and for freedom, had its higher source in the *soul* [*Gemüt*];[8] it is *the ethical power of the spirit* which *felt its own energy*, raised *its banner*, and expressed this *feeling* as a force and *power* in [the realm of] *actuality*. We must regard it as commendable that our generation has *lived, acted, and worked* in this *feeling*, a *feeling* in which *all that is rightful, moral*, and *religious* was concentrated. – In such profound and all-embracing *activity*, the spirit rises within itself to its [proper] dignity; the banality of life and the *vacuity* of its interests are confounded, and the superficiality of its *attitudes* and *opinions* is unmasked and dispelled. Now this *deeper seriousness* which has pervaded the *soul* [*Gemüt*] in general is *also the true ground of philosophy*. What is opposed to philosophy is, on the one hand, the *spirit's immersion* in the *interest* of necessity [*Not*] and of everyday life, but on the other, the *vanity* of *opinions*;

if the soul [*Gemüt*] is filled with the latter, it has no room left for reason – which does not, as such, pursue its own [interest]. This vanity must evaporate in its own nullity once it has become a necessity for people to work for a *substantial content*, and once the stage has been reached when only a content of this kind can achieve recognition. But we have seen this age in [possession of] just such a *substantial content*, and we have seen that *nucleus* once more take shape with whose further development, in all its aspects (i.e. political, ethical, religious, and scientific), our age is entrusted.⁹

Our vocation and business is to *nurture the development of philosophy* as the *substantial basis* which has now been *rejuvenated* and *confirmed*. Its rejuvenation, whose initial impact and expression were felt in political actuality, makes its further appearance in that *greater ethical* and *religious* seriousness, that *demand* for *solidity* [*Gediegenheit*] and *thoroughness* in general, which has gone out *to* [people in] *all walks of life*; the *most solid* [*gediegenste*] [kind of] *seriousness* is essentially [*an und für sich selbst*] *the seriousness of truth*.ᵇ This need, by which *spiritual* nature is distinguished from that nature which merely *feels* and *enjoys*, is for that very reason the deepest need of the spirit;¹⁰ – it is an inherently *universal need*, and on the one hand, it has been *stirred more profoundly* by the seriousness of our times, and on the other, it is a characteristic property of the *German* spirit. As for the *distinction of the Germans* in *philosophical* culture, the state of philosophical studies *among other* nations and the meaning which they attach to the term 'philosophy' show that, while they have retained the name, its *sense* has *changed* and the thing itself has been *debased* and dissipated to such an extent that scarcely a *memory* or *inkling* of it has *remained*. This science has sought refuge among *the Germans* and survived *only* among *them*; we have been given *custody* of this *sacred light*, and it is our vocation to tend and nurture it, and to ensure that *the highest* [thing] which man can possess, namely *the self-consciousness of his essential being*, is not extinguished and lost.¹¹ But even in Germany, the *banality of that earlier time* before the country's *rebirth* had gone so far as to believe and *assert* that it *had discovered* and *proved* that there is *no cognition of truth*, and that God and the *essential being* of the world and the spirit *are incomprehensible*

ᵇ *Translator's note: Werke* adds the words *zu erkennen* ('and of cognition') at the end of this sentence.

and unintelligible. Spirit [, it was alleged,] should stick to *religion*, and religion to *faith, feeling,* and *intuition* [*Ahnen*] *without rational knowledge.*[12] Cognition [, it was said,] has nothing to do with the *nature of the absolute* (i.e. of God, and what is *true* and *absolute* in nature and spirit), but only, on the one hand, with the *negative* [conclusion] that *nothing true can be recognised,* and that only the *untrue,* the *temporal,* and the *transient* enjoy the *privilege,* so to speak, of recognition – and on the other hand, with its proper object, the *external* (namely the *historical,* i.e. the *contingent* circumstances in which the alleged or supposed cognition made its appearance); and *this same cognition* should be taken as [merely] *historical,* and examined in those external aspects [referred to above] in a *critical* and *learned* manner, whereas its content *cannot be taken seriously.*[13] They [i.e. the philosophers in question] got no further than *Pilate,* the Roman proconsul; for when he heard Christ utter the word '*truth*', he replied with the question '*what is truth?*' in the manner of one who had had enough of such words and knew that there is no cognition of truth. Thus, what has been considered since time immemorial as *utterly contemptible* and *unworthy* – i.e. *to renounce the knowledge of truth* – was glorified before[c] our time as the *supreme triumph of the spirit.* Before it reached this point, this despair *in reason* had still been accompanied by *pain* and *melancholy*; but *religious* and *ethical frivolity,* along with that *dull* and *superficial* view of *knowledge* which described itself as *Enlightenment,* soon confessed its *impotence frankly* and *openly,* and *arrogantly* set about *forgetting higher interests completely*; and finally, the so-called *critical philosophy* provided this *ignorance* of the eternal and divine with *a good conscience,* by declaring that it [i.e. the critical philosophy] *had proved* that nothing can be known of the eternal and the *divine,* or of truth. This supposed cognition has even usurped the name of philosophy, and nothing was more welcome to superficial knowledge and to [those of] superficial character, and nothing was so eagerly seized upon by them, than this doctrine, which described this very ignorance, *this superficiality* and *vapidity,* as *excellent* and as the goal and result of all *intellectual* endeavour. Ignorance of truth, and knowledge only of appearances, of temporality and contingency, of *vanity* alone – this *vanity* has enlarged its influence in philosophy, and it continues

---

[c] *Translator's note: GW* reads *vor* ('before'); *Werke* reads *von* ('by').

to do so and still holds the floor today.[14] It can indeed be said that, ever since philosophy first began to emerge in Germany, the condition of this science has never looked so bad, nor has such a view as this, such renunciation of rational cognition, attained such [a degree of] presumption and influence. This view has *dragged on* [into the present] from the period before our own, and it stands in stark *contradiction* to that *worthier* [*gediegenern*]^d *feeling* and new, substantial spirit [of today]. *I salute* and invoke this *dawn of a worthier spirit*, and *I address myself to it alone* when I *declare* that *philosophy must have a content* [*Gehalt*] and *when I* proceed to expound *this* content to you. But *in doing so*, I appeal to the *spirit of youth* in general, for youth is that fine time of life when one is not yet caught up in the *system of the limited ends of necessity* [*Not*] and is inherently [*für sich*] capable of the *freedom of disinterested scientific activity*; nor is it yet affected by the *negative spirit* of *vanity*, by *purely critical drudgery with no content*. A heart which is still in good health still has the *courage* to demand truth, and it is in the realm of truth that philosophy is at home, which it [itself] constructs, and which we *share in by studying it*. Whatever is true, great, and divine in life is so by virtue of the *Idea*; the goal of philosophy is to grasp the Idea in its true shape and universality. Nature is confined to implementing reason only by necessity; but the realm of spirit *is the realm of freedom*. All that holds human life together, all that has value and validity, *is spiritual in nature*; and this realm of the spirit exists solely through the *consciousness* of truth and right, through the comprehension of Ideas.[15]

May I express the wish and hope that I shall manage to gain and merit your confidence on the path which we are about to take. But first of all, the one thing I shall venture to ask of you is this: that you bring with you a trust in *science*, *faith* in *reason*, and *trust and faith in yourselves. The courage of truth* and *faith* in the *power of the spirit* is the primary condition of *philosophical study*;[16] man should honour himself and *consider himself worthy of the highest* [things]. He cannot overestimate the greatness and power of the spirit; the closed essence of the universe *contains no force* which could withstand the courage of cognition; it must open up before it, and afford it the spectacle and enjoyment of its riches and its depths.

^d *Translator's note: Werke* reads *gediegenen*, but *GW* has the comparative *gediegenern*.

Address on the Tercentenary of the Submission of the Augsburg Confession (25 June 1830)[1]

Most excellent, illustrious, reverend men, most learned and congenial colleagues, most honourable companions in study, most esteemed listeners of every rank!

The most venerable Senate has instructed me to comment on the occasion and cause of the celebration with which the King has authorised this university to mark today's festival. Since that immortal act which we now commemorate concerned the profession and establishment of religious doctrine, it appears fitting that our admirable Theological Faculty should play the leading part in this festivity. Its estimable Dean will accordingly give us a fitting and learned account of the event in question and profoundly impress its significance upon us. But what happened at Augsburg was not enacted by an assembly of Doctors of Theology and leaders of the Church; nor did they embark on a learned disputation in order to determine the truth and to require the lay community to accept it as certain and observe it with dutiful obedience.[2] On the contrary, the main significance of that day was that the princes of the [German] states and the burgomasters of the Imperial Cities publicly declared that the Protestant [*evangelicam*] doctrine,[3] freed at last from a mass of superstitions, errors, lies, and all kinds of injustices and abuses, was now finally perfected and elevated above the uncertain outcome of disputations, above the arbitrary will, and above all worldly authority, and that they [i.e. the princes and burgomasters] had now taken up the cause of religion.[4] They thereby let it be known that those who had formerly been [classed as] laymen were now permitted to express opinions on religion, and they claimed this inestimable freedom on our behalf. Thus, if I am to say a few words on this matter by way of introduction to our festivity, I must [on the one hand] apologise for my lack of skill as a speaker[5] and crave the indulgence of my esteemed audience; but [on the other hand,] I would betray the cause of that liberty which was secured for us on the day which we now celebrate if I were consequently to apologise for speaking as a so-called layman on religious matters. It would rather appear that I was entrusted with this aspect of the celebration – and I gladly accepted the task – so that we might make use of the opportunity we had been given and publicly declare and testify that we possess it. And for this reason I have considered it my duty to say something about that freedom which those of us who are not theologians acquired [as a result of the Augsburg Confession].[6]

For before that time, the state of Christendom was such that it was divided into two classes, one of which had appropriated the rights and administration of that freedom which was conferred on us all by Christ, while the other, reduced to servitude, was the property of [those who enjoyed] this same freedom. But we understand Christian freedom to imply that everyone is declared worthy of it who turns to God as the object of his knowledge, prayers, and worship, that everyone determines his own relationship with God and that of God with man, and that God himself consummates this relationship within the human mind.[7] We are not dealing here with a God who is subject to the influences of nature,[8] but with one who is the truth, eternal reason, and the mind and consciousness of this reason. But it was the will of God that man should be endowed with this same rational consciousness, and that he should therefore be distinct from the unthinking animals; it was likewise his will that man should be in God's own image, and that the human mind, which is surely a spark of the eternal light, should be accessible to this light. Furthermore, since man is made in the image of God, God thereby revealed to the human race that the archetype [*idea*] of human nature is truly to be found in God himself; he also willed and permitted that human beings should love him, and he granted them the infinite capacity and confidence to approach him.

Subsequently, this highest good which God was able to give to man was again taken away from him, for the innermost sanctuary of the soul, the only possible basis and channel for that holy communion [with God], was polluted by terrors and fictions and obscured by foul superstitions, and human contact with God was cut off as if by a wall of brass. These obstacles, interposed between God and the [human] soul which burned with desire to approach him,[9] were the source and origin of servitude; for divine love is a free and infinite relationship [*commercium*], and if limits are imposed on it, it is reduced to the kind of relationship [*consortio*] which is customary between mortals. Thus, sacred things are reduced to the condition of common objects which can be physically possessed, controlled by force of arms, or even bought and sold.[10] In an association of this kind, domination and arbitrariness have their place; it produces all those qualities which we encounter in souls which are alienated from divine freedom, such as ambition, lust for power, avarice, hatred, and every kind of tyranny and stupidity. Thus, in the very lap of freedom, the Christian community was split up into masters and slaves,[11] an arrangement which seemed to have rendered the rule of impiety permanent and utterly invincible.

But the true consciousness of God and his infinite love broke these fetters asunder, and free access to God was restored to man. Indeed, what the leaders of Germany proclaimed at the Diet of Augsburg, in their own name and in that of the people, was that they disowned servitude and renounced their status as laymen, just as the theologians had renounced their clerical status, so that [both] these orders were completely abolished.[12] Thus, that unseemly division was removed [*sublatum*] which, since it was not [just] a conflict over the fortuitous authority of particular individuals, had disrupted and even subverted not only the Church, but religion itself. Admittedly, [secular] princes had also been present at [ecclesiastical] councils before that time, as at the famous Council of Constance. But they were not there to express, as it were, their own opinions, but in an administrative capacity in order to sign the decrees of the doctors [of the Church], and they subsequently served as executioners to translate the bloody significance of these decrees into reality by killing [those whom the Church had condemned]. But the Emperor who presided at the Diet of Augsburg did not act with equal right or equal freedom, i.e. he did not act with divine authority. Charles V, whose realms were so extensive that it was said that the sun never set on them, that same Emperor who, a few years earlier, had delivered up the city of Rome and the Papal See to his army to conquer, pillage, put to the torch, and destroy, with all manner of outrage and mockery directed at the Pope himself, now presented himself at Augsburg as a protector and patron of the Church – i.e. as a guardian of the Pope – and declared that his intention was to restore peace to the Church, and with it the threat of servitude as before. He was content with the spoils which ambition, bloodthirstiness, and licentiousness had brought back to him from the world at large, from Rome, and even from the captive Pope. But he left to others the immortal glory of defeating that tyranny which had usurped control of religion; and in his deafness, he was unable to perceive that God had *risen up*, and that it was *his trumpet* which now proclaimed the wondrous sound of Christian freedom.[13] He was not equal to the sacred inspiration [*ingenium*] of his age.

But those who did hear that sound and who now considered themselves emancipated were only freedmen [*liberi*] and not genuinely free [*liberti*], and the reason for this appears to be that the territorial princes and the burgomasters of the Imperial Cities had taken control of affairs.[14] For it is impossible for minds which have only just escaped from the shackles of superstition not to remain tied to those legal and political principles [*ratio*] which correspond to the precepts of the old religion. For religion cannot be shut away in the recesses of the mind and cut off from the principles of action or the organisation of life.[15] So great is its power and authority that all that pertains to human life is embraced and governed by it.[16] It is therefore essential that, if religion is reformed, the political, legal, and ethical system [*ratio civitatis et legum morumque*] should also be reformed. Thus, the things which our Luther set in motion were truly new. But since it was the princes and civil magistrates who solemnly concluded the business at Augsburg, they thereby testified that this was accomplished by public debate and volition, not through the pressure of the multitude, and that the majesty and authority of the laws and of the princes had not been contravened, but rather that the latter held sway over law-governed states [*civitates*] and obedient peoples.[17]

It is true that some are more critical in this respect, arguing that one must distinguish between the way in which something begins and the shape which it finally assumes; for even if the outcome and end [of the Reformation] gave it legitimacy, these critics maintain that it was none the less culpable [in its initial phase]; indeed, they deny that Luther's enterprise was concerned solely with doctrine, claiming rather that it was directed against the laws which had hitherto been in force. Indeed, they declare that it is close to sedition if we try to excuse such conduct and feign an appearance of justice by deferring judgement until the final outcome, treating the losing party as guilty and the victor as justified. Thus, even if the cause which triumphed was pleasing to God, it will plainly be displeasing to such Catos as this, because the defeated cause had once been legitimate. The doctrine they here put forward undoubtedly carries much weight – namely that nothing should be more sacred to the citizens than the obedience which they must show towards the laws, and the respect and fidelity which they owe to their ruler. May I nevertheless be allowed in this context to quote what Cicero said of Socrates and Aristippus: 'By no means', he says, 'should any individual fall into the error of supposing that, if these men acted and spoke against custom [*morem*] and civil convention, he may do the same himself; for they acquired the right to do so by virtue of their great and divine gifts'.[18] But how much greater and more divine are those benefits in whose acquisition we here rejoice than those gifts which Cicero describes as great and divine! And consequently, how much juster and more legitimate was that licence with which Luther and his friends – and not only they, but with them the princes and magistrates – transformed and renewed many things which were formerly considered just and legitimate in civil law! Those who condemn the Reformation of the evangelical religion in the manner described above should take heed lest, in denouncing Luther's sedition, they glory in their own obedience and zeal towards the laws and civil authorities merely because they deny divine truth altogether and ascribe all religious doctrine to human invention and opinion.

For the same reason, the same people deplore the fact that a *profession of faith* was drawn up at the Diet of Augsburg; for they maintain that those who declared themselves free were merely changing their fetters. They accordingly consider that there are no true [general] principles – unless one chooses to regard one's own opinions as certain – and that freedom consists essentially in dissenting from whatever doctrine is generally accepted.[19] But anyone who accuses those who introduced that Magna Charta by which the Evangelical Church proclaimed its foundation and constitution of thereby imposing fetters on it overlooks the fact that it was the very community which this charter established that gave birth to that tireless endeavour,[20] by physical and intellectual means, to explore the nature of all things divine and human as thoroughly as possible; and that, as a result of this endeavour, nothing was left untried or untouched by the human understanding [*ingenium*], and all areas of learning, of liberal arts and letters, were restored to humanity – and not merely restored, but strengthened and augmented by a new and infinite ardour. Day by day, they grow and expand with constant vigour; and at the same time, they are freely accessible to all, and everyone is necessarily invited, urged, and encouraged from all quarters to investigate for himself what is just, true, and divine. – But I shall say no more of those fetters which allegedly attach to all public doctrines, both because the difficulty of this topic would distract me for too long from my theme and because, in view of the multiple suspicions and odium already referred to, it would be too melancholy a subject, inappropriate to today's joyful occasion. It may suffice to point out that so superabundant a harvest could in no wise have arisen from servile origins. But already at the time when this process began, and certainly in our own day, it became obvious how great a potential the restored doctrines of religion possess for improving civil laws and institutions. Let us now look more closely at the nature of that evangelical doctrine which relates to the theme I was asked to discuss.

First of all, we note that the schism which brought discord into the innermost sanctuary of the soul and split the commonwealth [*respublica*] into two civil powers was abolished; we now understand that the commonwealth, by divine authority,[21] should be internally one, and that the laws [*iura*] pertaining to the state [*civitas*] and citizens and the precepts of virtue are divinely sanctioned. Princely power has been reconciled with the Church, and while the former is now at one with the divine will, the latter renounces all unjust authority. What strikes me as most noteworthy here is the fact that this was not some fortuitous and external agreement between princes and theologians; on the contrary, the precepts of religion and of the state [*civitas*] itself and the most fundamental principles [*rationes*] of truth came together in a genuine peace. The foundation which was then laid down developed more fully over the course of time until finally – for this can happen only very slowly – it penetrated and informed every area of human life and the rules which govern all human duties [*omnium officiorum*].

May I therefore invite my esteemed audience to recall what the duties of human life are, and how they were attacked and indeed corrupted by the doctrine of the older Church.[22] The duties in question are familiar to everyone: firstly, there are those which relate to the family, such as conjugal love and the mutual love of parents and children, then justice, equity, and benevolence towards others, diligence and honesty in administering property, and finally the love of one's country and its rulers, which even requires us to lay down our lives in their defence. The immortal examples of these virtues which the Greeks and Romans left behind for us to admire and imitate were described by the Church Fathers as 'splendid vices'. The Roman Church accordingly set up another principle [*ratio*] of living, in opposition and preference to these virtues and rules of justice and honesty – namely *sanctity*. And we must surely concede from the outset that Christian virtue, if it is based on the love of God, is far more excellent and holier than anything which does not come from this source. But we maintain and believe that those duties which relate to the family, to the commerce between human beings, and to one's country and its ruler are indeed based on the will of God, and that the corresponding virtues are certainly confirmed by Christian piety, i.e. by love of the divine will, and should in no way be looked down on, despised or dismissed by it. But these duties and virtues are weakened and destroyed by those which the Roman Church set up as rules of sanctity and imposed on its members; and in case these should appear vague and empty words, we shall now describe the rules in question specifically.

The [Roman] Church accordingly claimed that *the unmarried state and childlessness are holier in terms of love and piety* than matrimony itself.[23] We are indeed impelled to this [matrimonial] union by nature, but only mindless animals cling to what they are drawn to by nature, whereas it is characteristic of human beings to transform this impulse into a bond of love and piety. Surely the ancients, in supposing that Vesta or the Lares and Penates presided over the family, had a truer sense that there was something divine in it than did the Church, which discerned a special sanctity in contempt for marriage. We need not mention what moral abuses this rule of celibacy gave rise to, for it is well enough known that most of those clerics who were committed to sanctity of this kind, including those of the highest rank and authority, were the most licentious and openly dissolute of men. It is admittedly argued that such vices cannot be attributed to the law itself, but should be ascribed to human lust and depravity. But those duties which God imposed on men and wished them to regard as sacred apply to everyone, and he wishes to reveal himself in equal measure to those of every class [*ordo*] who love him. But if it follows from that law of righteousness – and this is surely absurd – that the entire human race could be forbidden to marry, the basis of all honesty and moral discipline would certainly be destroyed, for this is plainly to be found in family piety.

Then the [Roman] Church has taught that *poverty* is a sacred virtue. It consequently has a low opinion of industriousness and probity in the care and administration of property, and of diligence in the acquisition of [material] goods, which are not only necessary to sustain life but also serve to help others; it thereby rates idleness above work, stupidity above ingenuity, and carelessness above foresight and probity. As a result of the vow (or rather pretence) of poverty, the clergy was given leave to indulge in avarice and luxury; for it is plain that the possession and acquisition of wealth were condemned in order that the clergy alone might be rich and owners of all the wealth which others had acquired through folly or even wickedness.

To these two precepts, the [Roman] Church added a third to crown them all, namely *blind obedience and mental servitude*. This ensures that the love of God will not lead us into liberty, but will thrust us down into servitude, both in minor things which are subject to contingency and to the arbitrary will of the individual, and in major things, i.e. in the knowledge of what is just, honourable, and righteous and in the arrangement and conduct of our lives – plainly in order that those who present themselves as servants (or even as servants of servants)[a] may rule over private life and domestic affairs and be masters of the commonwealth [*respublica*] and its rulers.

---

[a] *Translator's note*: *servus servorum Dei* ('servant of the servants of God') was a title adopted by the Popes.

No one who is mildly and benevolently disposed towards those of differing religious views, and who wishes that the religious hatred which agitated the nations [*populos*] so long and so violently should finally be laid to rest and never again awakened, will deny that those rules which, as I said, are taught by the Roman Church embrace the entire basis [*ratio*] of human life, and that they confuse and confound all justice and honour within it. Consequently, the declaration of the German rulers [*civitatum rectores*] at Augsburg abolished not only that Holiness from which the Roman Pope borrowed his title, but also the much more oppressive, indeed pernicious rules of sanctity; it thereby proclaimed that the state [*civitas*] was reconciled with God, and God with the state.[24] Only then was the contradiction [*dissidium*] resolved whereby just and honest laws were supposed to be pleasing to human beings and something else to be pleasing to God, and only then was that ambiguity and duplicity removed [*sublata*] whereby the wicked could ask for indulgences for their crimes and offences, whereas the upright might either be led into revolt against authority and other misdeeds, or into folly and inactivity; only then did consciousness of the divine will cease to be different from consciousness of truth and justice.

Human beings can have no firm trust in the laws unless they are persuaded not only that the latter are not at variance with religion, but also that they have their source in it. There are indeed many highly placed and talented individuals in our time who believe that true wisdom consists in the separation of religion and the state [*civitas*]; but they are gravely mistaken.[25] For it is manifest that the supreme and most firmly based principle in our minds and the sole source of all our duties is the notion [*notio*] of God. Consequently, whatever does not depend on this and is not sanctioned by the idea [*species*] of the divine will can be regarded as contingent, as a product of the arbitrary will or of coercion, and no one can be truly bound or obligated by it. Thus, one cannot sufficiently censure the foolishness of those who believe that the institutions and laws of the state can be reformed without restoring the true religion to which the former correspond. The fruit of regained divine liberty, and of it alone, is civil liberty and justice. We may recall how the error of those who failed to comprehend the nature of this matter was forcibly refuted by that terrible teacher, the course of events [*eventus rerum*]. For in all those Catholic dominions in which those of higher station [*nobiliores cives*] had gained a truer knowledge of what is just and honourable, attempts were made to reform the laws and customs [*mores*] of society [*civitatis*]; but while some rulers assented to this and others dissented, religion remained opposed, so that all such attempts were vitiated from the start. They were subsequently overwhelmed by every kind of crime and evil, until they finally came to grief, to the most acute but ineffectual shame of their instigators.[26]

In our case, however, divine providence ensured that the precepts of the religion we profess are in accord with what the state regards as just.[27] This was accomplished three hundred years ago by the princes and peoples of Germany. But both they themselves and their successors then had to expiate the immense and ancient guilt of the perversion of Christianity by suffering the prolonged misfortunes and miseries of war, until they could at last secure what they passed on to us as our most precious heritage – namely the free concord of the state and religion, and particularly that evangelical religion of which, as already mentioned, this concord is characteristic. This concord gave rise to what we rejoice in as the main contribution to the common welfare of our times, so that all those propitious and useful steps could be taken which human ingenuity devised and inherent necessity required in order to increase freedom, to improve the laws, and to develop the institutions of the state in a more fruitful and liberal manner. All these things were accomplished peacefully, without internal convulsions and crimes, through the discernment and goodwill of those in whom supreme power is invested.[28] Most important of all, let me add that, if our princes are pious, we need not fear their piety like that ill-starred and terrible piety of the French kings, which drove them to frenzied action – even with their own hands – against their Protestant subjects, nobility and commoners alike, with carnage, plunder, and every kind of atrocity. They defiled the name of piety by such infamy, which was sanctioned by the religion of those who committed it. Thus the Protestant [*evangelici*] princes know that they are acting piously if they shape and administer the commonwealth [*respublica*] in accordance with the eternal rule of justice, and guarantee the security of the people; and they neither know nor recognise any kind of sanctity but this.

Thus, the piety of our princes fills us with confidence and security and assures them of our love. And whereas on the birthday of our most gracious King Frederick William,[29] we turn our eyes every year to the image of his virtues and remind ourselves of the benefits which he so richly bestows on this his university, let us today joyfully praise his exceptional piety, which is the source of all his virtues.[30] And since this directly concerns his subjects, let us cherish it, venerate it, and rejoice in it. Our joy and reverence gain considerable extra significance from the fact that the whole Protestant [*evangelicus*] world, both within Germany and beyond its frontiers, knows that our cause is an important one, and the admiration, trust, and pious wishes of all those good people who rejoice in this freedom join with us in turning to that person whom they recognise as the sure defender of the evangelical doctrine and of the freedom which goes with it. We have prayed, pray now, and shall not cease to pray to almighty God that he may favour our most gracious King and his whole illustrious [*Augustae*][b] house by preserving and increasing those blessings with which he eternally rewards piety, justice, and mercy.

[b] *Translator's note*: Hegel seems to be playing here on the similarity between the Latin name for Augsburg (*Augusta Vindelicorum*, usually shortened to *Augusta*) and the adjective *augusta* ('illustrious') to emphasise, at the conclusion of his address, the close relationship between the Prussian monarchy and the Protestant cause which he sees embodied in the Augsburg Confession. (The Prussian monarchs were in fact not themselves Lutherans, but Calvinists.)

Lectures on the Philosophy of History[1] (1827–1831), Part IV, Section 3: The New Age

[Editorial note: The following excerpt is from Part IV of Hegel's *Lectures on the Philosophy of History*, which is entitled 'The Germanic[2] World'. Parts I to III deal with the Oriental World, the Greek World, and the Roman World respectively. In his brief introduction to Part IV, Hegel argues that the Germanic people are the carriers of the Christian principle in Western civilisation, and that the Christian principle is constitutive of freedom in the 'new age'. This principle develops in the Germanic world in three distinct stages, the first of which stretches from the fall of Rome to the time of Charlemagne, and the second (i.e. the Middle Ages) from Charlemagne to the Reformation. The latter stage, Hegel argues, was characterised by Catholic corruption and by the Church's denial of the right of conscience, and a rigid separation was introduced between priesthood and laity and between spiritual and secular worlds. Most important of all, however, he contends that the ideals of Catholicism, and in particular those of celibacy, poverty, and obedience, rendered religion incompatible with *Sittlichkeit*, especially in its three essential moments of family, civil society, and the state.

In the extract translated here, Hegel discusses the third stage in the development of the Christian principle among the Germanic peoples. He attempts to show how the Reformation inaugurated a movement that led to the recovery of the realm of *Sittlichkeit* for Christianity. In his view, this recovery was initiated by Luther, but Luther's Reformation – the 'first' Reformation – failed to complete the process. As a philosopher of *Sittlichkeit* and of Protestantism, Hegel wishes to suggest how the process which Luther began might be completed in the present. The argument he advances in the following extract leaves no doubt that he pursued this end consciously and deliberately.]

We now come to the third period of the Germanic realm, and so enter the period in which the spirit knows itself as free inasmuch as it wills the true [*das Wahrhafte*], the eternal, and the universal in and for itself.

In this third period, three phases should again be distinguished. Firstly, we must consider the *Reformation* as such, the all-illuminating *sun* which followed the dawn at the end of the Middle Ages;[3] then the development of the situation after the Reformation; and finally, recent times from the end of the last century onwards.[4]

Chapter 1: The Reformation

The Reformation arose out of the *corruption of the Church*.[5] The corruption of the Church was not fortuitous, not just an abuse of power and authority [*Herrschaft*]. 'Abuse' is a term very commonly used to describe a corrupt condition; it is assumed that the foundation was good and that the thing itself was faultless, but that the passions, subjective interests, and contingent will of human beings in general made use of that good [foundation] as a means for their own ends [*für sich*], and that all that is necessary is to remove these contingent factors. On this view [*Vorstellung*], the thing itself is rescued and the evil is eliminated as a purely external element. But if something is abused in a contingent manner, only individual aspects are affected, whereas a great and universal evil in so great and universal a thing as a Church is a completely different matter. – The corruption of the Church developed out of the Church itself; its principle consists precisely in the fact that the This [*das Dieses*] is present in it in sensuous form [*als ein Sinnliches*], that the external is present as such within it. (The transfiguration of this element by art is [still] not sufficient.) The higher spirit, the world spirit has already excluded the spiritual from it; the Church does not share in it or occupy itself with it; it thus retains the *This* within it, as sensuous subjectivity or immediate subjectivity which it has not transfigured into spiritual subjectivity.[6] – *From now on, it falls behind the world spirit*, which has already moved beyond it; for it [the world spirit] has come to know [*wissen*] the sensuous as sensuous, the external as external, to be active in the finite [realm] in a finite manner and to be with itself [*bei sich*] in this activity as an indifferent and justified subjectivity.

This destiny, which is intrinsic to the Church, necessarily reveals itself as inner corruption as soon as it no longer encounters resistance and has become firmly established. Then the elements are released and fulfil their destiny. It is this externality within the Church itself which accordingly becomes evil and corruption, and develops as the negative within it. – The forms of this corruption are the manifold relations in which the Church itself stands, and into which this moment consequently introduces itself.

There is superstition throughout this [form of] piety, which remains tied to a sensuous object, a common thing. It assumes the most varied shapes: slavery to *authority* (for the spirit, as inwardly outside itself, is unfree and externally constrained); a *belief in miracles* of the most absurd and foolish kind (for the divine is thought to exist [*dazusein*] in a completely sporadic [*vereinzelt*] and finite way and for wholly finite and particular ends); and finally, lust for power, self-indulgence and all the corruptness of barbarism and vulgarity, hypocrisy and deceit. All of this opens up within the Church; for sensuousness in general is not restrained and cultivated in it by the understanding; it has become free, but only in a crude and savage manner. – On the other hand, the *virtue* of the Church, in negating sensuousness, is only abstractly negative; it does not know how to be ethical in this [sensuous] context, and therefore simply flees, renounces, and lacks vitality in the actual world [*in der Wirklichkeit*].[7]

These contrasts within the Church – crude vice and lust, and an all-sacrificing sublimity of soul – become even stronger through the energy which human beings now feel in their *subjective strength* in relation to external things, and in nature, in which they know they are free and hence acquire an absolute right for themselves. – The Church, which is supposed to save souls from corruption, makes this very salvation into an external instrument [*Mittel*] and is now reduced to performing this function in an external fashion.[8] The *remission of sins*, the highest satisfaction which the soul seeks in order to be certain of its unity with God, this profoundest and innermost [aspiration], is offered to human beings in the most external and frivolous manner – namely as something to be *bought with mere money*; and at the same time, this is done for the most external ends of self-indulgence. It is also true that one of these ends was the construction of St Peter's, the magnificent Christian edifice in the heart of the residence of that religion. But just as the supreme example of all works of art, Athene and her temple stronghold in Athens, was built with the money of that city's allies and yet deprived the city both of its allies and of its power, so did the completion of this Church of St Peter, and of Michelangelo's 'Last Judgement' in the Sistine Chapel, mark the Last Judgement and downfall of this proud edifice.

The old and well-tried *inwardness [Innigkeit] of the German people* had to produce this revolution out of its own simple heart. While the rest of the world made off to the East Indies or America – to amass riches or to build a secular empire whose territory was to encircle the globe and on which the sun would never set – it was a simple *monk* who discovered that the This [*das Dieses*] which Christendom had previously sought in an earthly sepulchre of stone lay rather in the deeper sepulchre of the absolute ideality of all sensuous and external things; that is, he found it in the spirit and showed it in the heart – the heart which, infinitely offended by this offer of the most external satisfaction for its innermost needs, recognises, pursues, and destroys this distortion of the absolute relation of truth in all its individual guises [*Zügen*]. Luther's simple doctrine is that the *This*, infinite subjectivity – i.e. true spirituality or Christ – is in no way present and actual in an external fashion; on the contrary, as something wholly spiritual, it is attained only through reconciliation with God – *in faith and in enjoyment*.[9] These two words express it all. It is not a consciousness of a sensuous object as God, nor even of something merely represented [*vorgestellt*] which is not actual and present, but of something actual which is not sensuous. This elimination of externality reconstructs all doctrines and reforms all the superstition into which the Church had consistently dissolved.[10] It concerns above all the doctrine of *works*; for works are what is somehow accomplished not in faith, in one's own spirit, but externally, on [the direction of] authority, etc.[11] But neither is *faith* just a certainty with regard to purely finite things – a certainty belonging only to the finite subject, as, for example, the faith that this or that person existed and said this or that, that the children of Israel passed dry-footed through the Red Sea, or that the trumpets had an effect as powerful as that of our cannons before the walls of Jericho; for even if none of this had been reported, our knowledge [*Kenntnis*] of God would be no less complete.[12] Faith is certainly not a belief in something absent and over and done with, but a subjective certainty of the eternal, of truth which has being in and for itself, of the truth of God. The Lutheran Church says of this certainty that only the Holy Spirit produces it – i.e. that it is a certainty which pertains to the individual not by virtue of his particular individuality, but by virtue of his essential being.[13] – The Lutheran doctrine is therefore wholly [identical with] the Catholic, with the exception of all that follows from that relation of externality already referred to (in so far as the Catholic Church affirms this externality). Luther could therefore do no other than make no concessions on that doctrine of the Eucharist in which everything is concentrated. Nor could he concede to the Reformed [Calvinistic] Church that Christ is a mere memory or recollection; on the contrary, he agreed on this question with the Catholic Church that Christ is a [real] presence, but in faith and spirit [alone]. He taught that the spirit of Christ does actually fill the human heart, and that Christ should not be regarded merely as a historical personage – on the contrary, human beings have an *immediate relation* to him *in spirit*.[14]

Now inasmuch as the individual knows that he is filled with the divine spirit, all relations of externality are abolished: there is no longer any distinction between priests and laymen, and no one class [*Klasse*] has exclusive possession of the content of truth and of all the spiritual and temporal treasures of the Church. It is instead the heart, the feeling spirituality of human beings, which can and should come into possession of the truth, and this subjectivity is that of *all human beings*.[15] Each must accomplish the work of reconciliation within himself. – The subjective spirit must take the spirit of truth up into itself and let it dwell within it. That absolute inwardness of soul which pertains to religion itself is thereby attained, as is freedom within the Church. Subjectivity now makes the objective content – i.e. the doctrine of the Church – its own. In the Lutheran Church, the subjectivity and certainty of the individual are just as necessary as the objectivity of truth.[16] For Lutherans, truth is not a ready-made object [*Gegenstand*]; on the contrary, the subject itself must become a true subject [*ein wahrhaftes*] by giving up its particular content in exchange for substantial truth and making this truth its own. Thus, the subjective spirit becomes free in truth, negates its particularity, and comes to itself in its truth. Thus Christian freedom is actualised. If we identify subjectivity solely with feeling, without this content, we remain at the [level of the] purely natural will.

At this point, the new and ultimate standard round which the peoples gather is unfurled, the banner of the *free spirit* which is with itself [*bei sich selbst*], and with itself in truth and truth alone. This is the banner under which we serve and which we bear aloft. The age from that time until our own has had no other work to do or yet to be done than to cultivate this principle and bring it into the world, so that reconciliation in itself [*an sich*] is achieved and truth also becomes formally objective.[17] Form pertains to culture [*Bildung*] in general; culture is the activation of the form of the universal, which is thought in general. Right, property, ethical life, government, the constitution, etc. must now be determined in a universal way so that they may accord with the concept of the free will and [so] be rational. Only in this way can the spirit of truth appear within the subjective will, in the will's particular activity; and as the intensity of free subjective spirit resolves to assume the form of universality, the objective spirit can [in turn] appear. It is in this sense that we should understand that the state is based on religion. States and laws are nothing other than religion as it appears in the relations of actuality.[18]

This is the essential content of the Reformation; human beings are by nature [*durch sich selbst*] destined to be free.[19]

. . .[20]

The *relation between the new Church and the secular realm* has already been discussed, and only the details have still to be specified. The development [*Entwicklung*] and progress of the spirit from the Reformation onwards consists in the fact that, by virtue of that mediation which takes place between man and God, the spirit, now conscious of its freedom and certain that the objective process is [part of] the divine essence itself, duly comes to grips with this process and follows it through in the further development [*Bildung*] of secularity.[21] The reconciliation which is thereby achieved gives rise to the consciousness that the secular is capable of embodying the truth, whereas it had formerly been regarded as merely evil and incapable of goodness, which remained a realm beyond [*ein Jenseits*].[a] It is now known that what is ethical and right within the state is also divine and commanded by God, and that, in terms of content, nothing is higher or more sacred. It follows from this that *marriage* is no longer inferior to celibacy. Luther took a wife to show that he respected marriage, without fearing the calumnies which he would thereby incur. It was his duty to do so, as it was to eat meat on Fridays, in order to prove that such things are right and permissible in contrast to the supposedly higher merit of abstinence. It is through the family that human beings enter into the community and into the relation of mutual dependence within society, and this union is an ethical one, whereas the monks, segregated from ethical society, formed as it were the Pope's standing army, just as the janissaries formed the basis of Turkish power. As soon as priests can marry, the external difference between laity and clergy also disappears. – Nor was [the state of] unemployment any longer regarded as sacred; on the contrary, it was rated more highly if human beings in a state of dependence made themselves independent through activity, through intelligence [*Verstand*] and industry. It is more meritorious [*rechtschaffener*] that someone who has money should spend it, even on superfluous needs, than give it away to idlers and beggars; for he gives it to an equal number of people, and there is at least the condition that they should have actively worked for it. Trade and industry have now become ethical, and the obstacles which the Church put in their way have disappeared.[22] For the Church had declared it sinful to lend money for interest; but the necessity of doing so led to precisely the opposite result. The Lombards (from whom the French expression *lombard* for 'loan office' is derived), and especially the Medicis advanced money to princes throughout Europe. – The third moment of sanctity in the Catholic Church, namely blind *obedience*, was likewise abolished

[a] *Translator's note*: The sense in which Hegel employs this adverbial noun becomes clearer when he introduces it again on p. 207 below.

[*aufgehoben*]. Obedience to the laws of the state, as the rational basis [*Vernunft*] of volition and action, was now made into a principle. In this obedience, human beings are free, for the particular [now] obeys the general. They themselves have a conscience, and should therefore obey freely. The possibility of reason and freedom developing and being introduced [into human affairs] is thereby posited, and reason and the divine commandments are now synonymous. The rational is no longer contradicted by the religious conscience; it can develop peacefully on its own ground, with no need to react forcibly to its opposite. But in the Catholic Church, this opposite has absolute authority [*Berechtigung*]. Princes may indeed still be bad, but they are no longer authorised and encouraged to be so by their religious conscience. On the other hand, the conscience may very well be opposed, in the Catholic Church, to the laws of the state. Regicides, political conspiracies, and the like have often been supported and carried out by the priests.

This reconciliation of Church and state has arisen *immediately* and of its own accord [*für sich*]. There is as yet no reconstruction of the state, the system of right, etc., for thought still has to discover what is right in itself. The laws of freedom first had to develop into a system of what is right in and for itself.[23] After the Reformation, the spirit does not appear at once in this complete state [*Vollendung*], for the Reformation is initially confined to immediate changes, as, for example, the dissolution of monasteries, bishoprics, etc. God's reconciliation with the world was initially still in abstract form, and had not yet developed into a system of the ethical world.

This reconciliation should first take place within the *subject* as such, in its conscious sensibility [*Empfindung*]; the subject should assure itself that the spirit resides within it, that – in the language of the Church – its heart has been broken and divine grace has become manifest within it. Human beings are by nature not what they ought to be; they arrive at truth only by a process of transformation.[24] The universal and speculative [element] consists precisely in the fact that the human heart is not what it ought to be. It was now required of the subject that it should become conscious of what it is in itself – that is, dogmatics wished human beings to know that they are evil. But the individual is evil only when the natural comes into existence in sensual desire and the will of the unjust [person] does so in an unrestrained, undisciplined, and violent manner; and yet the individual is supposed to know that he is evil, and that the good spirit resides within him; he should accordingly have and experience in an immediate sense [*Weise*] what in a speculative sense has being in itself. Once the reconciliation had assumed this abstract form, human beings were subjected to the torment of forcing the consciousness of their sinfulness upon themselves and knowing themselves as evil. The most ingenuous souls [*Gemüter*] and most innocent natures brooded over and explored the most secret stirrings of their hearts in order to observe them minutely. But this duty was also combined with an opposite duty whereby human beings were also supposed to know that the good spirit resided in them and that divine grace had become manifest within them. This in fact took no account of the great difference between knowing what has being in itself, and knowing what is [present] in existence [*Existenz*]. The torment of uncertainty arose as to whether the good spirit did reside in human beings, and the whole process of transformation was supposed to be known within the subject itself. We can still hear an echo of this torment in many religious poems of that era; the Psalms of David, which display a similar character, were also introduced as hymns at that time. Protestantism accordingly took this course of small-minded brooding over the soul's subjective condition and treated this preoccupation as important, so that it was long characterised by inner torment and wretchedness. In our own time, this has induced many people to convert to Catholicism in order to exchange this inner uncertainty for a broad formal certainty based on the imposing totality of the Church.[25] But cultivated reflection on [human] actions also found its way into the Catholic Church. The Jesuits brooded no less deeply over the ultimate sources of volition (*velleitas*); but they possessed a casuistry which could find a good reason for everything and so eliminate evil.[26]

This is connected with a further remarkable phenomenon common to both Catholic and Protestant worlds. Human beings were driven to inwardness and abstraction, and the spiritual was regarded as distinct from the secular.[27] The dawning consciousness of human subjectivity, of the inwardness of human volition, brought with it a belief in *evil* as a vast power in the secular realm. This belief is parallel to [that in] indulgences: just as one could buy eternal salvation for a sum of money, so was it now believed that one could exchange one's salvation for worldly riches and the power to gratify one's desires and passions by means of a pact with the devil. Thus arose the famous story of Faust who, dissatisfied with theoretical knowledge [*Wissenschaft*], plunged into the world and forfeited his own salvation in exchange for all its glory. According to the poet, Faust did enjoy the world's glory as his payment; but those poor women who were described as witches are supposed to have had only the satisfaction of petty revenge on their neighbour by stopping her cow's milk or making her child fall ill. But no account was taken of the extent of the damage through loss of milk or the child's sickness etc. in proceedings against them; on the contrary, the power of evil within them was pursued in the abstract. The belief in this separate and specific power of secularity, in the devil and his deceptions, led to an infinite number of *trials for witchcraft* in both Catholic and Protestant countries. The guilt of the accused could not be proved – it was merely suspected; it was therefore only on *unmediated knowledge* [*unmittelbares Wissen*] that this rage against evil was based. It was nevertheless considered necessary to proceed to evidence; but the basis of these trials was simply the belief that [certain] persons possess the power of evil. This was like a monstrous plague which ravaged the nations [*Völker*] in the sixteenth century in particular. The main incentive was suspicion. This principle of suspicion appears in just as terrible a form under the Roman Empire and under Robespierre's Reign of Terror, when dispositions [*die Gesinnung*] as such were punished.[28] Among the Catholics, it was the Dominicans to whom – along with the Inquisition in general – the trials for witchcraft were entrusted. Father Spee, a noble Jesuit (who also wrote a collection of splendid poems entitled *Trutznachtigall*), attacked them in a work which fully acquaints us with the terrible character of criminal justice in cases of this kind.[29] Torture, which was supposed to be administered only once, was continued until a confession was obtained. If the accused persons fainted through weakness under torture, it was said that the devil gave them sleep; if they went into convulsions, it was said that the devil laughed within them; if they held out steadfastly, it was said that the devil gave them strength. These persecutions spread like an epidemic through Italy, France, Spain, and Germany. The earnest objections of enlightened men like Spee and others already had a considerable effect. But the first to oppose this pervasive superstition with major success was Thomasius, a professor at [the University of] Halle.[30] The whole phenomenon is inherently [*an und für sich*] quite remarkable when we consider that we escaped from this fearful barbarity by no means long ago (as late as 1780, a witch was burned at Glarus in Switzerland). Among the Catholics, persecution was directed against heretics as well as witches; both were placed in roughly the same category, and the unbelief of the heretics was likewise regarded as evil pure and simple.

Leaving this abstract form of inwardness behind us, we now have to consider the *secular* aspect – the formation of the state [*Staatsbildung*] and the rise of the universal, the growing consciousness of universal laws of freedom. This is the second and essential moment.[31]

. . .[32]

Chapter 3: The Enlightenment and Revolution

In the Protestant religion, the principle of inwardness had arisen in conjunction with religious liberation and [the principle of] satisfaction within the self; this also led to the belief that inwardness is evil, and to the belief in the power of secularity. In the Catholic Church, the casuistry of the Jesuits also gave rise to endless investigations, as long-winded and hair-splitting as those of scholastic theology in earlier times, concerning the inner nature and motives of the will. In this dialectic, which rendered all particulars uncertain by turning evil into good and good into evil, nothing was finally left but the pure activity of inwardness itself, the abstract [aspect] of spirit, namely *thought*. Thought considers everything in the form of universality and is consequently the activity and production of the universal. In the scholastic theology of former times, the proper content of this theology – i.e. the doctrine of the Church – remained a realm beyond [*ein Jenseits*]. In Protestant theology, the spirit likewise retained its reference to a realm beyond; for on the one hand, the individual [*eigene*] will, the human spirit, the 'I' itself remains, and on the other, there is the grace of God, the Holy Spirit, and hence, in [the context of] evil, the devil. But in thought, the self is present to itself, and its content and objects are likewise absolutely [*schlechthin*] present to it; for when I think, I must raise the object [of my thought] to universality.[33] This is utter and absolute freedom, for the pure 'I', like pure light, is absolutely with itself [*schlechthin bei sich*]; thus diversity, whether sensuous or spiritual, no longer holds any terrors for it, for it is inwardly free and freely confronts it. A practical interest makes use of objects and consumes them; a theoretical interest contemplates them in the assurance that they are not in themselves different. – Consequently, the culminating point of inwardness is thought. Human beings are not free if they do not think, for their relation is then to an Other. This comprehending and grasping of the Other, [coupled] with an innermost self-certainty, contains the reconciliation in immediate form [*unmittelbar*]: the unity of thought with the Other is present *in itself*, for reason is the substantial basis both of consciousness and of the external and natural. Thus, what thought confronts [*das Gegenüber*] is likewise no longer a realm beyond, nor is it of another substantial nature.

Thought is the stage at which the spirit has now arrived. It [i.e. thought] contains reconciliation in its purest essentiality, because it approaches the external [world] in the expectation that this will embody the same reason as the subject does. The spirit recognises that nature and the world must also have an inherent reason, for God created them in a rational manner. A universal interest in contemplating and getting to know the present world has now arisen.[34] The universal aspect of nature is the species, genera, force, and gravity reduced to their phenomena, etc. Thus *experience*[b] has become the science of the world, for experience is on the one hand perception, but on the other hand, it is also the discovery of the law, the internal [dimension], the [underlying] force, inasmuch as it reduces what is given to its simple rudiments. – It was Descartes who first extracted the consciousness of thought from that sophistry of thought which renders everything uncertain.[35] Just as it was in the purely Germanic nations that the principle of spirit emerged, so were the Romance nations the first to grasp *abstraction*, which is connected with their character of inner division as described above.[36] Empirical science [*Erfahrungswissenschaft*] was therefore quickly accepted by them, in common with the Protestant English and the Italians in particular. It seemed to human beings as if God had only now created the sun, moon, stars, plants, and animals, as

---

[b] *Translator's note*: *Erfahrung*, which also carries associations of 'experiment'.

if the laws [of nature] had only now been determined; for only now did people become interested in these when they recognised their own reason in the reason inherent in them. The human eye became *clear*, the senses aroused, and thought went to work and explained. The laws of nature were used to confront the monstrous superstition of the age, as well as all notions of mighty alien powers which could be conquered only by magic. People everywhere – Catholics no less than Protestants – declared that those externals [*das Äußere*] to which the Church wished to attach a higher significance [*das Höhere*] are no more than externals: the Host is merely *dough*, the relic merely *bones*. Belief based on authority was countered by the autonomous rule of the subject, and the laws of nature were recognised as the only link between one external [thing] and another. Thus, all miracles were rejected; for nature was now a system of known and recognised laws, human beings were at home in it, and only what they were at home with was accepted as valid – they were free through their cognition of nature. Then thought was also directed to spiritual matters: right and ethical life were regarded as based on the present ground of human will, whereas they had formerly been present only as divine commandments imposed from without, as written in the Old and New Testaments, or in ancient parchments in the form of particular rights or privileges, or in [legal] treatises. It was known from empirical observation (as in the work of Grotius)[37] what nations acknowledge as right in their mutual relations; then those drives which nature has implanted in the human heart were regarded, in Cicero's manner,[38] as the source of existing civil and political right [*Staatsrecht*] – for example, the social instinct, and likewise the principle of personal security and security of citizens' property, along with the principle of the general good [*des allgemeinen Besten*] or reason of state. On the basis of these principles, private rights were on the one hand despotically disregarded, but on the other hand, universal political ends were enforced in opposition to the [merely] positive. Frederick II [of Prussia] may be named as the ruler under whom the new era attained actuality, the era in which the actual *political interest* acquired its universality and supreme justification.[39] He deserves particular emphasis because he grasped the universal end of the state by means of thought, and because he was the first ruler to hold firmly to the state's universal aspect and to take no further account of particulars if they were at variance with the end of the state. His immortal work is a domestic code of laws, the [Prussian] Common Law [*Landrecht*]. He furnished a unique example of how the father of a family energetically provides for and regulates the welfare of his household and dependants.

These universal determinations – i.e. the laws of nature and the content of what is right and good – based as they were on the present consciousness, were given the name of *reason*. The recognition [*das Gelten*] of these laws was known as *Enlightenment*.[40] It came over to Germany from France, and a new world of ideas [*Vorstellungen*] arose out of it. The absolute criterion which was applied to all authority of religious belief and positive laws of right (especially political right) was that their content should be understood by the freely present spirit itself. Luther had achieved spiritual freedom and a concrete reconciliation [of subject and object]; he triumphantly established that what is the eternal destiny of human beings should be enacted within themselves. But the *content* of what was to be enacted and what truth should come to life within them was taken by Luther as already given, as revealed by religion. The principle was now set up [by the Enlightenment] that this content should be a present one, of which I can become inwardly convinced, and that everything must be reduced to this inner ground.[41]

This principle of thought first emerges in its universal form; it is still abstract, and is based on the maxim [*Grundsatz*] of contradiction and identity. The content [*Inhalt*] is accordingly posited as finite, and the Enlightenment outlawed and eradicated all speculative elements [*alles Spekulative*] from things human and divine. But even if it is infinitely important that a manifold content [*Gehalt*] should be reduced to its simple determination in the form of universality, this as yet abstract principle still fails to satisfy the living spirit and concrete mind [*Gemüt*].

With this formally abstract principle, we come to the *final stage of history, to our world and our own times.*

Secularity is the spiritual realm in [determinate] being [*im Dasein*], the realm of the *will* as it comes into existence [*Existenz*]. Feeling [*Empfindung*], sensation [*Sinnlichkeit*], and drives are also modes of realisation of inwardness, but they are individually transient; for they are the variable content of the will. But what is just

and ethical belongs to the essential and inherently universal will
which has being in itself, and if we wish to know what is truly right,
we must abstract from inclinations, drives, and desires as particular
[things]; we must consequently know *what the will is in itself*. For
drives^c of benevolence, helpfulness, and sociability remain drives,
and various other drives are hostile to them. What the will is in
itself must rise above these particulars and opposites. But when it
does so, the will, as will, remains abstract. The will is free only in
so far as it does not will anything other, external, or alien (in which
case it would be dependent), but wills only itself as will.[42] The
absolute will is the will to be free. The will which wills itself is the
basis of all right and all obligation, and hence of all laws of right,
prescribed duties, and imposed obligations. The freedom of the will
itself is, as such, the principle and substantial foundation of all right;
it is itself absolute right, eternal in and for itself, and the highest of
all rights (in so far as it is compared with other, particular rights).
It is even that [quality] by which the human being becomes a human
being, and is consequently the fundamental principle of spirit. –
But the next question to arise is this: how does the will become
determinate?[43] For when it wills itself, it is merely identical self-
reference. But it also wills particular things: there *are*, as we know,
distinct duties and rights. We expect the will to have a content and
determinacy; for the pure will is its own object and content, which
is no object or content at all. As such, it is nothing more than a
formal will. But this is not the place to discuss the speculative process which leads on from this simple will to the determination of
freedom, and hence to rights and duties. It may simply be noted
here that, in Germany, the same principle was established theoreti-
cally by the *Kantian* philosophy. For according to the latter, the
simple unity of self-consciousness, the 'I', is inviolable and utterly
independent freedom and the source of all universal determinations
(i.e. determinations of thought), namely theoretical reason, and likewise the highest of all practical determinations, namely practical
reason as free and pure will; and the rationality [*Vernunft*] of will
consists simply in maintaining itself in pure freedom, in willing only

---

^c *Translator's note*: *Werke* has *Dem Triebe* ('To the drive'), which is incoherent in
grammar and sense. I follow Glockner's edition (vol. XI, p. 552), which has *Denn
Triebe* ('For drives'); Lasson's edition has *Die Triebe* ('The drives'), which also
gives a coherent sense.

the latter in all particular instances, in willing right purely for the sake of right, and duty purely for the sake of duty. With the Germans, [all] this remained tranquil theory; but the French wished to put it into practice. – Two questions now arise: why did this principle of freedom remain merely formal? and why did only the French, and not the Germans, set out to realise it?[44]

The formal principle was certainly supplemented [in France] by categories of weightier content – above all that of society and what is useful to it; but the aim of society is itself political, the aim of the state (see the *Droits de l'homme et du citoyen* of 1791), which is to uphold *natural rights*; but natural right is *freedom*, whose further determination is *equality* of rights before the law. The two are directly linked, for parity is [achieved] through the comparison[d] of many, but the many in question are human beings, whose basic determination is the same, namely freedom. This principle remains formal, because it arose out of abstract thought (i.e. the understanding), which is primarily the self-consciousness of pure reason and, being immediate, is abstract.[45] It does not yet develop anything further out of itself, for it still remains opposed to religion in general as the concrete absolute content.[46]

As for the second question (i.e. why did the French proceed at once from the theoretical to the *practical*, while the Germans went no further than theoretical abstraction?), one might say that the French are hotheads ('ils ont la tête près du bonnet'); but the reason lies deeper than this.[47] For in Germany, the formal principle of philosophy is faced with a concrete world and actuality in which the need of the spirit finds inner satisfaction and the conscience is at peace. For on the one hand, it was the *Protestant world* itself which had advanced so far in thought as to become conscious of the absolute apex of self-consciousness; and on the other hand, Protestantism is reassured, with regard to ethical and legal [*rechtliche*] actuality, by the *disposition*[48] [of its adherents], which is at one with religion and is itself the source of all the legal content of civil law and the political constitution. In Germany, the Enlightenment was on the side of theology; in France, it was at once directed against the Church. As far as secular life was concerned,

[d] *Translator's note*: Hegel underlines his point by exploiting the etymological affinity between *Gleichheit* ('equality') and *Vergleichung* ('comparison'); a similar affinity exists between the words 'parity' and 'comparison' in English.

everything had already improved in Germany as a result of the Reformation.[49] Those pernicious institutions of celibacy, poverty, and idleness had already been done away with; there was no dead wealth tied up in the Church, and no constraint on ethical life – a constraint which is the source and occasion of vices; there was not that unspeakable injustice which arises from the interference of ecclesiastical authority in secular right, nor that other injustice of the anointed legitimacy of kings (i.e. the doctrine that princely arbitrariness as such is divine and holy because it is the arbitrariness of the Lord's anointed) – on the contrary, their will is treated with respect only in so far as it wisely affirms right, justice, and the welfare of the whole. To this extent, the principle of thought was already reconciled; besides, the Protestant world was conscious within itself that, in the reconciliation which had previously been expounded [in theological terms], the principle was already present for the further development [*Ausbildung*] of right.

The abstractly developed consciousness of the understanding can leave religion on one side; but religion is the universal form in which truth exists [*ist*] for the non-abstract consciousness. Now the Protestant religion does not permit two kinds of conscience;[50] but in the Catholic world, there is the sacred on one side, and on the other, abstraction opposed to religion – i.e. to its superstition and its truth. This formal, individual [*eigene*] will is now treated as fundamental: right in society is what the law wills, and the will is *individual* in character. Consequently, the state, as an aggregate of numerous individuals, is not a substantial unity in and for itself or the truth of right in and for itself to which the will of individuals must adapt itself in order to be a genuine free will; on the contrary, the atomic wills are the point of departure, and every will is immediately represented as absolute.[51]

In this way, a *principle of thought* was discovered for the state – no longer just some principle based on opinion, such as the social impulse, the need for security of property, etc., nor on piety, like the divine appointment of authority, but the principle of certainty, which is identity with my self-consciousness. (It is not yet, however, the principle of truth, which must be clearly distinguished from it.) This is an immense discovery with regard to our innermost nature [*das Innerste*] and to freedom. The consciousness of the spiritual realm [*des Geistigen*] is now essentially fundamental, and sovereignty has now passed to *philosophy*. It has been said that the *French Revol-ution* arose out of philosophy,[52] and it is not without reason that philosophy was [once] called 'worldly wisdom' [*Weltweisheit*];[e] for it is not only truth in and for itself, as pure essentiality, but also truth in so far as it comes to life in the secular world. We should not therefore take issue with the assertion that the Revolution received its first impulse from philosophy. But this philosophy is at first only abstract thought, not concrete comprehension of absolute truth, which is immeasurably different.

Thus, the principle of freedom of the will asserted itself against existing right. It is true that, before the French Revolution, the great nobles[f] had already been suppressed by Richelieu and had their privileges removed; but like the clergy, they retained all their rights in relation to the lower class. The whole condition of France in those days was a chaotic aggregate of privileges contrary to all thought and reason, a senseless state of affairs which was at the same time associated with extreme ethical and spiritual corruption – an empire of injustice which, when consciousness begins to register it, becomes shameless injustice. The grinding oppression which weighed down on the people, and the government's embarrassment as it struggled to finance the luxury and extravagance of the court, were the prime causes of discontent. The new spirit became active; oppression provided a stimulus to investigation. It was noted that the sums extorted from the toiling people were not applied to the ends of the state, but squandered in the most senseless manner. The whole political system seemed one [great] injustice. The change was necessarily violent, because the transformation was not initiated by the government. But the government did not initiate it because the court, the clergy, the nobility, and even the parliaments were unwilling to give up their privileges either on grounds of necessity or for the sake of that right which has being in and for itself; also because the government, as the concrete centre of political power, could not make a principle out of the abstract wills of individuals and reconstruct the state on that basis; and finally because it was a Catholic government, so that the concept of freedom and rational laws was not recognised as ultimately and absolutely binding, for

[e] *Translator's note*: See note a to *The Relationship of Religion to the State* on p. 228 below.
[f] *Translator's note*: Compare p. 76 above.

the sacred and the religious conscience are divorced from it. The thought and concept of right asserted its claims *all at once*, and the old framework of injustice could offer no resistance to it.[53] A constitution was accordingly established on the basis of the idea [*Gedanke*] of right, and everything was supposed to be based on this foundation from now on.[54] As long as the sun has stood in the firmament and the planets have revolved around it, it had never been observed that man stands on his head – i.e. [that his existence is based] on thought – and that he constructs actuality in accordance with it. Anaxagoras was the first to say that the world is governed by νοῦσ;[55] but only now did people come to recognise that thought ought to govern spiritual reality. This was accordingly a glorious dawn. All thinking beings shared in celebrating this epoch. A sublime emotion prevailed in those days; an enthusiasm of the spirit swept through the world as if the actual reconciliation of the divine with the world had only now been accomplished.[56]

The following two aspects [*Momente*] must now engage our attention: (1) the course of the Revolution in France; and (2) how the Revolution became world-historical.

1. Freedom embodies a twofold determination. The first concerns the content of freedom, its objectivity – i.e. the thing itself; the second concerns the form of freedom, in which the subject knows itself as active; for the requirement of freedom is that the subject should know that it possesses it and is playing its part, for it is in the subject's own interest that the thing itself should be realised [*daß die Sache werde*]. Then the three elements and powers of the living state must be considered (although detailed consideration will be deferred until the Lectures on the Philosophy of Right).[57]

(a) The *laws* of rationality, of right in itself; objective or real freedom (including freedom of property and personal freedom): all lack of freedom resulting from feudal ties hereby comes to an end, and all provisions [*Bestimmungen*] derived from feudal law, such as tithes and tributes, are hereby abolished. Real freedom further includes freedom of trade or profession [*Freiheit der Gewerbe*], whereby people are allowed to use their abilities as they wish, and free access to all offices of state. These are the moments of real freedom, which are not based on feeling (for feeling allows even serfdom and slavery to remain in being), but on thought and on the self-consciousness of human beings of their spiritual essence.

(b) But the agency which actualises the laws is *government* in general. Government is primarily the formal exercise of the laws and the upholding of their authority; in foreign relations, it pursues the end of the state, which is the independence of the nation as one individuality in relation to others; and finally, in internal affairs, it has to look after the welfare of the state and all its classes [*Klassen*], which is administration.⁵⁸ For it is not just a matter of the citizen being able to practise a trade – the citizen must also profit from it; it is not enough that people should be able to use their abilities – they must also find an opportunity to apply them. The state accordingly incorporates a universal [element] and an application of the latter. This application depends on a subjective will, a will which resolves and decides. Even the making of laws – finding the determinations in question and giving them positive expression – is an application. Then the next stage is that of resolution and execution. Here, the question arises of whose will should make the decisions. The final decision rests with the monarch; but if the state is based on freedom, the many wills of individuals also wish to share in the resolutions. But the *many* are *everyone*, and it seems an empty expedient and a monstrous inconsistency to allow only *a few* to take part in these resolutions, since each wishes his will to participate in what is to be a law for him. The few are supposed to *represent* the many, but they often merely *trample them underfoot*.ᵍ Nor is the rule of the majority over the minority any less glaring an inconsistency.

(c) This collision of subjective wills leads us next to a third aspect [*Moment*], namely that of *disposition*.⁵⁹ This is the inner affirmation [*Wollen*] of the laws – not just custom [*Sitte*], but a disposition to regard the laws and constitution in general as firmly fixed, and to see it as the highest duty of individuals to subject their particular wills to them. There may be many different opinions and views concerning laws, constitution, and government, but there must be a disposition to regard all these opinions as subordinate to the substantial interest of the state and to abandon them in its favour; there must also be a disposition [to believe] that nothing is higher and more sacred than the disposition of the state itself – or that, even if religion is higher and more sacred, it contains nothing distinct

---

ᵍ *Translator's note*: It is impossible to reproduce in English Hegel's play on the morphological similarity between *vertreten* ('to represent') and *zertreten* ('to stamp on' or 'to trample underfoot').

from or opposed to the constitution. It is admittedly accepted as a basic article of wisdom that the laws and constitution of the state should be kept quite separate from religion, for fear that a state religion may lead to bigotry and hypocrisy; but even if religion and the state are different in content, they share the same root, and the laws receive their highest endorsement from religion.

Now it must be stated categorically [*schlechthin*] here that no rational constitution is possible under the Catholic religion.[60] For government and people must have this ultimate mutual guarantee of disposition, and they can have it only in a religion that is not opposed to a rational political constitution.

Plato, in his *Republic*, makes everything dependent on the government, and makes disposition into a principle, which is why he places the main emphasis on education. This is completely at variance with the modern theory, which leaves everything to the individual will. But this gives no guarantee that the will in question will also have the right disposition compatible with the state's continued existence.[61]

After these basic definitions we must now trace the course of the *French Revolution* and the transformation of the state in accordance with the concept of right. At first, only the wholly abstract philosophical principles were laid down, and no account was taken of disposition and religion. The first constitution in France was that of the *kingdom*: the monarch was to be head of state, and the executive power was to reside with him and his ministers; but the legislative body was to make the laws. This constitution, however, was from the outset internally contradictory, for the whole power of administration was invested in the legislature: the budget, war and peace, and the recruitment of the armed forces were the responsibility of the legislative Chamber. Everything was regulated by law. But the budget is by definition not a law, for it is an annual occurrence, and the power which has to present it is the power of government. (This is further connected with the indirect appointment of ministers and officials, etc.) The government was accordingly transferred to the Chambers, as in England to Parliament. – This constitution was also beset by absolute distrust: the dynasty was suspect, because it had lost the power which it formerly possessed, and the priests refused to take the oath. The government and constitution could not continue in this way, and they were overthrown.

Nevertheless, a government was still present. We must accordingly ask where it went to. In theory, it passed to the people, but in actual fact it passed to the National Convention and its committees. The abstract principles of *freedom* and (as it exists in the subjective will) *virtue* were now dominant.[62] Virtue now had to govern in opposition to the many who, in their corruption and attachment to old interests – or even through excesses of freedom and the passions – did not keep faith with virtue. Here, virtue is a simple principle which merely distinguishes between those who are virtuously disposed and those who are not. But disposition can only be recognised and judged by disposition. Consequently, *suspicion* prevails; but as soon as virtue comes under suspicion, it is already condemned. Suspicion acquired terrible power and brought the monarch, whose subjective will was in fact the religious conscience of Catholicism, to the scaffold. The principle of virtue was set up as supreme by Robespierre, and it can certainly be said that this man took virtue seriously. Now *virtue* and *terror* prevailed; for subjective virtue, whose rule is based purely on disposition, brings the most terrible tyranny in its train. It exercises its power without legal forms, and the penalty it imposes is equally simple, namely death. This tyranny had to perish; for all inclinations and interests, and rationality itself, were opposed to this terrible and consistent freedom which, in its concentrated form, behaved with such fanaticism. An organised government emerged once more, just like the previous one except that the head [of state] and monarch was now a variable Directorate with five members, who may have formed a moral unit but not an individual one. Suspicion prevailed among them too, and the government was in the hands of the legislative assemblies; it was therefore destined to collapse like its predecessor, for the absolute need for a governing *power* had been demonstrated. *Napoleon* established the latter as a military power, and in turn placed himself as an individual will at the head of the state;[63] he knew how to rule, and soon had internal affairs under control. He drove out the remaining lawyers, ideologists, and sticklers for principle, and distrust no longer prevailed but gave way to respect and fear. With his enormous strength of character he then looked outwards, subjugated the whole of Europe and spread his liberal institutions everywhere. No greater victories were ever won, and no campaigns of greater genius were ever conducted; but never did the powerlessness of victory appear in a clearer light than it did then. The disposition of the peoples – i.e. their religious disposition and that of their nationality – finally overthrew this colossus, and a constitutional monarchy, with the *charte consti-tutionelle* as its foundation, was in turn established in France.[64] But here again, the antithesis between disposition and distrust made its appearance. The French were lying to each other when they issued addresses full of devotion and love towards the monarchy and full of the blessings it bestowed. A farce was played out for fifteen years; for even if the *charte* was the universal banner on which both sides had sworn an oath, one side was of a Catholic disposition, which made it a matter of conscience to destroy the existing institutions.[65] Thus another breach occurred, and the government was over-thrown. After forty years of wars and immeasurable confusion, older people [*ein altes Herz*] might well rejoice at last to see all this come to an end and satisfaction restored. But although one main point has now been settled, there is still a breach within the Catholic principle on the one hand and among the subjective wills on the other. In the latter case, a major one-sidedness remains inasmuch as the universal will is also supposed to be the *empirically* universal will – i.e. individuals as such are supposed to govern or to have a share in government. Not content with the fact that rational rights and freedom of person and property are recognised, that there is an organised state encompassing spheres of civil life which have their own functions to perform, or that men of insight have influence among the people and the latter are filled with confidence, *liberalism* counters all this with the atomistic principle of individual wills, according to which everything should be governed by the latter's express power and with their express consent. With this formalistic view of freedom, with this abstraction, they [i.e. the liberals] do not allow any firmly based organisation to emerge. Particular rulings of the government are at once opposed by [appeals to] freedom, on the grounds that they are [expressions of] a particular will and consequently arbitrary. The will of the many overthrows the admin-istration, and the erstwhile opposition now takes office; but inas-much as this opposition is now the government, it is in turn opposed by the many. So the movement and unrest continue. This collision, this crux, this problem is what history now faces, and it must solve it at some time in the future.

2. We now have to consider the French Revolution as a *world-historical* event, for it is world-historical in *content* [*Gehalt*], and the conflict of formalism [which has just been discussed] must be clearly

distinguished from it. As far as its outward expansion is concerned, almost all modern states have been exposed to its principle through conquest, or this principle has been expressly introduced within them; liberalism has prevailed in all the Romance nations in particular, i.e. in the Roman Catholic world (*France, Italy,* and *Spain*).[66] But it became bankrupt everywhere: first the parent company in France, then in Spain and Italy – twice, in fact, in those states where it had been introduced. It was first introduced in Spain by the Napoleonic constitution, and then by that of the Cortes; in Piedmont when that country was incorporated into the French Empire, and then through internal insurrection; and in Rome and Naples, this also happened twice. Thus the abstraction of liberalism spread from France throughout the Romance world, but religious servitude kept that world in fetters of political unfreedom. For it is a false principle that the fetters which bind right and freedom can be cast off without the emancipation of conscience – i.e. that there can be a revolution without a Reformation.[67] – These countries accordingly relapsed into their old condition, with some modifications to the external political condition in Italy. Venice and Genoa, those ancient aristocracies – which, to be sure, were at least legitimate – vanished as rotten despotisms. External domination can accomplish nothing in the long run: Napoleon could no more coerce Spain into freedom than Philip II could coerce Holland into servitude.

These Romance nations stand in contrast to other nations, the Protestant ones in particular. Austria and England have remained outside the sphere of internal unrest and shown great, indeed enormous, evidence of their inner stability. Austria is not a kingdom but an empire, i.e. an aggregate of many political organisations. Its main territories are not Germanic in character and have remained untouched by Ideas. Unimproved by education or religion, the subjects have in some parts remained serfs and the nobles have remained in a state of repression, as in Bohemia; in other areas, while the condition of the subjects has remained the same, the barons have asserted their freedom in order to maintain their tyranny, as in Hungary. Austria has given up that closer association with Germany which went with the Imperial title and has divested itself of its numerous possessions and rights in Germany and the Netherlands. It now exists as a political power in its own right in Europe.

England, by great exertions, has also stood firm on its old foundations; the English *constitution* held its own amidst the general upheaval, although it was all the more susceptible to the latter inasmuch as its public Parliament, its custom of public gatherings for all social orders [*Stände*], and its free press made it easy for the French principles of liberty and equality to gain access to all classes [*Klassen*] of the people. Was the English nation culturally too obtuse to grasp these general principles?[68] But there is no country where freedom has been the subject of more reflection and public discussion. Or did the English constitution already allow such complete freedom, and were the above principles already realised in it to such an extent that they could no longer arouse any opposition or even interest? The English nation no doubt approved of France's liberation; but it was proudly confident in its own constitution and its own freedom, and instead of imitating the foreign [country], it reacted with its usual hostile attitude and was soon embroiled in a popular war with France.[69]

England's constitution is entirely composed of *particular rights* and special privileges. The government is essentially administrative – i.e. it looks after the interests of all particular estates [*Stände*] and classes; and these particular churches, parishes, counties, and societies look after themselves, so that there is in fact nowhere where the government has less to do than in England.[70] This is the main feature of what the English call their freedom, and the opposite of such centralised administration as is found in France where, down to the smallest village, the mayor is appointed by the ministry or its lesser officials. Nowhere are people less tolerant of other people's initiatives than in France: the ministry there incorporates all administrative authority, to which the Chamber of Deputies in turn lays claim. Conversely in England, every parish, every subordinate sphere and association has its own function to perform. In this way, the universal interest is concrete, and the particular interest is known and willed within it. These institutions based on particular interests completely rule out any universal system. This is also why abstract and universal principles mean nothing to the English and sound hollow to them. – These particular interests have their positive rights, which date from the old days of feudal law and have been more fully preserved in England than in any other country. With the utmost inconsistency, they are at the same time the height of injustice, and the institutions of real freedom are nowhere less in evidence than in England. They are incredibly far behind in civil law and freedom of ownership: we need only think of primogeniture, which means that military commissions or ecclesiastical appointments have to be purchased or arranged for younger sons.

Parliament rules, even if the English are reluctant to acknowledge the fact. We should note that what has always been regarded as the corrupt phase of a republican nation [*Volk*] is in evidence here, for parliamentary elections are decided by bribery. But even the fact that they can sell their votes or purchase a seat in Parliament is described by the English as freedom. – This utterly inconsistent and corrupt state of affairs does, however, have the advantage of making a government possible – i.e. a majority of men in Parliament who are statesmen, and who have devoted themselves since their youth to affairs of state and have worked and lived amidst them. And the nation has the right sense and insight to recognise that there must be a government, and hence to place its trust in a body of men who have experience of governing; for the sense of particularity also recognises that universal particularity of knowledge [*Kenntnis*], experience, and training which the aristocracy, who devote themselves exclusively to such interests, possess. This is the complete opposite of that sense of principles and abstraction which anyone can instantly acquire – principles which are in any case enshrined in all constitutions and charters. – What is in question is the extent to which the reform now proposed, if consistently implemented, will still allow for the possibility of a government.

England's material existence is based on trade and industry, and the English have taken on the major vocation of acting as missionaries of *civilisation* throughout the world; for their commercial spirit impels them to explore every ocean and country, to establish links with barbarous peoples, to stimulate needs and industry among them, and above all to create for them the conditions required for commerce – namely abstention from acts of violence, respect for property, and hospitality [towards strangers].

Germany was traversed by the victorious French armies, but the German nationality cast off this yoke. An important factor in Germany are the laws of right, even if these were the product of French oppression which clearly showed up the deficiencies of the previous institutions. The pretence [*Lüge*] of an Empire has completely vanished. It has broken up into sovereign states. Feudal obligations have been abolished, and freedom of property and personal freedom have been made basic principles. Every citizen is eligible to hold offices of state (although skill and aptitude are necessary qualifications). Government is in the hands of officialdom, and the monarch's personal decision stands supreme – for a final decision, as already remarked, is absolutely [*schlechthin*] necessary. But with firmly established laws and a specific political organisation, what is left for the monarch alone to decide is inconsiderable in point of substance.[71] It must nevertheless be regarded as highly fortunate if a people happens to acquire a noble monarch; but even this is less important in a large state, whose strength lies in its rationality [*Vernunft*]. The existence and security of small states is more or less guaranteed by the other states; they are therefore not truly independent, and they do not have to undergo the fiery ordeal of war. – As already mentioned, everyone with the required knowledge, training, and moral will can participate in government, which should be in the hands of well-informed people – οἱ ἄριστοι[72] – not of the ignorant or of presumptuous know-alls. – Finally, as far as disposition is concerned, it has already been pointed out that the reconciliation of religion and right was achieved by the Protestant Church. There is no sacred or religious conscience divorced from – let alone opposed to – secular right.

This is the point which consciousness has now reached, and these are the chief formal moments in which the principle of freedom has been actualised; for world history is nothing but the development of the concept of freedom. But objective freedom, the laws of real freedom, require the subjugation of the contingent will, for this will is completely formal.[73] If the objective is implicitly [*an sich*] rational, our insight must accord with this rationality [*Vernunft*], in which case the essential moment of subjective freedom is likewise present. We have considered only the progress of this concept, and have had to deny ourselves the pleasure of depicting in detail the fortunes of peoples, their greatest periods, the beauty and greatness of individuals, and the interest of their fates in joy and sorrow. Philosophy is solely concerned with the splendour of the Idea which is reflected in world history. It escapes from the tedium of the immediate passions and their movements in the actual world; its interest is to recognise the course of development of the Idea as it actualises itself – the Idea of freedom which exists [*ist*] only as the consciousness of freedom.

That world history, with its changing spectacle of [individual] histories, is this course of development and the actual coming into being of the spirit – this is the true *theodicy*, the justification of God in history.[74] Only *this* insight can reconcile the spirit with world history and with actuality – the insight that God is not only present in what has happened and what happens every day, but that all this is essentially his own work.

The Relationship of Religion to the State (1831)[1]

[Editorial note: The following excerpt is from the lectures on the philosophy of religion which Hegel delivered in the summer of 1831, only a few months before he died. He had, of course, been concerned for some time with the way in which Catholicism and Protestantism functioned as political ideologies in the modern world – for example, in *AC* and *PH*, and in the additions he made to the third edition of his *Encyclopedia of the Philosophical Sciences*. But although he had delivered his lectures on the philosophy of religion on several previous occasions, it was not until the 1831 series that he included the topic covered in this extract, namely 'The Relationship of Religion to the State'. For a full discussion of the place of this topic in the series as a whole, see Hodgson's remarks in Hodgson 1984: vol. I, pp. 77–81.]

1. The state is the true mode [*wahrhafte Weise*] of actuality; in it, the true ethical will attains actuality and the spirit lives in its true form [*Wahrhaftigkeit*].[2] Religion is divine knowledge, the knowledge which human beings have of God and of themselves in God. This is divine wisdom and the field of absolute truth. But there is a second wisdom, the wisdom of the world, and the question arises as to its relationship to the former, divine wisdom.[3]

In general, religion and the foundation of the state are one and the same thing – they are *identical in and for themselves*. In the patriarchal condition and the Jewish theocracy, the two are not yet distinct and are still outwardly identical. Nevertheless, the two are also different, and in due course, they become strictly separated from one another; but then they are once more posited as genuinely identical.[4] [That the two have then attained] that unity which has being in and for itself follows from what has been said; religion is knowledge of the highest truth, and this truth, defined more precisely, is *free spirit*. In religion, human beings are free before God. In making their will conform to the divine will, they are not opposed to the divine will but have themselves within it; they are free inasmuch as they have succeeded, in the [religious] cult, in overcoming the division [*die Entzweiung aufzuheben*]. The state is merely *freedom in the world*, in actuality. The essential factor here is that concept of freedom which a people carries in its self-consciousness, for the concept of freedom is realised in the state, and an essential aspect of this realisation is the consciousness of freedom with being in and for itself. Peoples who do not know that human beings are free in and for themselves live in a benighted state both with regard to their constitution and to their religion.[5] – There is *one* concept of freedom in [both] religion and the state. This one concept is the highest thing which human beings have, and it is realised by them. A people which has a bad concept of God also has a bad state, a bad government, and bad laws.[6]

To consider this connection between the state and religion at length and in its fully developed form is properly the business of the philosophy of world history.[7] Here, we need only consider it in the specific form in which it appears to representational thought, how it becomes involved there in contradictions, and how that opposition between the two [i.e. the state and religion] finally arises which constitutes the interest of the modern age. We shall therefore consider this connection first of all

2. as it is *represented*. Human beings have a consciousness of it, but not yet as that *absolute connection* as known in philosophy; they know it rather in general, and represent it to themselves. Now the representation of this connection expresses itself [in the assertion] that the laws, governmental authority [*Obrigkeit*], and political constitution are derived *from God*: this is their authorisation, which comes from the highest authority [*Autorität*] available to representation. The laws are the development of the concept of freedom, and this concept, which thereby reflects itself in existence [*Dasein*], has as its foundation and truth the concept of freedom as under-

stood in religion.[8] What is expressed here is that these laws of ethical life and of right are eternal and immutable rules for human conduct, that they are not arbitrary, but endure [*bestehen*] as long as religion itself. We find the representation of this connection among all peoples. This can also be expressed in the form that one obeys God by following the laws and governmental authority as the powers which hold the state together.[9] This proposition is correct in one respect, but it also runs the risk of being taken wholly abstractly, inasmuch as it is not specified how the laws are explicated and what laws are appropriate to the basic constitution. Expressed formally, the proposition thus runs as follows: one ought to obey the laws, *whatever they may be*. In this way, governing and legislating are left to the *arbitrary will* of the government. This situation has arisen in *Protestant* states, and it is only in such states that it can occur, for in them that unity of religion and the state [already referred to] is present. The laws of the state are recognised [*gelten*] as rational and as divine on account of this *presumed original harmony*, and religion does not have its own principles which contradict those which apply within the state. But if we go no further than the formal proposition, the way is left open for arbitrariness, tyranny, and oppression.[10] This became particularly apparent in England (under the last kings of the House of Stuart),[11] in that *passive obedience* was demanded and the proposition was accepted that the ruler is answerable only to God for his actions. This presupposed that the ruler alone also definitely *knows* [*wisse*] what is essential and necessary for the state; for in him and in his will is contained the more precise determination [*Bestimmung*] that his will is an *immediate revelation* of God. But in its further consequences, this principle was developed to the point where it turned *into its opposite*. For the distinction between priests and laity is not present in Protestantism, and the priests do not have privileged possession of divine revelation; still less does such a *privilege* belong exclusively to a single layman. The principle of the divine authorisation of the ruler is therefore opposed by the principle that the laity in general is similarly authorised.[12] Thus, a Protestant sect arose in England which maintained that revelation had informed it how the government should be conducted; and in consequence of such divine inspiration, they initiated a revolution and beheaded their king.[13] – Thus, even if it is generally accepted that the laws are willed by God, it is no less important to know [*erkennen*] this divine will, and this is not a particular prerogative [*nichts Partikulares*] but something open to everyone.[14] To know [*erkennen*] what is rational is a matter for cultivated thought and particularly for philosophy, which in this sense may well be described as 'worldly wisdom'.[a] It is quite immaterial what external appearance the laws have assumed in asserting their validity (e.g. whether they were forcibly extracted from the ruler or not); the progressive development [*Fortbildung*] of the concept of freedom, right, and humanity among human beings is necessary in itself [*für sich*]. – Thus, in considering that truth that the laws are the will of God,[15] it is particularly important to determine *what these laws are*: principles as such are merely abstract thoughts which acquire their truth only in their development [*Entwicklung*]; if they remain tied to their abstract form, they are completely devoid of truth [*das ganz Unwahre*].

3. Finally, the state and religion can also be *divorced from one another* and have *different laws*. The secular and the religious spheres are distinct, and a difference of principle may also arise. Religion does not simply remain in its own distinct sphere, but also affects the subject, issuing precepts with regard to the subject's religiosity and hence also to its activity. These precepts which religion issues to the individual may be distinct from the principles of right and ethical life which obtain within the state. This opposition can be expressed in the following form: the requirement of religion relates to *sanctity*, and that of the state to *right and ethical life*;[16] the one determination concerns *eternity*, the other *temporality* and temporal well-being, which must be sacrificed for eternal salvation. Thus, a *religious ideal* is set up, a heaven on earth, i.e. the *abstraction of spirit* as against *the substantial realm of actuality*; *renunciation* of actuality is the basic determination which emerges, and with it conflict and flight. To the substantial foundation, the true basis [*dem Wahrhaften*], something else is opposed which is supposedly higher.

The *first* [mode of] ethical life in substantial actuality is *marriage*. In [the realm of] actuality, love (which is God) is conjugal love. As the initial appearance of the substantial will in existent [*daseienden*] actuality, this love has a natural aspect, but it is also an ethical

---

[a] *Translator's note: Weltweisheit*, the older German term for 'philosophy' which was in use for most of the eighteenth century until around the time of Kant, when it was gradually supplanted by the modern term *Philosophie*.

duty. In opposition to this duty, renunciation or *celibacy* is set up as something sacred.

Secondly, human beings as individuals have to contend with natural necessity; it is an ethical law for them to make themselves independent [of it] by their activity and understanding, for they are by nature in many respects dependent. They are obliged to earn their sustenance by their mind [*Geist*] and their integrity [*Rechtlichkeit*] and so to liberate themselves from that natural necessity; that is [the nature of] human rectitude [*Rechtschaffenheit*]. A religious duty set up in opposition to this secular duty requires that human beings should not be active in this way and should not trouble themselves with such cares. The whole sphere of commerce and all activity relating to acquisition, industry, etc. is thereby repudiated, for human beings ought not to concern themselves with ends such as these; but in this case, necessity is more rational than such religious views. On the one hand, human activity is represented as unholy, and on the other hand, it is even required of people that, if they have possessions, they should not only refrain from increasing these by their activity, but should give them to the *poor*, and especially to the Church – i.e. to those who do nothing and do not work. Thus, what is held up as rectitude in life is thereby rejected as unholy.

Thirdly, the highest ethical life within the *state* depends on the activation of the rational universal will; [for] in the state, the subject has its *freedom*, which is actualised within it. In opposition to this, a religious duty is set up, according to which freedom may not be the ultimate end for human beings, who should submit instead to strict *obedience* and remain thenceforth without a will of their own; furthermore, they should be selfless even in their conscience and faith, and renounce themselves and practise self-denial even in their innermost being.

If religion claims exclusive control of human activity in this way, it can impose on us distinct precepts which are opposed to worldly rationality. These have been challenged by that *worldly wisdom*[b] which recognises the true [*das Wahrhafte*] in actuality; within the spirit's consciousness, the principles of its freedom have awoken, and the claims of freedom have duly come into conflict with the

---

[b] *Translator's note*: See note a above.

religious principles which demanded that renunciation [referred to above]. In the Catholic states, religion and the state thus stand in mutual opposition when subjective freedom makes its appearance in human beings.

In this opposition, religion expresses itself only in a negative manner and demands of human beings that they renounce all freedom; more precisely, this opposition means that, in their actual consciousness, they are in themselves generally *without rights*, and that, in the sphere of actual ethical life, religion recognises no absolute rights. This is the monstrous distinction which has arisen in the modern world through the very fact that the question is raised as to whether human freedom should be recognised as something true [*etwas Wahrhaftes*] in and for itself, or whether it can be rejected by religion.

It has already been mentioned that harmony can exist between religion and the state. In Protestant states, this is generally the case in principle, but [only] in an abstract way; for Protestantism demands that human beings should believe only what they know [*wissen*], and that their conscience, as something sacred, should [also] be inviolable. Human beings are not passive in [relation to] divine grace; they are essentially involved in it with their subjective freedom, and the moment of subjective freedom is expressly required in their knowledge [*Wissen*], volition, and faith. In states of a different religion it may conversely happen that the two sides are not in harmony, and that religion is distinct from the principle of the state. A broad range can be detected here – on the one hand a religion which does not recognise the principle of freedom,[17] and on the other, a political constitution which makes this principle its foundation. When we say that human beings are by nature free, this is a principle of infinite worth. But if we stick to this abstraction, it prevents the emergence of an organic constitution, for the latter requires an articulated structure [*Gliederung*] in which duties and rights are limited. The abstraction precludes that inequality which must arise if an organism – and hence true vitality – is to come into being.[18]

Principles of this kind are true, but should not be taken in the abstract. The knowledge that human beings are free by nature (i.e. in terms of the concept) belongs to the modern age.[19] But whether or not we stick to abstraction, it may happen that these principles are opposed by a religion which does not recognise them but regards them as devoid of right and sees only arbitrariness as rightful. Thus, a conflict necessarily arises which cannot be settled in any true way. Religion demands the suspension [*Aufheben*] of the will, whereas the secular principle treats the will as fundamental; if such religious principles come into play, the only possible course is for the government to resort to force and suppress the opposing religion or treat its adherents as a [political] party. As a church, religion may well be circumspect and outwardly compliant, but then an *inconsistency* arises in the minds [of its adherents]. The world remains attached to a specific religion and simultaneously adheres to principles which are opposed to it.[20] In so far as those concerned apply these principles while still claiming to belong to the religion in question, there is a major inconsistency. Thus the French, for example, who adhere to the principle of secular freedom, have in fact ceased to belong to the Catholic religion, for this religion can make no concessions but consistently demands unconditional submission to the Church in all matters. In this way, religion and the state are in mutual contradiction. So religion is left on one side to cope as best it can; it is treated as a purely individual matter with which the state need not concern itself, and it is further argued that religion should not become involved in the political constitution. To posit those principles of freedom [referred to above] is to assert that they are true because they are connected with the innermost self-consciousness of human beings. But if it is in fact reason which discovers these principles, the only way in which it can verify them (in so far as they are true and do not simply remain formal) is by tracing them back to the cognition of absolute truth, and this is the object of philosophy alone. But this cognition must be complete, and must go all the way back to the final [stage of its] analysis. For if it is not internally complete, it is exposed to the one-sidedness of formalism; but if it does proceed to the ultimate ground, it arrives at what is recognised as highest of all, namely God. So it is all very well to say that the political constitution should remain on one side and religion on the other; but there is then a risk that the above principles will continue to suffer from one-sidedness. Thus, we see that the world is at present full of the principle of freedom, and that this principle applies in particular to the political constitution. These principles are correct, but if they are afflicted with formalism, they are prejudices, because cognition has not proceeded to the ultimate ground; only there do we find their reconciliation with the wholly [*schlechthin*] substantial. –

Now the other point which arises in connection with this separation is this: if the principles of actual freedom are made basic and develop into a system of right, they give rise to enacted *positive laws*, and these assume the form of juridical laws in general with regard to individuals. The courts are entrusted with upholding the legislation. Whoever violates the law is brought before the courts, and the existence [*Existenz*] of the whole is vested [*gesetzt*] in this *juridical form* in general. Then opposed to this there is that *conviction* [*Gesinnung*] or inwardness which is the very basis of religion.[21] There are accordingly two opposing aspects, both of which belong to actuality – the positive legislation and the conviction in relation to it.

As far as the constitution is concerned, two *systems* are involved here. On the one hand, there is the modern system in which the determinations of freedom and its entire structure are upheld in a *formal* sense, with no regard for [individual] conviction. On the other, there is the system of *conviction* – the Greek principle in general, which we find developed in Plato's *Republic* in particular.[22] A few [social] classes [*Stände*] constitute the basis of this system, and the whole depends in other respects on *education* and culture [*Bildung*], which are supposed to proceed to science and philosophy. Philosophy is supposed to be the ruling principle by which human beings are led towards ethical life; all classes are to share in σωφροσύνη.[23]

These two aspects, conviction and the formal constitution, are *inseparable* and cannot do without one another. But modern times have seen the emergence of that *one-sidedness* whereby the constitution is supposed to be self-supporting on the one hand, while on the other, conviction, religion, and conscience are to be set aside as irrelevant on the grounds that whatever conviction and religion individuals may subscribe to have nothing to do with the political constitution. But just how one-sided this [view] is can be seen from the fact that the laws are administered by judges on whose rectitude and insight everything depends; for it is not the law which rules, but human beings who have to make it rule.[24] This activity is a concrete one, and human will as well as human insight must play their part in it. Consequently, the subject's intelligence must often make the decisions, for while the civil laws go a long way in their specifications [*das Bestimmen*], they still cannot touch on every particular. But conviction on its own is likewise one-sided, and Plato's republic suffers from this deficiency. Nowadays, we do not wish to place any reliance on insight, but prefer to see everything regulated by positive laws. We have witnessed a major example of this one-sidedness in recent current affairs.[25] We saw religious conviction at the highest level of the French government, a conviction of a kind which considered the state in general to have no rights at all and which adopted a hostile attitude towards actuality, towards right and ethical life. The latest revolution was accordingly the result of a religious conscience which contradicted the principles of the political constitution – although according to that same constitution, it is not supposed to make any difference what religion the individual belongs to. This clash is still very far from being resolved.[26]

Conviction does not necessarily take the form of religion; it may also remain in a more indeterminate condition. But among what is known as 'the people', ultimate truth does not take the form of thoughts and principles; on the contrary, what is supposed to count as right in the eyes of the people can do so only in so far as it is *determinate* and particular. Now this determinate quality of right and ethical life has its ultimate guarantee for the people only in the form of an *existing religion*;[27] and if the latter has no connection with the principles of freedom, a split and an unresolved division continue to be present, a hostile relationship which ought not to occur in the state especially. Under Robespierre, there was a Reign of Terror in France, specifically directed against those who did not share the conviction [*Gesinnung*] of freedom, because they were *suspect* (i.e. because of their conviction). Thus, the ministry of Charles X was also suspect. In formal constitutional terms, the monarch was not answerable to anyone; but these formal provisions did not stand up [to the challenge], and the dynasty was deposed. It is accordingly evident that, in a formally developed constitution, conviction is once again the ultimate safeguard which, though ignored by the constitution itself, subsequently reasserts itself with contempt for all [considerations of] form.[28] It is from this contradiction and the prevailing lack of awareness of it that our age is suffering. –

On the English Reform Bill[1]

The primary intention of the Reform Bill now before the English Parliament[2] is to bring justice and fairness into the way in which the various classes [*Klassen*] and sections of the populace are allowed to participate in the election of Members of Parliament.[3] This is to be achieved by introducing a greater degree of symmetry in place of the most bizarre and informal[a] irregularity and inequality which prevail at present.[4] It is numbers, localities, and private interests which are to be rearranged; but in fact, the change in question also impinges on the noble internal organs of Great Britain, on the vital principles of its constitution and condition. It is this aspect of the present Bill which merits particular attention, and the aim of this essay will be to bring together those higher points of view which have hitherto come up for discussion in the parliamentary debates. It is not surprising that so many voices were raised in opposition to the Bill in the Lower House, and that it gained its second reading only by the accident of a single vote; for it is precisely those interests of the aristocracy which are powerful even in the Lower House that are to be challenged and reformed. If the Bill were opposed by all those who stand to lose (or whose sponsors stand to lose) their former privileges and influence, it would most decidedly have the majority against it at once. Those who promoted the Bill could rely only on the fact that a sense of justice had now prevailed over entrenched privileges even in those whose advantage lay in these

---

[a] *Translator's note*: The words 'most bizarre and informal' occur in Hegel's manuscript, but not in the published text of 1831.

very prerogatives – a sense which was greatly reinforced by the disquieting impression produced among interested Members of Parliament by the example of neighbouring France;[5] and the almost universally expressed view in England concerning the need for reform is regularly invoked in Parliament as a motive of the highest importance.[6] But even if public opinion in Great Britain were quite unanimously in favour of reform to the extent, or within the limits, proposed by the Bill, there would still have to be an opportunity to examine the substance of what this opinion demands – especially since we have not infrequently discovered, in recent times, that such demands have turned out to be either impossible to implement or disastrous in practice, and that this universal opinion has meanwhile turned vehemently against what it seemed to demand and approve with equal vehemence a short time before.[7] Those ancients who, as members of democracies since their youth, had accumulated long experience and reflected profoundly about it, held different views on popular opinion from those more a priori views which are prevalent today.[8]

The projected reform begins with the indisputable fact that the grounds on which the share of the various counties and communities in parliamentary representation was [originally] determined had completely changed over the course of time, with the result that their 'rights to this share' were now completely at odds with the principles underlying those grounds themselves, and in contradiction to everything which, in this part of a constitution, strikes [even] the plainest common sense as just and reasonable. One of the most prominent opponents of the Bill, Robert Peel,[9] admits that it may well be easy to hold forth on the anomalies and absurdity of the English constitution; and its incongruities have indeed been fully and circumstantially described in the proceedings of Parliament and in the national press. It may therefore be sufficient here to recall the main points: towns with a small population, or indeed their councillors (who in fact appoint one another and act without reference to the citizens), and even boroughs which have declined to two or three inhabitants (themselves leaseholders), have retained the right to fill seats in Parliament, while many flourishing cities of more recent origin with 100,000 inhabitants or more are denied the right to elect candidates; and between these extremes, the greatest variety of other inequalities is also to be found. An immediate consequence of this is that the filling of a large number of parliamentary seats is in the hands of a small number of individuals. (It has been calculated that the majority of the House is controlled by 150 persons of eminence.) A further consequence is that an even more significant number of seats can be purchased, and are in some cases a recognised market commodity, so that possession of such a seat can be gained by bribery or by the formal payment of a certain sum to the electors, or is in general reduced, with numerous other variations, to a purely financial matter.

It would be difficult to discover a comparable symptom of political corruption in any other people. Montesquieu declared that *virtue*, the unselfish sense of duty towards the state, is the principle of the democratic constitution;[10] and in the English constitution, the democratic element has significant scope in the participation of the people in electing members of the Lower House (i.e. those politicians who have a major share of power in deciding matters of universal concern). It is probably a fairly unanimous view among pragmatic historians[11] that, if private interest and squalid financial advantage become the predominant factor in the election of heads of government within a given nation [*Volk*], this condition can be regarded as a prelude to the inevitable loss of that nation's political freedom,[12] the downfall of its constitution and of the state itself. In response to the pride of the English in their freedom,[13] we Germans may well point out that, even if the old constitution of the German Empire was likewise an amorphous aggregate of particular rights, it was only the external bond of the German territories, and political life within these, as far as the filling of seats in the surviving provincial assemblies[b] and rights to elect to them were concerned, did not display such anomalies[c] as those just mentioned, let alone that selfishness[d] which permeates all classes [*Klassen*] of the [English] people. Now even if, in addition to the democratic element, the aristocratic element is an extremely important power in England; even if purely aristocratic governments like those of Venice, Genoa, Berne,[14] etc. have been accused of maintaining their security and stability by submerging the people they govern in base sensuality and moral corruption;[15] and even if the ability to cast one's vote

[b] *Translator's note*: Reading *Landständen* ('provincial assemblies') for Hegel's *Ländern* ('territories').
[c] *Translator's note*: The manuscript version has 'absurdity'.
[d] *Translator's note*: The manuscript reads 'corruption'.

entirely as one pleases, irrespective of what motive determines the will, is counted as freedom – we must nevertheless acknowledge that it is a fair indication of the reawakening of the moral sense among the English people that one of the feelings which the need for reform has evoked is repugnance at the corruption[e] just referred to. It will also be acknowledged that the right way to seek improvement is no longer to rely simply on such moral means as representations, admonitions, or associations of isolated individuals designed to counteract the system of corruption and to avoid becoming indebted to it, but to change the institutions [themselves]. The common prejudice of inertia, which clings on to the old faith in the value of an institution even if the condition to which the latter gives rise is totally corrupt, has thus finally given way. The demand for a more thoroughgoing reform was all the greater, given that the proposals for improvement which were put forward in response to specific accusations of bribery at the opening of each new Parliament had produced no significant results. Even so commendable a proposal as the recent attempt to transfer to the city of Birmingham the franchise from a small community in which bribery had been proved, and thus to show a just inclination to remedy a glaring inequality – if only to a modest extent – was outmanoeuvred by ministerial tactics in Parliament, especially by those of Peel, a Minister otherwise acclaimed for his liberal sentiments. Thus, a great initiative which was taken at the opening session of the current Parliament was subsequently reduced to prohibiting candidates from distributing any further *badges* to their supporters among the electorate. Since the great majority of members of both Houses, who are the judges in criminal cases of this kind, are themselves involved in the system of corruption, and since most members of the Lower House owe their seats to this very system, accusations of bribery directed at a place entitled to elect [a Member of Parliament], and the ensuing investigations and trials, have been too openly and loudly denounced as pure farce, and indeed as shameless procedures, for anyone to expect even isolated remedies to emerge from this source.

The usual argument advanced on other occasions in Parliament against attacks on positive rights is based on the *wisdom of our ancestors*;[16] but it was not employed in this instance. For this wisdom,

---

[e] *Translator's note*: The manuscript reads 'depravity'.

which presumably distributed parliamentary constituencies in accordance with the then existing population of counties, cities, and boroughs or with their importance in other respects, contrasts too glaringly with the way in which the population, wealth, and importance of the different regions and interests have developed in more recent times. Another consideration which has not been mentioned is the fact that many individuals would suffer a loss of capital, while an even greater number would suffer a loss of income; for financial gain derived from direct bribery is illegal, although all classes [*Klassen*] are implicated in it either as givers or takers. The capital value lost to boroughs which are to be disenfranchised is based on the transformation, over the course of time, of a political right into a monetary value. And although the acquisition [of a seat in Parliament] at a price which is now falling was no less *bona fide* a transaction than the purchase of slaves, and although the English Parliament, when new laws are passed, usually pays particular attention to the preservation of real assets in such cases and, if these assets should suffer a loss, to [the need for] compensation, no claims of this kind have been made in the present instance, nor have any difficulties been raised in this connection, however strong a motive against the Bill this circumstance may furnish for a number of Members of Parliament.

On the other hand, another legal principle peculiarly characteristic of England is indeed attacked by the Bill, namely that *positive* character which predominates in English institutions concerned with constitutional and civil law [*Staatsrecht und Privatrecht*]. It is true that, in formal terms, every right and its [corresponding] law is positive, [that is,] decreed and laid down by the supreme political authority, and requiring obedience because it is a law. But at no time than today has the understanding of people at large [*der allgemeine Verstand*] been led to distinguish between whether rights are merely positive in their *material content*, and whether they are also right and rational in and for themselves; and in no constitution is the judgement so strongly impelled to observe this distinction as in that of England, given that the peoples of the Continent have allowed themselves to be impressed for so long by declamations about English freedom and by that nation's pride in its own legislation.[17] It is common knowledge that the latter is comprehensively based on particular rights, freedoms, and privileges which have been granted, sold, or bestowed by kings or parliaments – or wrested from them – on particular occasions. The Magna Charta and Bill of Rights, which are the principal foundations of the English constitution as further defined by subsequent Acts of Parliament, are forcibly exacted concessions or favours granted, agreements, etc., and constitutional rights [*Staatsrechte*] have retained that form of private rights [*Privatrechte*] which they originally possessed, and hence also the contingent nature of their content. This inherently incoherent aggregate of positive determinations has not yet undergone the development and transformation which has been accomplished in the civilised states of the Continent, and which the German territories, for example, have enjoyed for a longer or shorter period of time.[18]

England has hitherto lacked those elements which have played the greatest part in these glorious and auspicious advances.[19] Foremost among these elements is the scientific treatment of law [*Recht*], which on the one hand has applied general principles to the particular varieties of law and their complexities and implemented them throughout, and on the other hand has reduced concrete and special instances to more simple determinations. This made possible the [compendia of] common law and constitutional arrangements of the more recent continental states, which are for the most part based on general principles, while common sense and sound reasoning have also been allowed their proper share in determining the content of justice. For another even more important element in the transformation of law [*Recht*] must be mentioned, namely the broad vision of princes in making such principles as the welfare of the state, the happiness of their subjects, and general prosperity – but above all the sense of a justice which has being in and for itself – into the guiding light of their legislative activity, in association with the due power of the monarch, so as to gain acceptance for these principles and to endow them with reality in the face of merely positive privileges, long-standing private interest, and the incomprehension of the masses.[20] England has lagged so conspicuously behind the other civilised states of Europe in institutions based on genuine right, for the simple reason that the power of government lies in the hands of those who possess so many privileges which contradict a rational constitutional law and a genuine legislation.

It is on this state of affairs that the proposed Reform Bill is supposed to have a significant influence – but not, for example, by increasing the power of the monarchic element of the constitution.[21] On the contrary, if the Bill is not at once to encounter universal disapproval, jealousy of the power of the throne – perhaps the most intractable of English prejudices – must be treated with indulgence; and the proposed measure does indeed owe some of its popularity to the fact that the influence of the monarchy is perceived to be further weakened by it. What arouses the greatest interest is the fear felt by some, and the hope felt by others, that the reform of electoral law will bring other material reforms in its wake.[22] The English principle of positivity (on which, as already mentioned, the general legal arrangements of that country are based) is in fact undermined by the Bill in a way which is quite new and unprecedented in England, and there is an instinctive suspicion that more far-reaching changes will follow from this subversion of the formal basis of the established order.

In the course of the parliamentary debates, some mention has been made of these views (if only in passing). The proponents and friends of the Bill may either sincerely believe that it will have no further consequences beyond its own provisions, or they may keep their hopes to themselves in order not to provoke more violent reactions among their opponents – just as the latter will not hold up the object of their concern as a prize of victory; and since they own a great deal, they do indeed have much to lose. But the fact that no more has been said in Parliament about this more substantial aspect of the reform is due in large measure to the convention that, when important matters come up before that assembly, most of the time is invariably taken up by members' own expositions of their personal position; they present their views not as men of affairs, but as privileged individuals and orators.[23] There is wide scope for reform in England, encompassing the most important objectives of civil and political society. Its necessity is beginning to be felt, and some of the matters which have been raised on various occasions may serve to illustrate how much of the work which has been accomplished elsewhere still remains to be done in England.

Among the prospects for material improvements, hopes are primarily directed towards *economies* in administration [*Verwaltung*]. But however often the opposition urges that such economies are absolutely necessary in order to relieve the pressure and general misery suffered by the populace, it is also repeated on every occasion that all such endeavours have hitherto been futile, and that the popular hopes aroused by [successive] administrations [*Minis-terien*], and even in the speech from the throne, have invariably been dashed. These declamations have been repeated in the same way every time taxes have been reduced over the last fifteen years. Better prospects are held out for the eventual fulfilment of such hopes in a reformed Parliament where a greater number of its members would be independent of the administration [*Ministerium*], whose weakness, hardheartedness towards the people, [self-] interest, etc., have been blamed for chronic overspending. But if we consider the chief categories of public expenditure in England, there appears to be no great scope for *economy*. On the one hand, payments of interest on the enormous national debt cannot be reduced. On the other, the costs of the army and navy, including pensions, are intimately connected not only with political factors (particularly with the interest of trade as the basis of English existence, and with the risk of insurrection at home), but also with the habits and expectations of individuals who enter the armed forces that they will not be at a disadvantage in relation to other classes [*Ständen*] as far as luxury and affluence are concerned; consequently, there can be no savings in this area without risk. The figures brought to light by the outcry over the notorious sinecures have shown that even the complete abolition [*Aufhebung*] of these, which could not be effected without great injustice, would be of little significance. But we need not go into these material aspects; we need only note that the tireless efforts of Hume,[24] who scrutinised the finances in minute detail, have been almost uniformly unsuccessful. This cannot be ascribed solely to the corruption of the parliamentary aristocracy, which allegedly procures all kinds of advantages for itself and its relatives through sinecures (as well as generally lucrative positions in administration [*Verwaltung*], the armed forces, the Church, and at court), or to the indulgence with which this aristocracy is treated by the administration [*Ministerium*], which is in need of its support. The relatively very small number of votes which such proposals for reducing expenditure normally attract suggests that there is little faith in the possibility of (or scant interest in) such relief of the allegedly universal pressure, against which Members of

Parliament are in any case protected by their wealth. That section of them which is nominally independent tends to be on the side of the administration, and this independence sometimes seems inclined to go further than this section's usual attitude or the accusations of the opposition might lead one to expect, as on those occasions when the administration shows an express interest in approving a financial payment. Thus a few years ago, when the administration took great interest in its proposal that a supplementary payment of £1,000 be made to the highly respected Huskisson,[25] who resigned from a lucrative post because his salaried duties at the Board of Trade had become too onerous, the proposal was defeated by a large majority; and the same has not infrequently happened with proposals to raise the maintenance allowances of royal princes, which are not exactly generous by English standards. In these cases involving a personality and feelings of propriety, passion has overcome that lukewarm attitude which Parliament has normally displayed towards economies. – This much is certainly plain, that no Reform Bill can directly remove the causes of high taxation in England. Indeed, the examples of England and France might lead to the induction that countries in which the political administration [*Staatsverwaltung*] relies on the approval of assemblies elected by the people bear the heaviest burden of taxes. In France, where the aim of the English Reform Bill to extend the franchise to a greater number of citizens has been in large measure accomplished, the national budget has just been likened in the French press to a promising child which makes significant advances from day to day. To adopt radical measures to reduce the oppressive quality of the political administration [*Staatsverwaltung*] in England would require excessive interference with the internal constitution of particular rights. No power is available to take serious steps towards a substantial reduction of the huge national debt, despite the enormous wealth of private individuals. The exorbitant cost of the tortuous administration of justice, which allows only the rich to take cases to court, the poor-rate which no administration could introduce in Ireland, where necessity no less than justice demands it, the use of ecclesiastical assets (which will be further mentioned below), and many other major branches of the social union, presuppose that further conditions should be fulfilled by the political authority beyond those contained in the Reform Bill before any change can be made. – Passing reference has been made in Parliament to the abolition of church tithes and manorial hunting rights in France; all this, it was pointed out, occurred under the auspices of a patriotic king and a reformed Parliament. The implication of such remarks seems to be that the curtailment [*Aufhebung*] of rights of this kind is in itself a lamentable subversion of the whole constitution, quite apart from the fact that it has resulted in dreadful anarchy in France. But it is common knowledge not only that such rights have disappeared in other states without any such consequences, but also that their abolition has been regarded as an important foundation of increased prosperity and essential freedom.[26] Something more may accordingly be said about them here.

Firstly, as far as *tithes* are concerned, the oppressive nature of this tax has long been commented on in England. Apart from the particular odium which invariably attaches to this kind of tax, the feeling against it in England is not at all surprising, given that there are parts of that country where the clergyman has every tenth measure of milk collected daily from the cowsheds, a tenth of the eggs laid each day, etc. There have also been criticisms of the unfairness inherent in this tax, for the more the yield of the soil is increased by industry, time, and expenditure, the higher the tax becomes, so that instead of encouraging the improvement of agriculture [*Kultur*], in which England has invested large amounts of capital, it has imposed a tax on it. Tithes belong to the Church in England; in other countries, especially Protestant ones, they were abolished or made redeemable, without pomp and circumstance and without exploitation or injustice, either long ago (over a century ago in the Prussian territories) or in recent times, and church revenues were duly deprived of their oppressive character and collected in a more appropriate and decorous manner. In England, however, the nature of the original justification of the tithes has been essentially diminished and perverted in other respects too. Their function as a means of support for teachers of religion and for the construction and maintenance of the churches has largely changed into that of a dividend accruing from private property: the office of the clergyman has [taken on] the character of a benefice, and its duties have been transformed into rights to an income.[27] Disregarding the fact that a host of lucrative ecclesiastical positions, [such as] canonries, carry no official duties whatsoever, it is all too common knowledge how often it happens that English clergymen occupy themselves with anything but the functions of their office (with hunting, etc. and other kinds of idleness), consume the rich proceeds of their position in foreign countries, and transfer their official functions to a poor curate who receives a pittance which barely preserves him from starvation. A comprehensive impression of the relationship between holding an ecclesiastical office and drawing the income from it on the one hand, and fulfilling its duties and leading a moral [*sittlichen*] existence on the other, can be gained from an example which came before the courts some years ago. A suit was brought against a clergyman by the name of Frank to have him declared incapable of administering his estate because of insanity, and to have his estate placed under the guardianship of the court. He had a living of £800 [per annum], and other benefices of around £600 (i.e. somewhat less than 10,000 Reichstalers). But the lawsuit was brought by his son, on his coming of age, in the interests of the family. The evidence given in public over a number of days concerning this vicar's alleged madness, including numerous statements by witnesses, brought to light acts which he had committed, unchecked by any ecclesiastical authority, in the course of several years. For example, he had on one occasion, in broad daylight, made his way through the streets and across the bridge of his home town, in highly disreputable company,[f] followed by a crowd of jeering street urchins. Even more scandalous were the man's own domestic circumstances,[g] which were likewise confirmed by witnesses. This shameless behaviour on the part of a minister of the Church of England had caused him no difficulties in the tenure of his office or in the enjoyment of the income from his benefices. The Church is brought into contempt by such cases, most of all because, in spite of the institution of an episcopal hierarchy, it fails to take action to prevent such corruption and the scandal to which it gives rise. This contempt, like the greed of other clergymen in collecting their tithes, also plays its part in diminishing that respect which the English people are required to show for the Church's property rights. Because it is

---

[f] *Translator's note*: Instead of the preceding four words, Hegel's manuscript has 'on each arm a dissolute female from a house of ill repute'.

[g] *Translator's note*: Instead of the preceding five words, Hegel's manuscript has 'anecdotes of his relations with his own wife and a lover of hers who resided in his house'.

designated for a religious purpose, such property is wholly different in character from private property, which can be freely disposed of by the arbitrary will of its owners; this difference is the basis of a difference in legal status [*ein verschiedenes Recht*], and the enjoyment of such assets is conditional on the performance of associated duties; and in Protestant states, the [religious] purpose already referred to gives the political authority its justification for jointly ensuring that this purpose, and the duties for which payment is received, are fulfilled: principles such as these still appear to be completely alien and unknown in England. But it is too much to the advantage of that class [*Klasse*] which has the dominant influence in Parliament to stick to the abstract perspective of civil law [*Privatrecht*] in this context; for through its influence, it has links with the administration [*Ministerium*], which has the senior and most lucrative ecclesiastical posts in its gift, and the class in question has an interest in providing such benefices for those younger sons or brothers who are left without means, since landed property in England is generally inherited only by the eldest son. This same class is also likely to retain, or even to extend, its position in Parliament even after the Reform Bill [is passed], and it is consequently very doubtful whether it has any need to fear for its interest as far as the wealth of the Church and its patronage are concerned.

There is every reason why fears regarding a reform of such conditions in the Church of England should extend especially to its Irish establishment,[28] which has been so vigorously attacked for several years, chiefly in the cause of [Catholic] emancipation (which is itself concerned only with the political aspect).[29] It is well known that the majority of the Irish populace are members of the Catholic Church. The assets which formerly belonged to the latter in Ireland, the churches themselves, the tithes, the obligation of the parishes to maintain the church buildings in good repair, to supply liturgical accessories and pay the wages of vergers, etc. – all this was taken away from the Catholic Church by the right of conquest and transferred to the Anglican Church. In Germany, as a result of the Thirty Years War more than 150 years ago and of the growth of rationality in more recent times, each territory, province, town, or village has either been allowed to retain the assets belonging to the church of its inhabitants, or the needs of worship have been provided for in other ways; the religion of the prince and government has not requisitioned church assets belonging to another denomination within its territory. Even the Turks have in most cases allowed the Christians, Armenians, and Jews under their dominion to retain their churches; and even where they were forbidden to repair such churches when they became dilapidated, they were still given leave to buy permits to do so. But the English confiscated all the churches of the conquered Catholic population. The Irish, whose poverty, misery, and consequent degeneracy and demoralisation are a standing topic in Parliament which all administrations have acknowledged, are obliged to pay their own clergy out of the few pence they may possess, and to provide premises for their services. Conversely, they have to pay tithes on all their produce to Anglican clergymen, in whose extensive incumbencies, which may encompass two, three, six, or more parish villages, there are often very few Protestants (sometimes only the verger); and they are even obliged to pay for repairs to the churches which are now Anglican, and for the provision of liturgical accessories, etc. The enemies of emancipation have also made a point of holding up, as a means of intimidation, the prospect of a reform of such crying injustice as a likely consequence of this measure. But its friends, on the other hand, have in essence reassured themselves and their followers [with the reflection] that emancipation will both satisfy the demands of the Catholics and make the establishment of the Anglican Church in Ireland all the more secure. This situation, which is unparalleled in any civilised Protestant Christian nation, and the positive legal title [which upholds it], are sustained by self-interest,[h] and they have so far held their own against the presumable religious disposition of the Anglican clergy and the good sense [*Vernunft*] of the English people and their representatives. Admittedly, the Reform Bill does add a few more Irish members to the Lower House, and these may include Catholics; but this circumstance may be more than outweighed by the same Bill's provision whereby the representation of that class [*Klasse*] whose interest is linked with the present condition of the Church [in Ireland] will be increased.

Similar anxiety is felt that the reform will eventually extend to *manorial rights*. These have long ceased to include serfdom among the agricultural class [*Klasse*], but they weigh just as oppressively

---

[h] *Translator's note*: Hegel's manuscript has 'acquisitiveness'.

on the mass of such people as serfdom did, and indeed force them to endure even greater deprivation than that of serfs. In England itself, though disqualified from ownership of land and reduced to the status of leaseholders or day-labourers, they do find some work as a result of the wealth of England in general, or in its huge manufacturing industry in times of prosperity; but it is to a greater extent the poor law, by which every parish is obliged to look after its own poor, that preserves them from the consequences of extreme deprivation. In Ireland, on the other hand, the class which lives by agriculture is in general propertyless and does not have this protection. Both the descriptions of travellers and data supplied in parliamentary documents depict the general condition of the Irish peasantry as so wretched that it is hard to find comparable examples even in small and poor districts of civilised continental countries, or indeed in those where civilisation is less advanced. The propertylessness of the agricultural class has its origin in the laws and relationships of the old feudal system, which nevertheless, in the form in which it still survives in several states, does guarantee the peasant who is tied to the land a subsistence on the land he cultivates.[30] But while the serfs of Ireland do on the one hand have personal freedom, the landlords have on the other hand taken such complete control of property that they have disclaimed all obligation to provide for the subsistence of the populace which tills the land they own. This is the justification with which the landlords, if they happened to find more advantage in a mode of agriculture which requires fewer workers, drove out hundreds, indeed thousands, of those who had formerly cultivated the land, who were tied to it for their subsistence no less than the serfs had been, and whose families had lived there for centuries in cottages which they did not themselves own.[31] They thus deprived those who were already without possessions of their homes and of their inherited means of subsistence as well – all in due legal form. And it was again with the backing of the law that, in order to make sure that the peasants were well and truly evicted from their cottages (and to rule out any delay in their departure or any furtive return to such shelter), the landlords had the cottages burnt down.[32]

This cancerous affliction of England is brought to the attention of Parliament year in, year out. How many speeches have been made on it, how many committees have sat, how many witnesses have been questioned, how many circumstantial reports have been submitted, and how many measures have been proposed which have proved either wholly inadequate or wholly impracticable! The proposal to reduce the surplus numbers of poor by establishing colonies would have to remove at least one million inhabitants to have any chance of success. But how could this be effected? – not to mention the fact that the empty space thereby created would soon be filled in the same way as before if laws and circumstances remained otherwise unchanged. An Act of Parliament (the Sub-letting Act)[33] designed to restrict the division [of land] into small tenancies (the means whereby the fertile class of beggars is accommodated in Ireland, and the main cause of its multiplication) proved so inadequate a remedy for this evil that it recently had to be repealed after a few years of experiment. The moment of transition from feudal tenure to property has passed by without the opportunity being taken to give the agricultural class [*Klasse*] the right to own land; some scope for this might be achieved by changing the rights of inheritance, introducing equal distribution of parental assets among children, allowing property to be requisitioned and sold in settlement of debts, and in general by changing that legal status of landed property which involves indescribable formalities and costs in the event of sale, etc. But the English law of property, in these and many other respects, is too far removed from the freedom enjoyed in this area by the continental countries,[34] and all private relationships are too securely enmeshed in such fetters. Indeed, it would have only a very insignificant effect in relation to the whole if these laws were changed so as to make it possible for the agricultural class to acquire landed property. The power of the monarchy was too weak to oversee the transition [from feudal tenure to property] already referred to; and even after the Reform Bill, parliamentary legislation will remain in the hands of that class [*Klasse*] whose interests – and in even greater measure its ingrained habits – are bound up with the existing system of property rights. Hitherto, such legislation has always been designed merely to remedy the consequences of the system by direct means when need and misery became too crying, resorting to palliatives like the Sub-letting Act or to pious hopes that the Irish landlords might take up residence in Ireland, etc.

Mention has also been made of *hunting rights* as an area which could well be reformed – an issue close to the hearts of so many

English Members of Parliament and their circles; but the mischief and abuses have become so great that moves to change the relevant laws were inevitable. In particular, attention has universally been drawn to the increased number of assaults and murders committed by poachers on the person of gamekeepers, to the increasing loss of game suffered on the estates of landowners, and especially to the increasing number of poaching offences coming before the courts (although these are only a small proportion of those actually committed). Attention has also been drawn to the harsh and disproportionate penalties laid down for infringements of hunting rights and inflicted on those found guilty of them – for it was the same aristocrats who enjoy these rights who made the laws in question, and who in turn sit in court in their capacity as magistrates and jurors. The interest of hunting enthusiasts is also engaged by the extension of hunting rights in unenclosed [*offenen*] areas; a squire's son is entitled to hunt, and every parson counts as a squire, so that the son may enjoy this privilege even if the father does not himself possess it (unless he is himself the son of a squire), etc. A Bill to amend these laws has been brought before Parliament annually for several years past, but no such Bill has yet had the good fortune to prevail in face of the privileged hunting interests; the present Parliament also has a Bill of this kind before it. The extent to which the projected parliamentary Reform might have a significant influence on this legislation must still be regarded as problematic – [for example,] in reducing penalties, in limiting personal hunting rights, and in particular also – in the interest of the agricultural class – in modifying the right to pursue stags, hares, and foxes with a pack of hounds and twenty, thirty, or more horses and even more huntsmen on foot across sown fields and all cultivated unenclosed land. In many German territories, the damage done by game, the devastation of fields by hunting, and the consumption of crops and fruit by game used to be a standing article in the complaints discussed by the Estates. So far, however, English freedom has not yet imposed any restriction on these rights, which the German princes have long since relinquished for the benefit of their subjects.

The rambling confusion of English *civil law*, which even the English, proud though they are of their freedom, can bring themselves to call an Augean stable, might encourage the hope that it will eventually be sorted out. The little that Robert Peel accomplished a few years ago was deemed highly commendable and met with universal praise.[35] More far-reaching proposals for judicial reform which the present Lord Chancellor, Brougham,[36] subsequently put forward in a seven-hour speech, and which were received with much approval, did result in the appointment of committees, but have so far had no further consequences. The English nation has not yet achieved through popular representation what several centuries of quiet work in the cultivation of science [*der wissenschaftlichen Bildung*], and of princely wisdom and love of justice have accomplished in Germany; and the new Bill is in fact devoid of those particular elements which might allow well-founded insight and genuine knowledge to prevail over the crass ignorance of the fox-hunters and rural gentry, over an education acquired merely through social contacts, newspapers, and parliamentary debates, and over the skills of lawyers, which are mostly acquired by mere routine. The preconditions which must be fulfilled in Germany even by those of noble birth, wealth, and landed property, etc. before they can take part in the affairs of government and the state (whether in general or more specialised areas) – namely theoretical study, scientific education, practical training and experience – are as little to be found in the new Bill as they were imposed, under the previous dispensation, on members of an assembly in whose hands the most extensive powers of government and administration are vested.[37] Nowhere but in England is the prejudice so entrenched and sincerely accepted that if birth and wealth give someone an office, they also give him the intelligence [*Verstand*] to go with it. Even the new Bill contains no such conditions; it also sanctions the principle that a free income of £10 derived from landed property fully qualifies an individual for the task of judging and deciding on [a person's] capacity for the business of government and political administration with which Parliament is concerned. But the idea [*Vorstellung*] of boards of scrutiny composed of sensible and experienced men with official duties of their own (as distinct from a mass of individuals qualified only by an income of £10), like the idea of demanding evidence of competence from candidates for the legislature and political administration [*Staatsverwalten*], is too much at variance with the unconditional sovereignty of those who are entitled to take such decisions.

The need to secure those material interests of rational law [*Recht*] referred to above, as well as others which have already been secured in many civilised continental states (especially in the German territories), seems to be almost dormant in England. The need for reform has therefore not been brought to light by the experience that little or nothing has been done in this respect by [successive] Parliaments with rights of patronage in their existing form; England will endorse what the Duke of Wellington said recently in the House of Lords,[38] that 'from the year 1688' (i.e. the year of the Revolution which deposed the House of Stuart with its Catholic sympathies) 'to the present, the country's affairs have been conducted in the *best and most illustrious* manner through that union of wealth, talents, and manifold knowledge which represented the major interests of the kingdom'. National pride in general prevents the English from studying and acquainting themselves with the advances made by other nations in developing their legal institutions.[39] The pomp and circumstance surrounding the formal freedom to debate the affairs of state in Parliament and other assemblies of all classes and estates [*Klassen und Stände*] and to resolve such issues in Parliament, together with the unqualified right to exercise this freedom, prevent the English from grasping the essence of legislation and government through quiet reflection – or give them no incentive to do so. (Few European nations display so fully developed a capacity for reasoning [*Räsonnement*] to suit their prejudices and so little depth of principle.)[i] Fame and wealth make it superfluous to go back to the foundations of existing rights, whereas peoples who feel such rights oppressive have been driven to do so by external necessity and by the need of reason which this has awakened.[40]

We return [now] to the more formal aspects more immediately connected with the present Reform Bill. One aspect of great importance, which is also emphasised by opponents of the Bill, is the need for the various major interests of the nation to be represented in Parliament, and the changes which this representation would suffer as a result of the present Bill.

---

[i] *Translator's note*: Hegel's manuscript reads 'such shallowness in relation to principle'.

Views on this question appear to differ.[41] On the one hand, the Duke of Wellington maintains that, as a consequence of the Bill in question, the majority of voters would consist of shopkeepers, which would seem to confer an advantage on commercial interests.[42] On the other hand, there is a general view, which is strongly urged in the Bill's favour, that landed property and agricultural interests will not only lose none of their influence, but will rather undergo a relative expansion; for the projected cancellation of existing electoral rights will allot only twenty-five members to the major cities or commercial interests, while the remaining eighty-one will go to the counties and landed property, including smaller towns in which the influence of the landowner is also generally paramount. In this connection, it is particularly noteworthy that a number of traders, namely the leading London bankers who have connections with the East India Company and the Bank of England, have declared themselves against the Bill. Their reason for doing so is that, while this measure seeks to base the representation of the kingdom on the broad foundation of property and to extend this foundation further, it would have the practical effect of closing the *main avenues* through which financial, commercial, shipping and colonial interests, together with all other interests throughout the country and in all its foreign possessions down to their remotest regions, have hitherto been represented in Parliament.

These *main avenues* are the small towns and minor boroughs in which a seat in Parliament can be bought directly. It has hitherto been possible, by way of the usual trade in parliamentary seats, to ensure that bank directors, like directors of the East India Company, had seats in Parliament. The great plantation owners of the West Indies and other traders who dominate such great areas of commerce have likewise secured such positions in order to look after their interests and those of their association (which are admittedly also of great importance for the interest of England as a whole). The bank director Manning,[43] who had held a seat for many years, was excluded from the last Parliament because his opponent proved that he had employed bribery in his election. The view that the various major interests of the nation should be represented in its main deliberative body is characteristic of England, and in different ways, it has also been a fundamental part of the constitution of the older Imperial Estates and provincial assemblies in all the European monarchies, just as it still provides the basis on which parliamentary delegates are appointed under the Swedish constitution, for example. But it runs counter to the modern principle according to which only the abstract will of individuals as such should be represented.[44] It is also true that the subjective and arbitrary will of the nobility [*der Barone*] and others with electoral privileges furnishes the basis on which such appointments are made in England, so that the representation of [particular] interests is itself left to chance. Nevertheless, this procedure is regarded as so important an element that the most respected bankers are not ashamed to indulge in the corruption surrounding the sale of parliamentary seats, and to complain in a public declaration to Parliament that the Bill would deprive those major interests of their route to parliamentary representation, a route which was not exposed to accident since it was governed by bribery. Moral considerations give way before so weighty a point of view as this, but it is a defect in the constitution that it leaves a necessary measure to chance, and compels people to secure it by corrupt means which morality condemns. It is true that, if the interests are organically divided into estates [*Stände*] (for example, into nobility, clergy, citizens of towns, and peasants in the case of Sweden as mentioned above), they are no longer fully in keeping with the present situation in most states in which those other interests already referred to have become powerful, as in England. But this defect could easily be removed if the earlier basis of constitutional law [*des inneren Staatsrechts*] were once again understood – that is, if the real foundations of political life, which are genuinely distinct and whose distinct content[45] must be given essential consideration by the government and administration [*Verwaltung*], were also consciously and expressly highlighted and recognised, and, whenever they were discussed or made the object of decisions, permitted to speak for themselves without this being left to chance. In a constitution which Napoleon gave to the kingdom of Italy, he had this consideration in mind when he distributed the right to representation among the classes [*Klassen*] of *possidenti, dotti,* and *merchanti.*[46]

In the earlier parliamentary debates on proposals for very incomplete reforms, one of the chief grounds which was always cited against them (and which is again stressed in the present debate) was that all major interests were [allegedly] represented in Parliament as presently composed, and that issues rather than individuals as such should have an opportunity to be voiced and given a hearing. This argument seems to touch on a matter – though without enlarging on it – which the Duke of Wellington brought to the attention of the Upper House in his last speech as something which both Upper and Lower Houses had hitherto overlooked, namely that what had to be created was a *legislative assembly*, not a *corporation of electors*, a Lower House and not a new system for the constituents.[47] If it were not a question of voting rights and of who the constituents should be, but of the [end] result – namely the constitution of a legislative assembly and a Lower House – it might well be said that such a Lower House was already constituted in accordance with the existing right of representation. In the course of his speech, the Duke actually cites the testimony of a supporter[48] of the Reform Bill to the effect that the present Lower House is so constituted that no better one could be elected. And in fact, the Reform Bill itself contains no further guarantee that a House elected under its provisions and in violation of the existing positive rights would be any more excellent.

In his speech, the Duke likens these rights to the right whereby he could as little be deprived of his seat in the Upper House as the Prime Minister, Earl Grey, could be divested of his properties in Yorkshire.[49] The Bill does, however, contain the new principle whereby the electoral prerogative is no longer placed in the same category as actual property rights. In this respect we must acknowledge as correct the charge brought by the Bill's opponents, namely that, precisely because of this new principle, the Bill is internally utterly inconsistent. A personally more offensive charge lies in the allegation that the line of demarcation whereby privileged smaller towns will retain their electoral rights was deliberately drawn by the Bill in such a way that the boroughs belonging to the Duke of Bedford (whose brother, Lord John Russell, introduced the Bill in the Lower House) were left unscathed. The Bill is in fact a mixture of ancient privileges and the universal principle that all citizens – provided they meet the external condition of [drawing] a ground rent of £10 [annually] – are equally entitled to vote for those who are to represent them.[50] Since the Bill accordingly contains a contradiction between positive rights and a universal[j] principle of thought,

[j] *Translator's note*: Hegel's manuscript reads 'abstract'.

it brings the inconsistency of everything derived merely from old feudal law into much sharper focus than if all entitlements were collectively placed on one and the same footing as positive rights.

It is true that, in itself, this principle [of equal rights for all] opens the way for an infinite number of claims, on which the power of Parliament can certainly impose limits for the time being – although it would amount to a revolution rather than a mere reform if it were followed through consistently. But it seems unlikely that such further claims will be pursued with particular energy in the near future, given that the middle and lower classes in the three kingdoms appear to be very generally satisfied with the Bill. The so-called practical sense of the British nation (i.e. its preoccupation with earnings, subsistence, and wealth) seems so far to have been little affected by any need for the material rights just referred to.[51] It is even less likely to be influenced by purely formal principles of abstract equality, for the fanaticism associated with such principles is even more alien to it. It is true that this same practical sense stands to lose directly, in that a great mass of people will cease to profit from bribes if the electoral qualification is increased from forty shillings to five times that amount. [But] if this higher class* has hitherto reaped a material [*reellen*] benefit from its votes, it is not about to lose it. A Member of Parliament elected by Liverpool has just been excluded from the House because it was proved that the voters had taken bribes. The voters of this city are very numerous, and since the city is very rich, it may be supposed that those who did so also included many well-off people. Besides, just as surely as the big estate-owners managed to pass off hundreds and thousands of their propertyless tenants as owners of forty-shilling freeholds, so also will this peculiar method of acquiring votes be incorporated in the new [electoral] census and the same dependent people will appear in the guise of freeholders with an income of ten pounds. And despite the increased electoral qualification, it is also unlikely that the English rabble[52] will readily give up those weeks of feasting and inebriation in which it was encouraged and paid to indulge its unchecked savagery.^k In the election before last, it was

---

* *Hegel's note*: This higher class, with its £10 rent, has recently been given the name of 'paupers' in the Upper House.
^k *Translator's note*: Hegel's manuscript reads 'bestiality'.

stated that £80,000 sterling (i.e. nearly 560,000 Reichstalers) was spent in the populous county of York to elect a local landowner by the name of Beaumont.† But if it has been suggested in parliamentary debates that the costs of elections have become altogether excessive, the question arises of how the people will regard the fact that the rich wish to make economies at their expense. It is still uncertain how this aspect of material benefit will develop, and what new combinations will be devised by the tireless speculation of dealers in parliamentary seats; it would be premature to build conjectures on the change which this interest is undergoing. But the right to vote itself seems to afford a higher interest, for it automatically arouses the expectation and demand that it should be more widely distributed. Experience suggests, however, that the exercise of the right to vote is not attractive enough to generate powerful claims or the movements to which these give rise. On the contrary, a great indifference seems to prevail in this respect among the electors, despite the interest in bribes which goes along with it. No petitions against a Bill so disadvantageous to them have so far emerged from the numerous class of those who will lose their right to vote specifically because of the raised electoral qualification [*Wahlzensus*], or whose right is considerably weakened because their votes are lumped together with the general mass of voters in the county. The protests raised against it have come from those whose certainty or likelihood of gaining a seat in Parliament has been reduced or lost entirely. When the income required to qualify as an elector in Ireland was raised by Act of Parliament a year ago, a total of 200,000 individuals lost their right to vote without complaining about this loss of their entitlement to participate in the affairs of state and government. To all appearances, the electors regard their right [to vote] as a property which is chiefly of benefit to those who seek election to Parliament, and to whose personal discretion, arbitrary will, and interest all that this right contains by way of participation in government and legislation must be sacrificed. – The main electoral business on which the candidates employ agents conversant with the [relevant] localities and personalities and with how to deal with them is that of canvassing and mobilising electors,

† *Hegel's note*: In one of the last sessions of Parliament, the cost of the Liverpool election referred to above was given as £120,000 (i.e. over 800,000 Reichstalers).

and equally of inducing them – especially through bribery – to vote
for their patrons. The owners of great estates have hosts of their
tenants rounded up, with some of them (as already mentioned)
newly dressed up for the occasion as owners of the necessary freehold. At a previous election, Brougham wittily described a scene
where such people were made to camp in the courtyards with fires,
pudding, and porter and – to isolate them from the influence of the
opposition – locked up there until the moment when they were
required to cast their obedient vote. This indifference to the right
to vote and to its exercise stands in stark contrast to the fact that it
embodies the people's right to participate in public affairs and in
the highest interests of the state and government. The exercise of
this right should be a supreme duty, because the constitution of
an essential part of the state's authority, namely the representative
assembly, depends on it, and because this right and its exercise (as
in France) are in fact an enactment of the sovereignty of the people,
indeed its sole enactment. Such indifference towards this right can
easily invite accusations that a people is politically obtuse or corrupt,
as can its addiction to bribery in exercising this right. This harsh
view must, however, be moderated if one considers what must help
to produce such lukewarmness, and the obvious factor is the feeling
that the individual vote is really of no consequence among the many
thousands which contribute to an election. Of the approximately
658 members who are currently elected to the Lower House in
England, or the 430 elected to the Chamber [of Deputies] in France
(and the changes shortly to be made to these figures are of no consequence here), only *one* member is to be appointed [by a given con-
stituency], which is a very inconsiderable fraction of this total; but
the individual vote is an even more negligible fraction of the 100 or
1,000 votes which contribute to that member's election. If the total
number of voters to be registered under the new electoral law in
France is assessed at 200,000, while the number of members to be
elected by them is taken in round figures as 450, it follows that
the individual vote is one two-hundred-thousandth part of the total
electorate, and one ninety-millionth of one of the three branches of
the power which makes the laws.

   In these figures, the individual can scarcely conceive of how negligible his own influence is. Nevertheless, he has a definite sense of
this quantitative insignificance of his vote, and the quantitative

aspect, the number of votes, is in practice the only decisive factor here. The qualitatively important considerations of freedom, of the duty to exercise the right of sovereignty, and of participation in the general affairs of state may certainly be held up [as arguments] against apathy. But sound common sense likes to stick to what is effective; and if the individual is confronted with the usual argument that, if *everyone* took so apathetic a view, the state's continued existence would be put at risk, and freedom even more so, he is bound to be no less mindful of the principle on which his duty and his whole right of freedom is based, namely that he should not let himself be determined by any consideration of what others are doing, but only by his own will, and that his arbitrary will as an individual is the ultimate and sovereign principle which befits him and to which he is entitled. – In any case, this [electoral] influence, so negligible in itself, is limited to [the choice of] personalities, and it becomes infinitely more negligible because it has no reference to the *thing*, which is in fact expressly excluded. Only in the democratic constitution of the Year III in France under Robespierre,[53] which was adopted by the entire people (although it proved correspondingly ineffectual in practice), was it decreed that laws on public matters should also be submitted to the individual citizens for final decision. – Furthermore, the voters are not even mandators [*Kommittenten*] with powers to instruct their delegates. The programmes [*cahiers*] which the members of the National Assembly took with them on their [parliamentary] mission were at once set aside and forgotten by both parties, and it is recognised as one of the most essential constitutional principles in England and France that the elected members are just as sovereign in casting their votes as their electors were in casting theirs. In neither country do members have the character of officials in their deliberations and resolutions on public matters, and they share with the King what is sanctioned for him, namely that they are answerable to no one for the performance of their duties.

In keeping with the feeling that the influence of the individual is in fact negligible, and with the sovereign arbitrary will associated with this right [to vote], experience confirms that electoral meetings are not at all well attended. The numbers (as occasionally listed in the press) of those entitled to vote and of those who actually cast their votes at a given election are usually widely divergent, as happened even in the turbulent final years of Charles X's reign in France;[54] and in the most recent election held in Paris, the centre of political interest, in which the parties appear to have shown no lack of zeal in summoning the electors to cast their votes, it was reported that out of roughly 1,850 constituents some 600 did not put in an appearance. It might also be interesting in this regard to discover the average ratio of constituents to actual voters in other areas where all citizens have the right to vote and where this affects an interest much closer to them – for example, in meetings to elect town councillors in the state of Prussia. – In the earlier stages of the French Revolution, the zeal and conduct of the Jacobins at electoral meetings put peaceable and honest citizens off exercising their right to vote, or even made it dangerous for them to do so, and faction alone held the field. – While those great political bodies which are currently making decisions on the franchise believe they are fulfilling a duty of supreme justice by relaxing the external qualifications for this entitlement and granting it to a larger number of people, it may well escape their notice that they are thereby reducing the influence of the individual, weakening his impression of its importance and hence also his interest in exercising this right – not to mention the question of how any political authority comes in the first place to dispose of this right of the citizens, to take a sum of fifty or one hundred francs or so many pounds sterling into account, and to vary this right in accordance with such sums. The right in question was accepted as by definition sovereign, primary, inalienable, and generally the opposite of all that can be conferred or taken away.

Just as that sound common sense for which the English people are so renowned makes individuals realise how insignificant the influence of their single vote is on affairs of state, it also gives them a proper sense of their general ignorance and limited ability to judge the talents, business experience, skill, and education required for high offices of state. Is it then likely that they will regard a freehold of forty shillings or ten pounds, or [payment of] two hundred francs in direct taxes (with or without the additional centimes) as guaranteeing so great an enhancement of this ability? The rigour with which the French Chambers refuse to consider any ability apart from that which is supposed to reside in the two hundred francs (with or without the additional centimes), and ascribe it only to members of the Institute, is characteristic enough. Formalistic respect for the two hundred francs has prevailed over respect for the ability and good will of prefects, magistrates, doctors, lawyers, etc. who do not pay so much in taxes. – Besides, the voters know that their sovereign right exempts them from having to undertake a preliminary judgement, let alone examination, of the candidates as they present themselves, and that they have to reach their decision without any such preliminaries. It is therefore no wonder that a large number of individuals in England – and it still remains to be seen whether they are not the majority – need to be prompted by the candidates to make the undemanding effort of casting their votes, and have to be rewarded with badges, roasts, beer, and a few guineas by the candidates who thereby benefit. The French, who are newer in these political ways, have not yet resorted to this kind of compensation on a similar scale, no doubt also because of pressure from the central interests of their [political] situation, which has not yet been fully consolidated but is in fact exposed to the most fundamental danger. But inasmuch as they have been encouraged to take [political] matters and their share in them more seriously, they have secured their right and compensated themselves for the negligible share which their individual sovereignty has in public affairs by themselves participating in such matters through insurrections, clubs, associations, etc.[55]

The peculiarity – already touched upon – of [there being] a power in England which is supposedly subordinate and whose members at the same time make decisions on the entire business of the state without instruction, without accountability, and without being officials, is the basis of a relationship with the monarchical part of the constitution. The influence which the Reform Bill may have on this relationship, and on the executive power in general, calls for mention here. Before considering this matter, we must first recall the immediate result of the peculiarity in question, namely that it gives rise to a great difference in England between the power of the Crown and that of the executive. The power of the Crown controls the main branches of supreme authority within the state, particularly those which concern relations with other states, the authority to make war and peace, direction of the army, the appointment of ministers (though it has become etiquette for the monarch to appoint only the Prime Minister directly, and for the latter to

put together the rest of the Cabinet), the appointment of army com-
manders and officers, of ambassadors, etc. Now Parliament is
responsible for the sovereign decision on the budget (even including
the sum provided for the support of the King and his family), i.e.
for the whole range of means for making war and peace and maintaining an army, ambassadors, etc., so that a ministry can only
govern – i.e. exist – in so far as it affirms the views and will of
Parliament. Consequently, the monarch's share in the executive
power is more illusory than real, and its substance lies with Parliament. Siéyès[56] had a great reputation for profound insight into the
organisation of free constitutions, and when the constitution of the
Directorate was replaced by that of the Consulate, he was at last able
to extract from his portfolio his plan which would enable France to
enjoy the benefit of his experience and profound reflection. As
everyone knows, he placed at the head of the state a leader [*Chef*]
who would be charged with the pomp of representation abroad, and
with nominating the supreme Council of State and the responsible
ministers, along with the other subordinate officials.[57] Thus, the
supreme executive power was to be vested in the aforementioned
Council of State, whereas the *proclamateur-électeur* was to have no
share in it. We all know the soldierly verdict which Napoleon, who
felt he was made to be master and ruler, passed on this project for
a leader [*chef*] of this kind, in whom he saw only the role of a *cochon
à l'engrais de quelques millions* which no man of any talent and a
modicum of honour would ever be inclined to undertake. What this
project overlooked (in this case no doubt in good faith, though in
others with full awareness and complete deliberation) was that the
nomination of members of the Ministry and other officials of the
executive is in itself a powerless formality, and that the substance
is to be found wherever the power of government effectively lies. In
England, we see this power in Parliament. In the various monarchic
constitutions whose creation we have witnessed, the formal separation of the power of government, as the executive, from a 'merely'
legislative and judicial power is made explicit, and the former is
even invested with pomp and distinction. But ministerial appointments are always the focus of controversy and strife (even if the
right to make such appointments is ascribed exclusively to the
Crown), and what is described as the 'merely' legislative power is
[in fact] triumphant. Thus, even under the latest constitution in

France, amidst the daily questions and controversies, both political and non-political, there is an unmistakable tendency to compel the Ministry to move the government's headquarters[1] to the Chamber of Deputies, where it has itself been reduced to engaging in public controversies with its subordinate officials.

The fact that the executive power lies with Parliament has a direct bearing on an argument adduced by the opponents of the Reform Bill in support of those boroughs through possession of which many parliamentary seats are dependent on single individuals or families – namely that it was through this circumstance that the most distinguished English statesmen found their way to Parliament and thence to the Ministry.[58] It may indeed often happen that an outstanding and profound talent is recognised primarily as a result of private friendship, and is in a position to find its proper place only through individual generosity – a place which it might otherwise fail to attain in view of the inadequate resources and family connections of the mass of citizens in a [given] town or county. But such examples may be ascribed to the realm of chance, where one probability can easily be set against another, or a possible advantage against a possible disadvantage. – Related to this is another alleged consequence of greater importance, to which the Duke of Wellington drew attention.[59] (It is true that he is not renowned as an orator, since he lacks that fluent volubility, sustained for hours at a time and full of self-advertisement, through which many Members of Parliament have gained so great a reputation for eloquence. But despite those disjointed sentences for which he has been criticised, his speeches are not lacking in substance or in perceptions which go to the heart of the matter.) He expresses a fear that those men who are at present charged with looking after the public interest in Parliament will be replaced by very different men, and he asks on another occasion whether shopkeepers,[60] of whom in his view (as already mentioned) the great majority of electors will consist as a result of the new Bill, are the people who ought to elect the members of that great national assembly which has to make decisions on domestic and foreign affairs and on agricultural, colonial, and industrial interests. – The Duke speaks from his [own] observation

---

[1] *Translator's note*: Instead of 'amidst the daily . . . headquarters' Hegel's manuscript reads simply 'the government soon found itself compelled to move its headquarters'.

of the English Parliament, in which, above the mass of incompetent and ignorant Members with a veneer of the usual prejudices and a culture [*Bildung*] derived from conversation (and often less than that), there stands a number of talented men who are wholly devoted to political activity and to the interest of the state. The majority of these are also guaranteed a seat in Parliament partly through their own wealth and the influence which they themselves or their family possess in a borough, city, or county, and partly through the influence of the Ministry as well as their friends within the party.

Associated with this class [*Klasse*] is a large number of men who make political activity their life's work, whether out of personal interest and because they have independent means, or because they hold public positions which they have obtained through their connection with parliamentary influence. But even if they have obtained these positions in other ways, their official standing and general inner vocation are such that they cannot refrain from joining the class of politicians and one of its parties. If service to the state is not tied to other preconditions (for example, a course of specialised [*wissenschaftlicher*] study, state-approved examinations, preliminary practical training, etc.), the individual must be incorporated into this class.[61] He must gain some importance within it and he is supported by its influence, just as his own influence helps to support it in turn. Individuals isolated from such connections – for example, Hunt[62] – are rare anomalies; they may enter Parliament, but they do not cease to cut a strange figure in it.

The other commitments of [members of] this circle – their family connections, their political discussions and speeches at dinners, etc., their endless and worldwide political correspondence, as well as the social round of country houses, horse-races, fox-hunting, etc. – will certainly suffer no disruption. It is true that a major element of their power – namely their control of a large number of parliamentary seats – will undergo a significant modification as a result of the Reform Bill, and this may well have the effect which the Duke mentions, in that many other individuals will take the place of those who belong to the present circle of those who devote themselves to the government interest; but this is likely to have the further consequence of upsetting the uniformity of those maxims and attitudes which are prevalent in that class, and which constitute parliamentary wisdom. Admittedly, it does not appear that Hunt, for example, goes beyond the usual categories with regard to oppression of the people by taxes, sinecures, etc. But the reform may provide access to Parliament for ideas which run counter to the interests of the class in question, and which have therefore not yet entered the heads of its members – ideas which form the foundations of real freedom,[63] and which relate to those circumstances already mentioned concerning ecclesiastical property, the organisation of the Church, and the duties of the clergy, along with manorial and other bizarre rights and property restrictions derived from feudal relationships, and other areas within the chaos of English laws. In France, such ideas have become mixed with many further abstractions and associated with those outbreaks of violence with which we are all familiar, whereas in Germany, in less adulterated form, they have long since become firm principles of inner conviction and public opinion, and have produced an actual transformation – peaceful, gradual, and lawful – of the old legal relationships. Thus, we have already made great progress here with the institutions of real freedom; we have now finished work on the most essential of them and enjoy their fruits, while the executive power of Parliament [in England] has as yet scarcely been seriously reminded of them. In fact, England may well have cause to fear the greatest disruption of its social and political fabric from the pressing demands of those principles and the call for their rapid implementation. However enormous the contrast is within England between immense wealth and utterly abject poverty,[64] there is an equally great – or perhaps even greater – contrast between, on the one hand, the privileges of its aristocracy and the institutions of its positive right in general, and on the other, legal relationships and laws as reshaped in the more civilised states on the Continent and principles which, inasmuch as they are based on universal reason, cannot always remain so alien even to the English mentality [*Verstand*] as they have done hitherto. – Those *novi homines* who, as the Duke of Wellington fears, will supplant the present statesmen may likewise find in these principles the strongest support for their ambition and popular appeal. Since there can be no question in England of these principles being adopted and implemented by the executive power, which has hitherto been in the hands of the privileged class, members of this class would have to feature only as an opposition to the government and to the existing order of things;[65] and the principles themselves would have to feature not in their concrete and practical truth and application, as in Germany, but in the dangerous shape of French abstractions. That antithesis between *hommes d'état* and *hommes à principes* which at once emerged quite starkly in France at the beginning of the Revolution and which has not yet gained a foothold in England, may well be introduced when a broader route to seats in Parliament is opened. The new class [*Klasse*] can gain a foothold all the more easily because the principles themselves are, as such, simple in character, so that they can be grasped quickly even by the ignorant; and since these principles can in any case claim, by virtue of their universality, to be adequate for all [purposes], they are sufficient to enable anyone with some facility of talent and some energy of character and ambition to attain that aggressive eloquence which he requires, and to produce a dazzling effect on the reason of the masses (who are equally inexperienced in such matters). Conversely, it is not so easy to acquire the knowledge, experience, and business routine of the *hommes d'état*, although these qualities are equally necessary for applying rational principles and introducing them to actual life.

But the introduction of a new element such as this would disturb not only the class whose members have the business of state in their hands; on the contrary, the power of government [itself] might be thrown off course. This power, as already mentioned, lies with Parliament; and however much the latter is divided into parties and however violently these oppose one another, they are in no sense factions. They remain within the same general interest, and a change of administration [*Ministerwechsel*] has hitherto had more significant consequences in foreign affairs, in relation to war and peace, than in domestic affairs. The monarchic principle, on the other hand, no longer has much to lose in England. We know that the resignation of Wellington's administration came about when it found itself in a minority on a motion to regulate the King's Civil List[66] – an occasion of particular interest, since it concerned one of the few remaining elements of the monarchic principle in England. What was left of the Crown Estate (which in fact had as much the character of a family estate, of the royal family's private property, as did the family estates of dukes, earls, barons, etc. in England) was made over to the Exchequer in the previous century, and in compensation, a specific sum corresponding to its revenue was set aside within the overall budget which the Lower House had to approve each year. This Crown Estate, the meagre remnant of the Crown's formerly vast resources which had been so greatly reduced by extravagance (and especially by the need to purchase troops and baronial support during civil wars), had not yet been split up into what was to remain family property and what was to be devoted to the general purposes of the state. Now that character of family property or private property which belonged to one part of this remaining wealth had already been altered, at least in form, when it was converted from landed property into an indemnity included in the annual parliamentary budget. Nevertheless, a form of monarchic influence on this minor part of Great Britain's annual expenditure still remained, even if it was subject to [the approval of] Cabinet. But even this remnant of royal or monarchic control has been abolished by Parliament's recent decision to set aside one portion [of the Crown revenues] for the King to spend on himself and his family, and to place the rest (which has already been used in the past for the state's own purposes) at the disposal of Parliament. One cannot fail to notice in this context that, while the majority [of votes cast] against an interest involving the monarchy [*ein monarchisches Element*] was large enough to cause Wellington's administration to resign, the second reading of the Reform Bill, which is directed against the prerogatives of the aristocracy, was passed, as everyone knows, by a majority of only one.[67]

It can be seen as typical of the monarchic element's status that, both on the occasion of the Catholic Emancipation Bill and during the debates on the Reform Bill, the administration was reproached for having allowed the King's consent to these measures to become public. There is no question here of the monarch having exercised his absolute power, or of a so-called *coup d'état*; what was considered improper was merely the authority or influence which the King's personal opinion might exercise. On the one hand, this measure was certainly adopted out of delicacy, in order to avoid the embarrassment of going against the will of the monarch during debates on the Bill. But it is equally the case that, even with reference to that initiative which properly belongs to the monarchic element (i.e. the Crown), Parliament wishes to deal only with an administration [*Ministerium*] dependent on and incorporated in [Parliament] itself, and indeed only with its own members, for it is only in the latter capacity that Ministers can bring a Bill forward. In the same way, the right which belongs to the King, as the third branch of the legislative power, of approving or rejecting a Bill which both Houses have adopted now becomes purely illusory, inasmuch as the Cabinet is once again that same administration [*Ministerium*] incorporated in Parliament. Earl Grey has declared,[68] in response to the above reproach, that the royal consent was already implicit in the fact that the Bill was introduced by the administration; but he rejected the blame for having expressly announced that the Bill had the King's approval simply by saying that this report did not come from Ministers but from other sources.

The peculiar discord which the new men might introduce into Parliament would therefore not be [the same as] that conflict which invariably arose with each of the various French constitutions over whether the executive power should actually belong to the King and his Ministers as the party [*Seite*] to which it was expressly assigned. In the English political administration as it stands at present, the decision has long since been taken on what in France has always first required a decisive and authentic interpretation through insurrection and acts of violence by an insurgent populace. The innovation contained in the Reform Bill can therefore impinge only upon the effective power of government as established in Parliament. Under present conditions, however, this power suffers only superficial variations in the form of changes of administration, but no genuine conflict of principles, for a new administration belongs to the same class [*Klasse*] of interests and of statesmen as its predecessor did. It gains the necessary predominance which it requires as a party to some extent from that group of members who count as independent, but who on the whole side with the current administration out of a feeling that a government must be present; but it also gains it in part through the influence which it is able to exercise on the filling of a number of parliamentary seats. Now even if the so-called agricultural interest appears to have declared that it will receive its due under the new mode of election which is about to be introduced, and even if a large part of the existing patronage of parliamentary seats and of the combinations [of factors] involved in their purchase remains in place, it is inevitable that the class which has hitherto been dominant in Parliament, and which furnishes each administration with ready material for [perpetuating] the existing system of social conditions, will undergo modification when new people and heterogeneous principles are introduced.[69] The Reform Bill in itself undermines the present basis of this system, namely the principle of purely positive right which secures the continued possession of privileges, whatever relation these privileges may have to the rights of real freedom. Once claims of a new kind, which until now have barely found involuntary and incoherent expression (and rather as indefinite fears than as actual demands) come up for discussion in Parliament, the opposition will change its character; the parties will have another object than that of merely taking over the administration.[70]

If we take an example of an opposition of different character as it appears in its extreme form in France, this character finds its most revealing embodiment in the surprise which has been expressed there after every change of administration in recent times over the fact that those individuals who come out of opposition into government subsequently follow much the same maxims as their ousted predecessors did. In the newspapers of the French opposition, we read naive complaints that so many excellent individuals change course as they progress through government office, betraying the left wing to which they formerly belonged – i.e. that, while they may have previously conceded *in abstracto* that a government existed, they have now learned what government actually is, and that it involves something more than principles alone. The latter, as we know, consist in France of general notions [*Vorstellungen*] concerning freedom, equality, the people, popular sovereignty, etc. National legislation, for men of principle, essentially extends no further than those *droits de l'homme et du citoyen* which were prefixed to the earlier French constitutions. They do, of course, concede that further specific legislation is necessary, as well as an organisation of the powers of the state and of administrative agencies, and that the people must be subordinate to these public authorities, and this is duly put into effect. But that institutional activity which constitutes public order and genuine freedom is opposed by renewed reference to those generalities whose very demands for freedom render the basic law contradictory within itself. It is conceded that obedience to the law is necessary; but when this is demanded by the authorities (i.e. by [specific] individuals), it seems to go against freedom. The authority to issue commands, and the difference to which this authority – like commanding and obeying in general – gives rise is incompatible with equality. A mass of human beings can call itself 'the people' – and rightly so, for the people is this indeterminate mass; but the authorities and officials, and in general the members of the organised power of the state, are distinct from the people, and they therefore appear to be in the wrong [*in dem Unrecht*] for having rejected equality and taken a stance opposed to the people, which has the infinite advantage of being recognised as the sovereign will. This is the extreme contradiction within whose circle a nation revolves as soon as these formal categories have come to dominate it.[71] The members of the English Parliament under the present system, and the English in general, have a more practical approach to politics, and they do have a conception [*Vorstellung*] of what government and governing are; and at the same time, it is in the nature of their constitution that the government virtually refrains from all interference in the particular circles of social life, in the administration of counties, cities, etc., in ecclesiastical and educational matters, and in other matters of common concern such as the construction of roads. This freer and more concrete quality of civil life may increase the probability that formal principles of freedom will not find ready acceptance by the class [*Klasse*] above the lower one (although the latter is extremely numerous in England, and most receptive to such formalism), an acceptance which the opponents of the Reform Bill portray as an immediate threat.

But if the Bill, by its principle rather than by its provisions, should open the way into Parliament – and hence into the centre of political power – for principles opposed to the existing system, thus enabling them to assume greater importance in that institution [*daselbst*] than radical reformers have been able to attain in the past, the conflict would threaten to become increasingly dangerous. For no superior intermediate power would stand between the interests of positive privilege and the demands for more real freedom in order to restrain and mediate between them, because the monarchic element in England lacks that power which, in other states, has facilitated the transition, without convulsions, violence, and robbery, from an earlier legislation based solely on positive right to one based on principles of real freedom.[72] The other power would [in this case] be the people; and if an opposition were established on a basis hitherto alien to Parliament as at present constituted, and if this opposition felt unable to stand up to the opposing party in Parliament, it might well be misguided enough to look to the people for its strength, and so to inaugurate not a reform but a revolution.

Editorial notes

The Magistrates should be Elected by the People

1 This is the original title of the pamphlet to which this fragment belongs. Hegel later changed the phrase 'by the people' to 'by the citizens' for stylistic reasons.

2 Harris (1972: pp. 418 n 3, 427) explains how this title, which was not Hegel's, became the accepted title among Hegel scholars.

3 The political situation in Württemberg at the time Hegel wrote this essay is ably discussed by Harris (1972: pp. 419ff). The Duke of Württemberg, Friedrich Eugen, had been forced for financial reasons to call the Estates into session in early 1797 – something that had not happened since 1770. In those circumstances, opportunities for political reform abounded. This, Harris argues, prompted Hegel to become a 'political pamphleteer'.

4 This sentence expresses concisely Hegel's life-long rhetorical strategy for urging change upon his audience. Something within man (e.g. his soul or heart or spirit) will 'come to life' or 'awaken' and move him towards a 'destiny' which also involves a reconciliation with a 'reality' that itself has been changed to accommodate that destiny.

5 The phrase 'still robust' signals Hegel's intention to work for change within existing institutions once they have been purged of their corruptions.

6 In *GC* (see pp. 6–101), Hegel uses similar language to explain the lack of legitimacy in the German Empire.

7 Harris (172: p. 428) sees Hegel using the 'bogy' of Jacobinism in this paragraph to promote reform from above in lieu of revolution from below.

8 A famous German and Württemberg patriot, Friedrich Karl von

Moser (1723–98), had used the building metaphor in 1759 in one of his 'patriotic' writings (Gooch 1920: pp. 22–3). Moser's influence on Hegel needs to be examined by Hegel scholars.

9 The translation of the fragment in Hegel (1964) ends here. What follows in our edition are substantial quotations from Hegel that Rudolf Haym (1857: pp. 65–8 and 483–5) included in his account of the original manuscript which he apparently had before him. Rosenkranz did not include this material among the excerpts in his 1844 biography of Hegel.

10 For a discussion of the political culture and political institutions of Württemberg in so far as they relate to Hegel's life, see Dickey (1987, chapter 3).

11 While living in Berne, Switzerland, Hegel saw and reported upon the devious ways in which oligarchies manipulate representative institutions by co-opting government officials. In this fragment, Hegel makes a similar observation about Württemberg. In this respect, the anonymous translation he published in 1798 of J. J. Cart's *Confidential Letters*, the contents of which deal with the corruption of the oligarchy in Berne, addressed affairs in Württemberg as much as in Berne. On the Cart translation, see Harris (1972: pp. 158–9 and 421ff) and S. Avineri (1972: pp. 5–8).

12 The reference to 'priest' here is typical of Hegel. Throughout his life he used the label to delegitimise authorities – religious and political – who wished to conduct their business in secret, free from public scrutiny. Against this, he proposed a policy of 'publicity'. Not coincidentally, F. K. von Moser (cf. note 8 above) had published a short essay on 'publicity' in 1792. Echoes of it can be found in this essay.

13 It is probable that J. J. Moser, Friedrich Karl's father (note 8 above), was the 'right-minded' person whom Hegel had in mind.

14 In his account of the content of Hegel's original manuscript, Haym (1857: p. 67) indicates that Hegel referred to a speech of Charles James Fox, the English parliamentarian. Harris (1972: p. 430) has traced the reference to a speech of 26 May 1797, in which Fox expresses concern about the possible adverse effects of expanding voting rights in England. Hegel articulates a similar concern here. And with his remark about 'active and passive' citizenship, he also alludes to French debates about citizenship.

15 Harris (1972: p. 429 n 2) speculates about the institutional 'body' Hegel may have had in mind here. Was it, Harris asks, the Council, the Assembly, or a dictatorship of the *bourgeoisie*? At one point (p. 431) Harris thinks this body denotes an 'enlightened bour-

geoisie' who will represent the *Gemeingeist* of the community. Given what J. G. Fichte and F. Schlegel were saying at this time about constituting intellectuals as an ephorate, Hegel may have had something like that in mind too. But in *NL* (pp. 135 and 290 n 52) he is critical of Fichte's idea of an ephorate. Since F. K. von Moser and any number of other German thinkers had been urging German citizens and intellectuals to join together in 'patriotic societies' for several decades, Hegel could have been thinking along those lines as well. On Moser and the association movement, see Ulrich Hof (1990).

The German Constitution

1 According to Harris (1972), Hegel wrote various drafts for this essay between late 1798 and late 1802. Although the essay was not published in Hegel's lifetime, Rosenkranz included significant parts of it in his various works on Hegel in the mid-nineteenth century. Harris suggests that Rosenkranz had available to him more of the manuscript than we have at present. The version translated here was first published in 1893 by George Mollat who also gave the work its title. For the dating of the different drafts and for a helpful commentary see Harris (1972: pp. 434ff).

2 Harris notes that the phrase 'no longer a state' began to appear in the margins of Hegel's revision of his manuscript in 1800. The matter of whether or not Germany was a state had been a concern to Germans since the 1760s. Just as important, Adam Ferguson had offered observations similar to Hegel's about the Empire in his famous *Essay on the History of Civil Society* (1767), a book Hegel had studied as a youth. Ferguson had referred there to the circumstances that had reduced the Empire to the status of 'a mere title' (Ferguson 1995: p. 128). On the importance of Ferguson for the Germans, and especially on how he influenced F. H. Jacobi's thinking on the Empire in *Woldemar*, a philosophical novel published and revised between 1779 and 1794, see Fania Oz-Salzberger (1995: pp. 260ff) and N. Waszek (1988: pp. 108–9). Hegel had read this novel, in which Ferguson's political views are discussed, by 1794.

3 In an early draft of *GC* Hegel names Voltaire; see note 15 below.

4 Hegel liked to begin his criticism of social and political institutions by pointing out how such institutions, while having the 'semblance of unity', were in fact so constituted as to militate against true unity. He does so here. Later (p. 56), when he distinguishes

between a 'people' and a 'mass', he is making the same point. In his early theological writings (Hegel 1948: p. 278) he makes a similar distinction, contrasting a mere 'collection' (*Versammlung*) of human beings and a 'communion' (*Gemeine*) of multi-sided beings who share a similar spirit.

5 The references to war in this passage need to be read in the context of similar remarks about war in Ferguson rather than as anticipations of military developments in twentieth-century Europe. Indeed, the martial focus in both Ferguson and Hegel probably owes more to their interest in certain aspects of ancient liberty – in the idea of citizen-soldiers – than to any authoritarian political inclination on the part of either thinker.

6 Hegel frequently uses the word *Gemüt* (soul) to identify a disposition within individuals that can be realised only in a community of fellowship (see, e.g., *BIA* pp. 182–3). Very often, he links the word to an inward religious disposition (*Gesinnung*) that can be guided by philosophy towards a communal end in which individuals share a common ethical life. See glossary entry *Gemüt*.

7 The 'is' versus 'ought' formulation here anticipates Hegel's later famous/notorious rendering of the opposition between what is 'real' and what is 'rational' in *PR*. It seems clear that he is pushing here – in the drafts from 1800 on – for a political reform programme grounded in realism. In 1797–8, Harris argues, Hegel was more optimistic about the possibility of 'radical' political change in central Europe.

8 Discussion of the interplay between 'culture' and 'destiny' is Hegel's way of drawing attention to the tension between 'is' and 'ought' in history. Indeed, the point of the whole essay is to persuade Germans to draw on resources in their character that will translate into real political activity. Ferguson pursued a similar line of argument in his *Essay*.

9 The paragraph's reference to 'the [Germans'] . . . drive for freedom' is Tacitean in origin. In its original form, Hegel says (p. 63), Germanic freedom emerged from 'the forests of Germania'. Subsequently, it played a significant role throughout Europe in establishing feudalism as a 'system' (p. 64) of *social* organisation. Later in this essay (pp. 66, 77), Hegel explains how German freedom evolved in many European countries into a *political* system of 'limited monarchy' in which aspects of monarchical and aristocratic (i.e. representative) government were politically balanced. In seventeenth-century England, this system was associated with what Montesquieu, following English usage, called 'Gothic' liberty

(*SL*, Book XI, ch. 8). Among seventeenth-century English thinkers, especially among the 'ancient constitutionalists', Tacitus was viewed as a key spokesman for this kind of liberty. Hegel says, however, that neither France nor the German states in the Holy Roman Empire evolved in this way. Feudalism in the former, he claims, degenerated (p. 65) into absolutism; in the latter, feudalism remained mired in particularism because Germany failed politically to make the transition to limited monarchy and a more representative government. According to Hegel, the obstinacy (or stubbornness) of the Germans ensured that they would cling to their original 'freedom' in circumstances where it was imperative for them to give their freedom a political (i.e. a 'Gothic' and constitutional) face. Having failed to make the transition, the German Empire became 'a collection [of states] without a [unifying] principle'. In the Preface to *PR*, Hegel invokes the obstinacy argument again in order to criticise the anti-political aspects of Lutheran inwardness.

10 M. Westphal (1984: pp. 79f) discusses how the term 'obstinate' (*eigensinnig*) figures in Hegel's later account of the Protestant principle of freedom.

11 Hegel means, of course, to set civil liberty off against political liberty. In fact, the strength with which private rights were adhered to by the Germans was why Germany had encountered difficulty becoming a state. Privatisation and depoliticisation are connected in Hegel's mind. He draws the same connection in *NL* (pp. 148–9), but shifts the focus backwards in time to Roman history.

12 See glossary *Reichstag*.

13 Roman Months: a term used since medieval times to refer to payments made by the members of the Imperial Diet to the Holy Roman Emperor. These payments were used by the Emperor to cover expenses which he incurred while travelling to Rome to meet with the Pope.

14 The Latin translates: 'Let justice prevail, even if Germany should perish'.

15 The phrase 'legal anarchy' relates back to the second paragraph of the essay. Cf. note 3 above. Although Hegel has Voltaire in mind, many Germans held that view too (e.g. Samuel Pufendorf).

16 Hegel's discussion of the opposition between *Staatsrecht* and *Staat* indicates that he wishes to assign a value to the state that is distinctly *political*. For this reason, this essay strikes Carl Schmitt (1996: p. 62) as a fine example of the decisively 'political' character of Hegel's thinking.

17 In some of his other political writings, Hegel will argue, for example, that 'a people' is not 'a mass'. Here he wishes a 'mass' to become 'a people' in a strictly political rather than a cultural or social sense. In Fichte's *SR* (p. 265), a book that greatly stimulated Hegel in the late 1790s, there is a passage in which Fichte claims that, with the establishment of government, 'the people are no longer a people, a whole, but an aggregate of individuals'. Hegel wishes to reverse that argument. He engages Fichte more directly in several writings in 1801–3.

18 This paragraph illustrates how Hegel tries to limit the scope of the state's authority in order to ensure the integrity of what is political about it. Otherwise, the state would be either totalitarian or a tool of special interests in society. The final sentence may refer to events in France in the 1790s.

19 Hegel seems here to be addressing the matter of passive and active citizenship, a major focus of the political debate in France during the Revolution. He makes a more explicit reference to this in *M*, p. 5 above.

20 While Hegel recognises diversity here, he seems in the next two paragraphs to have done so in order to emphasise the importance of religion for human identity formation in the modern world. When he mentions 'religious unity' as a 'prerequisite of a state' he anticipates the references later in this essay to Theseus and to his own later arguments in his Berlin years about religion finding fulfilment in the state. He also referred to Theseus as an agent of unity in the early theological writings. See Hegel (1948), p. 146.

21 Until the end of his life, Hegel allowed for the interplay between religion (i.e. a 'holy community of Christians') and politics (i.e. 'secular power') in his thinking about the modern state. His concept of *Sittlichkeit* represents the intersection of the two.

22 Knox (in Hegel 1964: p. 159 n 2) detects a reference to Fichte's police state here as well as to the despotism of the French Revolution. For more on Fichte's police state, see note 23 below and notes 47, 48, and 111 to *NL*.

23 Again, Hegel's disdain for totalitarian politics (as practised in France? in Prussia? or both at once?) is evident. Yet he is also against equating the 'political' with popular sovereignty. A few paragraphs later, he will imply that the French are 'illiberal' (*unfreie*: p. 25) because they are enthusiasts of centralisation. As he goes on to show, the ideological danger is that French illiberalism, while representing itself in theory as the champion of 'rational principles', in practice 'extends no trust whatsoever

towards its citizens'. Hence, in the following paragraphs Hegel calls France a 'hierarchical state' and its current political system 'mechanistic' (pp. 24–5). Beginning in the early 1800s, he associates Fichte's political thinking with the idea of the machine state (*GW*, vol. IV, p. 58). Fichte discusses the state in 'mechanical' terms in *SR*, pp. 189–202.

24 Here the machine reference is to Prussia. But a few paragraphs later Hegel argues that France as well as Prussia is such a state. See *GG*, the entry on 'Staat und Souveranität' (pp. 21, 30–1), for the emergence of the idea of the machine state among German thinkers in the later eighteenth century.

25 We translate *Staatsbürger* as 'citizens' here. The German word began to acquire special political meaning from the 1770s on. See Vierhaus (1987: pp. 101–4) for a discussion of the evolution of the term. Very often it was used to call for more middle-class involvement in the exercise of rulership.

26 Hegel's doubts about the French Revolution are unmistakable here and elsewhere in this essay. As Wood and Nisbet have observed (*PR*: p. 397 n 3), Hegel continued to interpret the French Revolution in this way in *PR*. Since he reiterates this line of criticism throughout the 1820s, it must be viewed as characteristic of rather than as an exception to his attitude towards 1789.

27 At this point in his life, Hegel is quite hostile to Prussia and its former commanding 'genius', Frederick the Great. Unlike certain supporters of enlightened absolutism, Hegel did not accept the argument that Prussia was a 'free monarchy' (Vierhaus 1987: p. 29). In Berlin, between 1818 and 1831, he changes the way in which he talks about Prussia and Frederick. But in doing so he does not embrace the Prussia that 'is' so much as the Prussia that 'ought' to be. For more on this theme, see the introduction to this volume.

28 Harris (1972: pp. 456–7) discusses the lacuna at this point in the manuscript.

29 Imperial Register (*Matrikel*): a list prepared in 1521 at the Diet of Worms which enumerated the financial contribution each member of the Imperial Diet had to make to the Emperor to cover his military expenses.

30 In the early modern period of Europe history, the idea that money was the 'sinews' of war shaped much of the debate about the doctrine of 'reason of state'. In his own way, Hegel is taking up that issue here. He is especially concerned to explain why political unity is essential for the self-determination (as distinct from the independence) of a people.

31 See glossary.
32 See glossary.
33 See glossary.
34 This refers to the second Congress of Rastatt, held between 1797 and 1799, for negotiations between the Empire and France.
35 The catch was, however, that the real bear had still to be captured.
36 For an overview of the organisational structure and politics of the German Empire in the eighteenth century, see Klaus Epstein (1966: chapter 5). For how the Empire operated in the eyes of a Württemberger, see Mack Walker (1981).
37 Ferguson (1995: p. 128) says something quite similar.
38 Throughout this essay, the Peace of Westphalia is presented as a defining moment of German history. It is when German 'state-lessness became organised' in an institutional sense (p. 74).
39 The Peace of Nijmegen (or Nimwegen) was concluded in 1678–9.
40 1697.
41 1714.
42 1738.
43 1801.
44 By 'partial' associations Hegel has in mind short-term contractual relationships that independent states form to ensure their 'separateness' rather than their togetherness. The fact that such contracts never require states to become 'interlocking' prompts him to deny political status to such partial associations. His distinction between contractual and 'interlocking' relations is relevant to his later conception of civil society and the state as aggregation and association, respectively.
45 Here Hegel's argument seems to recognise the German propensity for oscillating between extreme forms of collectivism and individualism.
46 Throughout this essay, Hegel uses the term 'formality' to explain a mind-set that results in people mistaking 'aggregations' for associations (cf. also *PWE*, pp. 248–9, 263–4, and 267–8, where he uses the term 'aggregate' to illustrate why an atomistic society of privatised individuals is not really a society). Here, the German concept of the state is 'empty' because it is formal. Nonetheless, Germans have convinced themselves that what is merely formal is real rather than empty. On these grounds, it was impossible for them to think about forming a truly political association, still less for them actually to take the initiative for forming such an association. Hegel develops the idea of the *Gedankenstaat* to express the illusory quality of this kind of thinking. Harris (172: p. 467 n 1)

is excellent on how all this relates to Hegel's concept of 'fate', a concept he had developed in his early theological writings.

47 This entire paragraph contains key elements of what will later become associated with Hegel's critique of liberalism. For him, liberalism articulates a theory of the state that, in essence, is unpolitical because it denies the state real political (i.e. independent) authority. It is worth observing that repoliticisation is Hegel's answer in both situations.

48 In this paragraph, the line between the idealisation of political association and idolisation of the state's political authority is thin indeed. For more on this theme, see the general introduction to this volume.

49 Later (pp. 66–7) Hegel will discuss the transition that is being impeded here in terms of the failure of the 'feudal constitution' to develop 'into a political power'. Given all that he says, it is surely an English-style 'limited monarchy' that he has in mind here. For this reason, he can declare that it is not 'feudalism [per se] which has cut off the possibility of Germany becoming a state' (p. 56).

50 *Reichshofrat*: see glossary.

51 See glossary.

52 This should in fact read 'Jülich-Cleve', as Hegel himself correctly describes it later: see p. 71.

53 A measure introduced in 1495 by the Emperor Maximilian I, which finally took effect in the early sixteenth century.

54 There is a difference, then, between 'politics' and the 'political' in Hegel's thinking. That 'politics' exists in the Empire does not mean that the Empire is actually a state in Hegel's sense of the term. Nor, he adds later, does the existence of 'politics' mean that a transition has been made from feudal anarchy to the give-and-take of constitutionalism.

55 Napoleon, in 1797.

56 Here is where German freedom failed to become politically institutionalised in the Empire in the form of limited monarchy. Compare Ferguson (1995: p. 127).

57 The opening three paragraphs of this section appear to describe the course of the Reformation in Germany. It is interesting that Hegel co-ordinates, somewhat as had the Scottish historians W. Robertson and J. Millar before him, the religious breakthrough of Protestantism with economic and cultural developments. In each case, the result is a kind of individualism that privileges parts before wholes. *Bürgergeist* suggests, in this context, a more private

than public focus for middle-class activity. Hegel here anticipates his own argument in *NL*, in which he uses the French term *bourgeois* to draw attention to privatising tendencies in the ancient and modern world.

58 In Greek, the idea of being 'untamed' is the opposite of being civilised. Here, Hegel uses the term as a synonym for barbarian.

59 On these grounds, Hegel sees Lutheranism as a depoliticising agent. He hints at this in his early theological writings of the 1790s, and he is explicit about the connection in *FK* (1802). He continues to hold this view until later in his life, when he begins to argue that Lutheran subjectivism is an immature form of Protestantism.

60 Distinctions similar to the one Hegel draws between 'community of religion' and 'community of physical needs' can be found throughout Ferguson's *Essay* (1995: e.g., pp. 53–5).

61 Hegel's concern with Protestantism's fear of Catholicism has to be interpreted as part of his disappointment with orthodox Lutheranism's failure to carry the Reformation far enough – into the world, as it were. This failure, he reasons, gave rise to a stultifying alliance between throne and altar in German history. For more on this theme, see our discussion of the idea of a 'second Reformation' in the general introduction.

62 Echoes of Locke's view of the 1688–9 upheaval in England can be heard here. Indeed, it is the fact that society does not dissolve when the state does that prompts Hegel to begin to allot conceptual space to civil society in his thinking.

63 This sentence anticipates Hegel's attempt in Berlin to find a place for religious and political values in his concept of *Sittlichkeit*.

64 Namely Catholicism, Lutheranism, and Calvinism.

65 This happened in Württemberg, Hegel's homeland, in the eighteenth century.

66 The sequence discussed here is consistent with Hegel's view of how German freedom evolved into 'representative' governments from the 'old feudal constitutions' of Europe, all of which were founded on German freedom.

67 See note 49 above.

68 Hegel describes Prussia as a 'foreign power' because the Prussian dukedom was formerly not an estate of the Empire but a hereditary fiefdom of Poland, which did not recognise Prussia's independent sovereignty until 1657.

69 The context here shows that the relationship between wholes and parts in Hegel's political thinking is not simply a matter of his being an anti-individual collectivist.

70 Here and at several places later in the essay (pp. 69–73, 79–80, 87, 97–8) Hegel discusses the cosmopolitan/nationalism problem as he understood it. His argument is that rights-based individualism and cosmopolitanism are two sides of the same utopian political coin. Like some twentieth-century critics of the Enlightenment, he sees a dangerous 'indeterminacy of rights' (p. 70) arising from the interplay between the abstractionism of cosmopolitanism and the subjectivism of individualism.

71 As King George I.

72 Prussia.

73 In the next six paragraphs Hegel outlines the process by which German freedom became institutionalised in certain countries in western Europe. Sadly, Hegel says, Germany never made the transition from the one form of German freedom to the other.

74 Obviously, Hegel means here to use 'representative' government as the standard with which to measure the evolution of German liberty.

75 The separation of the 'individual' from the 'universal' is an important motif in *NL* (see pp. 102–80). However, it is developed there in a very different conceptual framework, one that has aspects of Hegel's later separation of civil society and the state about it.

76 Private right in its 'full force' is licence, not liberty. Later Hegel says that this is a lesson Europeans have learned from the French Revolution.

77 Among the ancients, there was a close connection between philanthropy and cosmopolitan thinking. As the next paragraph shows, reason/interest of state is very much on Hegel's mind here.

78 Cf. note 52 above.

79 'Blessed are the possessors!'

80 A league of Protestant states set up in the early sixteenth century.

81 The so-called *Fürstenbund*, set up under Prussian auspices in 1785, to oppose further extension of the Emperor Joseph II's Austrian power in German territories.

82 The reference is to Johannes von Müller, *Darstellung des Fürstenbundes* (Leipzig, 1787).

83 In the next four paragraphs, Hegel uses the Peace of Westphalia as a negative ideological backdrop against which he will develop an argument about the wisdom inherent in Machiavelli's theory of 'reason of state'.

84 Pseudonym of Bogislaus Philipp von Chemnitz, author of *De ratione status in imperio nostro Romano-Germanico* (Stettin, 1640).

85 The Emperor Ferdinand II.
86 Earlier (p. 65) Hegel spoke of the degeneration of feudalism into absolutism in France and particularism in Germany. He is reworking that point here, implicitly contrasting the two extremes with England's more moderately middling course of constitutional development.
87 Later in his life, Hegel will interpret Louis XIV's move against the Huguenots (i.e. French Calvinists) in 1685 as decisive for the outbreak of revolution in France in 1789.
88 Machiavelli is the statesman. Hegel will proceed to argue that Machiavelli is not advocating tyranny so much as advancing a set of 'idealistic' prescriptions (p. 81) for how a prince might politically unite a people into a state.
89 The following translation of Hegel's extract is taken from Machiavelli, *The Prince*, ed. Quentin Skinner and Russell Price (Cambridge, 1988), pp. 87–91. Hegel himself cites a French translation of *The Prince*.
90 Theseus is discussed again at the end of the essay. The role religion played in Theseus' political achievement, testified to by any number of ancient sources (e.g. Euripides, *Supplices* 201–13), was not lost on Hegel.
91 The Latin translates as: 'necessary wars are just wars, and when there is no other hope except in arms, they are holy' (Livy, Book IX, 1).
92 The reference is to Frederick the Great and his treatise *Anti-Machiavel* (1740).
93 Harris (1972: p. 471 n 1) and Oz-Salzberger (1995: p. 261) discuss the Cato reference.
94 I.e. Caesar.
95 I.e. Cesare Borgia (1476–1507), son of Pope Alexander VI, here euphemistically described as his 'uncle', whose pontificate lasted from 1492 to 1503.
96 Pope from 1503 to 1513.
97 Another reference to Frederick the Great.
98 The reference once more is to Frederick the Great and his treatise *Anti-Machiavel*.
99 The Emperor Frederick I (Barbarossa; *c.* 1123–90).
100 In 1508.
101 I.e. Bressanone, just over the Italian frontier south of Innsbruck.
102 Hegel is referring here to the status of the Free (or Imperial) Knights as subject only to the Emperor; see also the glossary entry *Reichsunmittelbarkeit*.

103 A body set up to demarcate the boundaries of French and Prussian influence.

104 The date simply indicates that this is a later draft of the essay.

105 I.e. Prussia.

106 The word εὔχετο means 'it boasted'.

107 There is a sense here that, as machine states, France and Prussia make life comfortable for the middle class but demand quietism from it.

108 The *corpus evangelicorum* was a Protestant organisation within the Imperial Diet that regulated relations between princes and subjects on religio-political matters.

109 Such *Reversalien* – religious guarantees usually arranged by the *corpus evangelicorum* – would have been familiar to Hegel from a famous episode in 1733 in Württemberg.

110 The paragraph refers to the religious situation in Prussia in the 1780s. See H. B. Nisbet (1982) for a discussion of the context.

111 Hegel will endeavour for the rest of his life to bring a 'third possibility' of freedom into existence.

112 Hegel's use of the phrase 'general will' in the context of an argument about participation in government through representative political institutions is revealing when read in the light of Rousseau's understanding of the general will, one of his most famous political concepts. Hegel appears to want, so to speak, to harness some of Rousseau's political radicalism here.

113 The paragraph should be read in the light of Hegel's previous discussion (p. 23) and subsequent discussion (p. 98) of the right of citizens to 'share' in government through representation.

114 Given what Hegel had said earlier in the essay about the dissolution of the state not entailing a corresponding dissolution of society, this statement should not be interpreted as referring so much to German society as to the German empire *qua* political institution.

115 This paragraph is interesting because of the way Hegel locates the impulse towards patriotism in 'human nature'. Throughout his life, he insisted on grounding political matters in human nature in order to be able to derive the 'real' from the 'rational' side of human nature as it develops in individuals, societies, and history. The active principle arises here, Hegel says, from a will that seeks fulfilment in co-operation and sharing. This is parallel to the ancient Greek view of man as *zoon koinonikon* – of man as a sharing/co-operating/communicating/communal being. In *NL* (pp.

159–60 and 295 n 99), written about the same time, Hegel favourably quotes a passage from Aristotle in which the concept of the *zoon koinonikon* is the measure of man and of community.

116 Regarding Hegel's commitment to the idea that citizens should be allowed to share in government, see notes 113 and 115 above. It is not an accident that, among Greek thinkers, the gathering of scattered groups into co-operative associations, in which human beings shared a life in common, constituted a key moment in the civilising process.

117 That is, cities which withdrew from the Imperial union could no longer be required to pay compensation to the latter for failure to fulfil their obligations to it.

118 Hegel's reservations in the 1810s about liberal efforts radically to decentralise political authority in Germany also follow from this. The differences in early nineteenth-century Germany between centralising and de-centralising liberals likewise come into play here.

119 As to who this conqueror might be see Harris (1972: pp. 475–6) and Knox (*KP*: p. 241 n 2). As both note, the reference is probably not to Napoleon.

120 On Theseus, who gathered the scattered Greeks together, see notes 20, 90, and 116 above.

121 Echoes of the Greek antithesis between *koinonia* (here 'common social intercourse') and *idiota* (here the madness of individuals living in 'isolation' from their fellows) pervade this paragraph. (In *FK* (p. 151), written about the time that *GC* was composed, Hegel actually uses the Greek word *idiota* to express a similar idea.) The idea of murderous madness, moreover, recalls the kind of *mania* that the Greeks thought led to hubris or to acts of criminal transgression that destroy community in a nation. The antithesis between *koinonia* and *idiota* parallels the one Hegel will later draw between *Sittlichkeit* and atomism.

122 In the early theological writings (Hegel 1948: pp. 182ff), Hegel discusses the theme of Jewish particularity at great length.

123 This sentence would seem to refer to the French Revolution.

On the Scientific Ways of Treating Natural Law, on its Place in Practical Philosophy, and its Relation to the Positive Sciences of Right

1 *NL* was published in Hegel's and Schelling's *Critical Journal of Philosophy* (henceforth *CJ*) in two parts between December 1802

and May 1803. At the time, Hegel was an unknown thinker who, before assuming a teaching position at the University of Jena in 1801, had not actually written, let alone published, anything philosophical. By contrast, Schelling, Hegel's old friend from his university days at Tübingen, had already won acclaim as a philosopher. Given their respective reputations, Hegel was perceived as the junior editor of *CJ*. Despite the difference in their achievements, they shared a common religious vision at this time. In fact, as H. S. Harris has observed (1985: pp. 252–3), *CJ* was established to disseminate that vision. For both thinkers, the vision included developing a new religio-philosophical theory of *Sittlichkeit*. For a detailed account of *CJ* as a philosophical enterprise, see Harris (1985).

2 The opening sentence is really a declaration. As will become evident in the essay, Hegel wishes to keep natural law within the domain of philosophy while, at the same time, giving philosophy a method that separates it from methodologies used in the natural sciences. Overall, his intention is to develop a philosophical framework for natural law in which the natural rights of individuals are de-emphasised in favour of the universal interest of society. Hyppolite (1996: p. 36) calls this an 'organic' conception of rights and (mistakenly, in our opinion) traces it to Romanticism.

3 Since at least 1793, Hegel had viewed the concept of 'understanding' with suspicion. Shortly before publishing *NL*, he confirmed that suspicion again in *FK*, which was also published in *CJ* in 1802. In both of the essays, his point is that a philosophical science founded on understanding will never yield more than subjective ways of thinking.

4 Hegel's note refers to J. G. Fichte's *Grundlage des Naturrechts nach Prinzipien des Wissenschaftslehre* (1796/97), which can be found in Fichte's *Werke*, vol. 1/3 (Stuttgart, 1966). For our purposes, the most relevant sections are 14–16, pp. 425–60. This work has been translated into English as *The Science of Rights* (henceforth *SR*).

5 In *FK* it is made clear that 'critical philosophy' signifies a philosophy of understanding which is Kantian in nature.

6 It is, of course, Hegel's task to restore 'these sciences to philosophy'. This will eventually involve moving the science of natural law from its Kantian base in *Moralität* to Hegelian *Sittlichkeit*.

7 The point of this complicated passage is to establish two successive foci for the study of natural law. Although both approaches to natural law are grounded in necessity, each operates in its own realm – in the empirical and the universal, respectively. The key,

however, is to realise that the two realms derive from the same subject – from the particular and universal aspects of human nature. Hegel's challenge in this essay is to redefine natural law so that the focus of natural-law thinking shifts from particularity to universality.

8 The reference to 'relations', and in the preceding sentence to the 'science' of such relations, allows Hegel to locate self-regarding and other-regarding drives in one and the same individual. As a result, love of self and love of others need not be formulated in terms of an opposition between the individual and society. A spectacular discussion of this theme can be found in Georg Simmel (1950: pp. 58–84).

9 Implicit in this paragraph is Hegel's life-long commitment to the separation of *Moralität* and *Sittlichkeit* as philosophical ways of viewing man's relationship to the world, and especially to his fellows. He associates the former with the 'science of right' and faults it for its inability to establish a 'positive' basis for the organisation of communal life. The word 'positive' here should not, however, be confused with the critique of 'positivity' that Hegel develops in many of his other writings.

10 The section numbers follow those in *Werke*. They are not in the original text.

11 Throughout this essay, Hegel associates the 'fixing of determinacies' with a science of society that organises social wholes around aggregations of individual entities (e.g. atoms or individuals). Against those who claim that such aggregations constitute unity in multiplicity, Hegel contends that the unity achieved by aggregation is a fiction. Later in this paragraph, when he says 'the organic is broken up by empirical or imperfectly reflected intuition', he is reiterating a point he had made in *FK* about how Lockean empiricism and Kantian philosophy have contributed equally to the ascendancy of subjectivism in modern culture.

12 Here and later in the essay, Hegel implies that, despite its declared hostility to empiricism, critical philosophy develops a view of knowledge that in the final analysis is quite similar to what it condemns.

13 Empirical knowledge is inadequate here because it operates with a false concept of infinity. That is, it cannot unite 'unconnected determinacies' because it privileges each determinacy itself rather than the 'original unity' to which each determinacy belonged before it was analytically separated from the whole. This gives rise to what Hegel, perhaps following Schelling (1978: pp. 92–3), calls

an 'atomistic' social system (*FK*, p. 152). As early as 1801 (*GW*, vol. IV, p. 58), Hegel depicts Fichte as a philosopher of atomism.

14 Compare Hegel's discussion here of formalism in philosophy with the way in which he discusses formalism in political thinking in *GC* (p. 41 above).

15 Just as atomism cannot explain the power of gravity in the physical world, so empiricism and critical philosophy cannot explain the need for community in the ethical world. If we substitute the word 'anarchy' for 'chaos' in this passage, it is easy to predict what social and political consequences will follow. Hegel defines these consequences in the next paragraph. In his Berlin period, atomism in fact becomes for him a defining feature of civil society.

16 The 'chaotic image of the necessary', which can only 'contain' multiplicity but not transform it, becomes the organisational principle of civil society in Hegel's later writings.

17 This marks the point at which Hegel makes metaphysics essential to his emerging conception of the state.

18 An example of what Hegel is referring to here would be the relation between private property on the one hand and the right to private property guaranteed by law on the other. Both recognise what is empirical, but each does so from its own separate sphere – respectively, from the political domain of the law and the economic domain of property. Later in the essay, Hegel will organise his discussion of the *bourgeoisie* as a social class around this intersection.

19 'Inner necessity for one another' is what Hegel finds lacking in civil society as a form of human association. It yields only 'negative unity'. *Sittlichkeit*, by contrast, is a form of association that recognises and subsequently grows out of that inner necessity. It is not just something that is 'added on' to multiplicity, as he points out later in the paragraph.

20 Hobbes is no doubt alluded to here.

21 Some scholars detect a reference to Napoleon here.

22 When 'fixed as particular essences', the 'fragmented moments of organic ethical life' correspond to what Hegel will later define as the essence of civil society.

23 The relation Hegel sketches here between 'ethical life' (*Sittlichkeit*) and 'ethical nature' (*sittliche Natur*) reveals how he grounded *Sittlichkeit* in the idea of a subject who has other-regarding as well as self-regarding dispositions. Similarly, in the next sentence, he separates 'the natural' from the ethical in order to avoid having to argue that human beings are 'by nature' what they ought to be.

For elaboration of the latter point, see note 19 to *PH* (p. 309 below).

24 The phrase 'non-subjugated oneness' clearly shows that Hegel is not an anti-individual collectivist.

25 What is 'nullified' (*vernichtet*) is not so much intuition *per se* as the intuition human beings have of their need to belong to a whole in order to be truly human. That becomes clear in the next few sentences, when Hegel derives the ethical architectonic from 'intuition [which] remains true to itself'.

26 Understanding confuses intuition by orienting individuals to *Moralität* rather than *Sittlichkeit*.

27 Hegel seems to be equating intuition with 'rational spirit' here. The fact that he also says that this spirit is 'invisible' (i.e. latent) may relate to what Schiller (1967: p. 15) says about 'invisible *Sittlichkeit*'. Later (p. 120), Hegel will identify intuition with 'ethical reason' (*sittliche Vernunft*) – which is why his concept of *Sittlichkeit* is sometimes referred to as 'social *Geist*'.

28 In the remainder of this paragraph, Hegel not only develops the opposition in philosophy between empiricism and formalism but also relates the latter to political tendencies which grew out of the French Revolution.

29 In the last two sentences, Hegel's criticism of metaphysical politics aims less at demystifying metaphysics than at ensuring that philosophy applies the right kind of metaphysics to politics.

30 In some sense, Hegel means to use the idea of the *becoming* of the individual to get beyond 'the being of the individual', whether that individual is conceptualised in terms of happiness (*Glückseligkeitslehre*) or Kant's more high-minded conception of *Moralität*. (For more on Hegel's view of happiness, see note 40 below.) Obviously, in this paragraph, Hegel means to associate the natural self with being and the spiritual self with becoming.

31 The reference to an 'absolute point of indifference' needs to be read in terms of Schiller's and Schelling's earlier discussions of this matter. On this theme, see Dickey (1987: pp. 246–8).

32 The last few sentences seek to say that multiplicity is primary to physical nature and unity primary to ethical nature. This allows Hegel to oppose the two aspects of nature to each other in the same way as he would later oppose atomism to *Sittlichkeit* and civil society to the state.

33 Later in the essay (pp. 158–60), Hegel will advance his famous distinction between *Moralität* and *Sittlichkeit*. This paragraph needs to be read in anticipation of that distinction. It is also

important to realise that in this paragraph, Hegel does not use the term *Moralität*, but he does identify a certain kind of *Sittlichkeit* as *Unsittlichkeit*. Translating *Unsittlichkeit* as 'immorality' captures very well what Hegel means when he later substitutes *Moralität* for what is here identified as *Unsittlichkeit*.

34 See Kant, *CPR*, pp. 97–8 (A 58–9). (Our translation differs slightly from the Norman Kemp Smith translation.)

35 In writings from the years 1830–1, Hegel will use this line of argument to explain why France had been prone to political revolutions since 1789.

36 See Kant, *CPrR*, p. 30 (Book I, Chapter I, section 7). (Our translation differs slightly from Lewis White Beck's translation.)

37 What results for Hegel from this privileging of the private is what Friedrich Schlegel (1991: p. 81) called a 'polemical totality' in which everyone talks but no one listens.

38 See Kant, *CPrR*, pp. 26–7 (Book I, Chapter I, section 4 and Remark).

39 Hyppolite (1996: p. 47) discusses the Kantian background of the 'deposit' argument. Kant puts forward the argument in the material cited in note 38 above.

40 'Eudaemonism' translates the German *Glückseligkeitslehre*, i.e. that system of ethics which makes happiness the criterion of rectitude. It is not insignificant that in 1758, J. H. G. von Justi suggested that the machine state would maximise the happiness of citizens. See *GG*, entry on 'Staat', p. 21, for particular details. Parry (1963) also discusses this theme.

41 Accordingly, as Hegel will later argue in *PR*, the law of property serves the particular interests of civil society rather than the universal interest of the state. As such, law and property work together to preserve and sanction an 'empirical multiplicity' – an aggregation – that cannot transform itself into unity.

42 Again, as in notes 25 to 27 above, Hegel derives the principle of *Sittlichkeit* from the disposition towards unity in intuition.

43 In this sentence, we see Hegel discussing subjectivity in terms of self-regarding and other-regarding tendencies.

44 One of the most important statements in *PR* is that in which Hegel refuses to allow political participation to be 'optional' (Hegel 1991a: p. 276). This sentence in *NL* goes far to explain both why he said this and why he is not a political pluralist.

45 In other words, Hegel wishes to separate the disposition towards rights-based individualism from the science of ethics and, by so doing, to make *Sittlichkeit* the measure of natural law.

46 Here, Hegel re-affirms the link between *Moralität* and subjectivity that he had discussed in such detail in *FK*.

47 The reference is to the opening sentence of section 14 of Fichte's *SR*, p. 192 (German edn as in note 4 above). Fichte develops the idea of a machine state in this section. H. B. Acton (1975: pp. 28–35) provides a good discussion of Hegel's view of Fichte as it emerges in *NL*.

48 There are hints in some of Hegel's early political writings (e.g. *GC*, pp. 17, 40, 50–1, 63, 74–5 above) that he is trying to explain the violence of the French Revolution by means of the argument on 'coercion' which he is developing here. In the next two paragraphs, in which he discusses Fichte, he runs together the arguments concerning 'coercion' and 'mechanical' systems of government, just as he had in *GC*. As in note 47 above, he has Fichte in mind – specifically the latter's so-called 'law of compulsion'.

49 Implicit in what follows is a critique of mixed government. Compare this with the positive things Hegel had said in *GC* about the Gothic polity as a mixed form of government.

50 A formula similar to this can be found in Schiller (1967: p. 19).

51 In *GC*, Hegel represents the general will as a power in need of representation rather than as a power with absolute authority.

52 The reference is to Fichte's discussion of the ephorate in *SR*, section 16, pp. 205–85, esp. pp. 259ff. Also compare Hegel's last sentence with two statements of Friedrich Schlegel around 1800 (1996: pp. 166–7): (1) 'Without *opinion publique*, no *volonté générale*; and no *opinion publique* without the ephorate of intellectuals and propaganda of reason'; and (2) 'There is no republic without an ephorate and only the spiritual class can execute this.' That Fichte's ephorate may be an agent of public opinion has been noted by scholars. For a nuanced discussion of Fichte and the ephorate, see A. La Vopa (1989), especially p. 158.

53 Hegel's critique of Fichte here is parallel to his critique of the French Revolution.

54 With the phrase 'remote from public life', Hegel may be thinking of the Greek definition of the demagogue. For what the Greeks said about the latter, Hegel says about public opinion as an 'irresponsible' political power.

55 The last two sentences disprove the charge (e.g. in Barker 1957: p. xvii) that Hegel's political philosophy aims to engulf individuals.

56 Hyppolite (1996: pp. 5–6, 51) regards this as a decisive point in this text, the point where Hegel begins to ground the absolute in the ethical life of a people. At this time, Hyppolite also notes (pp.

62, 84 n 6), Hegel had not yet distinguished absolute spirit from 'ethical totality'.

57 As he had done in *GC*, Hegel criticises cosmopolitanism here. The reference to perpetual peace may indicate that he has Kant, and his essay *Perpetual Peace* (1795), in mind.

58 As scholars now fully appreciate, Hegel's willingness to consider the interplay between ethical and economic tendencies in the modern world sets him off from other German thinkers of his age. In what follows, he begins to allow political economy to shape the discussion of *Sittlichkeit*. One of the results of this will be his recognition and construction of a 'system of reality' (i.e. a 'system of needs') that is organised in terms of negative unity. He will later assimilate this system to his conception of civil society.

59 Hegel later uses his understanding of this 'system of universal mutual dependence' to express the 'semblance' of social unity that liberals see in civil society. In his opinion, this semblance simply masks the atomism of a market society, and the blindness of liberals to this circumstance is one reason why he is himself anti-liberal.

60 The last three sentences contain Hegel's critique of civil society, in so far as civil society is understood as a realm of civil liberty and socio-economic inequality.

61 What Hegel means by the formally absolute becoming a 'living particularity' is what Habermas (1975: p. 76) seeks to evoke through his idea of 'civil privatism'.

62 This sentence shows that, for Hegel, political economy, after constituting itself as a system of social reality, inhibits the development of *Sittlichkeit* by confining ethics to a sphere of life dominated by economics.

63 Hegel appeals to Plato here (*Statesman*, 294a–c) in order to underpin his own criticism of formalism. Plato's original Greek is to be found in *GW*, vol. IV, p. 615; the translation is by H. N. Fowler in Plato, *The Statesman*, Loeb Classical Library (London, 1925), pp. 133–5.

64 A critique of what, in the twentieth century, becomes modern pluralism is evident in this sentence.

65 This recalls Hegel's contention on p. 141 above that political economy forms a system of reality which operates independently of the state and which is opposed to 'the goal of ethical perfection'.

66 As Hegel proceeds to argue, organic stands to inorganic as *Sittlichkeit* stands to *Moralität*.

67 Ultimately, civil society will constitute the 'inorganic nature of the ethical'.

68 An excellent example of Hegel's conception of subjectivity as both other-regarding and self-regarding.

69 In other words, self-regarding subjectivity must be contained. Political economy, however, naturally increases subjectivity. Thus, its expansive powers must be contained too.

70 The passages referred to in Aristotle (*Politics*, 1255b 35–7) and Plato (*Republic*, 473b and 484a–486a) discuss qualities of political leadership that lead to justice and promotion of the common good. *GW*, vol. IV, p. 616 reproduces the Greek originals.

71 Plato (*Statesman*, 308e–309a); again, the topic is political leadership. The translation is by Fowler (see note 63 above), p. 187.

72 Aristotle (*Politics*, 1254a, 13ff); the theme discussed by Aristotle is the implication for political leadership of relations between masters and slaves.

73 At this point, Hegel begins a criticism of Rome that focuses on the depoliticisation of Roman public life. This marks a decisive moment in his development as a political thinker, because he also begins here to discuss the decline of the public life of the *polis* in terms of the emergence of a form of individualism that he relates to issues of economic enjoyment and personal security. As will become obvious later in the essay, Gibbon's notion of the increasingly 'privatised' life of Roman citizens helped him to make this initial connection. But it is crucial to realise that, when he introduces the word *bourgeois* (p. 151) to characterise this privatised type of life, he is adding an economic dimension to the argument concerning privatisation, one that dovetailed with the view of Christianity as a 'private religion' which he had developed in his early theological writings. (In addition to Gibbon, Hegel's reading of Scottish works on political economy is also relevant here.) The point to grasp, then, is that, here and in the following pages, Hegel posits a connection between two long-term processes of historical development: (1) the depoliticisation of the idea of citizenship in the ancient world; and (2) the privatisation of life that Hegel (and Gibbon, according to J. Pocock (1977)) sees as anticipating developments in the modern world. In other words, Hegel here begins to address on a philosophical level the famous argument about ancient and modern liberty.

74 It is important to remember that, when the 'second' class becomes 'the people', the people in question are constituted more by their economic than by their political interests. That is why Hegel quotes Gibbon on private life, and why he later uses the French term *bourgeois* (p. 151) to express what he is talking about.

75 Edward Gibbon, *Decline and Fall of the Roman Empire*, ed. J. B. Bury (London 1925), vol. I, pp. 56–7. Gibbon is discussing what he calls (just before the passage which Hegel quotes) 'the latent causes of [Roman] decline and corruption'.

76 In this sentence, we see Hegel identifying Roman law as the source of the kind of rights-based individualism he associates with self-regarding subjectivity and social and political atomism. In his later discussions of the French Revolution (e.g. in *PH*, pp. 212), he projects the abstractionism inherent in Roman law forward in time and uses it to explain tendencies in French thinking (i.e. Natural Law theory during the Enlightenment) and French politics (i.e. the French Revolution). In the 1820s, he will also associate these tendencies with Catholic philosophical and political thinking.

77 The quotations from Plato are from his *Republic*, 425c–427e and 404e–405b. Hegel's rendering of the Greek into German is rather free: for example, he slips the word *sittlich* ('ethical') in ('provided that God grants them the blessing of a truly ethical constitution') where there is no linguistic justification for it (the Greek refers to the preservative – perhaps redemptive – character of law or *nomos*). Our English translation is accordingly based directly on Hegel's German, not on Plato's Greek. For comparison, the following is a modern English translation of the phrase in question by a classical scholar (B. Jowett, *The Dialogues of Plato* (New York, 1937), vol. I, p. 688): 'if God will only preserve to them the laws which we have given them'.

78 In this sentence, Hegel means to contrast private life and public life. But, because private life has a semblance of universality about it, it appears to be 'social' too. Again, Habermas's idea of 'civil privatism' is relevant here (cf. note 61 above). In the next two sentences, Hegel will identify this system of privatised life as *bourgeois*.

79 Hegel had discussed the idea of 'political nullity' in *GC* (pp. 6–101 above). There and here, his concern is that privatisation entails depoliticisation. Obviously, he wishes to reverse that process, or at least to contain it. During the rest of his life, he will suggest a number of ways of repoliticising citizens – that is, of turning the burgher as *bourgeois* into the burgher as *citoyen*.

80 Facing up to the 'right of the inorganic' – say, to the necessity of political economy – consequently does not entail eliminating it.

81 The relationship between Hegel's conception of tragedy and his view of *Sittlichkeit* has often been discussed by scholars (e.g. by

A. C. Bradley (1959: pp. 69ff). In what follows, he moves from language associated with Greek tragedy to language associated with the resurrection of Jesus Christ.

82 Aeschylus was the author of *The Eumenides*, the third play in the trilogy known as the *Oresteia*. C. Meier (1990: pp. 82ff) has ably discussed the political dimensions of this tragedy. Harris (1983: p. 219) relates the political meaning of the *Oresteia* directly to Aristotle. Hyppolite (1996: pp. 56–9) and Cassirer (1946: p. 318) relate the tragic motif directly to Hegel's political thinking. Hyppolite correctly argues that much of what passes for 'dialectic' in Hegel's thought is a reflection of his 'pantragic' vision of world history.

83 Hyppolite (1996: p. 83 n 67) argues that comedy represents depoliticised Greek thinking. In the next paragraph, Hegel hints at something similar. Harris (1983: p. 219) relates the comedy motif to depoliticised Protestantism.

84 Hegel discusses Dante in *GW*, vol. IV, pp. 486ff. See Harris (1983: pp. 218ff) for comments on his view of Dante.

85 A reference to Plato (*Statesman*, 302a). Plato is discussing the failure of political leaders to grasp the science of politics.

86 Hegel seems to be arguing here that a proliferation of cultural forms at one historical moment signals an impending dissolution of the political order.

87 Throughout the 1790s, Hegel had developed the idea of 'fate' as a way of explaining continuity and change in history.

88 According to the editors of *GW*, vol. IV, p. 617, the passage in question is to be found in the second canto of Klopstock's *Messiah*; in our opinion, the resemblance is not sufficiently close to warrant the attribution to Klopstock.

89 Clearly, in this sentence, Hegel links different kinds of consciousness with different types of character.

90 Plato, *Phaedrus*, 246c–d. Plato is discussing the mortal and immortal aspects of the soul. The reference to a *gemeinschaftlichen* God at the end of the preceding paragraph should be read in conjunction with the information in note 112 below.

91 According to Knox (1975: p. 110 n), Hegel derives the aether reference from Schelling's philosophy of nature.

92 Knox (1975: p. 110 n) sees a possible allusion here to either Aristotle or Plato.

93 The idea that spirit is higher than nature is a main theme of the lectures on the philosophy of history which Hegel delivered in Berlin between 1822 and 1831.

94 The first instalment of *NL* ends here. The remainder of the essay appeared in the next issue of *CJ* (vols. 2, 3, 1803).

95 The opening sentence sets up the distinction, soon to be discussed more fully, between *Moralität* and *Sittlichkeit*.

96 A cautionary note is needed here, because Hegel does not reduce *Sittlichkeit* to the simple matter of abiding by laws that are traditional and/or in accordance with custom (*Sitte*). In this respect, his view seems to be similar to that of Aristotle. See, for example, E. R. Goodenough (1928: p. 67) and Leo Strauss (1964: p. 25).

97 By 'allegiance', Hegel simply means that placing the private advantage of the individual before the common good will make it difficult for philosophers of *Moralität* ever to talk coherently about the 'ethical life of everyone'.

98 As was noted above (note 56), Hyppolite makes much of Hegel's grounding of *Sittlichkeit* in 'the spirit of a people'.

99 Aristotle (*Politics*, 1253a 25–9). Hegel's rendering into German of Aristotle's Greek raises fundamental questions about how we should interpret his own social and political theory. To begin with, he uses the German *Volk* for the Greek *polis*. That in itself could be interpreted as a depoliticisation of Aristotle's language, for Aristotle (*Politics* 1252b) is clearly discussing the *polis* as the 'final and perfect' partnership/association (*koinonia*) in which citizens pursue the 'good life' as distinct from 'mere life'. At 1253a 39, Aristotle links pursuit of the good life both to 'political partnership/association' (*politike koinonia*) and to a disposition within individuals that requires membership in such an association. Hegel also uses the German phrase *wer . . . nicht gemeinschaftlich sein kann* (literally 'who cannot belong to a community') to translate a phrase in which *koinonein* (to share) is the key word. Modern translations of Aristotle's Greek differ significantly here: 'unable to share in the blessings of political association' (Barker); unable to 'enter into partnership' (Rackham); or 'unable to live in society' (Jowett). With regard to Hegel's translation, the problem is twofold: (1) does *gemeinschaftlich* refer to a political partnership/association, or to a social and/or communal partnership/association that lacks a political dimension but in any case fulfils the human need for association; or (2) does it refer to a communal ideal whose political and/or social content Hegel deliberately leaves open? And how do we ourselves translate Aristotle's *koinonia* and (in its verb form) *koinonein*? For example, we confuse social and political spheres if we render *koinonia* at 1253a 28 as 'social' (as Jowett does), because that translation tends to make the political just one form of association among many equal forms of non-political partnership/association. This results in a depoliticisation of Hegel's language and

makes it seem as if he were a pluralist – which he is not. Similarly, to read political content into *koinonein* where Aristotle's Greek is indeterminate obscures the fact that Aristotle often (e.g. *Ethics* 1170b 10–14) used *koinonein* to express the idea of spiritual communion among human beings. Obviously, no single translation of Hegel's rendering of Aristotle can fully capture all the possible meanings. In the passage which Hegel quotes, however, Aristotle is clearly discussing membership in the *polis* and trying to distinguish political membership from membership of other kinds of association. There is, therefore, a political dimension in this passage. Barker's translation captures it, whereas the other two do not. Hegel's German needs to be read in this light. In view of these translation problems, the English version supplied in the text is based directly on his German version.

100 The last two sentences make it perfectly clear that Hegel thinks the doctrine of *Moralität* stands the ethical world upside down. Conversely, *Sittlichkeit* stands the world rightside up. Accordingly, Hegel associates *Sittlichkeit* with his refigured conception of natural law. This allows him to reserve the term *Moralität* for the kind of rights-based individualism that had begun to emerge in Germany in the late eighteenth century (see Klippel 1990).

101 Because *Moralität* is the *Sittlichkeit* of the *bourgeoisie*, it is an agent of depoliticisation, too. As such, it cannot be 'truly ethical' in Hegel's judgement.

102 In this paragraph, Hegel begins to alter his perspective on the relationship between citizen and *bourgeois*. Previously, the latter had arisen as the privatisation process undermined the 'ethical life' of the *polis*. Here, however, Hegel begins to view the private life of the *bourgeoisie* as simply lacking in *Sittlichkeit* rather than as something unalterably opposed to *Sittlichkeit*. In this respect, the *bourgeois qua* 'child' is potentially an 'ethical individual'. It follows that the mark of a mature individual is ultimately the ability to share in the ethical life of the community.

103 The reference to 'a Pythagorean' is to Diogenes Laertius, Book VIII, I. 16. See *GW*, vol. IV, p. 617 n.

104 This sentence is a good example of Hegel's commitment to ethical holism. 'Common being' here translates the German *gemeinsamen Sein*.

105 In the opening sentences of the paragraph, Hegel seems to draw a distinction between, on the one hand, custom *qua* unreflective obedience to what has been, and, on the other hand, living custom which is brought into line with an ever-changing reality through thinking. Cf. note 96 above.

106 It is noteworthy that, in the 1820s, Hegel went on to present *Sittlichkeit* as the active expression of a religious *cultus*.

107 So, instead of a struggle for hegemony between self- and other-regarding tendencies in natural law, Hegel separates the former, in the form of *Moralität*, from the science of natural law altogether. In this formulation, natural law becomes an agent of the other-regarding disposition in human nature.

108 In other words, while Hegel does not deny that natural law derives from subjectivity, he does derive what he means by natural law from a potential within subjectivity that points towards ethical life rather than towards atomism.

109 Here Hegel dissolves intuition into self- and other-regarding tendencies. In several of the texts translated below (e.g. *PH*), 'immediate intuition' will take the form of feeling and 'intuition raised to an intellectual level' will take the form of thinking. Both forms of intuition are rooted in subjectivity, but the latter has an other- as well as a self-regarding orientation.

110 The encroachment argument anticipates Hegel's growing concern with the possibility and political consequences of civil society invading the state. Especially worrisome to him is what consequences an economic encroachment upon ethics will have for communal life.

111 What Hegel says here about Fichte parallels the argument in *GC* (pp. 22 and 276–7 notes 22–4 above) about the despotic tendencies in the 'machine state'. The mention of a 'perfect police-force' indicates that Hegel may be referring to Fichte's *SR* (section 16, pp. 374–87), where Fichte proposes to use the law to police the 'intentions' as well as the actions of citizens.

112 If there is any basis for what scholars call 'middle Hegelianism' (Ottmann 1996), it is enunciated here, for Hegel clearly aims to situate his philosophy of *Sittlichkeit* between despotism on the one hand and the anarchy of moral subjectivism on the other. In this respect, his earlier reference to *The Eumenides* (p. 152 above) might be read in the light of Aeschylus's statement (lines 526–30):

> Neither a life of anarchy nor a life under a despot should you praise. To all that lies in the middle has a god given excellence.

We follow Hugh Lloyd-Jones's translation of the *Oresteia* (Berkeley, CA, 1979), p. 241. In Isocrates (*Panegyricus* 39), Athens is the earthly embodiment of this middle way. Theseus, the Greek leader invoked at the end of *GC*, also figures in Isocrates' account.

113 Hegel's holism is again evident, as is the outline of the future distinction between civil society and the state. As he says later in

the paragraph, philosophy must 'honour [the] necessity' of particularity as well as striving for universality.

114 In the last two sentences, Hegel explains how individuality *qua Einzelheit* is transformed into 'ethical individuality' (*sittliche Individualität*). Both are subjective conditions, but the latter is animated by what he variously calls 'ethical intuition', 'ethical consciousness', 'ethical nature', and 'ethical reason'.

115 The reference to the 'world spirit' (*Weltgeist*) moving through history needs to be read in anticipation of arguments which Hegel later makes about Germany becoming the custodian of philosophy and the agent of *Sittlichkeit* in Europe (See *BIA*, pp. 182–3).

116 There is an anticipation of Hegel's discussion of the master–slave relationship in the *Phenomenology* here (Hegel 1931: pp. 228ff).

117 'Living individuality', which is not the same as 'living particularity' (p. 142 above), recognises the embeddedness of individuals in society and of nations in history. It is not an accident that Hegel cites Montesquieu in this paragraph, for it was Montesquieu – followed by Herder – who popularised the idea of historical embeddedness in eighteenth-century Germany.

118 The foregoing paragraph elaborates themes alluded to in note 96 above. For Hegel, it comes down to a question of how to decide between what is living and what is dead in the customs of a culture.

119 That the 'dissolution' of Germany should be on Hegel's mind at this time is not surprising, for he was working on *GC* as late as 1802, the year in which *NL* began to appear in *CJ*.

120 As in all of his political writings of 1797–1803, Hegel condemns empty (i.e. abstract) freedom as political escapism.

121 As in *GC* (p. 281 n 70 above), Hegel is critical here of cosmopolitanism and rights-based individualism.

122 Hegel's language here is revealing. For by identifying the 'abstractions and formal constructions' as 'protestant and revolutionary', and by opposing 'ethical vitality' (*sittliche Lebendigkeit*) to both, he indicates that, for him, *Sittlichkeit* is an alternative to religious as well as political forms of abstract subjectivism. In *FK*, he had posited a similar connection between 'reflective philosophy' (i.e. Kantianism) and Protestant subjectivism. In that essay, he also associated reflective philosophy with the atomistic organisation of society. Here, he begins to absorb the French Revolution into his emerging understanding of how atomism unfolded as a historical force in European history. By the time he published the *Phenomen-*

ology in 1807, an ideological connection existed in his mind between Protestantism (religion), the Enlightenment (philosophy), and the French Revolution (politics). Between 1818 and 1831, these three historical moments become the basis of his philosophy of modern history (see pp. 197–224).

Inaugural Address, Delivered at the University of Berlin

1 As was customary for new faculty members, Hegel delivered an inaugural address upon arriving in Berlin in 1818. By many accounts, this speech reveals on a micro-historical level a philosophical attempt to fuse universalistic German cultural values with the Prussian state (see Meinecke 1970: pp. 23–33, 148–59, and 233ff; cf. Haym 1857: pp. 357–9).

2 See W. Jaeschke and K. Meist (1981: pp. 29–39) on the political tensions surrounding Hegel's appointment.

3 For many years, Hegel had sought a 'wider' audience for his philosophy. In 1816, before his return to university teaching at Heidelberg, he remarked upon this in a letter to a friend (Hegel 1984b: p. 462). In 1816, in *HIA*, he publicly announced his commitment to help extend 'the higher interest of science' to a wider audience. Freiherr K. S. von Altenstein, who oversaw (but did not initiate) the hiring of Hegel for the University of Berlin, saw Hegel's task in identical terms (see Altenstein in Hegel 1984b: pp. 457, 459, 467). Just as publicly, Hegel's *PWE* commends Germany's young people for the public spirit they had shown in the recent Wars of Liberation (Hegel 1964: pp. 259–65). Hegel insists in *PWE* that the 'independence' which German youth had helped Germany to win during the war of 1813–15 entitled it to participate 'in the political life of the state'. He also says there that a 'rational' political system requires the participation of the citizens, but he is careful to distinguish his own view of 'rationality' from the atomistic one that allegedly governed political behaviour in France.

4 The reference to the dismal status of philosophy in the rest of Europe as well as in Germany echoes *HIA*. Prior to arriving in Berlin, Hegel consistently pointed to the popularity of Fries's shallow philosophising as proof of the precarious condition of German philosophy.

5 In this sentence, Hegel refers to the upheavals of the wars that had disrupted Europe since 1789. It is important to note that his remark about 'the inner life of spirit' is not meant to countenance, as Arnold Ruge (1802–80) insinuated in the early 1840s, a

Protestant retreat from political life into Mandarinism (Ruge 1983: pp. 218 and 222ff). Rather, Hegel recommends 'turning inwards' so that mature (i.e. 'free') reflection on how to bring 'actuality' into line with rationality (i.e. 'insight and thought') can begin. Insight is not, as Ruge mistakenly insinuates, a substitute for political action for Hegel (1983: p. 223). Rather, insight is the point of departure for instilling rationality into the political process. The phrase which Hegel uses to describe this process in *HIA* is more apt: spirit turns inward in order to 'collect itself' before moving outwards again.

6 Hegel means to set 'insight and thought' off against 'feeling' here. For years, this had been his position and he always associated feeling with subjectivism both in philosophy (e.g. with Fries) and in religion (with Schleiermacher).

7 The state in question, obviously, is Prussia. The reference to its 'spiritual supremacy' acknowledges Prussia's commitment to the expansion of higher education throughout its university system. The next sentence indicates that Prussia's creation of the University of Berlin in 1809 is clearly in Hegel's mind. Altenstein was involved in that effort, and it had all along been his plan to put Hegel in the vanguard of a movement to cultivate 'the sciences' at the new university. This agenda suited the King of Prussia because, as early as 1807, just after Napoleon's defeat of Prussia at Jena in 1806, he realised that Prussia had to 'establish through spiritual power [*geistige Krafte*] what it . . . lost in physical power' (see *GW*, vol. XVIII, p. 411).

8 In designating the soul (*Gemüt*) as the ground of philosophy, Hegel makes the formation of 'spiritual culture' (*Geistesbildung*) the goal of his philosophy as a means of *Bildung*. In turn, the point of spiritual culture is to translate *Geist* into *Sittlichkeit* (or social *Geist*). The references in the remainder of the paragraph to the need for people to strive for 'substantial content' is Hegel's way of saying that only *Sittlichkeit* can meet the standard of political rationality set by the spirit of the age.

9 The second half of the paragraph identifies 'necessity' and 'the vanity of opinions' as obstacles to spirit's realisation of its proper (i.e. historically appropriate) form. In both instances, the obstacles arise because of 'spirit's immersion' in self-regarding subjectivity. Large parts of *PR* describe how self-regarding subjectivism manifests itself institutionally in the form of civil society.

10 Like Plato and Cicero before him, Hegel plays with the idea of 'need' here. The deepest needs are spiritual and communal, not

biological and personal. For that reason, Hegel sets philosophy the task of directing thinking towards the satisfaction of spiritual needs. But those needs cannot be met through either feeling or enjoyment, the two most prevalent forms of subjectivity in the modern world. Again, the outline of Hegel's theory of civil society is visible here.

11 Hegel is alluding here to the cultural mission of philosophy in Germany. In the 1790s, that mission had expressed itself in cosmopolitan terms among a variety of German thinkers (see Meinecke 1970: pp. 42–7 and 55–6). As we saw earlier, Hegel had already shown little patience with cosmopolitan thinking in *GC*. But in his writings after 1813, there is evidence that he thought circumstances in Europe after Napoleon's fall had become propitious for what the Germans had long awaited: a *translatio*, a shift of leadership within Europe towards Germany and, in this case, away from France (see Voegelin 1971; Butler in Hegel 1984b: pp. 122, 300–2, 317, and 324). In *HIA*, Hegel had alluded to a series of *translationes* by which the 'sacred fire' of religious insight had passed from one religious people to another. He mentions the Jewish contribution in particular here (perhaps as a rebuff to the rabid anti-semitism of Fries and his followers in the *Burschenschaften*). But he is also interested in using the idea of *translatio* to explain the shift of the 'world spirit' from Catholic France to Protestant Germany. From this time on, Prussia and Protestantism are intimately connected in his thinking by way of the *translatio* of the 'world spirit' from France to Germany.

12 Hegel is drawing attention to the subjectivist tendency in critical philosophy, especially as developed by the self-declared Kantian, Fries. As early as *FK* (1802), Hegel had denounced critical philosophy for its subjectivism.

13 This long sentence might have provoked the anger of Schleiermacher and/or Savigny, the two champions of historical thinking at Berlin. There is evidence that Altenstein planned to use Hegel to contest the hold which these two thinkers had on the university (see, for example, Toews 1980: p. 60).

14 Throughout the 1820s, Hegel discussed the difference between feeling and cognition. With Fries's subjectivist philosophy in mind, he here suggests that Fries collapses cognition into feeling. Hegel wishes to separate the two without making his own conception of cognition excessively rational.

15 The last three sentences measure the evolution of human consciousness in terms of reason's movement from necessity to

freedom. As consciousness evolves, it shifts its focus towards spiritual (i.e. ethical and divine) ends. While in Berlin, Hegel devoted much lecture time to fleshing out what such a progression entails.

16 Earlier in the address, Hegel had referred to 'the ethical power of the spirit' (*die sittliche Macht des Geistes*). Here and elsewhere in the address he simply alludes to the 'power of the spirit'. Throughout the Berlin years, the aim of his philosophy is to ground spirit in ethical life (*Sittlichkeit*). This demands an ethical turn outwards after spirit has 'collected itself' inwardly.

Address on the Tercentenary of the Submission of the Augsburg Confession

1 Hegel had been elected Rector of the University of Berlin in October 1829. He also held the position of 'State Plenipotentiary for the Control of the University'. This combination of official posts has prompted comments from scholars about how Hegel 'personified a veritable synthesis' of culture and politics in Prussian-German history (Safranski 1990: pp. 297–8). As Rector, he was invited by Altenstein to speak on the occasion of the tercentenary of the Augsburg Confession. On this august occasion, the oration was delivered in Latin. Although a German translation of Hegel's Latin has been available for some time, the address has never until now been translated into English.

2 Hegel always opposed 'lay' communities to communities controlled by 'priests'. As already noted in our comments on *BIA*, he associated the former with Protestant openness (i.e. publicity) and the latter with Catholic closedness (i.e. secrecy). In some of his letters of the 1810s, he indicates that his philosophy is meant for the 'laity' rather than for the 'monks' (Hegel 1984b: pp. 326–9). His understanding of the laity is important because, throughout this address, it has a bearing not only on the secular implications of Reformation theology but also on the evolution of religious consciousness among Protestants. His conception of modern freedom is organised around this interplay.

3 The use of the term *evangelicam* here, and later in the address, is interesting for two reasons. First, it was a term used by Lutherans to describe themselves before, but not after, 1580. And, as it turned out, the Augsburg Confession later proved decisive in dividing Protestantism into Lutheran and Calvinist branches. Second, in Hegel's day, the term was associated with the King of Prussia's (often heavy-handed) attempts to create a unified Prot-

estant (i.e. *evangelica*) Church in Prussia. That effort was central to the project of the 'Restoration' in Prussia.

4 In many interpretations of German history, the taking up of the religious 'cause' by secular authorities marks the point at which Lutheranism and Calvinism go their separate ways as political ideologies. The latter develops 'against' the state; the former develops 'through' the state.

5 Largely because of his Swabian accent, Hegel had a reputation as a poor public speaker.

6 As is evident in our extract from *PH* (see pp. 197–224), Hegel believed that modern freedom began with the religious sanction which Luther won for subjectivity (i.e. the rights of private conscience) in the course of the Reformation. But speaking three hundred years later, he also believed that Luther's subjective freedom had to be extended from matters of religious 'doctrine' (*Lehre*) to all areas of 'life' (*Leben*) – to all of 'lay' culture, as it were. For further comments on the distinction between doctrine and life see the introduction (p. xxv above) and note 16 below.

7 Later in the address, Hegel links the idea of God's presence 'within the human mind' to the collateral idea that 'man is made in the image of God'. In the history of Christian thinking, the latter reference is generally to Genesis 1.26. This passage, in turn, provides biblical support for a doctrine of Christian perfectibility (i.e. the doctrine of *homoiosis*) that humanists and reformers periodically invoked to make Christianity a socially more responsible religion in an ethical sense. In this context, it is important to remember that Hegel had been talking in this way about religion since the 1790s, and that in doing so on this public occasion, he was committing himself to religious views which were not popular either in the Prussian court or in orthodox Lutheran and neo-Pietist religious circles.

8 Hegel's reference to God's relationship to nature is consistent with the negative views he held on pantheism throughout the 1820s.

9 Catholicism, in other words, put 'obstacles' in the way of religious perfectibility (i.e. *homoiosis*) and hence in the way of further development of human freedom, especially among the laity.

10 Hegel surely has Luther's objections to the Catholic policy of indulgences in mind here. He is explicit on this point later in the address.

11 The reference to 'masters and slaves' echoes the famous section on that subject in the *Phenomenology*. In this context, however, the Catholic-versus-Protestant dimension of the relationship becomes fully evident.

12 In abolishing the status of priests, Christianity becomes for Hegel a lay religion.

13 Luther, of course, is the 'trumpet'.

14 The distinction between *liberi* and *liberti* is all-important. In note 4 above, we noted how freedom was realised through the state. Hegel here addresses that point more fully and from a more critical political perspective. He is arguing that an alliance between throne and altar had formed in Germany in the sixteenth century. Although essential to the survival of Protestantism, the alliance proved to be detrimental in the long run to the development of human freedom among Protestants. As J. Ritter (1982: p. 185) has observed, the Reformation in Hegel's thinking is a 'moment' in the evolution of human freedom. What Ritter does not stress – although W. Jaeschke does (1983: pp. 37–8) – is that, for Hegel, Luther's is the first of two Reformations, the second of which Hegel was calling for in his own day. On these grounds, the term *liberi* stands to the first Reformation as *liberti* stands to the second. For Hegel's views on the need for a second Reformation, see the extract from *PH* (pp. 197–224).

15 We have here an absolutely clear statement of Hegel's commitment to social religiosity, to making religion more worldly.

16 Hegel means that the 'power and authority' of religion should extend from 'doctrine' (*Lehre*) to 'life' (*Leben*). This was a move which he had called for as early as 1793 (Hegel 1984a: p. 55). Even before that time, the terms 'doctrine' and 'life' had long been associated with Protestant calls for a second Reformation: see the discussions of this topic especially by P. Munsch and W. Neuser, in H. Schilling (1986), and Martin Schmidt (1965: pp. 1898–1906).

17 Hegel's apology here for Lutheranism as a political ideology is carefully constructed, for it is limited to the events surrounding the first Reformation. He signals this by contesting the claim that Luther's enterprise initially involved more than 'doctrine'. Hegel's strategy, however, had the consequence of de-politicising the first Reformation, making it only a Reformation of doctrine, of abstract or theoretical freedom. Accordingly, it remained for a second Reformation to translate doctrine into life, into the actual practice of piety in the world. From this paragraph, it is difficult to tell just whom Hegel means to confront with the argument that Lutheranism was not a doctrine of political sedition.

18 The reference is to Cicero, *De Officiis*, 1. 148.

19 In the 1790s, Hegel had implied that, with the emergence of Protestant orthodoxy in the sixteenth century, Protestants had

exchanged Catholic fetters for ones of their own making. The reference to 'dissenting' suggests that he has Dissenters in mind. But the opening sentence of the paragraph indicates that these are 'the same people' whom he had been talking about in the previous paragraph. Can this be squared with the argument about 'obedience' in that paragraph?

20 As the rest of the paragraph shows, the 'tireless endeavour' refers to developments in the realms of learning and culture. At the same time, Hegel relates these developments to the secular 'potential' inherent in Protestantism's willingness to allow for free inquiry by individuals into the truths of the Christian religion. By proceeding in this way, Hegel becomes part of an old tradition of Protestant thinking which sees the Reformation as much as an event in the history of knowledge as in the history of religion. The tradition begins in the seventeenth century with Thomas Sprat's *History of the Royal Society* (1958: Part III, esp. p. 372), and then runs through English Latitudinarianism (e.g. Edmund Law 1745: pp. 49–199), to Charles Villers' famous book of 1804 on how Luther's liberation of private judgement in religion eventually carried over into critical thinking in science and the arts throughout Europe (Villers 1807: esp. pp. 229–35). Hegel draws upon that argument here and, in so doing, also expands its scope to include advances in key institutions of civil society. Throughout the Berlin period, he tries to explain how the need for the development of *Sittlichkeit* in civil society entails fulfilling the 'doctrine' of the Reformation in actual 'life' (i.e. in the social and political institutions of the world).

21 When Hegel says that 'the commonwealth, by divine authority, should be internally one', he is referring back to the 'potential' Protestantism has for social religiosity. That is what is being sanctioned here, not the authority of the state itself. To underscore the point, he makes it clear that this argument is not meant to sanction the exercise of 'unjust authority'.

22 The 'older Church' is the Catholic Church. The charges Hegel levels against it in this paragraph allow us to see quite clearly the connection that existed in his mind between, on the one hand, the argument he had developed in *PR* about family, civil society, and the state, and, on the other hand, the Protestant principles for political life that he develops here. (The connection is most clearly developed in changes he made in the 1827 and 1830 editions of the *Encyclopedia*: see, for example, Hegel (1971: no. 552, pp. 282ff).) Whereas Catholicism separates God from civil institutions – from

what Hegel calls *Sittlichkeit* in *PR* – he wants Protestantism, in the re-figured form he was now giving it, to embrace *Sittlichkeit*, because the perfection of those institutions is consistent with his understanding of God's plan for the redemption of human beings in history. In this respect, the pursuit of *Sittlichkeit* and the practice of 'Christian piety' are for him one and the same thing.

23 In this paragraph, Hegel begins to historicise the institutional themes he associates with *Sittlichkeit*. He starts by setting Catholicism and Protestantism off against each other. In subsequent paragraphs, he contrasts celibacy and the family, idleness and industriousness (i.e. he picks up the theme of civil society here), and political slavery with the liberty of 'the commonwealth'.

24 Given the context, the reconciliation of 'God with the state' reaches well beyond simply giving the state a religious sanction.

25 The mistake, of course, is not to realise that the 'true wisdom' of Christian piety leads to *Sittlichkeit*.

26 In this sentence, we learn much about Hegel's view of the French Revolution. He is arguing, as he does elsewhere (see the excerpt from *PH*, pp. 197–224 below), that the French Revolution went off course because of a mind-set peculiar to the religious circumstances in Catholic France. Throughout the 1820s, he increasingly discusses politics in terms of a Catholic-versus-Protestant opposition (see Jaeschke 1983: p. 38).

27 What the state regards as just is not, however, a decision left to the state alone. It is a decision that follows from the initiative of 'divine providence' on the one hand, and from that of a Protestant people in their capacity as free human beings on the other. This is consistent with Hegel's view of God's covenant with Protestant peoples, for the covenant runs from God, through them, to their rulers, and not – as in the doctrine of the divine right of kings – the other way round.

28 Since Hegel's address was delivered before the outbreak of revolution in France in 1830, he is referring here to the events leading up to 1789, not to 1830.

29 The King's birthday would be celebrated a few weeks later. Toews (1980: p. 217) describes the political tone of the celebration as it was shaped by German perceptions of the revolution that had occurred in July in France.

30 The King, Frederick William III, was by most accounts a pious prince. His piety, however, was governed by considerations very different from those that informed Hegel's thinking. Thus, two sentences later, when Hegel reminds the King of the Protestant

'cause', he is asking the King to live up to his (i.e. Hegel's) standard of Christian piety – not to the orthodox one championed
by leaders of the Restoration in Prussia. There are, in short, two
Protestant agendas here, not one. Jaeschke (1983) has appreciated
this well.

Lectures on the Philosophy of History

1 We still await a critical edition of the lectures on the philosophy
of history that will allow us to see how Hegel's thinking developed
as he delivered them, with respect to revisions, in Berlin in 1822–
3, 1824–5, 1826–7, 1828–9, and 1830–1. Such an edition now
exists for his lectures on the philosophy of religion, and a similar
edition of the lectures on the history of philosophy is in the process
of being published. A glimpse of what a critical edition of the
philosophy of history might look like can be found in the Nisbet–
Forbes (Hegel 1975) edition of the Introduction to his lectures on
that topic. For the history of the various versions of the lectures
on the philosophy of history, see the statements by J. Hoffmeister
and G. Lasson in Nisbet–Forbes (Hegel 1975: pp. 5–9 and 221–
6). The selection from the lectures that is translated here follows
the text in vol. XII of *Werke*. That edition is itself based largely on
the edition published by Karl Hegel in 1840.

2 Sibree's unfortunate translation (Hegel 1956) of *germanische* as
'German' rather than 'Germanic' helped to create the impression
that Hegel approached European history from the narrow vantage
point of German nationalism. It is clear from his argument here,
as well as in *GC*, that this is by no means the case. Indeed, the
term 'Germanic' in Hegel's usage encompasses many of the
nations of western Europe.

3 As the end of Part IV, Section 2, makes clear, 'the dawn at the
end of the Middle Ages' refers to the Renaissance.

4 As becomes clear at the end of this section, Hegel includes the
French Revolution of 1830 in his time-frame.

5 Hegel provides a more detailed account of Catholic corruption in
Part IV, Section 2.

6 As pointed out on various previous occasions, the two aspects of
subjectivity are crucial to Hegel's political thinking during his
Berlin years.

7 The escape into monasticism is what Hegel has in mind. *Sittlichkeit* is the Protestant corrective to that flight from the world.

8 In this and the next sentence, Catholicism stands to Protestantism

as external stands to internal. Later, however, Hegel's conception of *Sittlichkeit* will stand to orthodox Protestantism as external stands to internal.

9 Although Hegel praises Luther's 'doctrine' (*Lehre*) here, he will begin to criticise that doctrine later in the lectures for its excessively inward and abstract rendering of subjective freedom.

10 The 'elimination of externality' is historically necessary but, Hegel proceeds to argue, the development of spirit will soon require Protestantism itself to embrace externality in the form of *Sittlichkeit*.

11 Among German Protestants in the late nineteenth century, there was a dispute (e.g. between A. Ritschl and E. Troeltsch) over whether Luther's position on 'works' made him a 'modern' or 'anti-modern' figure in religious history. Ritschl argued that Luther supported works; Troeltsch denied this claim. Hegel seems to anticipate Troeltsch's view.

12 Throughout the eighteenth century, Protestants in Germany (e.g. H. S. Reimarus) and England (e.g. C. Middleton) tried to demystify Christianity. Liberal Protestants did this in order to accommodate Christianity to the modern world (e.g. to advances in scientific knowledge). Others did so as part of a Socinian effort to present Jesus as merely human. The last sentence of this paragraph places Hegel among the former.

13 Hegel's aim here is to link 'spiritual' subjectivity with man's 'essential being' and then to derive *Sittlichkeit* from that being. In *NL* (pp. 102–80 above), he explains how spiritual subjectivity differs from empirical subjectivity.

14 In his early theological writings, Hegel (1948: pp. 244–81) depicts Jesus as the constitutive agent of subjectivity in religious thinking.

15 In the last two sentences, Hegel democratises spirit as part of his effort to erase the distinction between 'priests and laymen'. But he will quickly distance himself from the doctrine that measures spirit in terms of 'feeling'. (He had indeed already declared in the Introduction to these lectures that he would do so (Hegel 1956: pp. 15–40).)

16 In the remainder of the paragraph, Hegel refers again to the two subjectivities (cf. note 6 above), but in this instance, the negation of the 'particular' entails negation of 'feeling', of the 'natural' rather than the spiritual will. In this respect, Hegel moves beyond 'the feeling spirituality' of Lutheranism and toward a view of spirituality in which the substance of *Sittlichkeit* figures prominently.

17 It is easy to misunderstand this paragraph. Hegel is no longer

thinking here about Lutheran inwardness or subjective feeling. He is discussing thinking spirit that has worked, and is still working, to ground religion in right, property, ethical life, government, the constitution, and the state. All this follows, in his view, when subjective will directs itself outwards – in the direction of the universal principles he associates with *Sittlichkeit*.

18 It is interesting and ironic that, while turning Hegel on his head, Arnold Ruge (1983: p. 233) will use an almost identical sentence to criticise Hegel for the supposedly apolitical character of his Protestant inwardness.

19 This is a tricky sentence. In the Introduction to these lectures (Hegel 1956: p. 40), Hegel had indicated that, while the ideal of freedom is 'original and natural' to man, freedom does not exist 'as original and natural' in man's mode of everyday existence. The ideal, he says, must be 'sought out and won'. His philosophy aims at reminding people what they are destined to be 'by nature', and what they should accordingly seek to be in actuality.

20 The five pages of *Werke* that have been omitted here discuss particular aspects of Luther's criticism of Catholicism. Hegel also explains how Luther's translation of the Bible made it a 'People's Book', accessible to all. He then contrasts Protestant openness to the Bible with the closed nature of Catholicism. On the basis of this contrast, he draws a distinction between the character and values of Romance and Germanic nations in order to demonstrate (1) that 'disharmony' (*Entzweiung*) pervades the 'spiritual consciousness' of Catholic nations; and (2) that disharmony explains why the French Revolution proceeded in the unseemly way that it did.

21 As will soon become evident – and as others of Hegel's political writings show – the objective process to which he is here alluding encompasses the three essential moments of *Sittlichkeit*.

22 Though the sense of this sentence is clear, its meaning is not, for what trade and industry bring into existence is a civil society which is 'ethical' in the limited sense of *Moralität*. As such, it does not meet Hegel's standard of *Sittlichkeit*, of what is truly ethical. Or to put it another way, the former is the ethic of an aggregation, not an association (cf. his fuller explanation in the *Encyclopedia* (Hegel 1971: no. 544, p. 272), distinguishing between *vulgus* and *populus*).

23 Few Hegel scholars have appreciated what is implied by this paragraph. What Hegel is doing is establishing a framework for explaining the 'laws of freedom' in terms of a movement from

Lehre to *Leben* – that is, from the 'first' Reformation to the 'second' (see the introduction, pp. xxv, xxvii f. above, for discussion of this theme). That same movement not only underlies much of his political thinking (especially with regard to *Sittlichkeit*), but has roots deep in Protestant traditions that date from at least the late sixteenth century. His contention that spirit achieves its 'complete state' in *Sittlichkeit* simply underscores the deeply Protestant character of his thinking on civil society and the state.

24 Up to this point in the paragraph, Hegel has expanded upon the theme discussed in note 19 above. In declaring that human beings 'are by nature not what they ought to be', he postulates a conflict between sin and perfectionism in Protestantism. In his opinion, orthodox Lutheranism becomes preoccupied with the former and, for that very reason, is incapable of moving Protestantism forward to a more mature (i.e. perfect) form of religious thinking and acting. His own version of how subjectivism operates requires a shift away from the 'wretchedness' of sin. As already demonstrated, the motive for the shift lies for him in the notion that God created human beings in his own image and likeness.

25 Hegel is referring here to the conversion of some prominent figures among the German Romantics (e.g. F. Schlegel).

26 Pascal became famous in the seventeenth century for indicting the Jesuits for their casuistry.

27 It is significant that orthodox Protestants and Catholics are now grouped together. Hegel's doctrine of *Sittlichkeit* is offered as a corrective to the religious views of both.

28 With this sentence, Hegel tars Jacobinism with the same brush he had used to condemn the religious views of Catholics and orthodox Lutherans. Blurring the lines between religious and political modes of discourse had been a typical strategy of de-legitimisation among opponents of the French Revolution (e.g. Burke, the theocrats, and Novalis). But whereas the counter-revolutionaries used this language to bring out the Protestant character of the Revolution, Hegel uses it to draw attention to the Revolution's Catholic character.

29 Friedrich Spee von Langenfeld (1591–1675), in his *Cautia criminalis* (1631).

30 Christian Thomasius (1655–1728), rationalist philosopher and progenitor of the German Enlightenment.

31 The 'second and essential moment' that Hegel says leads towards the state is that of *Sittlichkeit*.

32 Chapter 2, Section 3 of Part IV, which is not translated here, is

around twelve pages long. It is entitled 'Influence of the Reformation on the Formation of the State'. Much of the chapter rehearses arguments Hegel had already advanced in *GC* about the evolution of feudalism among the Germanic nations. At the same time, he elaborates on the 'secular complications' (*weltliche Verwicklungen*) that followed from the alliance of throne and altar that characterised the Protestant states in Germany in the sixteenth and seventeenth centuries. Like Edmund Burke, he traces several of the major political upheavals of the early modern period to 'enthusiasts' (*Fanatiker*) among various Protestant sects. He carefully separates this group of political Protestants from the politically more moderate ones who emerged in England in 1660 and 1689. Most revealing of all, however, is the effort he makes at the end of Chapter 2 to designate Prussia and its famous eighteenth-century leader, Frederick the Great, as agents of the Protestant principle in modern history. This appreciation of Frederick stands in marked contrast to the view which he had articulated in *GC*. In the late 1830s, several years after Hegel's death, liberal Protestants still appealed to Frederick's legacy while criticising the reactionary political and religious policies of the current regime in Prussia.

33 The point, again, is to move from feeling to thinking by identifying universality as the proper object of subjectivity.

34 With this statement, we arrive at a turning point in Hegel's thinking. In the closing sentence of Part IV, Section 2, he had noted how, towards the end of the Middle Ages, science (*Wissenschaft*) had helped orient thought towards universality. He reiterates that point here, alluding later in the paragraph to developments in the physical sciences (e.g. the theory of gravity). But he also includes 'spiritual matters' in what he calls 'the science of the world'. This allows him to shift the focus from how attraction works in nature to how it works where matters of spirit are concerned – for example, in the study of human relations in society and the state. *Sittlichkeit* is the term he uses to explain attraction in the two spheres. Social Newtonians in eighteenth-century Britain (e.g. George Turnbull and Thomas Pownall) had pursued a similar line of argument with respect to the physical and spiritual aspects of attraction.

35 René Descartes (1596–1650), French rationalist philosopher. The reference is to his *Discourse on Method* (1637), which contains the outlines of his system.

36 Hegel alludes to a section of *PH* which is not translated here. For the content of the missing section, see note 20 above.

37 Hugo Grotius (1583–1645), Dutch publicist and statesman. The reference is to his main work, the *De iure belli et pacis* (1625).

38 Marcus Tullius Cicero (106–43 BC), Roman orator and politician. The reference is to his political treatises *De republica* and *De legibus*.

39 See note 32 above on how Hegel prepared the way for this celebration of Frederick's achievement.

40 Hegel is one of the first to apply this term (German *Aufklärung*) to the entire phase of European thought and culture which now goes by that name.

41 The last two sentences suggest a connection between the Reformation and the Enlightenment: to wit, the spiritual form of the former finds philosophical expression in the latter's theorising as to what the content of spirit should consist in. But as the next paragraph makes clear, Hegel does not assign positive roles to the Reformation and the Enlightenment in the development of spirit, for in his view, both represent spirit in terms of abstract subjectivity rather than as something that must realise itself concretely and collectively. In this respect, both have contributed to that process of atomisation that Hegel talks so much about during his Berlin period.

42 The notion that, when the will wills itself, it wills something universal rather than particular is Hegel's means of deriving *Sittlichkeit* from subjectivity.

43 In the remainder of the paragraph, Hegel explains how the Kantian doctrine of *Moralität* results from the will willing 'particular things'. Since the early 1800s, he had aligned his criticism of Kant with a criticism of civil society as the sphere of *Moralität* and particularity.

44 After 1831, alleged parallels – inverted political ones – between developments in German philosophy and French politics became an important theme in critiques of Hegelianism in the 1830s – e.g. in 1831 in the work of Heinrich Heine (Heine 1985: pp. 245–57).

45 The connection Hegel draws between understanding (*Verstand*) and pure reason continues his critique of Kantianism.

46 The fact that Luther, the Enlightenment, and Kantianism each failed to 'develop anything further out of itself' means that their doctrines did not evolve in a worldly direction.

47 As the next paragraph shows, the deeper reason for French revolutionary activism in 1789 lies, according to Hegel, in a dialectic of power that is unique to Catholic France.

48 The disposition (*Gesinnung*) is 'at one with religion' because both are oriented towards *Sittlichkeit*.

49 The problem here is obvious, for Hegel has already argued that improving 'secular life' was the religious challenge facing Protestantism in modern times. In his view, the challenge had persisted down to his own day because Protestant progress towards worldly engagement had stalled under the leadership of orthodox Lutheranism. This was a common view among liberal Protestants.

50 In fact, however, Hegel's life-long struggle against Protestantism in its mode of self-regarding subjectivity meant that Protestantism did permit 'two kinds of conscience'. One remains for ever inward; the other – the other-regarding form of subjectivism that Hegel promoted – eventually turns outwards.

51 Although Hegel directs his criticism of atomism at Catholicism here, his earlier criticism in *FK* of Protestantism as atomistic is relevant here too.

52 Hegel is relating the Enlightenment to the French Revolution here. As friends and foes of the French Revolution had observed in the 1790s, 1789 translated the philosophical principles of the Enlightenment into political action. Hegel's view of this development, however, is quite negative. In this respect, his view is similar to that of Burke.

53 Hegel's conception of the power struggle in France between two forms of absolutist political thinking is illuminated by his discussion in the early theological writings of Jesus' relationship to Judaism (Hegel 1948: pp. 284–8). In both instances, what is at issue is the absence of what he calls a 'middle course'.

54 If there is any truth to the student report (of 1826) that Hegel commemorated the French Revolution each year by raising a toast to it, it is surely this aspect of the Revolution that he toasted.

55 Greek *nous* = mind or sense.

56 As will become evident in what follows, the course of the French Revolution did not, in Hegel's opinion, reconcile 'the divine with the world'. That is, it did not permit 'thought' to 'govern spiritual reality'. For that to have happened, he argues here, French thought would have had to abandon atomism for *Sittlichkeit*.

57 In 1830, after the revolution in France, Hegel extensively re-wrote sections of these lectures. He indicates here his intention of further co-ordinating the substance of these lectures with those on the philosophy of right which he began to deliver again in 1831 after a hiatus of a few years. See Nisbet–Forbes (Hegel 1975) for information on the extent of the revision.

58 The connection between 'administration' and 'welfare' fulfils what Hegel calls the 'police' function of government. Throughout the

1820s, he recognised that inequalities of wealth and opportunity in civil society had to be addressed through the 'police' function of government. In his view, however, this function of government was relatively narrow compared to the government's responsibility for preparing citizens for participation in the political life of the nation. It is crucial, therefore, to keep the two functions separate when discussing his theory of the modern state. This distinction, moreover, lies at the centre of his critique of the English government in *ERB*.

59 As was the case above (note 48), the disposition referred to here is one that has become oriented towards *Sittlichkeit*. In Hegel's mind, this orientation is new – it is not just what Germans have traditionally accepted as part of their duty to the state. As he proceeds to explain, the state derives its legitimacy and its sanction from religion. But the state that he is talking about here is not yet in existence – and it is certainly not the Prussian state, whose religious orientation was anathema to him.

60 That is why Hegel tended to view the French Revolution more as a religious than as a political event. Beyond that, he could also claim, in opposition to Novalis (1996: p. 71), that the French Revolution was not a 'second Reformation'. Indeed, France had never had a first Reformation, still less a second one – an observation that had gained currency among Protestants in the 1790s (see Saine 1982: pp. 244–8 and 251–2; and E. D. Junkin 1974: p. 538). In this respect, Hegel could declare the second Reformation an alternative to 1789, as well as a fulfilment of the first Reformation.

61 A paragraph similar to this one can be found in *RRS* (see p. 232). What comes out more clearly here is the way in which Hegel proposes to use Plato's emphasis on education to shape the orientation of 'the individual will' so that it will have the 'right [i.e. other-regarding] disposition'. Without cultivation of such a disposition, modern society will remain atomised.

62 With the reference to 'virtue' (*Tugend*), Hegel begins to criticise the French Revolution for its anti-individual collectivism. In the 1810s, Benjamin Constant (1988: pp. 309ff) had made this point about the Revolution, arguing that the revolutionaries' embrace of virtue grounded their politics more in an ancient than a modern conception of liberty. Hegel agrees; but, in an astonishing twist, he derives the impulse towards collectivism from modern subjectivism rather than from a longing for ancient virtue.

63 There is a sense in which Hegel sees Napoleon as part of an ongoing process of atomisation. See his remark on Napoleon as a 'thinking' atom in Nisbet–Forbes (Hegel 1975: pp. 79 and 205).

64 Hegel is referring to the French Charter of 1814.

65 The tension Hegel sets up between the 'Catholic disposition' and 'conscience' illuminates his view of the larger issue raised by the 1830 revolution in France. As he explains, individuals *qua* subjective wills are now charged in France with governing the nation. The problem is that these wills operate in accordance with the 'atomistic principle'. As such, they can neither form themselves into a truly political association nor tolerate the organisation of freedom by anyone else. For this reason, Hegel argues, revolutions will continue to characterise French politics in the nineteenth century. In *ERB*, he fears that this manner of thinking will enter British politics.

66 Just as Hegel had earlier discussed Romance and Germanic nations in terms of the religious values of Catholicism and Protestantism respectively, so does he here discuss these nations in terms of the 'unfreedom' of 'liberalism' and the political freedom of Protestant peoples. In this sense, he is anti-liberal because of the social orientation of his religious thinking.

67 Hegel makes this point in several other contexts during his Berlin years.

68 Compare Hegel's view of England here with the more positive one he advanced in *GC*.

69 Hegel might have Burke in mind here.

70 The comparison of the French and English regimes allows Hegel to position himself, respectively, between the political extremes of too much centralisation and too much decentralisation of government. The following critique of England carries over into *ERB*.

71 These last two sentences hardly constitute a ringing endorsement either of absolutism or of the Restoration.

72 Greek *oi aristoi* = the best.

73 The 'contingent' will is at once formal, abstract, self-regarding in a subjective sense, merely natural, oriented towards the particular, and atomistic. Conversely, the 'essential' will is other-regarding in a subjective sense.

74 In the Introduction to these lectures (Hegel 1956: pp. 15 and 20), Hegel refers to the idea of theodicy. He traces the idea to Leibniz's efforts to develop a 'harmonising' metaphysic. But what allows for the development of that metaphysic, Hegel says, is the 'insight' (*Einsicht*) we possess (as a gift from God) into God's plan for human redemption in history. Hegel claims that his own philosophy simply puts that religious conviction into the form of rational thought. Critics of Hegel (e.g. E. Voegelin 1968: pp. 40–4) point

to this way of thinking as typical of those 'speculative gnostics' who defile science and philosophy by claiming to know the direction of history. Hegel, however, never claimed to have knowledge of the future, and for this he was severely criticised in the 1830s.

The Relationship of Religion to the State

1 During the last thirty years, our understanding of Hegel's philosophy of religion has benefited greatly from the collaborative work of American and German scholars associated with the Hegel Archive in Bochum, Germany. Together, they have given us English and German editions of the lectures on the philosophy of religion that Hegel delivered in Berlin between 1821 and 1831. By publishing the lectures of 1821, 1824, 1827, and 1831 as independent units, these editions allow us to see Hegel's thoughts on religion developing over time.

2 Spirit (*Geist*) realises itself in the state (*Staat*) through the agency of ethical will (*sittliche Wille*).

3 As *AC* stresses, Hegel wishes to allocate space in the Protestant religious outlook for the three key worldly institutions, each of which constitutes a moment of *Sittlichkeit*: the family, civil society, and the state.

4 The first two sentences of this paragraph discuss the relationship of religion to the state in terms of a dynamic (i.e. unity, disunity, unity) that also characterises Hegel's philosophy of history.

5 Jaeschke (1983) explains how the interplay between 'conviction' and 'constitution' works in Hegel's thinking during his last years in Berlin.

6 The reference to 'a bad concept of God' is aimed at Catholic France. In the last two paragraphs of this extract, Hegel raises questions about the revolution of 1830 in France which follow from views he had held on French politics before that event.

7 Hegel's strategy here is to use the philosophy of history to explain how Protestantism developed from an immature (i.e. wholly subjective) to a mature (i.e. substantive) religion.

8 It is important to realise that, in the last three sentences, Hegel is not providing the state – 'laws, government authority, and political constitution' – with a religious sanction derived directly from God. Rather, these state institutions develop from a concept of freedom derived from a covenant which, in Hegel's view, God made with the people rather than with the head of the state (on covenant theology, see note 12 below). That is why he devotes so much time

in his theory of *Sittlichkeit* to explaining how subjectivity becomes substantive (which would hardly be necessary were the state or its ruler to receive a religious sanction directly from God).

9 The formulation 'one obeys God by following the laws and governmental authority' suggests that Hegel might be 'idolising' the state here. But what he says in the next few sentences discounts that possibility. On the idolisation theme, see also note 24 below.

10 In Hegel's mind, orthodox Lutheranism often supported arbitrary government. Although throughout the 1820s he proclaimed himself a Lutheran, he criticises orthodox Lutheranism for not having moved Protestantism beyond the restrictive and repressive framework of the alliance of throne and altar.

11 The Stuart kings ruled England for most of the seventeenth century.

12 In the last few sentences, in which he discusses the religio-political situation in seventeenth-century England, Hegel shows that he has knowledge of the political implications of what scholars call 'covenant theology' – the theology, that is, that is often associated with Calvinist resistance theory in the sixteenth and seventeenth centuries. Clearly, Hegel wants the covenant to run from God through the laity to the King, and not through the King to the laity. The covenant theme also figures prominently in *AC*.

13 The tension between the laity's authorisation of its political actions through an appeal to 'revelation', and what happened to the King as a result of the laity's political action is palpable. As the next sentence shows, Hegel accepts the former but not the latter. This explains, in part, why he should not be considered a 'speculative gnostic'.

14 The phrase 'open to everyone' is meant to check the action of the 'sect' referred to in the previous sentence. This is underscored in what follows, when Hegel introduces 'what is rational' as a check on what some will surely perceive as having been 'willed by God' through 'revelation'.

15 The laws Hegel has in mind derive from the ethical will as it gradually attains actuality in the state. That will, in turn, is 'rational' for two reasons: (1) it knows that *Sittlichkeit* is the substance of the laws willed by God; and (2) it has been shaped by *Bildung* (i.e. educational and cultural values) to that end. In the *Encyclopedia* (Hegel 1971: no. 552, pp. 290–1), Hegel equates this maturation process with what he calls 'self-realising subjectivity'. He then explains how this process links religious values to the state. In the Foreword to the third edition of the *Encyclopedia* (1830), he also

shows how the laws which govern the ethical will unfold in terms of 'an order of salvation' (*Heilsordnung*) that is fulfilled in *Sittlichkeit* (Hegel 1991b: p. 20).

16 The opposition between 'sanctity' and 'ethical life' that Hegel examines in this paragraph addresses Protestant extremists as well as Catholics. Both exclude *Sittlichkeit* as the substantial reality of actuality from their religious ideal. In the following paragraphs, Hegel reiterates why the rationality of *Sittlichkeit* should become part of a mature Protestant outlook.

17 The remark on religion not recognising 'the principle of freedom' alludes to Catholicism and its sowing of the political seeds that provoked the French Revolution. The second part of the sentence criticises the political illiberalism of the French revolutionaries.

18 As Hegel says in *PH* (p. 213 above), atomism follows from abstract formalism. By contrast, *Sittlichkeit* gives rise to an 'organic constitution' that balances rights and duties. Hodgson (1984: vol. I, p. 475 n 4) reads this paragraph in the same way as we do.

19 As pointed out in the introduction to this volume, Hegel exploits the ambiguity inherent in the phrase 'by nature' to move freedom away from 'arbitrariness' and towards more organised forms of liberty.

20 Beginning with this sentence, Hegel posits a contradiction between 'secular freedom' and the 'Catholic religion' in France. He then uses that tension to frame his critique of political developments in France from the Enlightenment through 1789 to the 1830 revolution. The contradiction in question, Hegel suggests, is a legacy both of Catholicism and of the abstract political response which Catholicism provoked among the *philosophes*.

21 See note 5 above.

22 This passage is filled with important themes. But the distinction Hegel tries to draw between Greek and modern conceptions of constitutions is difficult to follow in the terms employed here. Scholars have long known that, while Hegel was attracted to the *political* character of Plato's thinking, he also criticised him for his inability to make room for subjectivity in his political philosophy (see, for example, Inwood 1984). Christianity as well as developments within its history (i.e. the emergence of Protestantism), Hegel contended, requires political as well as religious accommodation to the principle of subjective freedom. In this scheme, Plato is the one who has 'no regard for [individual] conviction'. Here, however, things seem to be turned around, for it is the 'modern system' that exhibits such intolerance. For clarification, Hodgson

(1984: vol. I, p. 459) has inserted 'of the people' after 'conviction', whereas we have inserted '[individual]' before it instead. This choice follows from our sense that Hegel's use of 'formal' in the sentence requires an insertion consistent with his understanding of modern freedom as being formal because it only pays lip service to individual conviction. If we are right about Hegel's meaning here, then it would appear that he is trying to Protestantise Plato by turning him into a philosopher of *Sittlichkeit* who uses *Bildung* to direct conviction towards communal ends.

23 The Greek word is *sophrosyne*, which means 'moderation', most often in the form of prudent self-control. For a discussion of the word's meaning among the Greeks, see Helen North (1966). Plato frequently uses the term in the context of how an individual or a city becomes master of itself. (*Sophrosyne* does not mean, as it did in the Spartan *polis*, unreflective adherence to customary law or *nomos*.)

24 This comment speaks powerfully to the point raised in the introduction to this volume as to whether Hegel's political philosophy idealises or idolises the state.

25 In the remainder of the paragraph, Hegel is discussing political developments in France in the late 1820s.

26 The thrust of the last three sentences can hardly be interpreted as hostile to the French Revolution of 1830 *per se*. Indeed, the position which Hegel takes on the revolution is consistent with views he had articulated in Berlin lectures well before 1830. In the next paragraph, the reference to 'indeterminate' conviction signals what he thought was wrong with the revolution: namely, that it pursued abstract and formal political freedom rather than a more organised form of liberty. In the early 1800s, he had said similar things about the formalism inherent in the French Revolution of 1789.

27 In other words, if the 'existing religion' privileges 'conviction' and 'inwardness' in a Protestant sense, then freedom in the modern world will become 'determinate' in the form of *Sittlichkeit*.

28 While discussing the chronic instability of French politics from 1789 through to the revolution of 1830, Hegel uses the phrase 'reasserts itself with contempt for all form' in a way that reminds us of his earlier argument about the political action of 'a Protestant sect' in seventeenth-century England. In both instances, the 'conviction' that leads to revolution is characterised as a 'safeguard' against a tyrannical and catholicising government which ignored the rights of individuals. But in France in 1830, Hegel argues, the safeguard exercised by the sect expressed itself only negatively.

For without respect for constitutional 'form', conviction remains hopelessly indeterminate and a constant source of further political instability.

On the English Reform Bill

1 *ERB* appeared in the *Allgemeine Preussische Staatszeitung* (Prussian State Journal) in April 1831. Already in the early 1840s, Arnold Ruge (1983: pp. 218–19) interpreted the text as anti-democratic. He was followed in this by Rudolf Haym (1857: pp. 456–9), who popularised the notion that the essay was consistent with Hegel's reactionary (i.e. pro-Prussian) political views. Recent scholarship, however, has convincingly shown that Hegel's views on the Reform Bill closely follow lines of argument derived from his reading of liberal English and Scottish newspapers and periodicals during the 1810s and 1820s: see, for example, Petry (1976) and N. Waszek (1985). The text published in 1831 was censored by Prussian authorities. See note 55 below for particulars of the censorship.

2 Although there was much public debate about reform in the 1820s, the Reform Bill did not come before Parliament until early 1831. It was introduced in the House of Commons on 1 March 1831. Two other versions of the Reform Bill were introduced later that year.

3 Throughout *ERB*, Hegel develops the idea of 'class' interest, using it to explain the positions taken by socio-economic groups on political issues connected with the Reform Bill.

4 Petry (1976: pp. 58–9) produces evidence that Hegel drew some of his ideas about the irregularities of English law from the *Morning Chronicle*, a liberal English newspaper. This evidence takes the form of excerpts which Hegel copied from the *Morning Chronicle* during the 1820s. The date of the issue in question is 8 February 1828. Waszek (1985) shows that Hegel followed the English debate on constitutional reform through his reading of the *Edinburgh Review* in 1817 and 1818.

5 Hegel is referring to the revolution of 1830 in France.

6 Petry (1976) argues that James Mill and James Mackintosh are two of the reformers whose views are parallel to those of Hegel.

7 This observation is consistent with Hegel's overall view of the instability of French politics since 1789. See, for example, his comments in *AC* and *RRS* (pp. 194–5 and 231–3 above, respectively).

8 The phrase 'a priori views' refers, pejoratively, to the abstract

approach of French thinkers to the role of will in modern politics. See also note 44 below.

9 Robert Peel (1788–1850): Prime Minister of England in the 1840s. Appointed Home Secretary in Liverpool's 'liberal' government in 1822, Peel occupied the same position in Wellington's government of 1828–30. In the late 1820s, he worked with Wellington to pass the Catholic Emancipation Bill, an Act that split the Tory party. An excerpt which Hegel made from the *Morning Chronicle* (4 March 1831) refers to Peel's attitude towards the irregularities of the English constitution. See Petry (1976: p. 67).

10 The reference is to *SL*: Part I, Book III. Hegel discusses Montesquieu's view on this issue more fully in *PR*, pp. 308–12.

11 Hegel develops the idea of 'pragmatic' history in *PR*, p. 29.

12 Here Hegel recalls arguments from the early theological writings and from *NL* about the loss of *Sittlichkeit* in the ancient world.

13 Later in the essay, Hegel suggests that this pride turns into obstinacy (see note 39 below). He had said the same of German pride in *GC*. In both instances, pride supports private interest.

14 The reference to Berne recalls both Hegel's experience of oligarchy in Switzerland in the mid-1790s and his translation of, and commentary on, Cart's *Confidential Letters*.

15 Hegel uses *moralische* here and in the sentence that follows. The context suggests that he is using the term to denote a privatised outlook which will impede efforts to organise individuals for political action.

16 Hegel's disdain for unreflective traditionalism is apparent here.

17 Perhaps Hegel is alluding to the anglophile argument in his own earlier *GC* here.

18 Hegel's praise of the continental states has been cited by Haym (note 1 above) as proof both of his disdain for democracy and of his commitment to rule by government bureaucracy.

19 Hegel begins here to advance the case for England's 'political backwardness' relative to the continental states.

20 Hegel may be interpreted as developing two different arguments here. On the one hand, he was proud of the reforms that had been initiated throughout Germany by various groups of bureaucrats after 1789. In this, he is an advocate of what students of German history have long called 'revolution from above'. (In Britain, J. R. McCulloch, the great populariser of Adam Smith's views on political economy, published in 1828 a review essay on Prussia in the *Edinburgh Review* in which he praises Prussian bureaucrats for their role in advancing 'liberal' reforms.) On the other hand, it is

hard to believe that he was unaware of the connection between the agrarian component of these reforms and the deteriorating condition of agricultural workers in Prussia, especially eastern Prussia. If he were so aware, then this argument about agricultural conditions in Britain could be viewed as an indirect criticism of the Prussian government as well. See Beck (1995: pp. 1–30) on the 'pauperisation' of agricultural workers in Prussia after 1815. (In Britain, William Spence drew attention to the 'universal poverty and misery' in England in the Preface to his *Tracts on Political Economy*, 1822.)

21 The regret which Hegel seems to express here about the weakness of the English monarchy has prompted scholars to believe he was a dogmatic monarchist, clinging tenaciously and unreflectively to a pre-industrial political order. In fact, the role Hegel assigns the monarch is quite circumscribed (see, for example, the concluding paragraph of *ERB*). Petry (1976) detects parallels between James Mill's and Hegel's views on the reforming role of the monarchy in modern political life.

22 All his life, Hegel insisted that the material circumstances of citizens had to be attended to before citizens could be expected to cast informed votes. Jaeschke (1983: p. 42) and Petry (1976: p. 13) draw the correct inferences from this.

23 In other words, members of Parliament were not properly 'political' in Hegel's sense of the term.

24 Joseph Hume (1777–1855): friend and associate of James Mill, and a leader among radical reformers in Parliament during the 1820s. Hume was known for his expertise on how to wring economies from government budgets.

25 William Huskisson (1770–1830) became President of the Board of Trade in Liverpool's 'liberal' government in 1823. He had long been a champion of liberal economic reform.

26 Hegel seems to connect economic growth with the liberation of industry from feudal shackles. This is a typical liberal view. But he also traces much of the social distress of propertyless agricultural workers to the legislation that accompanied the transition from feudalism to property. Among Germans, the latter view was popularised by two different groups: (1) by liberal-minded civil servants; and (2) by social conservatives. According to Beck (1995: pp. 10ff), much of the so-called *Pauperismusliteratur*, which appeared after 1815, was written by the former. Beck (p. 29) places Hegel in this group rather than among the social conservatives.

27 Although Hegel does not develop the point further in *ERB*, he

implicates the economic concerns of the English clergy in the decline of community in English life. As he suggests in the next paragraph, a socially more engaged clergy would help to assuage some of the hardships experienced by England's rural communities.

28 As several scholars have critically noted, Hegel seems, selectively, to generalise Irish conditions – religious and otherwise – to all of England. Either this is the case, or he has confused – as Knox suggests (Hegel 1948: p. 316 n 1) – the Irish Reform Bill with the Reform Bill itself.

29 Throughout the 1820s, a series of Catholic Emancipation Bills were proposed in the Commons. These initiatives culminated in a Bill that was finally carried in 1829 when Wellington and Peel threw their support behind it. The King signed it and made it law on 13 April 1829.

30 Read in the light of Prussian history, Hegel may be alluding to legal protections (*Bauernschutz*) which Frederick the Great had insisted on preserving in order to ensure a steady flow of able-bodied recruits for his army. In Prussia, the protections were removed by liberal bureaucratic reformers in 1807, with the result that a pauper class – propertyless agricultural workers – emerged as a socio-economic problem in Prussia. The literature which addressed this problem often referred to the *Entsittlichung* of rural communities in Germany. See Beck (1995: pp. 6, 13–15).

31 Beck (1995: p. 13) notes similar conditions in Prussia.

32 Hegel condemns the use of 'due legal form' to legitimise social injustice. His views reflect those expressed in an excerpt he made from the *Morning Chronicle* (17 November 1827); see Petry (1976: pp. 51–3).

33 The Act was passed in 1826. In 1831, attempts were made in the House of Lords to change aspects of the original Act.

34 Hegel means to suggest that human beings have material rights which may, under certain circumstances, override individual property rights. This was the sense of the excerpt referred to in note 32 above.

35 Hegel appears here to follow another of his excerpts from the *Morning Chronicle* (8 February 1828) that refers to Peel's role in legal reform. See Petry (1976: pp. 58–9).

36 Henry Brougham (1777–1868) was, among other things, a legal and educational reformer and something of an economist who had close ties with James Mill and Jeremy Bentham. He became Lord Chancellor in the government which Grey formed in 1830. Hegel's

information again seems to come from an except from the *Morning Chronicle* (8 February 1828). See Petry (1976: pp. 58–9).

37 Z. A. Pelczynski, *KP*, p. 103, is excellent on the deep roots of this argument in Hegel's earlier writings, esp. in *PWE*.

38 The Duke of Wellington (1769–1852), who was a living symbol of Toryism during these years, became Prime Minister in 1828. One of Hegel's excerpts from the *Morning Chronicle* (29 March 1831) contains information on the speech which the Duke had delivered the day before. See Petry (1976: pp. 69–70).

39 These remarks echo a comment of Hegel's on one of his excerpts from the *Morning Chronicle* (8 February 1828). See Petry (1976: pp. 58–9) and note 13 above.

40 That reason should recognise material rights is a consideration that Hegel uses to explain why rationality in government requires an ameliorative response to the social question.

41 In the next paragraph, Hegel notes converging and diverging tendencies in groups comprising England's propertied class.

42 Hegel excerpted a piece from the *Morning Chronicle* (4 February 1825) in which a reference to shopkeepers occurs. See Petry (1976: p. 30). Knox (Hegel 1964: p. 312 n 1) has traced Hegel's remarks about Wellington to a speech of the latter (28 March 1831) which includes another reference to shopkeepers; one of Hegel's excerpts from the *Morning Chronicle* (29 March 1831) includes an account of this speech: see Petry (1976: p. 69). (Among the English, a pejorative sense had been attached to the idea of 'shopkeepers' since at least the 1750s when remarks about the 'Shopkeeper's Age' implied a decline in learning, taste, and morality. Although Josiah Tucker had often written about England's shopkeeper mentality, the idea of Britain as a 'nation of shopkeepers' became famous through Adam Smith's use of the phrase in 1776 in *The Wealth of Nations*: see Smith (1976, vol. II, p. 613).)

43 Hegel draws his information on William Manning (1763–1835) from an excerpt he made from the *Morning Chronicle* (15 March 1826). Petry (1976: p. 43) provides more pertinent information on Manning and the matter of corrupt elections in England.

44 The reference to the 'abstract will' as 'modern' relates back to the comment on 'a priori' views discussed in note 8 above.

45 The notion of genuinely political ideas can also be found in *GC*.

46 This probably refers to the moment – in April 1805 – when Napoleon declared himself ruler of the newly created political entity which he called the Kingdom of Italy.

47 Hegel excerpted information on this speech from the *Morning Chronicle*: see Petry (1976: pp. 69–70).

48 The supporter, according to Knox, was Lord Lansdowne.

49 Knox (Hegel 1964: p. 315 n 1) notes Hegel's confusion of Grey with Brougham here.

50 Knox (Hegel 1964: p. 315 n 1) corrects Hegel here: 'The basis of borough franchise laid down in the Bill was occupation, whether as owner or tenant, of property of £10 annual value.'

51 Between the excessively narrow British and the excessively broad French political attitudes, the Germans were supposed to occupy the moderate middle position.

52 Hegel develops the idea of the 'rabble' and its relationship to poverty as early as 1817, in his Heidelberg lectures on the philosophy of right: see Hegel (1995: p. 211).

53 The date referred to is 24 June 1793.

54 Hegel refers to the rule of Charles X in France from 1824 to 1830.

55 The remainder of *ERB* was suppressed as politically controversial by the Prussian censor and did not appear in the *Allgemeine Preussische Staatszeitung* (cf. note 1 above).

56 Emanuel Joseph Count Siéyès (1748–1836) was instrumental in the French Revolution and in the rise of Napoleon to power in France. His manoeuvring went far to pave the way for the 18 Brumaire – the date on which Napoleon gained control of the French government.

57 This occurred on 9 November 1799 (18 Brumaire, by the French calendar).

58 Later in the paragraph, Hegel will use his discussion of Wellington to introduce a political distinction between statesmen and 'new men' in the English Parliament.

59 On Wellington, see note 38 above.

60 On the shopkeeper reference, see note 42 above.

61 As Hegel has already noted throughout *ERB*.

62 Henry (the Orator) Hunt (1773–1835) had long been a leading radical in the reform movement. In the late 1820s, he aggressively called for universal suffrage.

63 It is not obvious what the political content of these new ideas is before their assimilation to French and German circumstances.

64 It is tempting to connect Hegel's concern with poverty here with his long-standing awareness that the division of labour can lead to the brutalisation of workers in industrial society. But in *ERB*, he seems deliberately to avoid discussion of industrial work, suggesting that he intended to focus here on the plight of paupers rather than the proletariat. While this might make him seem less modern, it has the advantage of making his critique of propertyless

agricultural workers in Britain more relevant to pre-industrial conditions in Prussia. Beck (1995) is helpful on the emergence of the pauper/proletariat distinction in German thought during the Restoration.

65 In other words, political activism will begin to be marked by negativism, the kind of negativism that Hegel associated with French political instability.

66 Wellington's Ministry resigned on 15 November 1830.

67 The vote of 302 for, 301 against, occurred on 22 March 1831.

68 Earl Grey (1764–1845) formed a Whig government after Wellington's resignation.

69 Hegel applies lessons drawn from his observations of the political situation in France between 1789 and 1830 to England.

70 The reference to 'indefinite fears' alludes to the radical ideas of 1789.

71 Hegel's fear is that, before Parliament accepts responsibility for tending to the material needs of the poor, the a priori/abstract/formalist principles of 1789 will gain a hold on public opinion, further complicating the shift which he thinks England must make in order to achieve the level of civilisation – and the 'police' function of government (see note 58 to *PH* on pp. 313–14 above) – already achieved by the continental states.

72 This confirms the view of monarchy which we discussed in note 21 above.

Glossary

Most of the words listed below are ones which present problems for the translator, including those which are liable to be confused, in English translation, with one or more near-synonyms, those which have technical or specialised meanings, and those for which, as used by Hegel, conventional English renderings are not always adequate. An asterisk denotes those English terms which, for one of the above reasons, are normally followed in the text by the original German term in square brackets. (Where the English term in question occurs more than once in the same paragraph, the German original is normally supplied only on the first occurrence, unless confusion with related terms is likely or the interval between occurrences is so great as to justify its repetition.) The second main category of words listed is that of names of institutions, events, or practices associated with the Holy Roman Empire which call for some historical elucidation.

Ahnen, Ahnung	inkling; idea* [cf. *Gedanke, Idee, Vorstellung*]; intuition* [cf. *Anschauung*]
Anordnung	ordinance [cf. *Ordnung*]
anschauen	to look at; to contemplate; to intuit*
Anschauen	intuition
Anschauung	intuition; perception; view* [cf. *Vorstellung*]
an sich	in itself; implicitly*
Ansichsein	being-in-itself
Armee	army [cf. *Heer*]
Aufgehobensein	supersededness; supersession [cf. *Aufheben*]
aufheben	to supersede; to overcome; to cancel*; to annul*; to nullify* [cf. *vernichten*]; to suspend*; to abolish* [This is, notoriously,

	one of the most difficult of all Hegel's terms to translate. In the systematic works of his maturity, *aufheben* (in such cases normally translated as 'to supersede') encompasses the meanings 'to remove (or cancel)', 'to raise up', and 'to preserve'.]
Aufheben, Aufhebung	supersession [cf. *Aufgehobensein*]
Aufnahme	[literally, 'taking up'] elevation; incorporation*
aufnehmen	to take up; to elevate; to incorporate*
Autorität	authority [in the most general sense; cf. the more concrete and particular *Gewalt*, *Herrschaft*, and *Obrigkeit*; also *Berechtigung* in the sense of 'authorisation']
Bedürfnis	need [cf. *Forderung*]
Begriff	concept
bei sich	with itself
Berechtigung	justification; authority* [in the sense of 'legitimacy' or 'authorisation'; cf. *Autorität*]
beschließen	to resolve
Beschluß	resolution
Besitz	possession; property* [cf. *Eigentum*]; ownership* [cf. *Eigentum*]
besonder	particular; special
Besonderheit	particularity
bestanden	surviving
bestehen	to subsist; to endure; to (continue to) exist*
Bestehen	subsistence; [continued] existence* [cf. *Dasein, Existenz*]
bestimmen	to determine; to define
bestimmt	determinate; definite; specific
Bestimmtheit	[a term much used by Hegel in the essay on *Natural Law*, often in a sense close to that of *Bestimmung* (q.v.), which is commoner in his later works] determinacy; determinate character, element, or thing*
Bestimmung	determination; definition; role*; function*; provision*
Beziehung	reference; connection; association*; relation(ship)* [cf. *Verhältnis*]; context* [cf. *Zusammenhang*]; aspect*
bezwingen	[a term used by Hegel on various occasions

	in the essay on *Natural Law*, usually in contrast with *zwingen* ('to coerce'), in order to denote that kind of constraint (e.g. as employed by a legally constituted authority) which, unlike simple coercion or *Zwang*, is compatible with the free will of those to whom it is applied] to constrain*; to overcome*; to suppress*; to dominate*
Bezwingen	constraint
Bildung	education [in the widest sense, as the development and formation of the whole personality; cf. the narrower term *Erziehung*]; formation; development* [cf. *Entwicklung*]; culture* [as the end result of the educative or formative process; cf. *Kultur*]
Bürger	citizen
bürgerlich	civil; civic
bürgerliches Recht	civil right
Bürgerlichkeit	middle class* [cf. *Bürgerstand*]
Bürgerschaft	citizenry; citizens' assembly*
Bürgerstand	middle class* [cf. *Bürgerlichkeit*]
Burgflecken	borough
corpus evangelicorum	[literally 'the body of Protestants', i.e. the body representing the Protestant territories or 'estates' (*Stände*; q.v.) within the Holy Roman Empire; or the estates themselves as a collective unit. Its Catholic counterpart was the *corpus catholicorum*]
darstellen	to present; to represent [in the sense of 'depict' or 'portray'; cf. *vorstellen*]
Dasein	[a near-synonym of *Existenz*, rendered by some translators as 'determinate being'] existence* [cf. *Bestehen*]; being* [cf. *Sein*, *Wesen*]
different	different* [cf. *Differenz*]
Differenz	difference*; differentiation* [a technical term used by Hegel in the essay on *Natural Law* to denote a state of internal division or differentiation, in contrast to the unity and

identity of *Indifferenz*; cf. *Unterschied*, the
normal, non-technical word for 'difference'
or 'distinction' in German]

eigen [adjective] own; individual*; distinct(ive)*
[cf. *eigentümlich*]

eigentlich [adjective] actual [in the sense of 'proper';
cf. *wirklich*]; [adverb] actually; in fact

Eigentum property [cf. *Besitz*]; ownership

eigentümlich distinct(ive) [cf. *eigen*]; proper [as used
before noun in English]; peculiar

Einrichtung institution; arrangement

Einssein oneness; identity* [in the sense of
'oneness']

Einzelheit individuality; individual characteristic,
quality, or unit; detail [usually in plural];
singularity*

einzeln individual

Empfindsamkeit sensibility* [also the eighteenth-century
literary tendency of that name; cf.
Empfindung]

Empfindung sensation; sensibility* [cf. *Empfindsamkeit*];
feeling* [cf. *Gefühl*]

Entfaltung unfolding; development* [as a synonym of
Entwicklung]

entwickeln to develop

Entwicklung development [cf. *Entfaltung*]

erkennen to recognise; to know* [through an act
of cognition; cf. *kennen, wissen*]; to
discover*

Erkennen, Erkenntnis cognition; recognition; knowledge* [as an
act of cognition; cf. *Kenntnis, Wissen,
Wissenschaft*]

erscheinen to appear

Erscheinung appearance; phenomenon* [as a synonym of
Phänomen]; manifestation*

Erwerb earning; livelihood; acquisition; gainful
employment*

Erziehung education [in the sense of 'upbringing' and/
or 'training'; cf. the more comprehensive
term *Bildung*]

Ethik ethics [cf. *Sittlichkeit*]

Existenz existence [cf. *Bestehen, Dasein*]

Faustrecht	right of private warfare* [literally 'right of the fist', enshrined in the constitution of the Holy Roman Empire in medieval times; cf. *Landfrieden*]
Flecken	borough [cf. *Burgflecken*]; community
fordern	to demand; to require
Forderung	demand; requirement; need* [cf. *Bedürfnis*]
für sich	for itself; inherently*; independently*
Fürsichsein	being-for-itself
Fürst	prince; ruler
Fürstentum	principality
Gedanke	thought; idea* [cf. *Ahnung, Idee, Vorstellung*]
Gedankending	work [i.e. product] of thought*
Gedankenstaat	state in thought* [i.e. a state which exists only in theory]
gediegen	sterling; solid*; worthy*
Gediegenheit	solidity*
Gefühl	feeling [cf. *Empfindung*]
Gegensatz	opposite [noun]; antagonism; conflict
Gegenstand	object; objective
Gehalt	content [in the sense of essential or substantial content, unlike the more neutral *Inhalt*, which can often be translated as 'contents']
Geist	spirit; mind* [cf. *Gemüt*]
Gemüt	[a difficult term to translate, because its wide and variable meaning cannot be rendered by any single English word; it denotes in particular the emotional aspects of mind, in contrast to *Geist*, which is both more comprehensive and more rational] mind; state of mind; disposition* [cf. *Gesinnung*]; inclination*; soul* [cf. *Seele*]
gesetzmäßig	lawful; statutory
Gesinnung	disposition [cf. *Gemüt*]; conviction*
Gestalt	shape; form*
Gewalt	force; power; authority* [cf. *Autorität, Berechtigung, Herrschaft, Obrigkeit*]
Glückseligkeitslehre	theory of happiness; eudaemonism
Grund	ground; reason [in the sense of (rational) ground]; basis

Grundsatz	principle [cf. *Prinzip*]; precept; maxim*
Heer	army; regiment* [to distinguish it when used in conjunction with its virtual synonym *Armee*]
Herrschaft	rule; authority* [cf. *Autorität, Gewalt, Obrigkeit*]
Ich	(the) 'I'
Idee	Idea [in its technical sense within Hegel's system]; idea [cf. *Ahnung, Gedanke, Vorstellung*]
Inhalt	content(s) [cf. *Gehalt*]
inneres Staatsrecht	constitutional law* [cf. *Staatsrecht*]
itio in partes	[Latin] literally 'going to the parties' [in a dispute concerning religion]: i.e. the right of any party involved in a religious dispute within the Holy Roman Empire not to be bound by a majority vote, but to have the matter settled by negotiation
(das) Jenseits	realm beyond [in the sense of a transcendental world or afterlife]
Kammergericht	see *Reichskammergericht*
Kammersteuer	cameral tax(es) [i.e. taxes paid by the constituent states (or 'estates') of the Holy Roman Empire to support the *Kammergericht* and *Reichshofrat*]
Kammerzieler	see *Kammersteuer*
kennen	to be familiar with; to know* [through an act of cognition; cf. *erkennen, wissen*]
Kenntnis, Kenntnisse	knowledge* [cf. *Erkennen, Wissen, Wissenschaft*]
Klasse	[socio-economic] class* [this more modern term was in Hegel's day increasingly displacing the older *Stand* (q.v.), which denoted a state or condition within the social hierarchy determined primarily by non-economic factors]
Kultur	culture [cf. *Bildung*]; civilisation*; agriculture*

Landfrieden	prohibition on private warfare* [literally 'territorial peace'; the prohibition finally took effect in the sixteenth century (cf. *Faustrecht*)]
Landrecht	law of the land; Common Law
Landschaft	landscape; provincial assembly* [cf. *Landtag*]
Landstände	Provincial Diet* [i.e. an assembly of Estates or *Stände* in a particular territory within the Holy Roman Empire]
Landtag	Provincial Diet [cf. *Landstände* and *Reichstag*]
mannigfaltig	manifold
Mannigfaltigkeit	multiplicity [cf. *Vielheit*]
Meinen, Meinung	opinion; supposition*
(der) Mensch	human being(s); man(kind) [of the human species as a collective unit]
Menschenverstand	common sense
Ministerium	Ministry, ministers [of government]; administration* [in the sense of 'government currently in office'; cf. *Verwaltung*]
Mittel	means; instrument*
Moment	moment [in the sense of 'essential component']; element; aspect*
Moral, Moralität	morality [used by Hegel of moral philosophies (e.g. that of Kant) which are less comprehensive than his own ethics of *Sittlichkeit* (q.v.)]
Nation	nation [cf. *Volk*]
Naturrecht	natural law
Nicht-Ich	(the) not-'I'
nichtig	null and void; insignificant*
Nichtigkeit	nullity [cf. *Nichts*]
Nichts	nothing(ness); nullity [cf. *Nichtigkeit*]
Not	privation; urgency; needs; necessity* [cf. *Notwendigkeit*]
Notwendigkeit	necessity [cf. *Not*]
Obrigkeit	authority [as a publicly constituted body

	within the state; cf. *Autorität, Berechtigung, Gewalt, Herrschaft*]
Ordnung	order; arrangement* [cf. *Anordnung*]
Phänomen	phenomenon [cf. *Erscheinung*]
Phantasie	imagination
Potenz	[literally 'potential' or 'power'; a term with scientific associations, used by Hegel in his essay on *Natural Law* to denote a stage, level, or area, with potential for further development, within a larger whole or system] level*; status*; area*; potentiality*
Prinzip	principle [cf. *Grundsatz*]
Privatrecht	civil law
Räsonnement	ratiocination; reasoning
Realität	reality
Recht	right; law* [as in *Privatrecht, Staatsrecht*, etc.]
rechtlich	legal*; in accordance with right
Rechtlichkeit	integrity*
rechtlos	lawless*
rechtschaffen	honest; meritorious*
Rechtschaffenheit	rectitude*
Rechtsgrund	legal title*; legality*
Rechtspflege	administration of justice; judicial procedure*
Rechtssache	legal case
Rechtswissenschaft	science of right
Rechtszustand	state of law*
reell	real; material*
Reellsein	real existence* [cf. *Existenz*]
Regierungsgewalt	executive power; power of government
Reichshofrat	Aulic Council [one of the two Supreme Courts of the Holy Roman Empire; the Aulic Council, which was based in Vienna, dealt with cases involving member states (i.e. 'estates') of the Empire, whereas the *Reichskammergericht* (q.v.), based in Wetzlar, dealt with cases involving individuals]

334

Reichskammergericht (or *Kammergericht*)	Supreme Court* (of the Holy Roman Empire) [in fact one of two Supreme Courts, the other being the *Reichshofrat* or Aulic Council (see preceding entry)]
Reichsoberhaupt	Imperial head; head of the [Holy Roman] Empire [i.e. the Emperor himself]
Reichstag	Imperial Diet [Estates Assembly (or Parliament) of the Holy Roman Empire, which met in Regensburg]
reichsunmittelbar	directly subordinate to the Emperor [as applied to heads of territorial governments within the Holy Roman Empire and to other individuals (such as the Free Knights) who owed allegiance to the Emperor alone]
Reichsunmittelbarkeit	direct dependence on the Empire (or Emperor) [see preceding entry]
Reichsverband	Imperial union [i.e. the Holy Roman Empire itself, as a federation of member states (or 'estates')]
Reversalien	undertakings [on the part of princes of the Holy Roman Empire] to protect the rights of subjects*
Sache	thing; cause [as a principle espoused]; substance* [cf. *Substanz*]; (plural) issues*
Schein	semblance; appearance* [cf. *Erscheinung*]
Schicksal	fate; destiny
schlechthin	purely (and simply); utterly; without qualification; absolutely*
Seele	soul [cf. *Gemüt*]
Sein	being [cf. *Dasein, Wesen*]
selbständig	self-sufficient; independent
Selbstgefühl	self-confidence
setzen	to posit
Sitte	custom; (plural) customs; manners; ethics* [cf. *Ethik, Sittlichkeit*]
Sittengesetz	moral law*
sittlich	ethical; moral* [when applied to narrower (e.g. Kantian) conceptions of ethics than Hegel's own theory of *Sittlichkeit* as ethical life in general]
Sittlichkeit	ethical life; ethics [cf. *Ethik, Sitten*]; morality* [see previous entry]

Staat	state [as a political unit; cf. *Zustand*]
Staatsgewalt	political authority; authority of the state [cf. *Autorität, Gewalt, Staatsmacht*]
Staatskörper	body politic
Staatsmacht	political power; power of the state; political authority* [cf. *Staatsgewalt*]
Staatsrecht	constitutional law; political right*; (plural) constitutional rights [cf. *inneres Staatsrecht*]
Staatsverfassung	(political) constitution
Stand	estate [(i) as a social 'class' in the older sense of a state or condition, not primarily determined by economic factors, within the social hierarchy (cf. *Klasse*); (ii) the traditional designation for a member state or constituent territory, with rights of representation, within the Holy Roman Empire]; class* [cf. *Klasse*]
Stände	[plural of *Stand* (q.v.)] Estates [as a parliamentary assembly]; estates [in one of the two senses specified under *Stand* above]; classes* [cf. *Klasse*]
Standpunkt	viewpoint; point of view
Substanz	substance [cf. *Sache*]
tapfer	valiant
Tapferkeit	valour; courage
Trieb	drive; initiative*
unsittlich	immoral* [see comment under *sittlich* above]
Unsittlichkeit	immorality* [see comment under *sittlich* above]
Unterschied	difference [cf. *Differenz*]; distinction
Verhältnis	relation(ship) [cf. *Beziehung*]; (plural *Verhältnisse*) relations(hips); circumstances
verkehrt	distorted
vernichten	to destroy; to nullify or annul [cf. *aufheben*]
Vernichtetsein	nullification; annulment
Vernichtung	destruction; nullification; annulment
Vernunft	reason [i.e. rationality in a universal sense; cf. *Grund*]

336

vernünftig	rational
Verstand	understanding; intelligence; ingenuity*; mentality*
Verwaltung	administration [i.e. the act of administering, or the body responsible for it; cf. *Ministerium*]
Vielheit	plurality; multiplicity* [cf. *Mannigfaltigkeit*]
Volk	people; nation* [cf. *Nation*]; state* [cf. *Staat*]
Völkerrecht	international law
vollendet	complete
Vollendung	completion; complete state*
vollkommen	perfect
vorstellen	[reflexive verb] to represent (to oneself) [cf. *darstellen*]; to conceive of*; to contemplate*
Vorstellung	representational thought; representation*; view [cf. *Anschauung*]; notion*; conception*; idea* [cf. *Ahnung, Gedanke, Idee*]; model*
Wahlkapitulation	electoral contract*
wahr	true [cf. *wahrhaft*]
wahrhaft	true [cf. *wahr*]; genuine
Wahrheit	truth
Weltweisheit	literally 'worldly wisdom' [the usual German term for 'philosophy' during the eighteenth century until it was displaced by *Philosophie*]
Wesen	essence; essential being (or nature); being [in the sense of 'creature' or 'living entity']; being* [cf. *Sein*]; character*
wesenlos	insubstantial
Willkür	arbitrariness; arbitrary will
willkürlich	arbitrary
wirklich	actual [in the Hegelian sense of 'fully realised'; cf. *eigentlich*]
Wirklichkeit	actuality
wissen	to know [in a passive sense, as with factual knowledge; cf. *kennen, erkennen*]
Wissen	knowledge [as defined in the previous entry; cf. *Erkennen, Kenntnis, Wissenschaft*]
Wissenschaft	science [i.e. systematic knowledge of every kind, including not only natural science, but

	all academic disciplines]; knowledge* [cf. *Kenntnis, Erkenntnis*]
wissenschaftlich	scientific [see the previous entry]
Wollen	volition; willing
Zufall	contingency; accident; chance
zufällig	contingent; accidental; fortuitous
Zusammenhang	context; framework; connection
Zustand	condition; state* [cf. *Staat*]
Zwang	coercion
Zweck	end; aim; purpose
zwingen	to coerce [cf. *bezwingen*]

Bibliography of works cited in this edition

Acton, H. B. (1975), 'Introduction' to Hegel's *Natural Law*, tr. T. M. Knox (Philadelphia, PA)

Avineri, Shlomo (1972), *Hegel's Theory of the Modern State* (Cambridge)

(1985), 'Feature Book Review: The Discovery of Hegel's Early Lectures on the Philosophy of Right', *The Owl of Minerva*, vol. 16, pp. 199–208

Barker, Ernst (1957), 'Introduction' to Otto Gierke's *Natural Law and the Theory of Society 1500 to 1800*, tr. E. Barker (Boston, MA)

Beck, Hermann (1995), *The Origins of the Authoritarian Welfare State in Prussia* (Ann Arbor, MI)

Beiser, Frederick (1992), *Enlightenment, Revolution, and Romanticism* (Cambridge, MA)

Berdahl, Robert (1988), *The Politics of the Prussian Nobility* (Princeton, NJ)

Bigler, Robert (1972), *The Politics of German Protestantism* (Berkeley, CA)

Bradley, A. C. (1959), 'Hegel's Theory of Tragedy', in *Oxford Lectures on Poetry* (New York), pp. 69–95

Brandes, Ernst (1808), *Betrachtungen über den Zeitgeist in Deutschland* (Hannover)

Cassirer, Ernst (1946), *The Myth of the State* (New Haven, CT)

Constant, Benjamin (1988), *Political Writings*, tr. and ed. Bianca-Maria Fontana (Cambridge)

Crouter, Richard (1980), 'Hegel and Schleiermacher at Berlin: A Many-Sided Debate', *Journal of the American Academy of Religion*, vol. 48, pp. 19–43

Dahrendorf, Ralf (1967), *Society and Democracy in Germany* (Garden City, NY) de Maistre, Joseph (1884), 'Réflexion sur le Protestantisme', in *Oeuvres Complètes*, vol. VIII (Lyons), pp. 63–97

Dickey, Laurence (1987), *Hegel: Religion, Economics, and the Politics of Spirit, 1770–1807* (Cambridge)
    (1993), 'Hegel on Religion and Philosophy', in *The Cambridge Companion to Hegel*, ed. Frederick Beiser (Cambridge), pp. 301–47

Epstein, Klaus (1966), *The Genesis of German Conservatism* (Princeton, NJ)

Ferguson, Adam (1995), *An Essay on the History of Civil Society*, ed. Fania Oz-Salzberger (Cambridge)

Gooch, G. P. (1920), *Germany and the French Revolution* (New York)

Goodenough, E. R. (1928), 'The Political Philosophy of Hellenistic Kingship', *Yale Classical Studies*, vol. I, pp. 55–102

Habermas, Jürgen (1975), *Legitimation Crisis*, tr. T. McCarthy (Boston, MA)

Harris, H. S. (1972), *Hegel's Development, vol. I: Toward the Sunlight* (Oxford)
    (1983), *Hegel's Development, vol. II: Night Thoughts* (Oxford)
    (1985), *Between Kant and Hegel*, tr. G. di Vioganni (Albany, NY)
    (1993), 'Hegel's Intellectual Development to 1807', in *Cambridge Companion to Hegel*, ed. Frederick Beiser (Cambridge), pp. 25–51

Haym, Rudolf (1857), *Hegel und seine Zeit* (Darmstadt)

Hegel, G. W. F. (1931), *The Phenomenology of Mind*, tr. J. B. Baillie (New York)
    (1948), *On Christianity: The Early Theological Writings*, tr. T. M. Knox (Chicago, IL)
    (1956), *The Philosophy of History*, tr. J. Sibree (New York)
    (1964), *Hegel's Political Writings*, tr. T. M. Knox (Oxford)
    (1971), *Philosophy of Mind, Being Part Three of the Encyclopaedia of the Philosophy of Sciences*, tr. W. Wallace (Oxford)
    (1975), *Lectures on the Philosophy of World History. Introduction*, tr. H. B. Nisbet, with an introduction by Duncan Forbes (Cambridge)
    (1979), *'System of Ethical Life' and 'First Philosophy of Spirit'*, tr. and ed. T. M. Knox and H. S. Harris (Albany, NY)
    (1984a), *Three Essays, 1793–1795*, tr. and ed. P. Fuss and J. Dobbins (Notre Dame, IN)
    (1984b), *Hegel: The Letters*, tr. C. Butler and C. Seiler (Bloomington, IN)
    (1991a), *Elements of the Philosophy of Right*, ed. Allen W. Wood, tr. H. B. Nisbet (Cambridge)
    (1991b), *The Encyclopedia Logic*, tr. T. Geraets, W. Suchting, and H. S. Harris (Indianapolis, IN)

(1995), *Lectures on Natural Law and Political Science*, tr. J. Stewart and P. Hodgson (Berkeley, CA)

Heine, Heinrich (1985), *The Romantic School and Other Essays*, ed. Jost Hermand (New York)

Hellmuth, Eckhart (ed.) (1990), *The Transformation of Political Culture* (New York)

Hodgson, Peter (1984), *Hegel's Lectures on the Philosophy of Religion*, vol. I, tr. R. Brown, P. Hodgson, and J. Stewart, ed. P. Hodgson (Berkeley, CA)

Hof, Ulrich (1990), 'German Associations and Politics in the Second Half of the Eighteenth Century', in *The Transformation of Political Culture*, ed. E. Hellmuth (New York), pp. 207–18

Hoover, Jeffrey (1988), 'The Origin of the Conflict Between Hegel and Schleiermacher at Berlin', *The Owl of Minerva*, vol. 20, pp. 69–79

Hyppolite, Jean (1996), *Hegel's Philosophy of History*, tr. B. Harris and J. Spurlock (Gainsville, FL)

Inwood, M. J. (1984), 'Hegel, Plato and Greek "Sittlichkeit" ', in *The State and Civil Society*, ed. Z. A. Pelczynski (Cambridge)

Jaeger, Werner (1961), *Early Christianity and Greek Paidei* (Cambridge, MA)

Jaeschke, Walter (1983), 'Hegel's Last Year in Berlin', in *Hegel's Philosophy of Action*, ed. L. Stepelevich and D. Lamb (Atlantic Highlands, NJ), pp. 31–48

Jaeschke, Walter and Meist, Kurt (1981), *Hegel in Berlin* (Bonn)

Junkin, E. D. (1974), *Religion versus Revolution* (Austin, TX)

Kaufmann, Walter (ed.) (1970), *Hegel's Political Philosophy* (New York)

Klippel, Diethelm (1990), 'The True Concept of Liberty', in *The Transformation of Political Culture*, ed. E. Hellmuth (New York), pp. 447–66

Knox, T. M. (1975), *Hegel's Natural Law*, tr. T. M. Knox (Philadelphia, PA)

Knudsen, Jonathan (1990), 'The Limits of Liberal Politics in Berlin, 1815–48', in *In Search of a Liberal Germany*, ed. L. Jones and K. Jarausch (New York), pp. 111–31

La Vopa, Anthony (1989), 'The Revelatory Moment: Fichte and the French Revolution', *Central European History*, vol. 22, pp. 130–59

Law, Edmund (1745), *Considerations on the State of the World with Regard to the Theory of Religion* (Cambridge)

Lessing, Gotthold Ephraim (1956), *Lessing's Theological Writings*, tr. Henry Chadwick (Stanford, CA)

McClelland, Charles (1971), *The German Historians and England* (Cambridge)

Macpherson, C. B. (1962), *The Political Theory of Possessive Individualism* (Oxford)

Meier, Christian (1990), *The Greek Discovery of Politics* tr. David McClintock (Cambridge, MA)

Meinecke, Friedrich (1970), *Cosmopolitanism and the National State*, tr. R. B. Kimber (Princeton, NJ)

Nicolin, Günther (ed.) (1970), *Hegel in Berichten seiner Zeitgenossen* (Hamburg)

Nisbet, H. B. (1982) ' "Was ist Aufklärung?": The Concept of Enlightenment in Eighteenth-Century Germany', *Journal of European Studies*, vol. 12, pp. 77–95

North, Helen (1966), *Sophrosyne* (Ithaca, NY)

Novalis (1996), extracts in *The Early Writings of the German Romantics*, ed. Frederick Beiser (Cambridge)

O'Regan, Cyril (1992), 'Hegelian Philosophy of Religion and Eckhartian Mysticism', in *New Perspectives on Hegel's Philosophy of Religion*, ed. D. Kolb (Albany, NY), pp. 109–29

Ottmann, Henning (1996), 'Hegel and Political Trends: A Criticism of the Political Hegel Legends', in *The Hegel Myths and Legends*, ed. Jon Stewart (Evanston, IL), pp. 53–69

Ozment, Steven (1969), *Homo Spiritualis* (Leiden)

Oz-Salzberger, Fania (1995), *Translating the Enlightenment* (Oxford)

Parry, G. (1963), 'Enlightened Government and Its Critics in Eighteenth-Century Germany', *The Historical Journal*, vol. 6, pp. 178–92

Petry, M. J. (1976), 'Hegel and the "Morning Chronicle" ', *Hegel-Studien*, vol. XI, pp. 11–80

Pocock, J. G. A. (1977), 'Between Machiavelli and Hume: Gibbon as Civic Humanist and Philosophical Historian', in *Edward Gibbon and the Decline and Fall of the Roman Empire*, ed. G. Bowerstock and J. Clive (Cambridge, MA), pp. 103–20

Riedel, Manfred (1984), *Between Tradition and Revolution: The Hegelian Transformation of Political Philosophy*, tr. W. Wright (Cambridge)

Ritter, Joachim (1982), *Hegel and the French Revolution*, tr. R. Winfield (Cambridge, MA)

Rosenberg, Hans (1958), *Bureaucracy, Aristocracy and Autocracy* (Boston, MA)

Rousseau, Jean-Jacques (1978), *On the Social Contract*, tr. J. Masters, ed. R. Masters (New York)

Royce, Josiah (1919), *Lectures on Modern Idealism* (New Haven, CT)

Ruge, Arnold (1983), 'Hegel's "Philosophy of Right" and the Politics of Our Times', in *The Young Hegelians*, ed. L. Stepelevich (Cambridge), pp. 211–36

Safranski, Rüdiger (1990), *Schopenhauer and the Wild Years of Philosophy*, tr. E. Osers (Cambridge, MA)

Saine, Thomas (1982), 'A Peculiar German View of the French Revolution: The Revolution as German Reformation', in *Aufnahme–Weitergabe*, ed. John McCarthy and Albert Kipa (Hamburg), pp. 233–61

Santayana, George (1968), *The German Mind: A Philosophical Diagnosis* (New York)

Schelling, F. W. J. (1966), *On University Studies*, tr. E. S. Morgan, ed. N. Guterman (Athens, OH)

(1978), *System of Transcendental Idealism*, tr. Peter Heath (Charlottesville, VA)

Schiller, Friedrich (1967), *On the Aesthetic Education of Man*, tr. and ed. E. M. Wilkinson and L. A. Willoughby (Oxford)

Schilling, Heinz (ed.) (1986), *Die reformierte Konfessionalisierung in Deutschland: Das Problem der 'Zweiten Reformation'*, (Gütersloh)

(1992), *Religion, Political Culture, and the Emergence of Early Modern Society* (New York)

Schlegel, Friedrich (1991), *Philosophical Fragments*, tr. P. Firchow (Minneapolis, MN)

(1996), extracts in *The Early Political Writings of the German Romantics*, ed. Frederick Beiser (Cambridge)

Schmidt, James (ed.) (1996), *What is Enlightenment?* (Berkeley, CA)

Schmidt, Martin (1965), 'Pietism', in *The Encyclopedia of the Lutheran Church*, vol. III (Minneapolis, MN)

Schmitt, Carl (1996), *The Concept of the Political*, tr. G. Schwab (Chicago, IL)

Schopenhauer, Arthur (1974), *Parerga and Paralipomena*, vol. I, tr. E. F. J. Payne (Oxford)

(1995), *On the Basis of Morality*, tr. E. F. J. Payne (Oxford)

Sheehan, James (1973), 'Liberalism and Society in Germany, 1815–48', *Journal of Modern History*, vol. 45, pp. 583–604

(1989), *German History 1770–1866* (Oxford)

Simmel, Georg (1950), *The Sociology of Georg Simmel*, tr. K. H. Wolff (Glencoe, IL)

Smith, Adam (1976), *An Inquiry into the Nature and Causes of the Wealth of Nations*, 2 vols., ed. R. H. Campbell and A. S. Skinner (Indianapolis, IN)

Smith, R. J. (1987), *The Gothic Bequest* (London)

Sprat, Thomas (1958), *History of the Royal Society* (St Louis, MO)

Stewart, Jon (ed.) (1996), *The Hegel Myths and Legends* (Evanston, IL)

Strauss, Leo (1964), *The City and Man* (Chicago, IL)

Toews, John (1980), *Hegelianism* (Cambridge)

Turgot, A. R. J. (1977), *The Economics of A. R. J. Turgot*, tr. and ed. P. D. Groenewegen (The Hague)

Vierhaus, Rudolf (1987), *Deutschland im 18. Jahrhundert* (Göttingen)

Villers, Charles (1807), *An Essay on the Spirit and Influence of the Reformation by Luther*, 2nd edn, tr. B. Lambert (Dover, NH)

Voegelin, Eric (1968), *Science, Politics and Gnosticism* (Chicago, IL)
    (1971), 'On Hegel – A Study in Sorcery', *Studium Generale*, vol. 24, pp. 235–68

Walker, Mack (1981), *Johann Jakob Moser and the Holy Roman Empire of the German Nation* (Chapel Hill, NC)

Waszek, Norbert (1985), 'Hegels Exzerpte aus der "Edinburgh Review" 1817–1819', *Hegel-Studien*, vol. 20, pp. 79–112
    (1988), *The Scottish Enlightenment and Hegel's Account of 'Civil Society'* (Dordrecht)

Westphal, Merold (1984), 'Hegel and the Reformation', in *History and System: Hegel's Philosophy of History*, ed. R. L. Perkins (Albany, NY), pp. 73–99

Wolin, Sheldon (1960), *Politics and Vision* (Boston, MA)

Index of names

Holy Roman Empire, xi–xiii, xlii, 6, 12–
13, 26–9, 31–41, 44–5, 47–9, 51, 53,
55, 57–8, 60–2, 64, 67, 73, 84–7, 89,
91, 97–100, 223, 236, 271, 273, 275,
278–80, 283
Holy Spirit, 201, 207
Homer, 153
Hook, Sidney, xxxiii
Hoover, Jeffrey, xxxviii–ix
Huguenots, 76–7, 282
Hume, Joseph, 241, 322
Hungary, 35, 62, 94, 220
Hunt, Henry (Orator), 263, 325
Huskisson, William, 242, 322
Hyppolite, Jean, xxxvii, 285, 289–90,
294–5

Imperial Diet, 12–13, 29, 33, 38, 45–6,
53, 55, 61, 91–2, 96–7, 99, 275, 283
India, 61
Innsbruck, 282
Inquisition, 206
Inwood, M. J., 318
Ireland, 242, 245–8, 256, 323
Isocrates, 297
Israelites (*see also* Jews), 79, 201
Italy, 39, 48, 62, 77–83, 98, 206, 208,
219, 253, 282, 324
itio in partes, 45–6, 53, 56

Jacobi, Friedrich Heinrich, 273
Jacobins, 259, 271, 310
Jaeger, Werner, xxxvii
Jaeschke, Walter, xxxviii–ix, xl, 299, 304,
306–7, 316, 322
Jena, xix, xxi, xliii, 285, 300
Jericho, 201
Jesuits, 90–2, 126, 205–7, 310
Jesus, xix, 184, 187, 200–1, 294, 308, 313
Jews (*see also* Israelites), xix, xxxix, 45,
101, 225, 246, 284, 301
Joseph II (Emperor), 46, 52, 72, 90, 96,
281
Jowett, Benjamin, 293, 295
Judaism, 313
Jülich-Berg, 46
Jülich-Cleve, 71, 279
Julius II, Pope, 82
July Revolution (1830), xxvi, xl, 233,
306–7, 313, 315–16, 318–20
Junkin, E. D., 314
Justi, J. H. G. von, 289

Kammerzieler, 31, 56, 96
Kammin, 37, 60
Kant, Immanuel, xxi, xlii, xlix, 118, 123–
4, 131, 211, 228, 285–6, 288–9, 291,
298, 301, 312
Kaufmann, Walter, xxxiii
Kehl, 38
Kemp Smith, Norman, 289
Klippel, Diethelm, xxxiv, 296
Klopstock, Friedrich Gottlob, 294
Knox, T. M., vii–ix, xxxiii, xlvi, l, 276,
284, 294, 323–5
Knudsen, Jonathan, xl
Koselleck, Reinhart, xlix
Kroeger, A.E., l

Landfrieden, 48–9, 70–1
Lansdowne, Henry, third Marquis of,
325
Lares and Penates, 192
Lasson, Georg, xlvii, 30, 211, 307
La Vopa, Anthony, 290
Law, Edmund, 305
League of Princes (*Fürstenbund*), 72–3,
281
Leibniz, Gottfried Wilhelm, 315
Leopold I (Emperor), 96
Lessing, Gotthold Ephraim, xxxvii
Liège, 47
Liguria, 87
Liverpool, 255–6
Liverpool, Robert, second Earl of, 321–2
Livy (Titus Livius), 282
Lloyd-Jones, Hugh, 297
Lombards, 203
Lombardy, 36, 79
Lorraine, 39
Louis XIV, 73, 282
Lucca, 48
Lunéville, Peace of, 39
Luther, Martin, xxiv–v, xxvii, 189–90,
198, 200–1, 203, 210, 303–5, 308–9,
312
Lutherans, Lutheranism, xxiv–vi, 201–2,
275, 280, 302–4, 308–10, 312, 317

Machiavelli, Niccolo, 79–83, 281–2
Mackintosh, James, xxxvi, 320
Macpherson, C. B., xxix, xl
McClelland, Charles, xxxv
McCulloch, J. R., 321
Magdeburg, 37, 60

Rastatt, Congress of, 32, 278
Ratzeburg, 37
Red Sea, 201
Reform Bill (British), x–xi, xiv–vii,
  xxxvi, xlviii–ix, 234–70, 320, 323,
  325
Reformation, xxv–viii, xxx, xl, 190, 197–
  8, 202, 204, 213, 220, 279–80, 302–
  5, 309, 311–2, 314
Reign of Terror, 206, 233
Reimarus, Hermann Samuel, 308
Renaissance, 307
Restoration, ix, xxiv, xl, 307, 315, 326
Rhine, 34, 39, 49, 86
Rhineland, 88
Richelieu, Armand Jean du Plessis,
  Cardinal, Duc de, 75–7, 101, 214
Riedel, Manfred, xl
Ritschl, Albrecht, 308
Ritter, Joachim, ix, xxxiii, xl, 304
Robertson, William, 279
Robespierre, Maximilien, 206, 218, 233,
  258
Roman law, *see* law (Index of Subjects)
Roman Months, 13, 32, 275
Romanticism, 285, 310
Rome, Romans, xix, xxix, 19–20, 36, 57–
  8, 81–2, 148–9, 189, 192, 197, 206,
  220, 275, 292–3
Rosenberg, Hans, xxxviii
Rosenkranz, Karl, xxxiii, 9, 272–3
Rousseau, Jean–Jacques, xl, 283
Royce, Josiah, xli
Ruge, Arnold, 299–300, 309, 320
Russell, Lord John, 254
Russia, 19, 39, 60, 93
Ryswick, Peace of, 38

Safranski, Rüdiger, 302
Saine, Thomas P., 314
St Peters (Rome), 200
Saint-Simon, Claude Henri de Rouvroy,
  Comte de, xxxvi
San Marino, 87
Santayana, George, xxxix, xli
Savigny, Friedrich Karl von, 301
Saxony, 28, 47, 55, 85, 90, 99
Schelling, Friedrich Wilhelm Joseph von,
  xxxviii, xlii–iii, 284–6, 288, 294
Schiller, Friedrich, xiv, xxxv, 288, 290
Schilling, Heinz, xxxix, 304
Schlegel, Friedrich, 273, 289–90, 310

Schleiermacher, Friedrich Ernst Daniel,
  300–1
Schmidt, James, xxxiv
Schmidt, Martin, 304
Schmitt, Carl, xxix, xxxii, xl–xli, 275
Schopenhauer, Arthur, xxxi, xxxiii,
  xxxix, xli
Schwerin, 37
Seven Years War, 34, 39, 61, 80, 84, 90
Sforza, 78
Sheehan, James, xxxvi, xxxviii
Sibree, J., xlvii
Sicily, 58
Sickingen, Franz von, 47
Siena, 48, 78
Siéyès, Emanuel Joseph, Comte de, 261,
  325
Silesia, 61, 73
Silesian War, First (War of the Austrian
  Succession), 83
Simmel, Georg, 286
Sismondi, Jean Charles Leonard
  Simonde de, xxxv
Sistine Chapel, 200
Skinner, Quentin, 282
Smalkaldic League, 72
Smith, Adam, 321, 324
Smith, R. J., xxxiv
Socinians, 308
Socrates, 153, 190
Sophocles, 153
Spain, Spanish, 37, 58, 62, 77, 79, 93,
  206, 219
Sparta, 319
Spee von Langenfeld, Friedrich, 206,
  310
Spence, William, 322
Sprat, Thomas, 305
Stewart, J. M., xlvii
Stewart, Jon, xxxiii–iv
Stone, Harold Samuel, l
Strauss, Leo, 295
Stuart, House of, 227, 251, 317
Sub-letting Act, 248
Supreme Court (*Reichskammergericht; see
  also* Aulic Council), 31, 45–7, 53
Sweden, 37, 39, 58, 60–2, 75, 83, 86, 90,
  253
Switzerland, Swiss, 35, 37, 79, 87, 97,
  207, 272, 321

Tacitus, Publius Cornelius, 274–5

Index of subjects

Index of subjects

freedom (*cont.*)
251, 258, 264, 268–9, 274–5, 280–1,
283, 298, 302–4, 308–9, 315–16,
318–19
French Revolution, *see* Index of names

geography, 173
government, xii–xiv, xvi–xvii, xxxvi–vii,
xlii, 7, 16–17 21–3, 91, 94, 133–5,
202, 214, 216–19, 221–3, 226–7,
231, 233, 236, 239, 245, 250–1, 253,
256–7, 261, 263, 265, 267–9, 272,
275–6, 280–1, 283–4, 309, 314–17,
321–2, 324–6
grace (*Gnade*), 52–3, 67, 204–5, 207, 230

happiness, xii, 118, 239, 288–9
history (*see also* world history), x–xi, xiii,
xviii–xix, xxii–iii, xxv–viii, xxxi,
xxxiv, xxxix, xli–xlv, 39, 63, 81, 86,
92, 105, 111, 171, 173, 176–7, 197,
210, 219, 224, 236, 274, 278, 283,
294, 298–9, 301–3, 306–8, 311, 315–
16, 318, 321, 323
holism, 296–7
hunting, 243–4, 248–50, 263

Idea(s), 6, 102–6, 108, 114–15, 119–20,
155–6, 161, 163–4, 169, 171, 174–5,
179, 182, 185, 220, 223–4
imagination, 110, 136, 165, 168
immorality (*Unsittlichkeit*), 122, 125–6,
129–30, 289
individualism, xxvii, xxix, xxxiii, 278,
281, 292, 296, 298
indulgences, 205, 303
infinity, 104–5, 108, 114, 118, 120–22,
130–2, 134, 136, 138–41, 144–6,
156–7, 159, 162, 170, 179, 286
intelligence, 157–8
intuition (*Anschauung*), 103, 106, 108,
114–17, 128–30, 141, 143, 158, 162,
165, 169, 172, 179–80, 184, 286,
288–9, 297–8
itio in partes, see Index of names

justice, xvii–xviii, xxxi, 2–3, 9, 12–13,
17–18, 24–5, 44, 46–7, 53, 60, 69,
95, 98, 143–4, 150, 155, 170, 190,
192, 194–6, 206, 213, 234, 239, 242,
250, 259, 275, 292

Landfrieden, see Index of names
landowners, xiv
language, 19–21, 25, 159, 294
latitudinarianism, 305
law (*Recht*), 14, 16, 18, 23–4, 34, 44, 52,
71, 111, 113–14, 143, 145, 166, 168,
174, 176–8, 193, 208, 212–13, 232,
239–40, 247–8, 251, 268, 287, 289,
293, 297, 319, 323; civil, 12, 44,
170–1, 190, 212, 222, 238, 245, 249;
constitutional, 6, 10–15, 17, 28, 34–
5, 41, 43–4, 46, 54, 56, 59, 116,
170–1, 175, 238–9, 253; criminal,
116; English, 320; Imperial, 29, 46;
international, 170–1; moral, 122–5,
160, 229; natural, 21, 102, 104–7,
116, 118, 130, 159–60, 163, 166,
170, 285–6, 289, 293, 296–7; public,
12; Roman, 18, 293
laws, 2, 7, 9–10, 16–18, 21, 25, 28, 31,
33–4, 41–3, 46, 51, 53, 59, 66, 73,
77, 94, 107–8, 114–17, 143–4, 149–
50, 162, 164, 167, 175–8, 189–91,
194–5, 202, 204, 207, 209–11, 215–
17, 223, 226–8, 232–3, 238, 248–9,
258, 264, 293, 295, 309, 316–18
legislation, 18
liberalism, vii–ix, xvi–xviii, xxvi, xxx,
xxxiii–iv, xxxvi, xxxix, xliii, 219–
220, 237, 279, 284, 291, 311, 313,
315, 320–3
liberty (*see also* freedom), xii–xiii, xv,
xviii, xxviii–ix, xxxi, xxxiv, 16, 80,
187, 193–4, 221, 274–5, 281, 291–2,
306, 314, 318–19

machine state, xiv, xxxv, 22–5, 277, 283,
289–90, 297
magic, 209
marriage, 192–3, 203, 228
metaphysics, vii–x, xxxi, 102, 116, 287–
8, 315
Middle Ages, *see* Index of names
middle class, xvii, 50, 63–6, 89, 277, 280,
283
miracles, 199, 209
monarch, xvi, 12, 14, 21, 28, 36, 61, 63,
76, 82, 90, 94, 216–18, 223, 233,
239, 260–1, 266, 322
monarchy, xiii, xv, xvii, xxxv, 12, 14, 65,
76–8, 84, 88, 92–3, 96–7, 170, 219,

354

Index of subjects

Protestantism, Protestants, *see* Index of
  names
providence, 11, 195, 306
provincial assembly, *see* assembly
psychology, 110, 116
public, xi–xii, xxiii–iv, xxviii–xxx, xxxii,
  xxxiv, 69, 73, 83, 94, 147, 221, 235,
  257–8, 262, 264, 268, 272, 290, 293
publicity (*Publizität*), xi, 272, 302
punishment, 107, 116, 139–40, 166, 168

rabble, xxxv, 79, 255, 325
reason (*Vernunft*), xxi, 80, 108, 115–26,
  128, 130, 154, 158, 163–4, 172, 175,
  183–5, 187, 204, 208–12, 214, 231,
  251, 264–5, 288, 290, 298, 301, 312
rebellion, right of, 54
reflection, 112, 117, 130, 205, 221
reform, xi–xiii, xviii, xxxvi–vii, 2–3, 46,
  116, 222, 234–71, 274, 320–1, 323,
  325
Reform Bill, *see* Index of names
Reformation, *see* Index of names
religion, viii–ix, xix–xxviii, xxx, xxxiv,
  xxxvii–xl, xlii–iii, xlv, 10, 20–1, 25,
  38, 49, 50–6, 59–60, 62, 67, 72, 75,
  84, 90–1, 98, 132, 156, 172, 178,
  184, 186–97, 200–1, 207, 210, 212–
  13, 216–17, 220, 223, 225–33, 243,
  245, 276, 280, 282, 285, 292, 299–
  301, 303–5, 307, 309, 312, 314, 316,
  318–19
Renaissance, *see* Index of names
representation, representational thought
  (*Vorstellung*), 105, 111, 113, 226
republicanism, republics, xii, xxxvi, 63,
  77, 87, 179, 222, 233, 290
Restoration, *see* Index of names
revelation, 227, 317
revolution (*see also* Index of names:
  French Revolution, July
  Revolution), xii, xiv, xvi, xviii,
  xxxvi, 56, 220, 227, 233, 251, 255,
  270–1, 289, 319, 321
right, rights (*Recht*), ix, xv–xvii, xix,
  xxxi, xxxv, xxxvii, xliii, 3, 8–9, 11–
  13, 15, 17–21, 23, 29, 34, 36–8, 41–
  4, 46, 49, 51–4, 56, 58–60, 67–72,
  75, 77, 82, 86, 89–92, 95–6, 102,
  107–10, 114, 117, 123–4, 126, 131,
  135, 141–2, 144–6, 148–9, 151–2,
  154, 160, 162–4, 168, 170, 175, 179,

185, 187–8, 190, 202, 204, 209–15,
  217, 219–23, 227–8, 230–3, 236–9,
  242–4, 246, 248–9, 251–60, 264,
  267–9, 275, 281, 285–7, 289, 296,
  298, 303, 306, 309, 313, 318–19,
  323–5

science, xxxix, 6, 12, 102–9, 111, 115–6,
  120, 130–1, 141–3, 153–4, 159, 161,
  163, 165–6, 168–9, 171–2, 176, 178,
  181–3, 185, 208, 232, 250, 285–6,
  289, 294, 297, 299–300, 305, 308,
  311, 316
senses, 156–7, 209
sin, xix, 310
Sittlichkeit (see also ethical life), viii–x,
  xvi–xxiii, xxv–xxxiii, xxxix–xli, 197–
  8, 280, 284–9, 291, 293, 295–8, 300,
  305–6, 308–10, 312–13, 317–19, 321
slavery, 188, 193, 303, 306
society (*see also* civil society), xxvi, xxx–
  xxxii, 10, 21–22, 57, 113, 195, 203,
  212, 240, 276, 278, 280, 283, 286,
  295, 298, 311, 314
sovereignty, xxxii, 35, 37–9, 64, 76, 78–
  9, 83, 95, 97, 99, 250, 257–8, 260,
  268, 276, 280
spirit (*Geist; see also* world spirit), xx–
  xxi, xxiii, xxviii, 2, 5, 7–8, 10, 20,
  23, 25–6, 41, 50, 62–3, 74, 79, 84,
  91, 115, 135, 147–8, 154–6, 158–60,
  162, 179–80, 182–5, 198–202, 204–
  5, 208, 210–12, 214–15, 224–6, 228–
  9, 271, 288, 291, 294–5, 299–300,
  302, 308–12, 316
state (*see also* machine state, police state),
  viii–ix, xi, xvi–xvii, xxiii–iv, xxvi,
  xxx–xxxiii, xxxvi, xxxix, xli, 6–7, 9–
  26, 28, 30–41, 43–4, 48–51, 53–4,
  56–89, 91, 94–101, 111, 113, 116,
  139, 142, 159–60, 170, 179, 181–2,
  186, 189, 191, 194–5, 197, 202–4,
  207, 209–10, 212–20, 223, 225–33,
  236, 239, 243, 247, 250–1, 253, 256–
  61, 263–6, 268–9, 273, 275–83, 287–
  9, 291, 297, 299–300, 304–6, 309–
  11, 314, 316–17, 319
subject, subjectivity, xx, xxxi, xxxiii,
  xxxviii, 113–14, 129–32, 138, 166,
  171, 199–202, 204–5, 209, 215, 287,
  289–90, 292, 297, 300–1, 303, 307–
  8, 311–13, 317–18

356

Cambridge Texts in the History of Political Thought

Titles published in the series thus far

Aristotle *The Politics* and *The Constitution of Athens* (edited by Stephen Everson)
 0 521 48400 6 paperback
Arnold *Culture and Anarchy and other writings* (edited by Stefan Collini)
 0 521 37796 X paperback
Astell *Political Writings* (edited by Patricia Springborg)
 0 521 42845 9 paperback
Austin *The Province of Jurisprudence Determined* (edited by Wilfrid E. Rumble)
 0 521 44756 9 paperback
Bacon *The History of the Reign of King Henry VII* (edited by Brian Vickers)
 0 521 58663 1 paperback
Bakunin *Statism and Anarchy* (edited by Marshall Shatz)
 0 521 36973 8 paperback
Baxter *A Holy Commonwealth* (edited by William Lamont)
 0 521 40580 7 paperback
Beccaria *On Crimes and Punishments and other writings* (edited by Richard Bellamy)
 0 521 47982 7 paperback
Bentham *A Fragment on Government* (introduction by Ross Harrison)
 0 521 35929 5 paperback
Bernstein *The Preconditions of Socialism* (edited by Henry Tudor)
 0 521 39808 8 paperback
Bodin *On Sovereignty* (edited by Julian H. Franklin)
 0 521 34992 3 paperback
Bolingbroke *Political Writings* (edited by David Armitage)
 0 521 58697 6 paperback
Bossuet *Politics Drawn from the Very Words of Holy Scripture* (edited by Patrick Riley)
 0 521 36807 3 paperback
The British Idealists (edited by David Boucher)
 0 521 45951 6 paperback
Burke *Pre-Revolutionary Writings* (edited by Ian Harris)
 0 521 36800 6 paperback

Christine de Pizan *The Book of the Body Politic* (edited by Kate
Langdon Forhan)
  0 521 42259 0 paperback
Cicero *On Duties* (edited by M. T. Griffin and E. M. Atkins)
  0 521 34835 8 paperback
Conciliarism and Papalism (edited by J. H. Burns and Thomas M.
Izbicki)
  0 521 47674 7 paperback
Constant *Political Writings* (edited by Biancamaria Fontana)
  0 521 31632 4 paperback
Dante *Monarchy* (edited by Prue Shaw)
  0 521 56781 5 paperback
Diderot *Political Writings* (edited by John Hope Mason and Robert
Wokler)
  0 521 36911 8 paperback
The Dutch Revolt (edited by Martin van Gelderen)
  0 521 39809 6 paperback
The Early Political Writings of the German Romantics (edited by Frederick
C. Beiser)
  0 521 44951 0 paperback
Early Greek Political Thought from Homer to the Sophists (edited by
Michael Gagarin and Paul Woodruff)
  0 521 43768 7 paperback
Erasmus *The Education of a Christian Prince* (edited by Lisa Jardine)
  0 521 58811 1 paperback
Ferguson *An Essay on the History of Civil Society* (edited by Fania
Oz-Salzberger)
  0 521 44736 4 paperback
Filmer *Patriarcha and Other Writings* (edited by Johann P. Sommerville)
  0 521 39903 3 paperback
Fletcher *Political Works* (edited by John Robertson)
  0 521 43994 9 paperback
Sir John Fortescue *On the Laws and Governance of England* (edited by
Shelley Lockwood)
  0 521 58996 7 paperback
Fourier *The Theory of the Four Movements* (edited by Gareth Stedman
Jones and Ian Patterson)
  0 521 35693 8 paperback

Locke *Political Essays* (edited by Mark Goldie)
o 521 47861 8 paperback
Locke *Two Treatises of Government* (edited by Peter Laslett)
o 521 35730 6 paperback
Loyseau *A Treatise of Orders and Plain Dignities* (edited by Howell A.
Lloyd)
o 521 45624 X paperback
Luther and Calvin on Secular Authority (edited by Harro Höpfl)
o 521 34986 9 paperback
Machiavelli *The Prince* (edited by Quentin Skinner and Russell Price)
o 521 34993 1 paperback
de Maistre *Considerations on France* (edited by Isaiah Berlin and Richard
Lebrun)
o 521 46628 8 paperback
Malthus *An Essay on the Principle of Population* (edited by Donald
Winch)
o 521 42972 2 paperback
Marsiglio of Padua *Defensor minor* and *De translatione Imperii* (edited by
Cary Nederman)
o 521 40846 6 paperback
Marx *Early Political Writings* (edited by Joseph O'Malley)
o 521 34994 X paperback
Marx *Later Political Writings* (edited by Terrell Carver)
o 521 36739 5 paperback
James Mill *Political Writings* (edited by Terence Ball)
o 521 38748 5 paperback
J. S. Mill *On Liberty*, with *The Subjection of Women* and *Chapters on
Socialism* (edited by Stefan Collini)
o 521 37917 2 paperback
Milton *Political Writings* (edited by Martin Dzelzainis)
o 521 34866 8 paperback
Montesquieu *The Spirit of the Laws* (edited by Anne M. Cohler,
Basia Carolyn Miller and Harold Samuel Stone)
o 521 36974 6 paperback
More *Utopia* (edited by George M. Logan and Robert M. Adams)
o 521 40318 9 paperback
Morris *News from Nowhere* (edited by Krishan Kumar)
o 521 42233 7 paperback
Nicholas of Cusa *The Catholic Concordance* (edited by Paul E. Sigmund)
o 521 56773 4 paperback

Nietzsche *On the Genealogy of Morality* (edited by Keith Ansell-Pearson)
  0 521 40610 2 paperback
Paine *Political Writings* (edited by Bruce Kuklick)
  0 521 36678 X paperback
Plato *Statesman* (edited by Julia Annas and Robin Waterfield)
  0 521 44778 X paperback
Price *Political Writings* (edited by D. O. Thomas)
  0 521 40969 1 paperback
Priestley *Political Writings* (edited by Peter Miller)
  0 521 42561 1 paperback
Proudhon *What Is Property?* (edited by Donald R. Kelley and Bonnie G. Smith)
  0 521 40556 4 paperback
Pufendorf *On the Duty of Man and Citizen according to Natural Law* (edited by James Tully)
  0 521 35980 5 paperback
The Radical Reformation (edited by Michael G. Baylor)
  0 521 37948 2 paperback
Rousseau *The Discourses and other early political writings* (edited by Victor Gourevitch)
  0 521 42445 3 paperback
Rousseau *The Social Contract and other later political writings* (edited by Victor Gourevitch)
  0 521 42446 1 paperback
Seneca *Moral and Political Essays* (edited by John Cooper and John Procope)
  0 521 34818 8 paperback
Sidney *Court Maxims* (edited by Hans W. Blom, Eco Haitsma Mulier and Ronald Janse)
  0 521 46736 5 paperback
Spencer *The Man versus the State* and *The Proper Sphere of Government* (edited by John Offer)
  0 521 43740 7 paperback
Stirner *The Ego and Its Own* (edited by David Leopold)
  0 521 45647 9 paperback
Thoreau *Political Writings* (edited by Nancy Rosenblum)
  0 521 47675 5 paperback
Utopias of the British Enlightenment (edited by Gregory Claeys)
  0 521 45590 1 paperback